A VOYAGE
AROUND THE WORLD
WITH THE ROMANZOV
EXPLORING EXPEDITION
IN THE YEARS 1815-1818

Adelbert von Chamisso. Engraving of a drawing by Franz Kugler, 1828. Reproduced with permission of Walther Migge from Adelbert von Chamisso, *Reise um die Welt*, ed. Walther Migge.

# A VOYAGE AROUND THE WORLD WITH THE ROMANZOV EXPLORING EXPEDITION IN THE YEARS 1815–1818 IN THE BRIG *RURIK*, CAPTAIN OTTO VON KOTZEBUE

BY Adelbert von Chamisso

Translated and Edited
by Henry Kratz

UNIVERSITY OF HAWAII PRESS

Honolulu

**Library of Congress Cataloging-in-Publication Data**

Chamisso, Adelbert von, 1781–1838.
A voyage around the world with the Romanzov exploring
expedition in the years 1815–1818 in the brig Rurik,
Captain Otto von Kotzebue.

Translation of: Reise um die Welt mit der
Romanzoffischen Entdeckungs-Expedition in den Jahren
1815–1818.
Bibliography: p.
Includes index.
1. Rîurik (Ship)  2.  Voyages around the world.
I.  Kratz, Henry.  II.  Title.
G420.R48C4513    1986      910.4'1      86–11255
ISBN 0–8248–0983–1

End sheets: An interview between Kamehameha and the *Rurik* party. Water-color by Louis Choris. On the king's right are John Elliot de Castro, Capt. Otto von Kotzebue, Eschscholtz, Chamisso, and Choris. From Louis Choris, *Vues et paysages des régions équinoxiales*.

Cover: Vues dans les îles Radak. Watercolor by Louis Choris. Honolulu Academy of Arts. Gift of the Honolulu Art Society, 1944.

IN MEMORY OF

# LYNN KRATZ HARTY

## (1953–1979)

# CONTENTS

# A NOTE ON THE SPELLING OF NAMES

IN general I have retained Chamisso's spellings of proper names but with some exceptions. Mostly I have transliterated Russian names in the present English fashion and not in Chamisso's German style. However, some names have become so established in the literature that I have retained them: thus I have used *Rurik*, even though it would more properly be transliterated *Ryurik*, and *Romanzov*, which should be *Rumiantsev*. Hawaiian names constitute a special problem, as they circulated in many different forms before the language was codified by the missionaries. It should be noted especially that *t* often appears where modern spelling demands *k*, and *r* where today we have *l*. For instance, Chamisso writes *Kamehameha* as *Tameiameia* and *Lanai* as *Ranai*. On top of that, there are many forms that are garbled almost (sometimes completely) past recognition. While in general keeping Chamisso's spelling, I have put the modern form in square brackets when the word is first used. I have done the same with the other Hawaiian words Chamisso uses occasionally: thus, "*Arocha* [*Aloha*]."

# ACKNOWLEDGMENTS

I wish to express my gratitude to the Honolulu Academy of Arts for permission to reproduce on the dust jacket Louis Choris' previously unpublished painting "Vue dans les îles Radak" and in the text his watercolor of Kadu, and especially to Sanna Deutsch and Hilda Randolph for the assistance they provided; to the staff of the Hawaiian and Pacific Collection of Hamilton Library, University of Hawaii, who were most helpful in providing the map of the Great Ocean that appeared in Choris' *Voyage pittoresque autour du monde* and his painting of the meeting between Kamehameha and the *Rurik* party that appeared in his *Vues et paysages des régions équinoxiales;* and to Dr. Walther Migge of Grosserlach, Germany, for permission to reproduce an engraving of a drawing by Franz Kugler that appeared as the frontispiece in Albert von Chamisso, *Reise um die Welt*, edited by Walther Migge. Above all, I wish to thank Damaris A. Kirchhofer of the University of Hawaii Press for her invaluable assistance. This book owes very much to her devoted expertise and attention to detail.

HENRY KRATZ

# INTRODUCTION

MAGELLAN'S expedition traversed the Pacific in the early sixteenth century, and his path around the world was followed by Sir Francis Drake and others, but the vast expanse of the South Seas remained terra incognita to Europeans for a long time thereafter. The lush, palm-studded islands of Polynesia and Melanesia and the blazing atolls of Micronesia slumbered on for a couple of centuries, unseen by European eyes, unmolested by European guns, uncorrupted by European mores. While Luther defied Pope and Empire, while Shakespeare wrote *Hamlet*, while Louis XIV basked in the magnificence of Versailles, while England, France, Spain, Holland, and Portugal divided up the American continents among themselves, indeed, while Washington's army shivered at Valley Forge, the South Sea islanders continued to live in thatched huts and worship idols, even as their ancestors had done for centuries before. The marvelous small vessels they constructed continued to ply the local waters as they too had done for centuries. It was not really until the eighteenth century that the comparative serenity of South Pacific culture was rent asunder and destroyed forever by the advent of European explorers, warships, and missionaries.

The eighteenth-century Enlightenment in Europe brought with it a new respect for learning and a new curiosity about the wonders of nature and the inhabitants of the remote corners of the earth. Traveling and travelogues became popular, and explorers headed into the unknown depths of continents and seas. It became customary to send scientists along on these expeditions to report on the phenomena of nature they encountered. In this spirit, and also, of course, motivated by the hope of mercantile gain and geopolitical considerations, European exploration of the Pacific began to increase in intensity toward the middle of the eighteenth century. Much of the exploration took the form of voyages around the world, the vessels generally proceeding westward from Europe around Cape Horn,

then across the Pacific, around the Cape of Good Hope, and so
northward to home. On one such expedition Samuel Wallis (1728–
1795) landed at Tahiti and what became known as the Wallis Islands.
Louis Antoine de Bougainville (1729–1811) headed the first circumnavigation of the globe under the French flag (1766–1769), for which
history has rewarded him by naming after him an island of the Solomons, two straits, one in the Solomons and one in the New
Hebrides (Vanuatu), and a tropical flower.

Probably the most famous of the eighteenth-century explorers
was Captain James Cook, who headed three British expeditions
around the world that excited the imagination of all Europe. On the
first (1768–1771) he visited Tahiti and charted the coasts of New
Zealand, Australia, and New Guinea. On the second (1772–1775) he
sailed to the edge of Antarctica in search of a lost continent believed
to exist in the South Pacific, visited Tahiti again, as well as Vanuatu,
and was the first European to land at New Caledonia. On the third
voyage (1776–1779) he discovered the Hawaiian Islands for Europe
(1778) and charted the northern coast of North America. When he
returned to Hawaii in 1779 he was killed by the natives.[1]

Other voyages around the world followed and continued into the
nineteenth century. Among them was one under Adam Johann von
Krusenstern (1770–1846), an Estonian by birth, though of German
ancestry, who led the first circumnavigation of the world under the
Russian flag in the ships *Nadezhda* and *Neva* in the years 1803–
1806.[2]

One of the persistent hopes and goals of exploration in these days
was the discovery of a subarctic navigable passage across the North
American continent, a passage that would make the journey from
Europe to the Pacific much shorter than the tedious and dangerous
transit around the tip of South America. This route was known
either as the Northwest Passage, if it was approached from the east,
or the Northeast Passage, if it was approached from the west. Cook
and Captain George Vancouver, a fellow English explorer, sought
this passage in vain.[3] Nikolai Petrovich Rumiantsev (Romanzov, as
Chamisso spells it), a Russian nobleman and statesman, was so
enthralled by the idea of finding it that he underwrote the voyage
that is the subject of this book, which was captained by Otto von
Kotzebue (1787–1846), a lieutenant in the Russian Navy. Even
though Rumiantsev financed the expedition, the brig *Rurik* (more
properly, *Ryurik*) was a vessel of the Russian Navy, manned by Russian naval men, carrying cannon; technically a man-of-war, it was
entitled to the treatment accorded any other naval vessel when it
called at foreign ports. Kotzebue's father was August von Kotzebue

(1761–1819), the most successful German playwright of his time, whose name, as Chamisso's narrative shows, was known all over the world. Otto, too, was a man of no small talents. He had participated in the Krusenstern expedition and, at a relatively young age (twenty-eight when the expedition started), he successfully brought his vessel around the world, discovering some islands in the Marshalls hitherto unknown in Europe and exploring the country beyond the Bering Strait. A few years later (1823–1826) he headed another globe-circling expedition and continued his explorations.

On board the *Rurik* there was another person who gained renown, the artist Louis Choris, whose paintings made during the expedition were published along with a short account of the voyage.[4] It is he who painted the famous portrait of Kamehameha I of Hawaii in a red vest and that of Kadu, the native of the Carolines of whom Chamisso writes so much.

The *Rurik* set out from Kronshtadt on July 30, 1815, and on August 9 arrived in Copenhagen, where Chamisso joined the crew. From Copenhagen it went to Plymouth to make final preparations for the long voyage ahead. The brig sailed from Plymouth via the Canary Islands, the Cape Verde Islands, and the coast of Brazil around Cape Horn to Talcahuano, Chile, where it spent a few weeks getting reprovisioned. From Talcahuano it proceeded across the Pacific, stopping only at Easter Island and Sala-y-Gómez before arriving at Petropavlovsk on the Kamchatka Peninsula. It entered the Bering Strait, where preparations were made to return the next summer for a more extended exploration, and then continued to San Francisco Bay, staying there a month before moving on to the Sandwich Islands (Hawaii). After a visit of three weeks, the *Rurik* set sail for the Marshall Islands; it was in these waters that the atoll chain of Ratak was discovered. After sojourning there for over two months, the ship turned toward Kamchatka and Alaska again. Crippled by a severe storm, it was forced to put in for extensive repairs at the island of Unalaska in the Aleutians. His own ill health and severe weather caused Captain Kotzebue to abandon the search for the Northwest Passage and turn homeward. On the way across the Pacific the *Rurik* called again at the Sandwich Islands and Ratak and afterwards at Guam and Manila, where again extensive repairs were made on the ship. From there the brig cruised westward to Cape Town, north to St. Helena, Portsmouth, Reval, Kronshtadt, and St. Petersburg, arriving there on August 3, 1818.

The author of the work presented in this volume, Adelbert von Chamisso, was the resident naturalist or "titular scholar," as he is called, on board the *Rurik*. He was born Louis-Charles-Adelaide de

Chamisso on January 30, 1781, in the ancestral castle of Boncourt in the Champagne, the scion of a noble French family that fled to Germany in 1792 to escape the guillotine. When he embarked on the *Rurik*, Chamisso was thirty-four years old and had never gone to sea before. He had served a hitch in the Prussian Army, having been granted a commission after being a page to Friederike Louise, Queen of Prussia and consort of the notorious Frederick William II. He was unhappy in the army, as he was primarily an intellectual. He frequented the literary salons of the Berlin Romanticists and joined the *Nordsternbund*, the "North Star Alliance," a literary society among whose members were Julius Eduard Hitzig, who remained Chamisso's lifelong friend, Karl August Varnhagen von Ense, and Baron de la Motte Fouqué. He also became acquainted with such major figures in the German Romantic movement as Johann Gottlieb Fichte, Friedrich Schleiermacher, Ludwig Tieck, and August Wilhelm Schlegel, whose Berlin lectures made an especially strong impression upon the group. Together with von Ense, for three years (1803–1806) Chamisso edited a literary magazine called the *Musenalmanach* or "Muses' Almanac," which was patterned after a journal with the same name previously edited by Schlegel. He had traveled to France and Switzerland (he enjoyed a close friendship with Madame de Staël) and had studied botany at the University of Berlin.

Chamisso had attained a degree of fame as a result of the publication in 1814 of his fairy tale *Peter Schlemihls wundersame Geschichte*, the story of a man who sold his shadow to the Devil and refused to sacrifice his soul in order to get it back.[5] Roaming the world in his seven-league boots to gather botanical specimens, Peter strangely prefigures Chamisso himself on the cruise of the *Rurik*.

An account of the voyage written by Kotzebue appeared in 1821 in two volumes, to which was appended as a third volume a number of essays on more or less scientific subjects by Chamisso called *Bemerkungen und Ansichten* ("Notes and Opinions").[6] In 1835 Chamisso wrote his own account of the voyage, *Reise um die Welt* ("Voyage Around the World"), which he published in 1836 as the first two volumes of his collected works.[7] The first volume bears the subtitle *Tagebuch* ("Journal"), and the second volume is a reprint, virtually unchanged except for spelling and the deletion of a few short articles on South America, of the *Bemerkungen und Ansichten*.

*Tagebuch* is a misnomer, for the work is written from the perspective of some twenty years after the fact, although it is partly based on notes and letters written on the expedition. It is in some measure a reaction to Kotzebue's record of the voyage, as well as his account of a later voyage around the world that appeared in 1830.[8]

As is understandable in view of three years of too-close contact in cramped quarters, occasionally there was friction between Chamisso and Kotzebue, and to some extent Chamisso attempts to set the record straight. Thus, he gives his views on Kotzebue's controversial decision to turn back prematurely from exploring in Alaskan waters and indicates his dissatisfaction with Kotzebue's refusal to allow him to stay for a year on Oahu. In the same vein, Chamisso decries Kotzebue's use of *Wilde* ("savages") to refer to Polynesians and other native peoples, even though, it must be admitted, he himself uses the term in the "Notes and Opinions" to refer to Indians and Papuans. It was in his declining years that he wrote the "Journal" of his voyage around the world, at a time when he was no longer able to keep up his professional activities as a botanist. There is, of course, a strong element of nostalgia in it.

While narratives of voyages in the golden age of exploration in the Pacific are often fascinating reading, they tend to be written by sea captains or other members of the crew whose style lacks literary finesse. In Chamisso's "Voyage" we have the unusual phenomenon of a narrative by a literary person who is at the same time a naturalist. The author thus combines the interest of the humanist with the sharp eye of the scientist and couches what he has to say in the smooth, flowing, and idiomatic style of a master of literary prose.

While his task on the expedition was to examine and report on fauna and flora and other scientific phenomena, as one steeped in European culture Chamisso was interested in everything he encountered. He was interested in people first and last. This interest extended not only to the governmental officials and scientists he met in the civilized enclaves they visited but also and perhaps even more so to the primitive people he encountered. He had a sense of history and tradition, and a good eye for details. He was sensitive to moods and feelings in others. He had a literary man's interest in literature and a Romantic's interest in folkways and folklore. Thus his work is crammed full of vignettes and anecdotes of the societies that flourished in the places the *Rurik* visited.

The *Rurik* went to Chile at a time when the Chilean independence movement, which had made great strides during the French occupation of Spain (1808–1814), was at a low ebb. In 1814 the rebels had been defeated by Royalists through the help of troops from Peru. The extremely repressive Ferdinand VII was securely ensconced on the throne of Spain, and in governmental circles, the high society of Chile—as Chamisso shows us—the revolutionaries were in low repute. The Spanish régime was not to last much longer, however: in 1817 a large army, which had been formed in Argentina under the Argentina-born José de San Martín, decisively defeated the Royalist forces and established Chilean independence.[9]

Alaska in these days was under Russian rule. When Russian ships, sailing from Kamchatka under the command of the Dane Vitus Bering (1680–1741), discovered the coast of Alaska, they also discovered the wealth of furs available in the area. In the ensuing years fur traders gradually spread out through the Aleutian Islands and to the Alaskan coast. The most prosperous of the fur-trading companies was founded by Grigori Ivanovich Shelikhov. This company and others were consolidated into one and licensed by the tsar in 1799 to engage in monopolistic trading in the area under the name of the Russian-American Company. Under the management of Aleksandr Andrevich Baranov ("governor" until 1818), it flourished and founded forts and settlements throughout the Aleutians and the northwest coast of North America as far south as Fort Ross, just north of San Francisco.[10] As a Russian ship, the *Rurik* and its crew received full cooperation from the Russian-American officials. Chamisso draws sharp portraits for us not only of the Russians but also of the Aleuts and Eskimos as they subsisted in subservience to the company.

When the *Rurik* dropped anchor in San Francisco Bay, Alta or Nueva California (so called to distinguish it from Baja or Antigua California) was still ruled by the Spanish. Beginning in 1769 with a mission at San Diego, the land had been thinly dotted by a number of missions, forts, and towns that stretched along the coast and a few miles inland to a point a little north of San Francisco. The land was divided into four districts centering on the presidios at San Diego, Santa Barbara, Monterey, and San Francisco, the central government being located at Monterey. Chamisso found that the Franciscan missionaries and the military there to protect them were two separate entities. The missionaries enjoyed a better situation because they had taught the Indians to till the soil for them. The military depended on supplies from Acapulco, which were slow and often late in coming, so that the soldiers were forced to beg for supplies from the missionaries. The Spanish military was spread so thin over this vast land that they were virtually powerless, even unable to displace the Russians from their trading post at Fort Ross.[11] Chamisso was especially interested in the California Indians and the distressful way they were treated by the Spanish. In general he is sharply critical of the Spanish régime in California but at the same time has good things to say about the individuals he met there.

In the Sandwich Islands we are treated to a description of premissionary Honolulu (Hana-ruru, as Chamisso writes it), and of Kamehameha I. But even more interesting is the author's account of his adventures when roaming the countryside looking for botanical specimens. According to archeological evidence, the Hawaiian Islands, two thousand miles from any other land mass, were settled by Polynesian colonists between A.D. 300 and 700, possibly from the Marquesas. A second wave from the Society Islands about the thirteenth century is often claimed but today is much disputed. Hawaiian tradition does retain the memory of settlement from a distant Kahiki, the Hawaiian form of Tahiti. Connections with the other islands were broken off, however, and for centuries Hawaii was isolated from the rest of the world.[12] This isolation came to an end in 1778 when Captain James Cook arrived. After this first contact with Europe, the Sandwich Islands, as Cook called them, after the Earl of Sandwich, his patron, were visited by ships from many European nations, and a number of Europeans gradually settled there.

The islands were ruled by a caste of chiefs (ali'i) and priests (kāhuna) who held absolute dominion over the common people. The people were subject to a body of religious and social regulations and prohibitions that were strictly observed and the infraction of which was very severely punished: the taboo (or *kapu*, the Hawaiian form of the word) system. Before Cook the islands had been ruled by a number of petty kings, often at war with each other, and no one had ever acquired sovereignty over all of the islands. In the years after contact a young chieftain called Kamehameha, "the silent one," gained control of his native island of Hawaii and, with the aid of European artillery and European ships, gradually extended his sway over the other islands. In 1810, when the king of Kauai swore fealty to him, his sovereignty was complete. He ruled until his death in 1819, all this time preserving the ancient laws and customs. After Kamehameha's death the kapu system was abolished, and in 1820 life in the islands changed radically when American missionaries were allowed to establish themselves there.[13] The monarchy lasted until Hawaii's last sovereign, Queen Liliuokalani, was forced to abdicate in 1893.

At the time the *Rurik* visited Hawaii the Russian flag was extremely unpopular because of an adventure undertaken by Georg Anton Schäffer, a representative of the Russian–American company. He had been sent by Baranov to Hawaii to rescue the cargo from a Russian ship that had been shipwrecked off the coast of Kauai and also to set up a Russian trading post in the islands. He intrigued with Kaumuali'i, king of Kauai and reluctant subject of Kamehameha, receiving grants of land in Kauai as well as half of the island of Oahu, over which Kaumuali'i exercised no sovereignty. Schäffer proceeded to Oahu, where he built a fort and raised the Russian flag. He was driven back to Kauai by incensed Oahuans, and such was the situation when the *Rurik* arrived. Eventually Kamehameha and the other European traders were able to pressure Kaumuali'i into expelling Schäffer, and nothing more ever came of the Russian presence in the islands.[14]

Chamisso was especially interested in and impressed by the natives of Ratak, whom he found unspoiled by any previous encounter with the white man. He furnishes detailed descriptions of his day-to-day encounters with them. We also are provided descriptions of life in Manila of the day, where again Chamisso was busy not only in botanical pursuits but also in attempts to gather information about Philippine and other Austronesian languages. On the way home, at Cape Town, Chamisso was visited aboard ship by an old acquaintance, who introduced him to other scientists in the city. Back in England, Chamisso toured London. He gives us his impressions of that great bustling city and contrasts it with the conditions in St. Petersburg.

Chamisso, as a child of his times, had read Rousseau, Herder, and Chateaubriand and was imbued with the idea of the "noble savage." He thus started out on the expedition with a feeling of sympathy toward primitive peoples, whom he considered to live in a state of pristine and childlike innocence uncorrupted by European civilization.[15] He had a respect for their traditions and customs and a disgust for their exploitation by Europeans. This is registered on numerous occasions in the *Voyage Around the World* with reference to a number of different groups.

Unlike most of the other European Romantics, Chamisso was able to test the ideal of the noble savage against the reality of actual peoples. He found something very close to this ideal in the inhabitants of Ratak, of whom he says: "The sensitivity, the delicacy of the manners, the extreme cleanliness of this people are expressed in every slightest aspect, only the smallest number of which are suitable to be described."

If the inhabitants of Ratak were the incarnation of the noble savage for Chamisso, in the person of Kadu he found the noblest savage of them all. Kadu was a native of Woleai, an atoll in the Western Carolines. He and three companions had been tempest tossed and blown far out of their way to the Marshalls, where they had settled among the Ratakians. Kadu was highly regarded by them and had taken two wives from among them, by one of whom he had sired a daughter. When he encountered the *Rurik* he immediately decided to ship on board with the Europeans, sailing with them to Alaska and ultimately back to Ratak via California and the Hawaiian Islands. Chamisso soon became fast friends with Kadu, describing him as "one of the finest characters I have met in my life, one of the people I have loved most." Much of the information about Ratak and the Carolines he imparted in his "Notes and Opinions" was obtained from Kadu. When we reflect that neither knew the other's tongue, it is clear their conversations could not always have been easy. They seemed to have conversed in a kind of pidgin composed "of the dialects of Polynesia that Kadu spoke, and a few European words and expressions." In the face of the added difficulty, as Chamisso complains, that Kadu seldom volunteered any information beyond a bare answer to a question, it would seem that the accuracy of some of his information was somewhat questionable.

At any rate, Chamisso draws a charming portrait of his friend: he stood out from the Ratakians by his lighter color, curlier hair, smaller stature, and less obtrusive tattooing. In fact, Choris' portraits of him, the best of which appears as a frontispiece to the 1836 edition of the "Notes and Opinions," depict a delicately featured and handsome young man, if one is not disturbed by the long, pendant earlobes, split and stretched to make possible the insertion of rolled-up leaves or other finery. But Kadu's outstanding qualities were not limited to such superficialities: he had, Chamisso tells us, "heart, understanding, wit," was "generous in his poverty and grateful in his heart." His two most prominent virtues were his detestation of killing and warfare (although he bore scars from wounds received defending Ratak) and his sensitive modesty.

Not that Chamisso presents him as a character without flaws; he deplores his laziness, for instance, which was so great according to Chamisso that all he really liked to do was sing and sleep. Chamisso praises his adaptability and, indeed, to the detached observer it seems that that might have been his most outstanding quality, although it is not out of the question that he may have propounded many views because he knew that they met approval from Chamisso. And then again, there was the problem of communication.

At any rate, the Ratakians, as they appeared to Chamisso at least, and the personality of Kadu, as it appeared to him, were tough competition for the Hawaiians, and in Chamisso's eyes they suffer by contrast. This does not mean to imply that Chamisso was by any means repelled by the boisterous Hawaiians, for he has many good things to say about them. He has high praise for Kamehameha I (or Tameiameia, as he writes it), who received the leaders of the *Rurik* expedition on the island of Hawaii, and for his advisor, Kalanimoku or Kālaimoku (he writes Kareimoku). In fact, Chamisso boasted that he had shaken hands with three outstanding men of the era, Kamehameha, Sir Joseph Banks, and Lafayette. In spite of the trouble he had had with Schäffer and the Russian trading ships, Kamehameha received them well and generously promised to maintain them gratuitously while they were in his domain. He bestowed upon them a handsome feather cloak as a present for Tsar Alexander. During their second visit to Hawaii, the *Rurik* party paid their respects to the king at a rude camp by the shore where he had gone to catch bonito. The king appeared after the day's fishing clad only in a *malo* and graciously bestowed his catch upon them. He then donned the red vest made famous by Choris' painting and joined them in a sumptuous meal.

Chamisso seems to have gotten along well with the rank and file of the populace. He praises the lightheartedness and friendliness of this "people of joy and pleasure." However, he was greatly bothered —or at least he says he was—by their sexual promiscuity.

Chamisso was very concerned about the deleterious effects of European culture upon primitive cultures. In "Notes and Opinions," he contended that "in the islands of eastern Polynesia Christianity can be founded only upon the collapse of everything existing." In the "Journal" he recalled Kotzebue's later remarks on the subject:

> I observed with regret, in my daily visits to Hanaruro, that the Wahuanere had lost the simplicity and innocence of character which formerly distinguished them. The profligate habits of the settlers of all nations among them, and of the numerous foreign sailors with whom they constantly associate, have most prejudicially affected their morals. Fraud, theft, and burglary, never heard of in Tamearmea's time, are now frequent. . . .

> This once industrious and flourishing people are rapidly acquiring confirmed habits of idleness and dissipation. A great part of the well cultivated tarro-fields, which formerly surrounded Hanaruro, now lie waste. On the great market place, horse and foot races are proceeding all day long, and give occasion to extreme gambling.[16]

When in 1825 Kotzebue paid his last visit to the islands some eight months after the one mentioned above, he found the land much changed because of the tyranny, he asserts, of missionary Hiram Bingham (whom he calls Bengham):

> The inhabitants of every house or hut in Hanaruro are compelled by authority to an almost endless routine of

> prayers; and even the often dishonest intentions of the for-
> eign settlers must be concealed under the veil of devotion.
> The streets, formerly so full of life and animation, are now
> deserted; games of all kinds, even the most innocent, are
> sternly prohibited; singing is a punishable offence; and the
> consummate profligacy of attempting to dance would cer-
> tainly find no mercy. On Sundays no cooking is permitted,
> nor must even a fire be kindled: nothing, in short, must be
> done; the whole day is devoted to prayer, with how much
> real piety may be easily imagined![17]

Chamisso assures us that he is a "man of progress" who believes in
the beneficial effect of Christianity, but he agreed with Kotzebue
that in Hawaii it was practiced in an uninspired way.

All aspects of Hawaii's culture were of interest to Chamisso, who
felt it was high time that it was thoroughly studied before it became
too late. This sentiment sounds very modern to us. Indeed, Chamisso had the soul of an anthropologist as well as a botanist. Many of
his observations about life in Hawaii were presented in "Notes and
Opinions" and later in the "Journal." There is an enthusiastic
description of a hula ("hurra-hurra") in which he compares it to the
"chorus of the Greeks, to tragedy before dialogue had entered," and
contrasts the grace of the dancers to what he calls "the repulsive
gyrations that we admire in our danseuses under the name of
ballet."[18]

As a guest of Kalanimoku he attended what he called a "Tabu-
pori" in a *heiau*, which he terms *Morai* (Tahitian *marae*). He was
startled at the lack of solemnity in the proceedings. However, the
lack of solemnity by no means blinded Chamisso to the realities of
taboo and human sacrifices to the gods. The *Rurik* party had, in fact,
seen the corpse of a woman floating in the bay who had been killed,
they were told, for having entered her husband's eating house
(strictly kapu) unwittingly in a state of intoxication. Much as he
deplored human sacrifice, he found excuses for the Polynesians
when he contrasted them to Europeans.

But Chamisso was not drawn solely to the more exotic manifestations of the culture. He notes the clothes Hawaiians wear, the tat-
toos they bear, the food they eat, the houses they live in, the canoes
they paddle. He discusses their social and political institutions at
length, demonstrating that he was fully aware of the caste structure
and the economic system that invested all the land in its king. He
realized that Kamehameha was the first to assume control over all
of the islands and was convinced the kingdom would crumble at his
death. It must be remembered that these interests were pursued in
addition to Chamisso's main task of gathering scientific data on

fauna and flora. His greatest regret was the amount of material he was unable to obtain before it became too late; he notes that he had volunteered to remain in the islands until the ship returned, but that the captain had vetoed his proposal.

Chamisso was interested in languages. Although his native language was French, he did most of his writing in German, the language of his adopted country. His German apparently never became accent-free, and his German syntax, particularly in his earlier writings, occasionally shows French influence. He had taught himself some Spanish and was able to act as interpreter in the Spanish-speaking countries the *Rurik* visited. He knew some English but notes that Englishmen tended to laugh at his pronunciation whenever he opened his mouth. He once started to learn Russian but soon gave it up, claiming at one point in his writings that it was an advantage for him not to have to listen to the babble that went on around him.

The languages of the Pacific attracted him, and he made an effort to learn Hawaiian and Marshallese. He was aware of the connections between Polynesian languages and the other Austronesian languages—in fact, he uses the term *Polynesian* to refer to the entire group. In Manila he tried to get as much material as he could about Tagalog, Bisayan, and other Philippine languages. He learned a certain amount of the Caroline Islands dialect of his friend Kadu.

Like his contemporaries, Chamisso believed that primitive peoples spoke simple, childlike languages, and he places Hawaiian in that category in his "Notes and Opinions." Later, when he came to know more about it, he changed his mind. On the basis of translations by American missionaries of some of the books of the Bible into Hawaiian he later wrote the first grammar of Hawaiian ever published, a work that, for all its imperfections, according to Samuel H. Elbert was "far in advance of contemporary writers on Tongan and Maori, and of Lorrin Andrews, his junior by 14 years."[19] (Andrews was the author of a Hawaiian grammar published in 1854.) Chamisso also gave an accounting of his further Hawaiian studies, promising a supplement to the grammar, which he never finished, and explaining why he had given up a projected Hawaiian dictionary.[20]

Chamisso lived some twenty-one years after returning to Germany from his circumnavigation of the globe. His position as naturalist on the voyage bestowed a certain prestige upon him, and he was able to secure employment as a botanist, as one of the curators of the Berlin and Schöneberg herbariums. He published a number of scientific articles and was highly regarded in his field.[21] He married a foster daughter of his friend Hitzig's and settled down to a busy and happy life. Gradually he returned to literary activities, joining a new literary society, the *Mittwochgesellschaft* or "Wednesday Society," started by Hitzig and including some of the former members of the North Star Alliance. He became a political liberal, and this is reflected in his poetry, which changes from the Romantic mode to one of greater social consciousness. Toward the end of his life his poetry became quite popular, and in 1836 he published a complete edition of his poems. In this period he produced a couple of hundred poems, but only a handful have any reference to his Pacific journey or deal with Pacific subjects. Of these, the only one that could be said to proceed directly from experience is *Salas y Gómez*, a long strophic poem that appeared in the *Musenalmanach* for 1830.[22] It deals with the bleak island near Easter Island inhabited only by birds, which the *Rurik* visited in 1816. Chamisso peoples it with a shipwrecked mariner who ekes out the rest of his days in miserable isolation, subsisting on birds' eggs. *Idylle* ("Idyll") is an adaptation of a Tongan poem, and Chamisso makes it into a paean of praise for the lotus-eating life of the natives of the South Seas.[23] *In malaiischer Form* ("In Malayan Form") consists of three poems written in imitation of Malay folk poems dealing with love and nature.[24] *Ein Gerichtstag auf Huahine* ("A Day of Judgment on Huahine") is based on an episode narrated by William Ellis in his *Polynesian Researches* with regard to Huahine, one of the Society Islands.[25] It concerns the clash of the old order with the new one imposed by the missionaries, and Chamisso here somewhat surprisingly emphasizes the virtues of the new Christianity-based law, which secured justice for a commoner from the queen after she had caused a breadfruit tree belonging to him to be cut down. Chamisso used this poem as evidence that he did not oppose missionary activity when it was carried out sensibly.

Scholars have debated the question of why Chamisso did not write more poems about the Pacific, which made such an impression upon him, and have come to varying conclusions.[26] I think the basic reason lies in Chamisso's poetic nature. He is not a poet whose inspiration comes primarily from his own experiences: the great majority of his poems are translations or adaptations of other poems or are poetic retellings of legends, folktales, or other miscellaneous works he read. Except for *Salas y Gómez*, this holds true for the Pacific poems as well. Thus, there were few poems by Chamisso about the Pacific because there were few poems and other literary works about the Pacific written at that time that might have inspired his muse. His claim to fame rests on *Peter Schlemihl* and the charming travel narrative that is presented in these pages.

This volume contains Chamisso's "Journal" in its entirety and selected chapters from the "Notes and Opinions," which have already been published in translation. I have included here all the material on California and Hawaii but have limited the other chapters to material that is still of some interest today. Material of anthropological, literary, or general human interest has been left in, but I have excluded much of the scientific data Chamisso furnished, so outdated today that they are of little value.

# A Voyage Around the World
# in the Brig *Rurik*

# PART I
## Journal

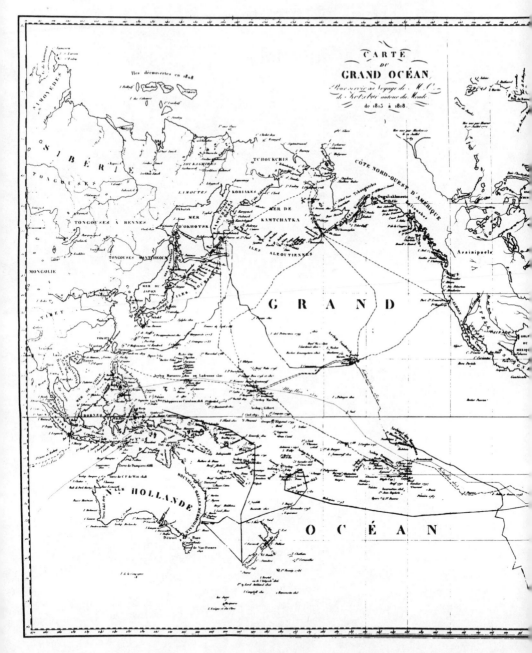

Map of the Great Ocean. From Louis Choris, *Voyage pittoresque autour du monde*.

# Table of Contents.

# By Way of Foreword.

THE book by Otto von Kotzebue, lieutenant in the Russian Imperial Navy, entitled *Voyage of Discovery to the South Seas and to the Bering Strait for the Discovery of a Northeast Passage, Undertaken in the Years 1815–1818 at the Expense of His Excellency Imperial Chancelor Count von Romanzov in the Ship Rurik* (Weimar, 1821, quarto), contains in the third volume the "Notes and Opinions" that I made with regard to this voyage, in which I participated as a naturalist.

The only advantage I could hope for for my endeavors as naturalist during and after this voyage was to see these memorabilia of mine appear in a well-printed, worthy form before the public for which they were designed. The result did not conform to my expectations. What I wrote was defaced and made incomprehensible in many places by innumerable sense-distorting typographical errors, and I was firmly refused permission to note them in an errata notice. In a separate treatise, which could be and has been ascribed to me, Eschscholtz again expressed traditional views about the coral islands, the refutation of which I considered an important contribution of mine.[1] The publishing house had spoiled the chance of a French translation, which a scholar friend of mine wished to make, by refusing him the galley proofs he had requested for this purpose.[2] Finally, Sand's miserable act cast its dark shadow over the book as it appeared, and left only the name which it bore on its forehead to shine forth in the light of partisan politics.[3]

I have seen only one favorable review of this travel narrative, and this only of the nautical part (*Quarterly Review*, 1822).[4]

And nevertheless I consider some parts of my work not altogether unworthy of being rescued from oblivion. What an honest man notes down briefly, what he has seen and investigated with his own eyes, deserves to be deposited in the archives of science; it is only the book that has been copied and collated from other books that ought to be replaced and obscured by later more complete or more clever ones.

If I were now to devote a new investigation to the subjects I dealt with then, it would be incumbent upon me to compare and examine the testimonials and statements of my numerous successors. That, however, is the task of the latest investigator in the same field who has the complete data. I might add: the task of the latest traveler. The reports of past circumnavigators of the world are generally true, but only the testimony of one's own eyes can lead the way to an understanding of them.

In my childhood Cook had lifted the curtain that still concealed an enticing world of marvels, and I could not imagine that extraordinary man in any other fashion than clothed in light, in the way that Dante's ancestor Cacciaguida appeared to him in the fifth heaven.[5] At least I was still the first one who undertook such a voyage from Berlin. Now it seems that a trip around the world is a requisite of a scholarly education, and in England they are said to be outfitting a passenger ship to take idlers on Cook's trail for a small amount of money.

I have often had opportunity to bestow a piece of advice upon young friends that as yet no one has seen fit to follow. I would, I told them, if I were again to return home from a scientific voyage that I had to report about, completely suppress the scholar in me in my narrative and seek only to present the strange land and the strange people, or rather present myself in the strange surroundings to the participating reader, and if the success were in proportion to the intent, then everyone would have to dream along with me wherever the voyage took us. This part would perhaps be best written during the voyage. I would then write a separate work to present to the scholars all the trivial or important matters that I might have had the good fortune to discover or accomplish.

No one requested a narrative of my own voyage, and, not being one who enjoys writing all that much, I was glad to leave it to others, Mr. von Kotzebue and the painter Choris (*Voyage pittoresque autour du monde*, Paris 1822, folio), each of whom composed one of his own. I have only written in a plain fashion my "Notes and Opinions" about the countries we touched upon, and I shall incorporate several of them into this collection in spite of their often unavoidable dryness. And, frankly, this is what impels me to make up for lost time and address these lines to you, my friends, and friends of my muse. I do not picture myself standing before strangers but rather only before friends as I set about speaking freely about myself and reciting a goodly piece of my life story.

But will the dew not have evaporated from the flowers, will not their fragrance have blown away? Since then almost twenty years have gone by, and I am no longer the vigorous youth but an almost old man, and a sick and tired one. However, my mind has stayed fresh and my heart has stayed warm, so let's hope for the best. The very disease that is breaking down my strength and is making me unfit for more serious tasks furnishes me with the necessary leisure for this confidential conversation.[6]

# By Way of Introduction.

ANYONE who wishes to accompany me sympathetically on this great journey must first find out who I am, how fate played with me, and how it transpired that I boarded the *Rurik* as a titular scholar.

Descended from an old family, I was born in the chateau at Boncourt in the Champagne in January 1781. The emigration of the French nobility drove me from the soil of my mother country as early as the year 1790.[1] The memories of my childhood are an informative book for me in which that passionately aroused time now lies open to my more penetrating eye. The opinions of a boy belong to the world that is reflected in him, and I sometimes ask myself: Are those of the man any more his property? After considerable traveling around in the Low Countries, Holland, and Germany, and after having endured considerable privation, my family was finally cast ashore in Prussia. In the year 1796 I became a page of the Queen Consort of Frederick William II, and in the year 1798 I entered military service in an infantry regiment of the Berlin garrison under Frederick William III.[2] In the beginning of the century the milder rule of the First Consul permitted my family to return to France, but I remained behind.[3] So in the years when a boy matures into a man I was alone, and completely without any education; I had never seriously attended a school. I wrote verses, first French and later German. In the year 1803 I wrote *Faust*, which I have included in my poems as a grateful reminder.[4] This almost boyish metaphysical-poetic attempt brought me by chance close to another youth who, like me, was attempting to write poetry, K. A. Varnhagen von Ense.[5] We swore oaths of brotherhood, and thus immaturely the *Muses' Almanac* for the year 1804 came into being, which, as no publisher would take it on, was published at my expense.[6] This indiscretion, which I cannot regret, became the rewarding turning point of my life. Even though the poetry I wrote at that time may well have consisted only in the filling out of the poetic forms that the so-called new school recommended, the little book nevertheless aroused some interest. It brought me into association with fine youths who grew up to be excellent men, and on the other hand it drew upon me the benevolent attention of some important men, among whom I will mention only Fichte, who honored me with his paternal friendship.[7]

Adelbert von Chamisso and K. A. Varnhagen's *Muses' Almanac* was followed by two more years of the same, for which a publisher had been found, and the book ceased to appear only when political events separated the editors and collaborators.[8] In the meantime I was studying hard, first the Greek language—only later did I take up Latin and occasionally the living languages of Europe. The decision matured within me to leave military service and devote myself completely to my studies. The fateful events of the year 1806 hindered and delayed me in my resolutions. The university in Halle, where I was to follow my friends, no longer existed,[9] and my friends themselves were scattered abroad in the wide world. Death had robbed me of my parents. Confused within myself, without position and profession, bowed and bent, I passed a gloomy time in Berlin. The most devastating effect was exerted upon me by a man who was one of the greatest minds of the time and toward whom I felt sincere devotion. A mere word, a mere gesture from him would have sufficed to lift me up, but he (and this is still incomprehensible to me) took it upon himself to trample me down.[10] At that time a friend wished that I would commit some kind of mad act, so that I would have something to atone for and would regain my vitality.[11]

I was rescued from the dejection in which I was sinking by a call, which I unexpectedly received in the fall of 1809 through the offices of an old family friend, to be a professor in a lyceum in Napoléonville.[12] I traveled to France, but I did not assume my professorship. Chance, Fate, the all-powerful, again decided my lot: I was drawn into the circle surrounding Madame de Staël.[13] I spent the winter of 1810–1811 following her expulsion from Blois with the prefect Prosper de Barante in Napoléon, and in the spring of 1811 I followed the great lady to Geneva and Coppet; in 1812 I was a participating witness to her flight.[14] I spent unforgettable days with this absolutely wonderful woman, met many of the most important men of the day, and experienced a portion of the history of Napoleon, his enmity toward a power which would not be subservient to him; for nothing independent was allowed to exist around or below him.

In the fall of 1812 I left Coppet and my friend Auguste de Staël in order to devote myself to the study of nature at the University of Berlin.[15] Thus for the first time I put an active and determining hand to my history and designated the direction in which it has advanced continually ever since.

The world events of the year 1813, in which it was not given me to participate actively (I no longer had a fatherland, or rather, I still had no fatherland), tore me apart repeatedly without turning me from my path. That summer, to distract myself and amuse the children of a friend, I wrote the fairy tale *Peter Schlemihl*, which was favorably received in Germany and has become a part of folk culture in England.[16]

Hardly had the ground become solid again and the sky arched blue above again, when in the year 1815 the storm rose again, and the call to arms was sounded again.[17] What my closest friends had to shout at me at the time of the first mustering I now told myself: these times held no sword for me. But it is painful to be forced to remain a spectator when such a popular movement to shoulder arms was abroad.

Prince Max von Wied-Neuwied was now making preparations to undertake his voyage to Brazil.[18] I conceived the idea of joining him. I was suggested to him as an assistant, but he could not expand the company he had already settled upon, and I was unable to afford the cost of the voyage out of my own pocket.

Then one day at the house of Julius Eduard Hitzig by chance I came across a newspaper article in which the confused news of an impending Russian exploratory expedition to the North Pole was given. "I wish I was at the North Pole with these Russians," I cried out petulantly, and probably stamped my foot at the same time. Hitzig took the paper out of my hand, read the article and asked me, "Are you serious?"—"Yes."—"Then get me testimonials as to your studies and your capabilities at once. We'll see what can be done."

The paper named Otto von Kotzebue as the leader of the expedition. Hitzig had at one time been associated with Councillor August von Kotzebue, who now lived in Königsberg, and had remained on a friendly footing with him. With the next post Hitzig sent to Councillor von Kotzebue letters and testimonials from my teachers, whom I was proud to count among my friends, and in the shortest possible time his answer was followed by a letter dated June 12, 1815, at Reval, from his brother-in-law, Admiral (then Captain) von Krusenstern of the Imperial Russian Navy, the manager of the outfitter of the expedition, Count Romanzov.[19] I was appointed in place of Professor Ledebour, whose ill health had caused him to resign, naturalist on the discovery expedition that was to be undertaken to the South Seas and around the world.[20]

# CHAPTER I

## Anticipation. Voyage to Copenhagen via Hamburg.

NOW I was really on the threshold of the most wonderful dreams, dreams I had scarcely dared dream in my boyhood years, dreams that had hovered over me in *Peter Schlemihl,* and for the realization of which, having matured into a man, I had not dared to hope. I was like the bride who with the myrtle wreath in her hair watches her beloved approach. This is the time of true happiness. Life always makes a deduction when it pays out the face value of a draft, and perhaps that person should be numbered among the favored few here below who is called away before the world translates the extravagant poetry of his future into the common prose of the present.

Conscious of my joyful vitality, I looked into the world that lay open before me, eager to enter the fray with my beloved nature, and to wrest her secrets from her. Even as in the few days before my embarcation countries, cities, and people that I was to become familiar with appeared to me in the favorable light which emanated from my own joyous bosom, I must also have left the most favorable impression on those people who saw me at that time; for the appearance of a happy person is a thing of joy.

The letter from Mr. von Krusenstern contained in very plain expressions the immediate information that I needed to know. Time was pressing: the *Rurik* was to leave St. Petersburg on July 27, and Kronshtadt on the first of August. Under favorable conditions it could dock at Copenhagen as soon as August 5. It was left up to me whether to join the expedition in St. Petersburg or Copenhagen. In case I should prefer the former, I should find the passport necessary for entry into Russia waiting for me at the border. No prospects for fame or treasure were dangled before me, but rather I was referred for reward to the knowledge of having participated in a famous enterprise. The ship was apparently exceptionally well constructed and especially well equipped for comfort. My cabin, so the words read, in spite of the small size of the ship was much better than that of Mr. Tilesius on board the *Nadezhda*.[1]

After mature consultation with my friends it was decided that I should go aboard in Copenhagen and that I should utilize and enjoy the three weeks till the middle of July in Berlin.

In these days I received a letter from Auguste de Staël dated Paris, May 15, but delayed because of the necessary detours, and I could lay it aside only with great melancholy. The die was cast, and I looked only forward, not sideward.

My friend's thoughts had turned from Old Europe to the New World, and he was preparing for a journey to found Neckerstown in the tract of wilderness that his mother possessed on the St. Lawrence River.[2] It was his desire to link my future to his. He outlined to me his far-seeing plan, the details of which would be ironed out later, and indicated the role that he had ascribed to me in their execution. I was to join him in New York the next spring with hired laborers. I could only explain to him my newly acquired commitment, distressed at refusing my cooperation in a plan that never was executed. I never found out what caused him to give it up.

My chief occupation now, using time and the good nature of scholars industriously, was to inquire what gaps in our scientific knowledge a voyage such as the one in prospect might hope to fill. I asked questions particularly in order to hear what sorts of things it would be best to collect. I could only ask in general terms, as Mr. von Krusenstern had said nothing about the goal and plan of the voyage, and I did not know what coasts we should touch at.

Niebuhr designated a stretch of the east coast of Africa where geography is still deficient and noted that conditions might easily allow it to be surveyed on the return trip.[3] I answered meekly and somewhat startled that that would be a matter for the captain alone to decide. He however ascribed some importance to the counseling voice of the scholar in such affairs. What a scholar is on such a voyage of discovery will become clear from these pages.

The poet Robert said to me: "Chamisso, collect away, and for others bring home stones and sand, seaweed, leaf moulds, Entozoa and Epizoa, that is, as I've heard, intestinal worms and vermin; but don't disdain my advice. Also collect money on your trip if the opportunity presents itself, and lay it aside for yourself. But bring me back a savage's pipe."[4] Indeed, I did bring him back a pipe made by the Eskimos, and he took great pleasure in it; but I forgot about the money.

At this point I might add that on board the *Rurik* I found a treatise by Dr. Spurzheim, who, less practical, recommended for the advancement of craniology that the heads of savages should be shaven and the impression of their skulls be taken in plaster.[5]

I left Berlin on July 15, 1815, on the ordinary stagecoach for Hamburg. The description of what was then called an ordinary stagecoach might be in order here and now, as the progress of history has also rid us of this monstrosity. But, without endangering my credibility, I can cite Lichtenberg, who has compared this torture machine to the cask of Regulus.[6] The German stagecoach, I wrote at the time, seems to be specially equipped for the collecting botanist, as one can only survive outside of it, and its speed is calculated to allow one plenty of time to walk ahead or behind. Nothing is missed at night either, as in the morning one is approximately at the same point one was on the evening before.

The ostler who took care of the team at the first stations, a tall jolly ex-gendarme, in the five and a half years since his retirement had covered about 8,524 German miles on his mail stretch of about 10 miles, going back and forth with the mail. The circumference of the earth measures only 5,400 miles.[7]

The passengers were insignificant. In Lenzen we were joined by a man of the people, a handsome, vigorous, jolly old man who was now a sailor on Elbe River boats but had formerly sailed out of Hamburg and had often visited the northern polar glacier, in the end as a harpooner on seal and whale hunts.[8] Once his ship along with several others had sunk after running afoul of ice, and he himself, after seventeen hungry days on an ice floe, had reached Greenland. He had lived with the "savages" for seventeen months and learned the "language of the savages." A Danish ship with a crew of five had taken him aboard along with twenty of his comrades in misfortune and brought them back on short rations to Europe. Of about 600 men only 120 returned home. He himself had sacrificed several fingers. This man, with whom I soon made friends, gave me more pleasure than a book. He related what he had seen, experienced, and suffered in a simple and lively fashion. I listened to him attentively and in my mind's eye I saw the fields of ice, the icebergs, and the coasts of the Arctic Sea into which I hoped to penetrate from the Bering Strait, and in which sea it might be my lot to experience and suffer the same things he had suffered.

On July 18 I reached the dear city of Hamburg, where I took care of my business, visited old friends, and made new worthwhile acquaintances. Friedrich Perthes was especially kind and helpful to me, and it was in his bookstore that the following amusing incident took place.[9] The houseservant, who saw his master on such a friendly footing with me and had heard me discoursing of distant

journeys with reference to the globe of the world, asked one of the
clerks who the dark foreign gentleman was for whom he had to run
so many errands. "Don't you know?" the clerk answered. "It's
Mungo Park."[10] And happy and proud, like a newspaper that has a
great piece of news to proclaim, the literary errand-boy ran his
errands throughout the town, stopping everyone whom he knew to
inform him that Mungo Park had not died, he was here, he was at
his master's house, he looked like such and such, and told a lot of
stories about his trips. Now, alone or in groups, the good Ham-
burgers came running to Perthes' shop and clamored to see Mungo
Park. In *Schlemihl*, in the fourth section, I wrote: "Must I confess?
it flattered me, to have been regarded as the revered head."

On the evening of the 21st I took an extra stage to Kiel. At that
time Hamburg was the northernmost limit of the known world for
me, and pressing forward beyond to Copenhagen (I had never
boarded a ship before) I was engaged in a voyage of discovery. I really
studied northern nature faithfully in Copenhagen, where, arriving
on the *Rurik*, my colleague Eschscholtz, who had never ventured so
far south before, at the same time began to study southern nature,
enraptured when for the first time he caught sight of *Vitis vinifera
sub Dio*, a grapevine growing in the open. South and north are like
youth and old age: everyone likes to think himself between both of
them as long as he can. No one wants to be old and belong to the
north. I once had to eliminate the word "old" from a poem to a re-
tiree, and a Lapp preacher once told me about his transfer to the
south, to Torneå [Tornio] just below the Arctic Circle.[11]

Having arrived in Kiel on July 22, I felt at home there right away,
even as I found the gift within myself of feeling at home wherever I
may be. Some of the men whom I had hoped to see had already left
for Copenhagen for the coronation. A friend introduced me into a
circle of friends, and I savored the enjoyment of the moment while I
waited for the departure of the packet boat, to board which I was
summoned on July 24. I had inquired with fearful concern if it was
at all conceivable that the packet boat, detained or blown astray by
contrary winds, could take more than eight days to get to Copenhagen, and I was assured that in the worst possible event I would land
on time on the Danish islands.

An inlet of the sea turns, like the shore of a lake, inward to Kiel,
bordered by hills that are resplendent in the most gorgeous green of
creation. An inland sea without ebb and tide, into the smooth surface of which the green garb of the earth dips, does not have the
splendor of the ocean. Nettelbeck dubs the Baltic a duckpond.[12] On
the trip from Kiel to Copenhagen one does not even get into the

middle of it, as one never loses sight of land. But it became quite apparent how the seas are really the roads of the land in the face of all the sails one could see round about, and of which we never counted fewer than fifty between the green plain of Sjælland and the low coasts of Sweden.

We had gotten under way on July 24. In the evening the wind came up and the night was stormy. When the ship, a galleass with a crew of five, began to roll, the initially loud passengers became silent, and I myself paid my first tribute to the sea.[13] But I recovered the next day, and thought that I had gotten off more cheaply than I had feared. Along with this experience I also obtained something else on this prelude to circumnavigating the globe, which propriety prevents me from naming. This became evident later on, when I was unhappy at finding what I nonetheless had been busily seeking. In an apothecary's shop where I, ignorant of Danish, unfolded my best Latin requesting help, the apprentice answered me in much better German and handed me the salve I had requested. At noon of July 26 in a complete calm we were towed into the harbor of Copenhagen by our own boat.

In Copenhagen, I spent perhaps the most joyous and happiest days of my life, making myself at home right away, with dear, sympathetic friends and in friendly and informative conversations with men who were the honor of their country in science and the arts. Hornemann was absent at the time, but Pfaff from Kiel was in Copenhagen.[14] Oehlenschläger was just then busy translating Fouqué's *Undine*.[15] The theater, as is usual in the summer months, was closed. Libraries, collections, gardens kept me busy during the daytime, and my evenings were devoted to sociability.

I attended the anointment, or the coronation as we call it, of the very popular King Frederick VI of Denmark in the castle at Frederiksborg.[16] I note in passing that my friends obtained the necessary ticket of admission for me from a Jew who had some for sale.

In Copenhagen I did not get to eat any horseflesh, which as a naturalist I would have liked. My friends made the effort in vain. For the time I was there no horses were slaughtered in the Veterinary Medicine School, which alone has the prerogative.

Lieutenant Wormskiold, who had already made valuable contributions to natural history on a journey to Greenland, and who was now applying for permission to join the Romanzov expedition as a voluntary naturalist, sought me out soon after my arrival.[17] I received him warmly with open arms, happy to be able to conduct another worker to the beckoning harvest, and people congratulated me on the industrious assistant I should have.

In the early morning of August 9 I received the pleasing communication from the Admiralty that a Russian brig had just been
sighted.

Perhaps here is the place, before I conduct you on board the *Rurik*,
for a few lines that I wrote at the time about Copenhagen and Denmark. When you read them, think of the English attack and the loss
of the fleet in the year 1807, and of the latest events, the forced ced-
ing of Norway to Sweden, Norway's independent defense under
Prince Christian of Denmark, and the final treaty whereby as an
independent kingdom with its own laws it subjected itself to the
king of Sweden.[18]

Copenhagen does not seem to me to be any larger or more populous than Hamburg. Broad streets, new architecture without character. The new city hall is built in the Greek style of bricks covered
with stucco. The Danes have always hated the Germans: only
brothers can hate each other. But now they hate the Swedes first,
then the English, and their hatred toward the Germans is receding.
They are striving for their own identity as a people and are humbled.
Many do not like Napoleon for this reason, but all recognize, and
who would deny it, that they were the victims of others' sins. They
share France's fate because France's power held the balance against
the power of their oppressors, the English. From Copenhagen the
view is that Norway, even less than the German provinces, was a
*possession* of Denmark's but rather by language, family ties, and
history really the other half of the kingdom. The fleet however was
the palladium. At the symposia I attended the Norwegian popular
song "Sinclair Song" was generally sung fiercely and sadly, and the
toast "To the first successful battle at sea!" was proposed.[19] The
king is loved with sincere attachment, and the misfortune of the
times is not attributed to him. The ceremony of anointment, at
which he appeared with crown and scepter with his knights around
him in ancient garb, was not a mere spectacle or carnival, as the
Danes' hearts were in it, and a national popular spirit still animated
the old venerable forms. Those who think justly attribute that
which was undertaken and really attained with regard to Norway to
Prince Christian with grateful love; the unjust attribute to him the
fault for that which was not accomplished, and deprecate him. In
Kiel the professors are disposed toward Germany, the students
toward Denmark.

# CHAPTER II

## The *Rurik*.   Departure from Copenhagen.   Plymouth.

ON the morning of August 9, 1815, I reported to the captain on board the *Rurik* at the wharf in Copenhagen. Lieutenant Wormskiold did the same along with me, and Mr. von Kotzebue, apparently influenced by the harmony he saw reigning between us, agreed to take him on. According to his travel account he seems not to have acted completely independently in this matter. He handed me a flattering letter from Count Romanzov and another from Mr. von Krusenstern and left me otherwise temporarily without instructions and commands as to my actions. I asked for them in vain. I was not advised as to my duties and prerogatives and obtained no information as to arrangements on shipboard that I would have to fit myself into. In my position on the *Rurik* things went for me the way they did elsewhere in the world, where only life teaches life. We were ordered to be on board with our gear within three days. However, the date of departure dragged on until the 17th. On the 13th the envoys of several courts visited the ship and when they left they were saluted with thirteen guns.[1]

Here is the place to give a preliminary account of the isolated little world to which I now belonged, and of the nutshell enclosed and compressed in which it was destined to be rocked across the huge spaces of the ocean. The ship is the home of the seafarer: in a voyage such as this he spends about two-thirds of the time floating in complete isolation between the blue of the sea and the blue of the sky. For not quite one-third of the time it lies at anchor in sight of land. The goal of the long voyage might be to reach a foreign land, but that is hard, harder than one imagines. Everywhere the ship that holds a person is the old Europe from which he strives in vain to escape, where the old faces speak the old language, where tea and coffee are drunk in traditional fashion at set times, and where the whole misery of a completely unembellished domesticity holds him fast. As long as he can still see the banners of his ship from foreign soil this

sight holds him to the old soil as if by magic spell. And still he loves
his ship!—like the inhabitant of the Alpine hut who willingly
allows himself to be buried in it for a part of the year. (This is the
case in Trient in Savoy.)

Here is what I wrote at the beginning of the voyage about our
wandering world. As part of the names the first names and patro-
nymics by which we were called on the ship in the Russian fashion
are given.

The captain, Otto Astavich von Kotzebue. First lieutenant, Gleb
Simonovich Shishmarev, a friend of the captain's, an older officer
than he, speaking only Russian; a merrily beaming full moon of a
face that it is a joy to look into; a powerful, healthy nature; a person
who never forgot how to laugh.[2] Second lieutenant, Ivan Jakovle-
vich Sakharin, sickly, irritable, but good-natured; understands some
French and Italian.[3] The ship's doctor, naturalist, and entomologist,
Ivan Ivanovich Eschscholtz, a young physician from Dorpat, almost
reserved, but noble and true as gold. The naturalist, I myself,
Adelbert Loginovich. The painter, Login Andrevich Choris, a German by origin, who, while still very young, had accompanied Marshal von Bieberstein as an artist on his journey to the Caucasus.[4]
Volunteer naturalist, Martin Petrovich Wormskiold. Three mates:
Khramchenko, a very good-natured, hard-working youth; Petrov, a
small, moodily merry fellow; the third, Koniev, less close to us. Two
boatswains' mates and twenty seamen.

The seamen, chosen from among those who had volunteered for
the expedition, are an extremely worthy group; tough men, completely obedient to the strictest discipline, but otherwise of capable,
ambitious turns of mind, proud of their profession of global sailors.

The captain, who in his earliest youth accompanied Krusenstern
on his voyage around the world in the *Nadezhda*, is the only one on
board who has crossed the Equator. I am the oldest one in years.

The *Rurik*, which the tsar had allowed to fly a naval flag on this
voyage of discovery, is a very small brig, a two-master of 180 tons,
and carries eight small cannon on the deck. Below deck the captain's cabin takes up the rear of the ship. From it the main cabin is
separated by the common hatchway, which is situated at the foot of
the large mast. Both get their light from above. The rest of the ship's
hold up to the kitchen at the foot of the foremast serves as a dwelling for the sailors.

The main cabin, incidentally, is twelve feet square. The mast, at
the foot of which there is a fireplace, makes an indentation into it.
Opposite the fireplace is a mirror, and below it, one side fastened to
the wall, is a square table. On each of the two side walls there are

two berths, really closets built into the wall and equipped for sleeping, six feet long and two and a half wide. Under them there is a ledge for sitting that runs the length of the wall and makes space for drawers, four of which belong to each berth. A few footstools complete the furnishings.

Two of the berths belong to the officers, the other two to the doctor and me. Choris and Wormskiold sleep in the forecastle in hammocks. My berth and three of the drawers under it comprise the only space on the ship that belongs to me. Choris took possession of the fourth drawer. In the narrow room of the cabin four people sleep, six live, and seven eat. At the table coffee is drunk at seven o'clock in the morning, a meal is eaten at twelve o'clock noon, and then the dishes are washed. At five o'clock tea is drunk and in the evening at eight the leftovers from the noon meal are served again. The duration of every meal is doubled when an officer has a watch on deck. In the intervals the artist takes up two sides of the table with his drawing board, the third side belongs to the officers, and only when they leave it unoccupied may the others compete for its use. If one wishes to write or engage in some other occupation at the table, he must wait and seize the scarce fleeting moments, then utilize them greedily. But I can't work that way. One seaman is in charge of serving the captain, by the name of Shafekha, a little Tatar, a Mohammedan. Another is in charge of the main cabin, Sikov, one of the most efficient, a Russian of almost Herculean stature. Tobacco may be smoked only in the cabin. It is against the ship's rules to leave anything standing outside of the space allotted to each one. Incidentally, the captain protests against collecting on the voyage because the ship's space does not permit it, and an artist is at the disposition of the naturalist to draw whatever the latter might desire. The artist, however, protests that he has to take orders only directly from the captain.

In Copenhagen, beyond the cited number of the crew, a cook was hired, a derelict son of the sea. By his facial features he looked to be an East Indian or a Malayan, but by language, which was compounded of a confused blend of all the dialects spoken by man, he was hardly a human being. Besides him a pilot was taken on board for the passage through the Channel to Plymouth, and the latter brought the number of our table company to eight, so that we no longer all fit at the table.

The *Rurik* had sailed out of Kronshtadt on July 30, 1815 (two days sooner than I had been told), and arrived at the wharf in Copenhagen on August 9. We weighed anchor on the 17th at 4:00 A.M., but we had to drop anchor four hours later outside of Helsingør.[5] The wind, which alternates between holding the gate open to sail in or to sail out, did not become favorable to us until the morning of the nineteenth, on which day we sailed through the sound at ten o'clock in the morning, as did more than sixty other ships at the same time, all having waited for the same moment. We saluted the fort, without waiting for a boat, which was rowing toward us from the port authority's ship. Sailing faster than the merchant ships around about us, we soon overtook the leaders, and soon we had the entire fleet behind us. The moment was really fine and exhilarating.

On our passage through the North Sea we had contrary winds almost incessantly, along with cold, wet weather and cloud-covered skies. After much tacking about, we had to be shown the lightship at the mouth of the Thames, which we had not yet discovered, by a ship that we hailed. I was called on deck in the night of August 31–September 1 to view the fires on the French coast, which were burning at Calais. The impression did not quite meet my expectations. In the morning a favorable breeze brought us through the Straits of Dover. Albion with its high white cliffs lay close to our right, while far to the left France lay murky in the fog. We gradually lost sight of it, and it never became visible again. On the same day we had to cast anchor for a few hours. At noon of August 7 we anchored at Cathwater off Plymouth.

The period of this passage was a hard apprenticeship for me. I came to know seasickness, with which I struggled constantly, without ever overcoming it. However, the condition in which we are placed by this illness is a miserable one. Without interest in anything, one can only lie in his berth, or subject himself to the wind on deck at the foot of the main mast where motion, next to its center, is less perceptible. The close air of the cabin is unbearable, and the mere smell of food excites unspeakable disgust. Even though the lack of food I could keep down perceptibly weakened me, I still did not lose courage. I listened to tales of others who had suffered more than I had, and about Nelson, who had never gone to sea without getting sick.[6] I endured this trial without grumbling for the sake of the happy goal.

In the meantime Wormskiold had undertaken to observe the meteorological instruments. His knowledge of life at sea gave him a great advantage over me, and I, uninitiated in these new conditions, aroused disadvantageous prejudices against myself by many an infraction of the rules. I did not know, for instance, that one must not visit the captain in his cabin without having been summoned, and that, when he is on deck, the leeward side belongs exclusively to him, and that one is not allowed to address him there, either; and that this side, when the captain does not claim it, belongs to the officer on watch. I was unaware of many such things, which I only gradually learned.

I had not noticed that with respect to service a distinction was made between the officers and the rest of us. As we sailed into Plymouth I gave my shoes to Sikov to polish. He took them from my hand and put them right back in the place from which I had taken them. I was told that he was obliged to serve only the officers. From that day on I was forced to do without the small services which up until then he had voluntarily performed for me. The good fellow liked me a good deal; I think he would have gone through a hail of fire for me, but he would not have touched my shoes again. Choris was able to get other seamen to perform such services. Eschscholtz knew how to perform them himself. But I knew how to put myself above them, and do without them.

As soon as the ship lay at anchor I was summoned to the captain. I stepped into his cabin. He addressed me earnestly and sharply, admonishing me to weigh my decision carefully. We were now in the last European port where it would be easy to turn back. He begged me to consider, *that as a passenger on board a warship I might not make any demands, as none could be fulfilled.* I answered in surprise that it was my inalterable decision to make the voyage under any conditions that might be imposed upon me, and if I were not discharged would not resign from the expedition.

The captain's words, which I have repeated here as I wrote them down at the time just as they were spoken and as they still resound unforgettably in my ears, were very depressing for me. I did not believe that I had given any cause for them. However, I cannot blame the captain on this occasion. It seems so natural that a titular scholar, participant in a learned undertaking, would demand to be a figure of authority, that a ship's captain cannot be blamed for anticipating such demands and heading them off. For two authorities cannot coexist on a ship. This is also demonstrated by the experience of merchant vessels, where generally things do not proceed amicably when along with the captain a supercargo as representative of the owner is aboard. This is taken into consideration where seafaring is understood. In France and England no titular scholars are taken along on voyages of discovery anymore; instead, it is seen to that all the participants in the expedition are scholars. On American merchantmen the head of the ship is at the same time the merchant, and the mercantile companies have trading posts so that the captain of a ship has unimpeded authority, his only obligation being to sail his ship between these trading posts and the mother country. Even if it lies in the nature of things, it is nonetheless regrettable that the scholar, who as a rule is well off on a merchantman, should be so hemmed in in the very place where a wider sphere of activity seems to open for him. Full of joy and hope, full of a thirst for action he goes there, and the first thing he must learn is that the chief task he has to accomplish is to make himself as inconspicuous as possible, to take up as little space and to be around as little as possible. He has dreamed of high and noble battles with the elements, dangers and deeds, and instead finds the usual boredom and the never-ending small change of domestic misery, unpolished shoes, and the like.

Nor was my next experience exactly encouraging. Through foresight I had made myself acquainted with the principle and the construction of the filter fountain and offered to construct one. The water, which had been drawn from the Neva River at an inopportune time and was already smelling abominably, seemed to support my proposal. Nevertheless it found no interest. There was no room and no time for it, other necessities were lacking, and finally the captain was of the opinion that "filtering would deprive the water of its nutrient parts, and make it less healthful." I saw that I had to drop the matter.

Plymouth is situated on an inlet of the sea, which behind the stretch of higher coastal land divides into arms and penetrates far inland. Old and new cities, villages, shipyards, arsenals, fortresses, magnificent country mansions all cluster around these shores. The whole region is one city, Plymouth itself being merely a section of it. The land round about is everywhere divided by walls and hedges into fields. The white walls, the fine dust, the architecture, the gigantic inscriptions on the houses, and the placards make one think involuntarily of the environs of Paris. Such a sea of houses is Paris, too, but it lacks the great roadway, the sea. The sea here bears in its own harbors and at anchoring places innumerable ships, over there warships (Plymouth Dock) and here (Plymouth, Cathwater) merchant ships of all nations. At the time a gigantic operation was being carried out, the building of the breakwater, a dam that was to partially close off the entrance of the sound and protect the waters within from the onslaughts of the outer waves. Over sixty-two vessels were continuously engaged in transporting the huge amounts of rocks that were incessantly being blasted off in the stone quarries on the shores of the fjord. The thunder of these charges, the signal shots, the saluting of ships often evoked the picture of a beleaguered city in the very midst of peace.

I was and remained a stranger in Plymouth. Nature attracted me more than the people. It has an unexpectedly southern character and the climate seems to be especially mild. The southern European oak *(Quercus ilex)* forms the pleasant groves of Mount Edgecomb, and *Magnolia grandiflora* blooms on trellises in the open.

The sea is perfectly magnificent with its high rocky shores and tides of a height hardly observed anywhere else in the world (the coast of New Holland). At high tide the sea climbs as much as twenty-two feet up the transitional limestone and clay cliffs, and at ebb tide the richest, most marvelously enigmatic world is unveiled to the eye of the naturalist. Since then I have seen nowhere else a shore so rich in seaweed and seaworms. I recognized hardly any of these animals. I couldn't find them in my books and I was appalled at my ignorance. I did not learn until later that the most of them remain unknown and undescribed. In the course of the voyage I missed a lot in this way, and I am dutifully noting it here as a lesson for my successors. Observe, my friends, collect and store away for science everything you can get your hands on, and don't be led astray by the idea that this or that must be known, and you just don't know about it. Indeed, among the few land plants that I took away from Plymouth as a memento was a species that was new to English flora.

We were favored by the brightest sun. On one of my walks I met two officers of the 43rd Regiment, who, curious to see our ship, followed me to it. They invited the captain and all the rest of us to join their regimental mess table. Things are so arranged that on one or two days of the week a more sumptuous meal than usual is served, and every one of them may bring guests. The captain and I accepted the invitation. I don't think I ever saw a more richly laden table. A lot was eaten, and even more was drunk, while no compulsion was imposed upon the foreign guests. However, no merriment reigned. In the evening those who invited us escorted us back to the ship, and one of them relieved himself of the wine he had consumed without disturbing propriety.

I have made no further mention of the political events that brought me to this voyage, and which faded into the background as soon as the call had been issued to me. Plymouth reminds me, the friendly contact with the officers of the 43rd Regiment reminds me, of the man of destiny whom, shortly before our arrival, the *Bellerophon* had transported from here to St. Helena, so that he who had once subjected and ruled the world should there decline pitifully amidst miserable disputes with his guards.[7] The enthusiasm for the conquered enemy that resounded in our ears from all classes of the people, especially the military, was uniformly general. Everyone tells when and how often he saw him, and what he did, in order to join in with the homage of the multitude. Everyone wore his medals, everyone praised him and angrily cursed the arbitrary action that had deprived him of the benefits of the law. In what contrast to the attitude prevailing here was the base abuse of the Spaniards in Chile who eagerly sought to be the beast of the fable who wishes to give the lion the last kick! The *Bellerophon* lay at anchor far into the Sound, and the Emperor became accustomed to showing himself on the deck between five and six. At this hour innumerable boats surrounded the ship, and the multitude waited eagerly for the moment to greet the hero and to become intoxicated with the sight of him. Later the *Bellerophon* had gone under sail and, crossing the Channel, waited for the equipment he was still lacking. A story was told of a suit directed against Napoleon for debt, and the subsequent issuance of a subpoena by a justice of the peace, which subpoena, if it could have been brought aboard the ship while it lay at anchor, would have had the consequence that the accused would have had to be brought before the judge. But if his foot had touched the English soil he could no longer be deprived of the protection of the law.[8]

At the time Miss O'Neill was appearing in the Plymouth theater in guest roles in performances at higher prices than usual. I saw her twice, in *Romeo and Juliet* and in *Menschenhass und Reue (The Stranger).*[9] Upon our return in the year 1818, I also saw Kean in London, and in the role of Othello.[10] I gratefully acknowledge it as a special favor bestowed on me by Fate that I have known both the French and the German theater, both in their fullest splendor, I might say before their decline, and was also privileged to see some of the greats of the English stage, even if only briefly. Miss O'Neill did not satisfy me in the role of Juliet, in which role she seemed to me to be too massive. However, I had no fault to find with her Eulalia, and the gift of tears, which has often been admired in her, stood her in excellent stead.[11] In general the actors seemed to perform Shakespeare almost just the way Hamlet did not wish his "Mousetrap" to be given.[12] Kotzebue entitles us to lesser demands, which are fulfilled more satisfactorily. In general the English actors all have good presence, speak the verses correctly, and endeavor with visible exertion to pronounce the words clearly and distinctly, contrary to the habits of everyday life. They seem to me comparable in this to the French actors, who find indispensable a training that includes everything that even those not given the gift by God can fashion from within themselves and into themselves. Artists endowed with a talent by God are rare all over. Maybe our Germany has a comparatively large number of those, but seldom does one see those on our stages who have trained themselves up to the point that is demanded of the French performers. And the common arti-sans, which make up the majority of them—what should one say about them?

As I have just had to report that in Shakespeare's own country I saw our Kotzebue performed by the foremost artists, and in a more satisfactory manner than their own hero, I will also testify right away, in order not to have to come back to it, that for those who rec-ognize *de facto* governments, Kotzebue is the poet of the world. How often in the far ends of the earth, namely on O-Wahu [O'ahu], Guaján [Guam], etc., have I been praised for my small share in the enterprise of his son, in order to cast a hem of the mantle of his fame over me. Everywhere we heard his name mentioned. American newspapers reported that *The Stranger* had been performed to extra-ordinary applause.[13] All the libraries in the Aleutian Islands, as far as I have investigated them, consisted of a single volume of the Rus-sian translation of Kotzebue. The viceroy of Manila, paying homage to the Muse, commissioned his son to deliver a gift of the most expensive coffee to his father, and on the promontory of the Cape of Good Hope the Berlin naturalist Mundt learned of the arrival of the *Rurik*, knowing me to be aboard and expecting me, from a sailor who could tell him only that the recently docked ship's captain had a comedian's name. At such a distance from home I heard nothing of *Alarcos*, of *Ion*, and their authors.[14]

The American merchants, for whom no sea-washed coast is inac-cessible, but for whom the sun of Romantic poetry has not yet risen, are the wandering apostles of Kotzebue's fame; for them he is the fit surrogate of poetry. The facts demonstrate that he possesses a requirement that many more eminent than he lack. For what good does it do Roland's mare to be so incomparable and flawless when it is, unfortunately, dead?[15]

As a rule we found the opinion prevalent that the great writer no longer was alive. That is natural, for who would look for Homer, Voltaire, Don Quixote, and all the other great names in veneration of which he has grown up, among the living? But people claimed to have seen the notice of his death on O-Wahu and in other places in American newspapers. This rumor, which made me uneasy, came to the captain's ears, who laid it to the death of one of his brothers, who died gloriously in the campaign of 1813.[16] In the course of these pages it will be seen that people in Europe had to believe us lost and perished because we missed the mailboat in Kamchatka, so that the father had every reason to mourn his hopeful son. Finally the *Rurik* arrives unexpectedly and unhoped for; and, ahead of any possible news about him, Otto Aslavich hurries to conduct his young wife, whom he has just married, to his father—he finds the bloody corpse on the bier!

I shall come back from this digression, which led me rather far astray, to Plymouth again, and hasten toward our departure. Time, not always appropriately utilized, passed very quickly. Each one of us had to complete his outfit (and/or equipment). In these distracting surroundings nothing held us together. Everyone provided for himself what he would and could. Much could have come about more efficiently and quickly if it had been discussed in concert and carried out according to a plan. A couple of dinners to which I was invited along with the captain offer me no material for further observations. The manners of the English, who excite respect more than they attract us by their friendly kindness, are described in all the books. I tasted the gooseberry wine for which the house of the *Vicar of Wakefield* was famous, and found it similar to champagne, only a little sweeter.[17] I have sat at the bare table with them after the tablecloth was removed and drunk with them and seen them drink, seriously, calmly, and taciturnly, the one bowing by turns to the other, an expression of respect and good will that one must not fail to reciprocate. In general I have never seen Englishmen laugh except when I tried to speak English with them, and in this way to my own joy I have produced joyful faces. Later on the ship I taught Choris English, who repaid me by from thenceforth serving me as interpreter among Englishmen. Where he got the pronunciation to go with my English I never found out. In general I found the English courteous and ready to oblige. The seamen's hospital, which I visited, causes me to testify that everything that the books say about the plentifulness, cleanliness, and beauty of such English institutions, and of the order and abundance that prevails in them, is far surpassed by the impression that an actual inspection provides.

On September 22 the *Rurik* was ready to sail. The observatory, which had stood under a tent on Mount Batten, a desolate peninsula in our vicinity, had been put on board again, and the steam bath dismantled which had been assembled in another tent for officers and men. It was here in Plymouth that I first met up with and adopted the Russian manner of bathing.

We were supposed to weigh anchor the next day, and still the letters from my dear ones, and a small capital in letters of credit that I hoped to take with me on the voyage, remained in the Russian Embassy in London, to which I had had them addressed, and all the steps I had taken to have them sent to me had been in vain. Since then I have learned that even where official business is concerned matters are rarely taken care of with any greater dispatch, and I never again chose this method of communication. Letting things lie, which may be an excellent means of dispatching many items of business, is not equally suited to the needs of all items. At the time I regretted that the captain had not carried out his original plan of putting me ashore at Dover or some other point on the English coast, from where I would have traveled to Plymouth via London. Only after we had twice started on our way, and twice been beaten back into the harbor by the gale, did my letters arrive. The equinoctial storms must have taken pity on me in my distress and concern.

On a long voyage, even as whatever possible is provided for the health of the men, such as fresh food, etc., similar provision is made for their entertainment, for the most killing thing is boredom. A seamen's singing group was furnished with the instruments of a janissary band, and our Bengal cook possessed a fiddle. Nevertheless, the captain was anxious to make provision for even more music. Ivan Ivanovich played the piano, and it was decided to procure him a psaltery or some other larger instrument if space would permit. Martin Petrovich undertook to do this with extraordinary zeal. On the last day he came enthusiastically up to the ship and reported that he had found a really excellent organ, which he had measured and which could be set up in the ship's hold at the foot of the mainmast, and all they wanted for it was twenty-one pounds. A person doesn't want to back down when the majority has decided, and for my three pounds I became a patron of the noble art of music, as did the rest. The captain went ashore on business, and Martin Petrovich as well, to fetch the instrument, which he soon brought back along with a workman to set it up. Our officers looked on with amazement and dismay but in silence as at the prearranged place a large machine, a church organ, was set up, which covered the hatchways to the lower hold. Otto Astavich, when he came aboard just as the work was finished, was incensed, and would have liked to vent his anger on the officer on watch for having permitted such a thing. But he himself had given the command. So there was nothing left for him to do but to order that within a half hour the organ should either be put ashore or thrown overboard. The former arrangement was made. One is punished in accordance with his sin: it amuses me to think that I, the opposite of a musical person, should have not one, but two shares in this property of ours sitting in England—for I bought Martin Petrovich's at a discount when he left us in Kamchatka.

On September 23 we weighed anchor, only to have to drop it again immediately, as the wind reversed direction. Not until the morning of the 25th did we set sail again with a weak land breeze, but right at the exit from the sound the south wind caught us from off the ocean and, blowing against us with ever-increasing force, caused us to tack about along the coast. In the night it swelled to a mighty storm, and we suffered some damage to the ship and had a man injured. We thus considered ourselves fortunate to regain our old anchorage at dawn of the 26th. In so doing we endangered an English merchantman at anchor next to us, causing it to incur some damage to its rigging, so that its captain appeared on deck cursing, in shirtsleeves and a bib, his face half covered with shaving soap and half shaved.

But the *Rurik* fought against the fury of the storm on a dark autumn night between the lighthouse at Eddystone, which cast its blinding light on the scene, and the coast of England, on which she was in danger of going aground, driven by the fact that she carried many sails. You are familiar with the Eddystone lighthouse from your long-discarded children's books, this magnificent work of modern architecture that rises from a single stone lost in the Channel to a height that you perhaps know, and which I do not care to take the time to look up.[18] You know that in a fierce storm the foaming crest of the wave is hurled up to the lantern itself. You note that all the conditions are here united to make a storm really beautiful, and you expect a really poetic description from me. My friends, after I had emptied the contents of my stomach, I lay quietly, quite quietly, in my bunk, troubling myself about nothing in the world, and hardly noticing the noise that table, chairs, boots, and drawers were making round about me as they did their own restless dance to and fro in the cabin, keeping time to the howling music and its booming rhythm up on deck. What a miserable creature a seasick person is you can see from the fact that our good doctor, normally as industrious and conscientious in his duties as anyone in the world, being now called, sent for, commanded to help the injured seaman, stayed quietly and motionless in his berth until everything was over.

Did you ever, as I did, have the house in which you were living burn down around you some fine night? Did you then act calmly and rapidly, taking care of wife and child and your possessions, neglecting nothing that should have been done? This is the situation the officer at sea faces when a storm comes up. With increased activity he wages war against the elements, and whether he wins or loses, he is pleased with himself, and after the danger is over he is the richer for the joyous demonstration of his own powers. It is the same feeling that makes a soldier lustful after a battle. For a passenger, however, a storm is only a period of the most inexpressible boredom. I will relate briefly here how things generally went at such times during the voyage. At a certain command which sounded above decks we in the cabin knew: war is declared! Thereupon everyone nailed his drawers shut and saw to it that his movable possessions were made fast. We lay down in our berths. When the next wave hit the deck and entered the cabin through the portholes, the latter were covered with tarred cloth, and we were blinded. Then I was generally requested to make the attempt to dredge up some as yet untold anecdotes out of my supply. But soon we were all silent, listening to each other take turns yawning. Meals stopped. We ate biscuits and drank brandy or a glass of wine. The naturalist hardly dares venture on deck, impelled by his sense of duty to take a quick look at the waves, for if a wave drenches him he is completely helpless, having no means to change his outer clothing or his linen, or even to dry himself. Moreover, the matter did not even have the attraction of danger. Danger is never present for direct observation and could at best only be determined intellectually by means of ratiocination. The unloaded pistol whose mouth I hold before my eye, shows me danger; I never looked it in the face that way on our little wave-rocked house of planks.

Early on the 30th we again set sail, and, caught by the storm and driven back, we again had to seek refuge behind the breakwater, where we cast anchor. Our pilot, whom, because of his striking similarity to the caricatures, we called John Bull, must have thought us like the revenant humpback in the *Arabian Nights.*

Not until October 4 did we succeed in getting out to sea.

# CHAPTER III
## Voyage from Plymouth to Tenerife.

WE sailed out of Plymouth Sound on October 4, 1815, toward ten o'clock in the morning. We caught a favorable wind, but the sea was still agitated from the preceding storms. We remained in sight of land all day long. When I came up on deck the next morning and looked in the direction of Cape Lizard it had disappeared, and nothing was to be seen except sky and waves. Our homeland lay behind us, before us lay hope.

At the beginning of this voyage and up until about the fourteenth of October I suffered continually and severely from seasickness worse than I had ever had before. However, I retained my cheerfulness and tried to keep busy. I read an act of *Earl Hakon* in Danish with Martin Petrovich, and read the rest of it without any assistance. I owe Oehlenschläger much pleasure and comfort. I always found *Correggio* moving, and Earl Hakon, the renegade Christian, the only believing heathen I have ever encountered in our literature, always filled me with great respect.[1]

With mostly favorable winds we followed the great trade route which leads southward out of the Channel to the Mediterranean, or past the entrance to it, to both of the Indies. Seldom did a day go by without our seeing several sails, and from the land, the closest points of which remained about 300 sea miles to the east, frequent messengers came to us when there was a NW wind and a clear sky.[2] On the 9th a small lark landed on our ship, where for three days it enjoyed the hospitality we gladly extended toward it, and three other land birds hovered around us at various times. The Atlantic Ocean never seemed wide to me. I always felt as if I were on a well-traveled stretch whose shores I did not have to see in order to feel them. On the contrary, the seas we had sailed on hitherto, the coastal fires of which, like the lanterns in a city, we seldom lost sight of, and where you have to fear that you will run another ship down or be run down yourself, seemed to me to be too narrow. The sky afforded us a great, awe-inspiring spectacle with all its changes. Behind us the North Star sank down in the sky, and the Great Bear, still ἄμμορος ὠκεανοῖο in Homer,[3] hovering above the saline depths, dropped its stars one after another into the sea, while before us the father of light and life arose.

On October 13 and the days following at 39°27′N latitude we had a perfect calm for almost five days. The sea leveled off to a smooth mirror, the sails hung down slack from the yardarms, and no motion could be felt. It is remarkable that even then water currents played imperceptibly with the ship, which kept changing its direction with respect to the sun, so that on deck one could see his shadow circle around at his feet and pass now to one side, now to the other side of his body. In the same manner a boat that was launched kept changing its position with respect to the ship, coming closer to it at one point and drawing farther away from it the next. If my imagination were to create a picture more horrible than a storm, shipwreck, or fire at sea, it would condemn a ship on the high seas to a calm which allows no hope that it will ever cease.

However, the naturalist who during a favorable wind, his gaze turned forward, idly dreams of the next coast on which he will land, in a calm is aroused to a new activity. The sun coaxes the lowly animals of the sea to the surface of the water, and he can easily gain possession of these most fascinating enigmas of nature. At other times we could only hope to catch similar animals from the deck of the ship with a net of canvas on a pole when our speed did not exceed two knots (that is, two miles an hour).

Here it was the salpas especially that attracted Eschscholtz and me, and it was here on these transparent mollusks of the high seas that we made the discovery that seemed important to us: that among them one and the same species appears in two radically different forms in alternate generations; that namely a free-swimming solitary salpa differently shaped bears young alive that are chained together almost like polyps, each one of which members of this little republic again brings free-swimming solitary animals into the world in which the form of the preceding generation recurs. It is as if the caterpillar bore the butterfly and the butterfly then in turn bore the caterpillar.[4]

I always studied, observed, and collected together with my faithful Eschscholtz. In complete harmony, we never distinguished between mine and thine. One of us would take pleasure in his own discovery only when he had called the other in as witness, as participant. Why must I say this? With Lieutenant Wormskiold this was not the case. He preferred a jealous rivalry, which unfortunately is not unknown among scholars, to the relationship I had offered him and into which I had entered with Eschscholtz. The fact that he considered me a natural philosopher, a class of people who were in bad repute with him, may have estranged him from me. He may also have thought to have too much of an advantage not to decline a cooperative effort to which he brought more than he would have garnered. I can smile now at the profound distress, at the despair that overcame me because of this, and of which the letters I wrote from Tenerife, Brazil, and Chile bear ample witness. I made every effort to convince myself and others that I was without any fault in what I considered a bad situation. Now as an old man, my passion having cooled, and having repeatedly reviewed the facts in the case, I can be the judge of myself and say: I really was without fault. Following his refusal it was still no comfort to me that Wormskiold lived on bad terms not only with me but also with the artist Choris, a situation that life at sea can easily cause to arise, and which then develops according to the character and the peculiarities of the people involved. I remember that, in sight of the coast of North America, I gazed over at the dreary, naked cliffs and could almost wish that the small boat would transport me to that wintry desolation and there deposit me, in order to free myself from the torture of the present.

Moreover, Lieutenant Wormskiold had stated at Plymouth that he would perhaps leave the expedition at Tenerife. On the crossing from Tenerife to Santa Catarina he declared that in Brazil he would disconnect his destiny from ours. Once he had arrived there—the land cools off the gall heated up by the sea—I advised him in a friendly fashion to choose this exceedingly rich field of investigation for his harvest, and in order to make it easier to carry out, I placed my cash at his disposal. He was now of a different mind. He intended to stay in Chile, but Spanish photophobia was opposed to his decision and placed insuperable obstacles in his path. He did not leave us until Kamchatka.

It was as grievous to my heart to write these lines as it is to make confession, and I shall not again refer to the subject, which I just could not leave unmentioned. There is something very peculiar about life on a ship. Have you read Jean Paul's biography of the twins whose backs were joined together at birth?[5] That is something similar, but not the same thing. External life is monotonous and empty, like the surface of the water and the blue of the sky above: no stories, no events, no news. Even the ever-identical mealtimes which twice daily divide up the time become more of an annoyance than an enjoyment. There is no way to get away, no way to avoid each other, no way to harmonize discord. If one day our friend says "Good day" instead of the "Good morning" we are used to hearing from him, we brood about this novelty all day long, and darkly cultivate our trouble, for there is no space on the ship to discuss the matter with him. In turn one or the other is subject to melancholia. Also, one's relationship to the captain is a quite special one to which nothing on land can be compared. The Russian proverb says, "God is high and the tsar is a long way away." On board his ship this man is a more unlimited monarch than the tsar, he is always present, so that one is as good as joined to him back to back, as one can not escape him, one cannot avoid him. Mr. von Kotzebue was amiable and kind. At the top of his many praiseworthy characteristics was his conscientious sense of justice. But he had to produce intellectually the strength necessary for his position of command: he had no strength of character, and he had his moods. He suffered from intestinal complaints, and on shipboard we could tell how his digestion was without its being mentioned. In view of the deficiency just deplored, especially in the later period of the voyage, when his indisposition increased in intensity, he may well have felt himself endangered by someone who was going about his work energetically and without duplicity. On the voyage across the Atlantic Ocean he had discarded the prejudices he may have felt, and I came to be looked upon as his favorite. I myself was almost passionately attached to him. Later he turned from me, and his disfavor rested upon me.

With the help of Login Andrevich I had begun to study Russian, at first indolently under the beautiful sky of the tropics, then more seriously when we headed toward the north. I had progressed to the point where I had read several chapters in Sarychev, but after due consideration I gave up the endeavor and learned to consider myself fortunate that the language was a kind of barrier that imposed itself between me and my immediate surroundings.[6] I never forgot anything else as quickly and as completely as I did my Russian. There were many occasions when during meals (by chance I had the middle seat at the table) I choked down my food in silence, my eyes riveted glassily on my image in the mirror, wrapped up in my linguistic ignorance, as alone as I was in the womb.

But let me return to the time period from which I digressed. With weak, varying winds we headed slowly toward the midday sun, and recurring calms slowed our passage down even more. The climate had also changed along with the stars of the nocturnal sky, and the consciousness of existence was no longer evoked by physical pain, as is the case in our north, but instead breathing had become a pleasure. Sea and sky rejoiced in a deeper blue, a brighter light surrounded us; we enjoyed a uniform benevolent warmth. On deck, cooled by the pleasant sea breeze, the heat is never burdensome, although in the closed-in cabin it can indeed become oppressive. We had taken off those articles of clothing which at home, once the nice, warm days of summer arrive, become even more intolerable to us than even the hostile cold of the winter air. A light jacket and pantaloons, a straw hat on our heads, light shoes on our feet, no stockings, no necktie: this is in general the appropriate costume for all Europeans to receive the benefits of the sun in the tropics. The only exception are the English, for whom everywhere the customs of London have the validity of the laws of nature. During the midday heat a canopy was erected, and at night we slept on deck under the stars. Nothing can be compared to the beauty of such nights, when, rocked gently to and fro and cooled by the wind, one looks up through the swaying rigging to a sky sparkling brightly with stars. Later we passengers were deprived of this pleasure, because the mates were forbidden to allow us to make use of the old sailcloth we needed for our couch.

Among the beauties of this sky I shall reckon a spectacle that one is called upon to observe much more frequently in the tropics, where more time was spent on deck, and which there occurs in much greater splendor. I mean the phosphorescence of the sea. This phenomenon never loses its charm, and at the end of a three years' journey one still looks at the phosphorescent furrow of the wake with the same pleasure as on the first day. The normal phosphorescence of the sea, as observed by Alexander von Humboldt and myself, has its origin from particles in the water that seem to become luminous only when struck or shaken, and seem to consist of organic inanimate material.[7] The ship, plowing through the sea, ignites this luminous dust round about it under the water, which otherwise only becomes bright through the action of the waves when they break into foam. Apart from this light spectacle we had another one here. There seemed to be a light shining up from some depth below the surface of the water, and this light was sometimes of some duration. This luminescence seemed to come from animals (jellyfish) in which an organic development of light can be assumed.

On October 23 we were becalmed at 30°36′N latitude, 15°20′W longitude (about 300 miles away from the coast of Africa). The remains of a huge swarm of locusts (Gryllus tataricus L.) covered the sea around us. These remains accompanied us for three days. On noon of the 25th we caught sight of the Salvages,[8] cruised in their vicinity on the 26th, and on the 27th saw the peak of Tenerife unveil itself at a distance of about 100 miles, its great height apparent even at this distance. The wind rose during the night and pushed us toward our goal.

During this passage I had let my mustache grow the way I had formerly worn it in Berlin. As we approached the landing place the captain besought me to cut it off. I had to make the sacrifice and leave the hair behind.

At eleven o'clock on the morning of the 28th we dropped anchor at the dock of Santa Cruz.

The purpose of our landing in Tenerife was to take aboard provisions, chiefly wine, as until now we had drunk only water. For this business three days were deemed sufficient, and we were at liberty to use them for an excursion into the interior of the island.

Tenerife has been visited and described by scholars like no other point on the globe. Alexander von Humboldt has been on this island; and Leopold von Buch and Christian Smith, whom we regretted not finding here any longer, had just finished a long stay during which they made the entire chain of the Canary Islands the object of their investigations.[9] We needed only to make our own discoveries and soak up the forms of life of tropical nature with our thirsting eyes.

One might expect that travelers who are transferred directly from northern nature to a southern one would be affected by the immediate contrast to such an extent that it would exercise an almost fairyland charm upon him. However, that is not the case. The series of impressions gained in the north lie completely closed off behind us, and a new series of different impressions begins, which is completely separated from the first, and is not connected with it by anything. The intermediate links that would unite both ends into a chain, both groups into one picture, are lacking from a total impression. When at the end of our winters we have seen the trees slowly and hesitantly budding out and then see them suddenly develop blossoms and leaves after a warm rain, and the spring appears in all its glory, then we revel in the fairy tale that nature tells us. When in our Alps we climb upward from the region of tilled fields through that of the deciduous and coniferous forests and that of the alpine meadows to the snowy mountain peaks and from these down again into the fertile valleys, the changes we see have a charm for us that is lacking in the contrast of different kinds of nature that the ship takes us to. But the change of the stars in the sky and the change in temperature belong to the former category. Let me add another observation by way of elucidation. When we are standing on a high point we can get dizzy if our glance rests on the wall of the tower or on intermediate objects in the depths below us, but the balloonist may look down on the earth below without being subject to vertigo.

Only a few date palms raise their heads, and only a few banana plants raise their broad leaves over the whitewashed walls of the gardens of the little city of Santa Cruz. The landscape is desolate, the tall jagged cliffs on the coast toward the east are bare, only sparsely covered with the gigantic, pale, cactuslike Canary Island spurge. Clouds rested on their tops. A few dromedaries could be seen plodding along on the road from Laguna.

I had used the first opportunity to go ashore. The learned mineralogist Escolar, whose acquaintance I made, was kind enough to secure a guide for me the next morning. On the morning of October 29 Eschscholtz and I began our excursion. We wished to avoid the paved road to Laguna. Señor Nicolás, our guide, led us astray in the desolate, rocky eastern valleys. Around a few widespread settlements one could see dracaena and the American agave and *Cactus opuntia*.[10] Most of the characteristically tropical forms of nature were foreign growths brought here by man. After three o'clock we arrived in Laguna. It began to rain. We ate grapes and visited the learned Dr. Savignon, who gave us a recommendation to Mr. Cologan in Oratava: "No queriendo privar a la casa de Cologan de su antiguo privilegio de proteger los sabios viajeros, etc." ("Not wishing to deprive the house of Cologan of its ancient privelege of protecting the learned travelers, etc."). We found a shelter for the night and grapes to eat at the house of a very talkative and jolly old woman. There are only two inns on the island, in Santa Cruz and Oratava. On the morning of the 30th the rain was pouring down. We started out on the road to Oratava. It goes through Matanza and Victoria, two names that, often recurring on the maps of the Spanish colonies, characterize the fate of the native peoples: slaughter and victory. Not until Victoria does one come to the vineyards that form the pride and the wealth of the island. The view of the mountains and the coast, the peak and the sea, is exceptionally beautiful, especially in the way it presented itself to us in the play of clouds and evening sun. The clouds were formed on the shore below and from time to time passed across the slope of the mountains toward the heights. The peak of the high mountain could be seen through the mist, covered by freshly fallen snow. However, I could not tell the great height of this mountain by looking at it: the impression did not meet expectation. Perhaps the snow line in our Swiss Alps has impressed itself upon me as a measure of height, and where this is not applicable I am unable to judge.

We were late, and would have been able to spend only the night hours in Oratava. We found it advisable not to go any farther. I smoked, *votum solvens* (to absolve an oath), a pipe under a palm tree, cut off a frond as a souvenir, and used the rib as a walking stick. We sought a shelter for the night. We had to go back to Matanza, where we found grapes in a hut and the bare earth for a bed. In order not to do completely without animal food, we had bought a few hen's eggs in different houses.

On the 31st, the rain continuing, we returned to Santa Cruz by way of Laguna, where we visited another garden. Accommodatingly, various informed citizens invited us to see gardens, collections of naturalia, *guanche* mummies; unfortunately, our time had run out.[11]

On our excursion the people in general had seemed extremely poor and ugly to us, at the same time possessed of a happy disposition and of great curiosity. Spanish dignity, which is expressed in their linguistic forms, we here encountered for the first time among rags. "Your grace" is of course the usual mode of address among the lowly people as well.[12]

First in Tenerife, as later on over the whole circumference of the earth, the inquisitive people with whom I, likewise inquisitive, came into contact, took pains to study the Russian national character in me, the Russian who was only a German and as a German really only a born Frenchman, a *Champenois.*

# CHAPTER IV
## Journey from Tenerife to Brazil.
## Santa Catarina.

ON November 1, 1815, we weighed anchor and left the docks of Santa Cruz. We ran into a calm, or at best a very light breeze, in the channel between Tenerife and Canaria.[1] We observed that the mountaintop was completely clear of clouds, but in the course of the morning the vapor collected around it again and enshrouded it. On the 3rd we caught the northeast trade wind outside of the channel, and as it was blowing unusually briskly it advanced us on our way with a speed of six to eight knots (so many miles the hour). Let me remark in passing that the speed of a ship is a matter in regard to which every sea captain's statement is as unreliable as that of a woman who is asked to state her age. At 4:00 A.M. on the 6th we crossed the Tropic of Cancer. On this day we saw porpoises and on the 7th the first flying fishes.

These creatures, which are similar in size and shape to herring, have pectoral fins that, adapted to flying rather than swimming, are as long as their bodies. They fly with outspread fins in an arc fairly high and far above the waves, into which they must dive again to maintain the suppleness of their flying equipment. As they do not have or need the eyes of birds, because nature places no obstacles in their path in flight, they do not know how to avoid ships and frequently fall on board those that, like the *Rurik*, do not rise higher above the waves than their flight. It is understandable that a North European to whom this information has never penetrated should consider the flight of the fish gruesome, as a perversion of nature. The first flying fish that fell onto the deck and into the hands of our sailors was cut into pieces by them while the utmost silence was preserved, after which they cast the pieces into the sea in all directions. That was supposed to prevent the impending evil. Very soon, however, this phenomenon receded and took its place among the everyday events in nature, and lost its mysteriousness for our people. The flying fish fell upon our ship so often both in the Atlantic and in the Great Ocean that they served not only us, but also, if I remember right, a few times the crew, too, as an excellent food.

In Tenerife we had taken on board a cat and a small white rabbit. The two lived together in great harmony. The cat caught fish, and the rabbit ate the bones that she left him. I mention this because it surprised me to see the rabbit, in the manner of mice and other rodents, living completely from animal food. The rabbit, however, died before we crossed the Equator, nor did the cat reach Brazil.

On the 9th we had reached the latitude of the northernmost of the Cape Verde Islands. At noon of the 10th Brava appeared through the fog, already at a very high angle of elevation. Toward half past one o'clock we had this high island ten miles to SE by SSE and, more to the east, two other lands appeared at a very slight angle, the easternmost with a seemingly volcanic peak in the center. In the evening we came too close to the island of Brava with the prevailing wind, of which however it suddenly divested us. Above the bank of clouds that rested on its heights, the peaks of the more distant island of Fogo appeared for a short time at an almost identical angle. Between us and Brava innumerable schools of porpoises were playing, but they probably did not perceive us, as they did not approach the ship.

The Cape Verde Islands, under Portuguese authority, are mostly inhabited by poor Negroes. However, the inhabitants of the different islands are described very differently to us. The inhabitants of San Iago, who are infused with white blood, are represented as being ignorant and predatory, while the poor and good Negroes of Brava remind one of the Negroes Mungo Park has taught us to know and love.[2]

Legend relates that the first people to land on Fogo were two Christian priests who desired to lead a hermit's contemplative life there, pleasing to God. The island did not yet burn with any subterranean fires. It is not known whether the new arrivals were alchemists or magicians, but they found gold in the mountains and built their cells there. They dug for gold and gathered a treasure together, after which their hearts turned toward the world again. The one, who seized power over the other, took most of the gold for himself, whence their mutual hatred and their feud. The flames, which their black magic bestowed upon their thirst for revenge, ignited the entire island, and the both of them found their destruction in the general conflagration. Then the power of the fire receded, retreating to the center of the island.

Lost in the contemplation of these islands, on which to my knowledge no naturalist has ever resided, I could dream that it might be reserved for me to some day make them the goal of a special voyage and to accomplish what still was left there to be done for science.

At any rate neither smoke nor flame betrayed the volcanoes of these islands to us, although former travelers had seen them on fire; and Cook, who landed on San Iago, also makes no mention of volcanic activity.

The northern trade wind, which we flattered ourselves would be with us down to 6°N latitude, left us on November 13 at only 10°. On the other hand on the 18th between the 7th and 8th degree north latitude we caught the southern trade, which we had not hoped to catch until we reached the vicinity of the Equator. Within these limits and during this time we had inconstant weather: calms, interrupted by frequent squalls of wind and rain. Twice there was lightning, and thunder was heard. Once, on the afternoon of the 17th, a phenomenon that resembled a waterspout was perceived. A few times sudden rainfalls disturbed our night's rest on deck. Messengers brought us notice of the land that lay $5^{1}/_{2}$ degrees to our east. On the 15th a beautifully red-feathered land bird lit on our bowsprit, and then flew away from us. On the 16th three herons circled above us, one of which, as it attempted to light upon the ship, fell into the water. The others continued their flight. On the 17th we were followed all morning by a duck (Anas sirsair forsk.), which was shot down. Finally on the 18th another duck appeared.

During this time various sharks were hooked and provided us with desired fresh food. I might say, I have never eaten a better fish than shark, for it tends to be caught on the high seas, when it is greatly desired.

On the 18th the wind held fast between S and SE, and we steered a very western course. On the 19th we saw a "sea bubble" (Physalia arethusa), perhaps the strangest of all animals that inhabit the surface of the sea.[3] We saw only the one north of the Equator, but in the southern hemisphere they became frequent. On the morning of the 21st we spotted two sails, and at noon we were hailed by a third ship, a homeward-bound East Indian, who sent a boat over to us to beg news from Europe. He gave us some from St. Helena, where Napoleon had arrived. On the 22nd and 23rd we were surrounded by schools of porpoises.

At eight o'clock on the evening of November 23 we crossed the Equator for the first time. The flag was hoisted, all cannon were fired, and a party was held on the Rurik. The crew, all of whom were first-timers, didn't quite know what to do, and their Neptune was silly. But growing merriment prevailed among them, and a comedy they performed closed the day enjoyably at a late hour. Sufficient quantities of punch had been granted them.

The applause this play garnered impelled them to put on a second performance, which took place on December 3, and turned out even better. The boatswain's mate Petrov this time was the author of the play and one of the chief actors. It was a sentimental play, but conceived and performed with suitable irony. The hymn that accompanied the consecration of the loving couple consisted of a litany of all the ropes and canvas of the ship, directed by the mate.

In general Sundays were devoted to the recreation of the crew. The janissary instruments were brought forth, and there was singing.[4] Incidentally, I might note that one of the Russian national songs that we caused to resound in all the five parts of the world was "Marlborough." I do not doubt that if today a similar Russian expedition is at sea their singers will strike up Holtei's "Cloak Song" among their popular songs.[5]

On November 24, 25, and 26 we observed a ship, an English brig, which had lost the topgallant mast from the main.

Also, since we reached the southern trade wind, we frequently sailed under clouds and experienced light passing showers. The wind, which had gradually changed from south to east, turned to the north on November 30 and left us entirely on December 1. After a short period of calm the south wind sprang up. On the 5th the sun was directly overhead. We crossed the Tropic of Capricorn on the 6th. During these days several bonitos were harpooned and provided us with fresh food. Also, butterflies repeatedly brought us notice of the American continent, which lay 120 miles to the west of us. A few ships were sighted.

On November 7, about one and a half degrees south of Cape Frio we observed a phenomenon that was repeated more strikingly on the 9th.[6] As far as one could see, wind and current had caused the surface of the sea to take on a variegated appearance, with two colors of water, straw yellow and green, sharply differentiated from each other and giving a ribbonlike effect. We investigated the water of these colored rivers or highways that our course traversed. The pale-yellow water was discolored by a pale-green pollen or a microscopic chaff with which it was densely covered. The coloring agent proved under the microscope to be free-floating, straight-rodded divided algae. The water investigated on the 7th also contained a very small proportion of green slimy material and finer, very small reddish animals of the same class as crabs, which, swimming around, frequently pulled threads from the surface and drew them to the bottom. The bands of green water observed on the 9th were as a rule less broad than the grayish yellow ones. They spread a very striking foul odor abroad. The pure green color stemmed from an infinite number of infusoria, which thickened the water.[7] These

*Planaria*-like animals could barely be distinguished with the naked eye.[8] Sometimes the Channel of Santa Catarina was similarly colored, especially when there was a south wind, and had a similar foul odor, but these animals were not present.[9]

On the 10th a storm overtook us in the vicinity of the harbor. On the 11th we saw the land, and on the afternoon of the 12th at four o'clock we lay at anchor in the Channel of Santa Catarina on the side of the mainland and in the vicinity of Fort Santa Cruz.

I, a passing traveler, who just about set foot in this country, only to be amazed at the colossally proliferating abundance of organic nature in it, will not presume to say anything edifying about Brazil. I should merely like to convey the impression that it made upon me, which it left in me, to my friends; but even here words fail me.

The island of Santa Catarina lies in the southern hemisphere below the Tropic of Capricorn, at the same southern latitude as Tenerife in the north. There the rocky ground is only partially and sparsely covered with verdure, only a few strange forms of plant life mixed with the European ones, and the most striking of them foreign to this soil, too. Here a new kind of creation surrounds the European, and in its abundance everything is striking and colossal.

When you turn into the channel that separates the island of Santa Catarina from the mainland, you get the impression that you have been transferred into the realm of a still untrammeled nature. The mountains, which rise in smooth lines from both shores, are covered with jungle and are a part of it, so that one scarcely perceives the works of recently arrived man at their feet. In the interior higher peaks rise in the form of cones and domes, and to the south the view is limited by a large ridge.

The human settlements lie mostly along the shore, shaded by orange trees which attain or surpass the height of our apple trees. Around them there are plantations of bananas, coffee, etc., and fenced areas in which some of our kitchen vegetables, accompanied parasitically by many European varieties of weeds, are unostentatiously cultivated. The papaya and a kind of palm *(Cocos Romanzoffiana M.)* project from these gardens.[10] If man neglects to defend the portion of land he has wrested from nature against it, the ground is immediately covered by a profusion of tall, wild shrubs, among which beautiful *Melastoma* varieties stand out, surrounded by purple-blossoming begonias.[11] If one attempts to go aside from here to penetrate the dark tangle of the jungle, the hewn-out path one starts on soon deserts him, and the crest of the next hill is unattainable. Almost all conceivable kinds of trees stand forth in great variety. I will mention only the acacias, with feathery leaves, tall trunks, and branches extended like fans. On the ground among them, above the moldering trunks of fallen trees, there is a profusion of grasses, semigrasses, ferns, broad-leafed heliconia, etc., far taller than a man. Between them there are dwarf palms and treelike ferns. From the ground an intricate network of climbing vines rises up to the tops of the trees and hangs down from them. Many varieties from all the natural families and groups of the kingdom of flora take on the characteristic form of lianas in this natural setting. High on the branches of the trees air-swept gardens of orchids, ferns, Bromeliaceae, sway in the breeze, and the *Tillandsia usneoides* is interspersed in the heads of aging trees like silvery locks on an old man's head.[12] Broad-leafed Aroideae grow in abundance at the edges of brooks.[13] Gigantic pillarlike cacti form separate rigid groups apart from the rest. Ferns and lichens cover dry stretches of sand. Over moist areas wind-swept palms lift their crowns, and the unifoliate mangrove *(Rhizophora)* gregariously covers with verdure the inaccessible morasses into which merge the inlets of the sea. The rock of the area, a coarse-grained granite, never shows through the surface of the earth and is only occasionally to be seen on the shore and the cliffs that tower up out of the channel.

I must remark that nowhere, neither in Brazil nor in Luzón or Java, so far as I could survey the adjacent coast from the ship, did I see palm trees assert the ascendancy over other forms of plant life to tower over the forest and determine the character of the landscape. The only exception that could be cited is the most beautiful of palms, the slender, wind-rocked coconut palm on the islands of the South Seas, planted by man and belonging to him. But palms are said to predominate between the Tropics of Cancer and Capricorn in the broad, flat, often flooded plains through which the great rivers of America pour.

Although America has no counterpart to the gigantic animal forms of the Old World, from elephants to boa constrictors, in the Brazilian forests the multifarious abundance seems to equalize this deficiency. The animal world is in harmony with the plant world. There is a correspondence between the liana form of plants, the climbing foot of birds, and the prehensile tail of the mammals, with which even the predators are equipped. There is life everywhere. Herds of crabs inhabit the moister spots of the land in the vicinity of the sea and withdraw into their holes, swinging their larger pair of shears above their heads. The greatest wealth and the greatest splendor prevail among the insects, and the butterfly vies with the hummingbird. When night sinks upon this green world the animal world round about ignites its luminous fire. Air, bushes, and earth are filled with gleams that outshine the sea. The elater carries two points of constant light in its straight flight, two nerve-equipped glowing organs on its thorax. Fireflies whiz through the air in erratic flight, the glow of their underbodies increasing and decreasing by turn, and along with this fabulous glow resound the croaking and the rumbling of the froglike amphibians and the strident note of the locust.

The inexhaustible wealth of the flora of Brazil can be seen from the years of endeavor devoted to it by Auguste de Sainte Hilaire, Martius, Nees von Esenbek, Pohl, Schlechtendal, and myself, and to some degree also by de Candolle and Adrien de Jussieu.[14] Everything was new to science. The work of so many men has still only dealt with a fraction of the material, and if one scholar reviews a family that another has already worked upon, this second working often does not contribute much beyond the first.

On November 13, the morning after our arrival, the *Rurik* was brought closer to land, and I then accompanied the captain to the city Nostra Senhora do Destero, on the island about nine miles away from our anchorage, situated on the narrowest part of the channel.[15] I visited it repeatedly, but it left no clear memory in my mind, nor do I retain a clear picture of the people with whom I came in contact there. It was nature, colossal nature alone that exerted lasting impressions upon me.

On the 14th the observatory was put ashore and a tent set up there. A ramshackle house and the tent served as a dwelling for the captain and the members of the ship's company that he took with him, while Gleb Simonovich remained on the ship and took over its command.

I learned that Lieutenant Sakharin, who had become more and more indisposed on the passage over, wished to subject himself here, and on the very next morning, to a terrible surgical operation; and Eschscholtz, who was to perform it, revealed to me that he counted on my assistance for it. It was, I confess, one of the most serious moments of my life, when after having received instructions and made preparation I stepped up to the patient's bed along with Eschscholtz and said to myself, "Be firm and attentive. A human life depends on your keeping your composure." But when the bloody work was about to start the doctor found that conditions had changed for the better. The operation was not performed, and the patient really did recover and could subsequently carry out his duties again.

Even if it was not the rainy season, which comes in September in this part of Brazil, we had almost constant rain, and among the people the arrival of the Russians was probably connected with the unusual weather. In the meantime my whole supply of paper was already used up by the plants I had collected, which were hard to dry. The ship's company that slept in the tent, artist, mate, and seamen, made use of my plant packets as part of their beds and as pillows. I had not been asked about this and would have tried in vain to oppose this arrangement. But on a rainy night the tent was knocked down, and the first thing on everyone's mind was not to get my plant packets to a dry place. In this way I lost not only a part of my plants but also a part of my paper—an irreplaceable loss and all the more sensitive as my supply was only small, I having been misled into counting on someone else but instead having to use my own supply for a second person's needs, for Eschscholtz, who was completely out.

Krusenstern, on whose ship Otto von Kotzebue had sailed, had been in this same harbor twelve years ago with the *Nadezhda* and the *Neva* at the same season of the year, had dropped anchor approximately at the same spot, and had had his observatory on the little island of Atomery, on which Fort Santa Cruz is situated. At that time a Prussian by birth by the name of Adolph, a resident of San Miguel, four or five miles from our tent, had received Krusenstern and his officers in a most hospitable manner, and lived with them in a very friendly way.[16] Otto Astavich remembered his host with affection. He inquired about him. He was told that he had died but that his widow was still alive, and he decided to visit the well-remembered, friendly woman. We made the pilgrimage to San Miguel. This widow was not the woman whom Otto Astavich had known, but a younger woman whom Adolph had married as his second wife after the death of the first. She had given lodging to a male friend from her own country in the newly stuccoed house. At the time they were there the Russian officers had scratched their names on the hospitable inside wall: the inside walls had been smoothed over and whitewashed, and the spot where the names had been was no longer ascertainable. No one knew anything about it, and the memory of Adolph, who had just died in the preceding year, as well as that of the Russians, seemed to have been completely forgotten.

On such excursions we were regaled with fruit by the local inhabitants whom we addressed or who accommodatingly drew us into their houses and were offered whatever their supply allowed them. When we offered to pay for what we had consumed they did not understand us. Overpopulation has still not diminished their natural hospitality.

We found the slave trade still flourishing here. The government of

Santa Catarina alone needed five to seven shiploads of Negroes every year to replace those who died on the plantations. The Portuguese themselves introduced them from their colonies in the Congo and Mozambique. The price of a man in his best years was 200–300 piasters. A woman was much less valuable. To use a person's entire strength quickly and then replace him with a new acquisition seemed more advantageous than to raise slaves in one's own house. I hope these simple words of a planter of the New World may sound unusual to your ears. The sight of these slaves in the mills, where they free the rice of its husk in wooden mortars with heavy pestles, grunting the rhythm for the work in a strange manner, is painful and depressing. In Europe such services are performed by wind, water, and steam. And already in Krusenstern's time there was a water-power mill in the village of San Miguel. Those in their masters' houses in general and those in poorer families naturally grew up closer to the whites than those whose strength is used up in mechanical tasks. We never witnessed any cruel mistreatment of them. Christmas, which everywhere is the holiday for children, here seemed to be also the holiday for blacks. They marched from house to house through the region in troops, fantastically decked out, and played and sang and danced for small gifts, given over to exuberant merriment. This green world of palm trees and oranges at Christmas! Everywhere outside there were banners and torches, songs and dances, and the joyous stomping of the fandango. In the last few days my comrades had made acquaintances with whom they were going to celebrate the holiday—I was so alone on this evening!

One finds connections everywhere. A tailor lived in the city who was born in my province, even my hometown, Châlons-sur-Marne. He must have known my name. He looked me up. I don't know how it came about, but I never saw him.

Perhaps this is the right place for the following note. The name *armação* designates the royal fisheries that carry out whaling, of which there are four in this government.[17] The catch takes place in the winter months outside the entrance to the channel. Only open wooden boats go out, manned with six oarsmen, a steersman, and a harpooner. The fish that is acquired is pulled ashore and there cut apart. Each *armação* is said to bring in about a hundred of them each winter, and we were assured that the number could increase considerably if the payment of wages, which were three years overdue, would occur more punctually. Provinces farther to the north also take part in the whaling. It is said that these fish can already be found at the twelfth degree of southern latitude. It is probably the sperm whale *(Physeter)* that is hunted under such a hot sun along the coast of Brazil.

In a letter I wrote from Brazil to Berlin I find the record of a discovery that hardly belongs in a travel account, which, however, I shall note here because it seems amusing to me that a native-born Frenchman had to travel around the world to announce it to the Germans. At any rate, on the trip to Brazil I discovered that in the "Bride of Corinth," one of Goethe's most perfect poems, one of the jewels of German and European literature, the fourth stanza has one foot too many![18]

> "Dass er angekleidet sich aufs Bette legt"
> ("That he lay down on his bed fully clothed")

Since then I have found no German, neither poet nor critic, who himself had made this discovery. I have read commentaries on the "Bride of Corinth," idolizing ones and deprecatory ones, and found in them no notice of the cited supernumerary foot. The Germans often take too many pains to talk about things they have taken too few pains to study! I still consider my discovery something new.

On December 26, 1815, the instruments were placed on board, and we ourselves got aboard. Stormy weather kept us in the harbor on the 27th, but we left it on the next day.

# CHAPTER V

## Voyage from Brazil to Chile.
## Sojourn in Talcahuano.

AT five o'clock in the morning of December 28, 1815, we got under way with a light wind in our sails. As we left the channel we could see, as was the case on November 7 when we sailed into it, that the water was discolored by the microscopic algae, and the little red crabs could be seen in it too. The wind rose during the night and in the morning we had lost sight of land.

Ships that sail around Cape Horn normally keep to a SSW course in these latitudes and follow the American coast at a distance of five to six degrees. They head between the mainland and the Falkland Islands without seeing land.[1] The current drives them toward the islands. The sea is not deep there, and the plummet finds the bottom of gray sand at 50 to 60 fathoms. Farther to the south they head more toward the east in order to sail around Cape San Juan, the easternmost point of Staten Island, the only point of the land that they desire to see.[2] On the voyage along the coast they hope for favorable northern winds. In more southern latitudes generally west winds and storms set in. Even as in the tropics the east winds are constant, in the region of variable winds toward the poles the west winds are decidedly predominant. Fighting against them, the ships seek to attain a higher latitude (up to the 60th degree, and from there, after they cross the meridian of Cape Horn, to head northward again. It is not unknown that ships struggling long and unsuccessfully against the western storms, giving up hope of circumnavigating Cape Horn, have exchanged their western course for an eastern one, to sail around the Cape of Good Hope into the Great Ocean.

The course described was also ours, except that the captain decided to head in a more westernly direction when sailing around Cape Horn and not to attempt to find higher latitudes if not forced to. And still—at the time I was justified in assuming that the purpose of our voyage would keep us occupied in the Arctic Sea for some time, and it seemed to me that the southern ice, the southern polar glacier, which our course at this point brought us so close to, would offer us an instructive point of comparison for the investigations soon to occupy us and could be well adapted to attract our curiosity. Mr. von Kotzebue did not go along with this idea, which I had the temerity to subject to his opinion. Not until two years later did the *William*, under Captain Smith, make the discovery of New South Shetland Island, which honor, if the captain had shared my views, might have fallen to him.[3]

On the morning of January 19, we sighted Cape San Juan and sailed around it on the following night. On the 22nd we crossed the meridian of Cape Horn at 57°33′S latitude, reached the latitude of Cape Victoria on the 1st of February,[4] on the 11th at ten o'clock in the evening had a view of land by moonlight; and after a trip of only forty-six days, on the 12th we sailed into Concepción Bay.

I will enumerate in a few words some of the occurrences of our trip. Please be indulgent with me. As in the life of a prisoner a fly, an ant, a spider take on important dimensions, for the seafarer the sight of a bit of seaweed, a turtle, a bird is a very important event.

In Brazil we had taken aboard a few birds (young *Ramphastos*) and a monkey *(Simia capucina).*[5] The birds died with the first gusts of wind that hit us on the high seas, but the monkey remained the most entertaining companion on board until we got to Kamchatka.

On December 30 we saw a ship that was probably bound for Buenos Aires, the only vessel to cross our path on this lonely voyage. Some ocean turtles were observed on various days at a distance of 300 miles and more from land. I did not see them myself. The north wind left us at a longitude of about 41°, and at +12° Reaumur (15°C) the cold became unpleasant.[6] We brought forth our winter clothing, and the cabin was heated. At Cape Horn, where the minimum temperature was +4, we had become accustomed to the cold and insensitive to it. South winds brought us clear weather, north winds rain. We saw the first albatrosses at a latitude of about 40°. A little farther to the south the gigantic seaweeds of the south appeared: *Fucus pyriferus* and *F. antarcticus*, a new species that I depicted and described in Choris' *Voyage*.[7] I had collected many examples of the different forms of these interesting plants, and I was allowed to put them in the crow's nest to dry. But later, when the ship was cleaned, my little treasure was pitched overboard without notice, and all I preserved was one leaf of *Fucus pyriferus*, which I had preserved in alcohol for other purposes.

Whales and other mammals of the sea, porpoises with white bellies *(Delphinus peronii)*, were sighted on different days. On the 10th the mate Khramchenko claimed to have seen on his morning watch a boat filled with people fighting against the sea. On the same day the storm rose from SW and endangered us almost incessantly for six days between 46° and 47°S latitude. In the afternoon at four o'clock a huge wave hit the stern with such force that it caused considerable damage and swept the captain overboard. Fortunately he was caught up in the rigging, hovered for a while over the deep, and then managed to swing himself back to the deck again. The railing was smashed, even the strongest pieces of the breastwork were splintered, and a cannon hurled to the other side of the ship. The rudder was damaged, a chicken coop with forty chickens in it was hurtled overboard, and almost all our remaining poultry drowned. The water had penetrated through the damaged sheathing into the captain's cabin. Chronometers and other instruments remained undamaged, but a part of the ship's biscuit, which was stored in the hold under the cabin, was soaked through and ruined.

The loss of the chickens was a serious one. On board ship eating takes on an importance the dimensions of which one cannot dream of on land: it is the only break in the day's monotony. In this respect we were in bad straits. The *Rurik* was too small to take aboard other animals, such as pigs, sheep, or goats and poultry. Our Bengalese, as Mme. de Staël asserted of her cook with less justification, was a man without imagination. The meal he served up to us on the first day out was repeated without variation for the entire duration of the passage, except that the fresh provisons, soon reduced by half, finally gave out entirely. If the crazy fellow was commanded never again to serve a dish we had become sick of, he begged with tears in his eyes for the favor of being allowed to make it again. The last of the live animals taken aboard are generally saved for an emergency, and if this does not occur, it generally happens that they grow closer to the people and obtain the rights of house pets. At the time we still had on board a pair of the hogs taken on at Kronshtadt, and I will have more to say of them later.

On one of these stormy days we had thunder and hail. Besides porpoises and albatrosses we also saw a seal that swam very rapidly under water, rose above it in high leaps, and, the way that porpoises do, came toward the bow of the ship. It was hit by the harpoon, but we did not secure it. At the latitude of the Falkland Islands we had very inconstant weather, storms and calms. The seal was sighted again. A small falcon came aboard and allowed itself to be caught by hand.

Tierra del Fuego, which lay before us on January 19, is a high land with very craggy bare peaks. In its western interior part snow lay on the slopes. Separated by the Strait of Le Maire from Tierra del Fuego,

Staten Island is its eastern extension. It rises in smooth lines, having two secondary peaks along with the higher mountain of the interior, and the eastern promontory slopes down gently to the sea. In the vicinity of Cape San Juan seaweed is most plentiful, and in the midst of it there floated a doubtful body of matter, animal or plant, which excited our curiosity without our being able to secure it. Numerous albatrosses swam around the ship. Several of them were fired at, but the lead did not penetrate their thick feather armor.

While sailing around Cape Horn and in its meridian we experienced storms from the southwest that lasted several days and produced the highest waves that we had yet seen. The sea was without phosphorescence. No whales, or only a few. No polar lights were observed.

Travelers are accustomed to saluting the Southern Cross with the lines from Dante's *Purgatorio*, which, however, containing a more mystic meaning, scarcely should be applied to it.[8] Travelers are inclined generally to exalt the stars in the sky of that hemisphere for splendor and glory far above the northern one. To have seen it is a privilege that is not granted to those who have not traveled there. Osages, Botocudos, Eskimos, and Chinese can be seen much more conveniently at home than abroad;[9] all the animals of the world, the rhinoceros and the giraffe, the boa constrictor and the rattlesnake, are exhibited in menageries and museums, and whales are driven upstream to satisfy the curiosity of our great cities. The Southern Cross can only be observed *in situ*. The Cross really is a beautiful constellation and a splendid hand on the southern stellar clock; but I still cannot join in the extravagant praise of the southern sky—I prefer the one we have at home. Do I give that preference to the Big Dipper and Cassiopeia that the Alpine dweller preserves for the snowy peaks that limit his horizon?

When we headed north the seaweed disappeared. On January 31, 1816, my thirty-fourth [thirty-fifth] birthday, or rather baptismal day, was celebrated in the vicinity of Cape Victoria. (When or if I was actually born at all is not documented; witnesses can no longer be procured, and it is only probability that speaks for it.)[10] I had saved a few oranges from Brazil, and the captain donated a bottle of port from his own supply.

Sailing northward along the western coast of America at a distance of about two degrees, we had lovely bright weather and south winds of the kind that are expected at this season of the year.

For the view that the coast of Chile affords at Concepción, I refer the reader to the essay found in my "Notes and Opinions," and which contains a few other descriptions and notes.[11] Pages written on the spot, which the captain requested and received from me about each port of call immediately after we left it, form the basis for those writings.

At noon of February 12, 1816, we sailed into Concepción Bay, and tacking about against an unfavorable wind, at three o'clock we came into sight of Talcahuano. We showed our flag and requested a pilot in accordance with maritime custom. But we were shyly and fearfully reconnoitered from afar. We did not understand what was called out to us and could not make ourselves understood. Night fell and we cast anchor. At daybreak we perceived a boat observing us. Finally we succeeded in enticing it to come near us. Our flag was unknown here, and their fear of corsairs from Buenos Aires, against whom they would hardly have known how to defend themselves, was great. We were now piloted to the anchorage before Talcahuano, and the captain immediately sent Lieutenant Sakharin and myself to the commandant of the place.

Ferdinand VII was master of Chile at the time.[12] In the authorities and the military with whom we naturally first came into contact, Coblenz of 1792 appeared before me, and the book of my childhood lay open and comprehensible before me.[13] I saw an old officer in the enthusiasm of unpretended loyalty throw himself on the ground before a portrait of the king, which the governor was showing us, and kiss the feet in the picture, shedding tears of sentiment the while. What is expressed in this feature, raised hieroglyphically above many others, the self-denial and the sacrifice of himself to an idea, even if it is only a phantom, is the exalted and beautiful side of man that becomes apparent in times of political partisanship. But the reverse side, in a triumph of arrogance, is cruelty, the thirst for revenge, which is satisfied only bestially. *Vae victis!* There was a trace of that here, too. At the ball the governor gave for us, I saw his natural son, an unmannered boy of thirteen to fourteen years, kick and spit on the ladies who, wrapped in mantillas, had attended as spectators according to the local custom, because they were pa-triots,[14] and what the boy did was acceptable. Deported persons who had not yet left the land, patriots not imprisoned, or others under suspicion, together with their families, were treated like suppressed people without legal rights, all burdens, deliveries, transports, quar-terings being imposed upon them. The formula that prevailed was: they are patriots.

The latest world events were known here, and we were honored by their attributing their outcome solely to Russian arms. It was natural to honor the friendly flag and the captain who flew it, but in their expressions of praise the Spaniards knew no limits or degree, and I could only view with amazement the strange position in which the highest authorities of the province placed themselves before the young Russian navy lieutenant.

The commandant of Talcahuano, Don Miguel de Rivas, came aboard the *Rurik* immediately and invited us to his house that evening. In response to a messenger whom he sent to Concepción, an adjutant of Governor-Intendant Don Miguel María de Atero appeared immediately, and the next morning the governor himself came to pay the first visit to Lieutenant von Kotzebue on board his ship. As on the one hand we had saluted the Spanish flag, and on the other the governor, in respect to the shots that had reference to the flag a misunderstanding came about, which had to be negotiated, and in which Spain hastened to retreat. An honor guard of five men was sent on board for the captain with a letter the words of which were high-flown and stilted in the Spanish fashion and the sense of which was almost fawning. Before the house placed at the captain's disposal, and in which he set up his observatory and moved into on the 16th with me as the only other member of the ship's company, an honor guard was set up.

But I must also show you the military that was involved here. For this, instead of a full muster an anecdote may suffice for the time being. The captain had dexterously accustomed the commandant and his officers to our well-set table. We were the hosts, they our daily guests who seldom missed a chance to appear. The commandant, Don Miguel de Rivas, whom we called "Frondoso" after a song he often sang, *"nello frondoso d'un verde prado,"* was not an adherent of a political party but a good, joyous man and our devoted friend with all his heart and soul.[15] When he once started to leave after dinner hand in hand with the captain, it turned out that the man on guard had found the threshold of the door in front of which he was supposed to stand a comfortable couch for his midday nap. We wondered tensely: what will Frondoso do? Frondoso stepped up to the comfortable sleeper, observed him for a while with an easy smile, then carefully and quietly stepped over him and offered the captian his hand in order to help him out of the courtyard into the street in the same manner, without disturbing the soldier at his rest.

We had made arrangements with Don Miguel de Rivas to ride to Concepción on the 19th in order to pay the governor a return visit. However, the latter requested the captain to wait until the 25th so that he could make arrangements to receive him in a worthy manner. The compromise was made that we would visit him as friends on the 19th and receive the honors he aimed at the Russian captain on the 25th.

In the meantime we were repeatedly invited to pleasant evening parties and balls at the house of Don Miguel de Rivas. In Concepción we met the first men of the province: the bishop, superior to any of the rest in culture and learning; Don Francisco de Rines, governor of Valdivia;[16] Don Martín la Plaza de los Reyes with his seven charming daughters, and others. I looked up the worthy old missionary, Pater Alday, who was glad to tell me a good deal about the eloquent Araucanians and prepared me for the great enjoyment I should find in reading Molina's *Civil History of Chile*.[17] I do not believe that the work has been translated into German, and still it is a book comparable to Homer. It depicts men at about the same stage in history, and deeds worthy of a heroic time.

On the 25th upon our advent we were saluted with seven guns. A banquet was prepared for us at the house of the governor, and in the evening a splendid ball. We were given quarters for the night elsewhere, because *el palacio*, the house inhabited by the governor, was not equipped to lodge strangers. The table was spread luxuriously, an abundance of ices at hand. The bishop sat with the governor and Mr. von Kotzebue in the place of honor. A cleric attended him. Toasts were made to the accompaniment of the thunder of cannon and the blare of trumpets. Verses were improvised by a number of the guests, for which a hearing was requested by a beating on the table and a cry of *"Bomba!"*[18] I cannot say of these impromptu poems that they were of any great quality, except that the bishop distinguished himself with a successful stanza in which Alexander and Ferdinand, Biobio, and the Chilean national poet Ercilla were mentioned in resonant tones.[19] Choris put on a little intermezzo for my amusement. It occurred to him to want some vinegar, which was not on the table. He couldn't make himself understood. I was nearby and had to serve as interpreter, but the word had slipped my mind. I was aware that *aceite* doesn't mean *"acetum"* but rather "oil," and I tried in almost too learned a manner, to make a Spanish word out of ὀξύς and wasted my time.[20] I was unable to break off the unhappy discussion, new auxiliary troops appeared, and at the head of the table the rumor was spread that the guests on that other wing of the table felt a lack of something they were unable to express in words. The governor rose up, the bishop rose up, indeed, there was a general uprising, and now finally the less remote word *vinagre* occurred to me, vinegar was sent for, and the rising flood subsided into its bed again. But when the vinegar came the one who had started all the commotion had already consumed the food that he had wanted it for, and refused to drink it.

In the evening the most splendid society gathered for the dance.

The ladies, among whom there were many of exceptional beauty, were in the majority, preservers of more refined manners, visibly endeavoring to please, and indeed pleasing by their charm.

The captain invited the governor to a return festivity and commissioned him to invite all of those who belonged to his social circle. Later, March 3 was fixed upon as the date of our festivity.

On February 27 the Spaniards celebrated the capture of Cartagena.[21]

On the 29th the only member of the crew we were to lose on the voyage through death died of consumption. The captain would have liked to see him buried in the common cemetery with clerical honors. He spoke of this with our friend the commandant, who, however, retreated, and said that this was a matter for the clergy, in which he could not interfere. Whatever was in his power, military honors, were at our disposal. Fortunately, this appeased the captain, and a detachment of soldiers appeared at the appointed hour to follow the bier. It seemed dangerous to have entrusted powder to such rabble. Some of them shot their weapons off in our courtyard without paying any attention to what they were aimed at. Finally they followed the cortege of our crew, and the authorities had demonstrated their good will. When the next day members of our crew went to plant the Greek cross, which had been carved out on the ship, on the gravesite, it was evident that the latter had been tampered with: the planing chips that had lain in the coffin were strewn about. The captain didn't press the matter. I later told Don Miguel de Rivas about it in a conversational tone. He was horrified at the crime and, crossing himself, took two steps backward.

The 3rd of March came upon us, and our guests arrived. They were taken over in groups on our boats by our festively adorned crew to inspect our ship. A shed adjacent to our house had been converted into a myrtle bower and equipped as a dance hall whose floral magnificence would have excited admiration in Europe. It was illuminated with wax candles, and not stingily, and it was this illumination, its splendor unknown in Chile, that excited an admiration which nothing can surpass. *"Cera de España, cera de España!"* This outcry resounded above everything else, and the governor, when we left Chile, requested of the captain and obtained, along with some Russian shoe leather, the gift of ten pounds of wax candles (*cera de España* "Spanish wax"). Choris had contributed two transparent paintings to the magnificence of the festival. The intertwined hands and names of monarchs along with laurel wreaths and a genius of victory or fame who hovered above the globe with blue wings. The unfortunate idea of depicting the earth as seen from the South Pole had furnished us with a Cape Horn pointing upward that I would have been ashamed to look at. The question often directed at us by the most informed of our guests, as to what harbor we had sailed from, Moscow or St. Petersburg, I find quite natural; that as to whether that flying figure represented Tsar Alexander, is much better; but the crowning glory was the one that a black-bronze bust of Count Romanzov on the *Rurik* occasioned. It is worthy of note if only from the circumstance that it was asked not only in Chile but also in California, and with the same words by a missionary there, namely this question, "Why does he look so black? Is Count Romanzov a Negro?"

Courtyard and gardens were amply illuminated by lampions for which the shell of a mussel that is eaten here, *Concholepas peruviana*, had served. Fireworks were ignited in the garden; the tables were set up in the somewhat narrow rooms of the house; our crew's chorus and the artillery on the *Rurik* did their part. Everybody was extraordinarily merry at our party, and very well satisfied with it, except for the curious, among whom outside the doors a little conflict arose. The next morning the shed was half torn down by the rabble, just so they could look in and see where the ball had been.

I have mentioned *Concholepas peruviana*. I ate this mussel almost every day during my sojourn in Chile, and I liked the taste very much. When for the purpose of our illumination a whole load of the shells was dumped at our door, I picked out a handful of the nicest examples, and on the *Rurik* I distributed about half of these to the others who were interested, for everyone wanted to make his own collection. Not until later—don't cast that stone, friends, but take note and consider modestly that on such a trip, if not the same thing, then definitely something similar would have happened to you, too—not until later did I learn that at the time the *Concholepas* animal was completely unknown and the object of a debate important for natural history and that the mussel, still very rare in those collections, stood at a very high price. I am far from desiring to ask about the value in money that such things have; and as I gave all of my natural history collection to the Berlin Museum, I would have derived no advantage from them.

Our guests from Concepción spent most of the next day with the friends who had given them lodging, and Talcahuano, overfilled by that festive crowd, took on an unusually animated appearance. Groups of ladies and gentlemen sauntered about, music sounded forth from all the houses, and in the evening a number of dances were given. The captain and I had returned home late, and we had gone to bed and were already asleep when music was heard under our windows, a guitar, voices. The captain stood up in annoyance and looked for a few piasters to satisfy these disturbers of the peace and get rid of them. "For heaven's sake," I cried out, more familiar with the local customs than he, "this is a serenade. They may well be our most prominent guests." And, peeping out of the window, I recognized the two daughters of our friend Frondoso among four young ladies protected by a young man. We threw on our clothes and soon had a candle burning. We invited the somnambulists in, and there was playing, singing, and dancing until later in the night, for it was no longer early. But what kind of dance did the Misses de Rivas dance? Oh, my friends! Do you know the *fricassée*? No, you certainly do not know the fricassée, you're much too young for that. In the years 1788–1790 in Boncourt in the Champagne I saw the fricassée danced by old people who had learned it in their youth from others who were already old at that time. Since then I was only reminded of the fricassée once, briefly, in Geneva, but I remember it very well from Boncourt: two cavaliers meet each other, greet each other, quarrel with each other, draw their swords against each other, and stab each other to death, and all of this to a melody I would sing to you if I could sing at all. What then, did these Misses de Rivas dance but this very fricassée! The next day we discovered to the horror of the captain, that our chronometers, which we had forgotten when the fricassée took place, had perceptibly changed their setting because of the shaking-up they had been subjected to.

I joined the nocturnal perambulators when they left the observatory, and we wandered through the streets of Talcahuano for a long time, engaging in various small persiflages. We rapped on the windows of houses where young gentlemen and officers resided, and one of the girls broke out in the voice of a toothless hag with whimsically jealous and still tender reproaches against her faithless lover and performed the most entertaining scenes with exceptional talent. For the most part the men answered only with some grumbling, and nowhere did we obtain the same reception that they had obtained at the observatory.

We were preparing for departure when, on the 6th, Shafekha, the captain's body servant, was missed. Because of this deserter, new discussions were held with the governor. It was to be assumed that, concealed in some remote hiding place, he would not put in an appearance before the *Rurik*'s departure. I was incensed when I held in my hand the assurance in black and white, signed by the governor of Concepción, Don Miguel María de Atero, that this absconder, if apprehended, would be imprisoned and sent under arrest to St. Petersburg for punishment. This was of course something that was easier to promise than to keep, but what a promise! Should a South Asian, a Mohammedan Tatar, not find safety from Greek Orthodox despotism in another hemisphere, the western, the southern one, but rather should Catholic Spain be the Russians' henchman in the New World on the border of the territory of the free Araucanians?

In such negotiations, with the French that I was fluent in and the Spanish I had learned in order to read *Don Quixote*, I was useful and convenient to the captain, for whom I carried out the correspondence, and that was good. But I will not conceal the last news we had of our deserter. Upon our return in the year 1818 the captain heard in London that Shafekha had presented himself before the Russian Embassy there as a repentant sinner and had requested a passport for St. Petersburg. In view of the conservative way in which business is carried out there the passport could not be made out immediately, and the applicant never again appeared to take care of the matter.

Could the story of a sow, which I can't resist telling here, impel a writer of novellas to spin it out in an embellished form to a length suitable for a literary journal? Imagination could not improve upon it. In Kronshtadt young hogs of a very small species had been taken on board for the officers' mess. The crew had jocularly given them their own names. Blind Fate chose now one, and now the other, and, like the companions of Odysseus, the men saw themselves slaughtered and devoured in the persons of their animal namesakes.[22] Only one pair came via the African islands and Brazil around Cape Horn to Chile, one of them the little sow that bore the name Shafekha, destined to outlast her godfather on board the *Rurik*. Shafekha, the sow, was put ashore at Talcahuano and taken aboard again, sailed to Polynesia with us, came to Kamchatka, and there, in Asia, she gave birth to her first litter, which she had conceived in South America. The young pigs were eaten, and she herself traveled northward with us. She enjoyed a guest's privileges at the time, and it was no longer conceivable that she could be slaughtered, unless starvation was impending, in which case people even eat each other. But our ambitious crew, jealous of their honor as world travelers, were already grumbling that an animal, that a sow, should share the same fame and glory as themselves, and their displeasure grew more threatening with time. So matters stood when the *Rurik* sailed into the harbor of San Francisco, New California. Here a conspiracy was plotted against Shafekha the sow. She was accused of having attacked the captain's dog and subsequently summarily condemned and slaughtered unheard. She, who had seen all five continents, in North America, in the midst of the peaceful harbor, was slaughtered, a sacrifice to envious human rivalry.

Now that I have reported on the hogs with respect to Shafekha, perhaps I may narrate the lesser affairs of the scholar on board. In

Brazil a moss mattress of mine had become so soaked and in consequence of this so lumpy and musty that it could no longer be used. I could expect no help from our crew, who were subordinate only to their officers and even reluctant to wait on them, being only happy when they were on watch and did their sea duties. In Chile, where I was closer to the captain, I complained to him, the *patushka*, the father of the house, about the trouble with my mattress, and he commanded Shafekha to take care of it. My mattress disappeared along with Shafekha, and I never heard it mentioned again, nor did I mention it myself. The empty space in my bunk that this loss occasioned is the only thing I owed to the crew on the entire voyage.

In these last days our crazy cook also got the idea of staying in Talcahuano. In order to dissuade him our friend Don Miguel de Rivas made him a long sermon with Spanish dignity, in which he addressed him by *usted* (the usual "your grace"), and let him hear some very fine things, of which this silly person probably didn't understand a word; nonetheless, he desisted from his intention.

I would like to etch in with a light, fine point a few more characters in the series of Chilean portraits I have tried to draw for you.

The first: Don Antonio, a tall, thin, lively Italian, who, as our supplier, provided us with all our needs, intervening cleverly and energetically everywhere and supplying everything that we wanted, but at the same time cheating us excessively in everything while, to allay our suspicions, he constantly derided the Spanish. Don Antonio's greatest disappointment was that he could not read and write, which skills would certainly have come in handy for him in view of his double bookkeeping.

The second: a shabby fellow (I think he was a tavernkeeper) in whose tavern the seamen drank a wine that transformed them into a state similar to insanity. The man forced himself upon me with all sorts of favors and small gifts. Later and hesitantly he came out with his proposal. He was a born Pole and had completely forgotten his mother tongue. He expected of me, who was a Russian, with whom he could make himself understood in Spanish, that I would have the kindness to teach him his forgotten Polish again.

The greatest punishment I saw inflicted upon the crew on board the *Rurik* was to be beaten with switches by the hand of the two petty officers. The captain conducts the examination, makes the judgment, and has the punishment applied in his presence, independently and without the involvement of his officers. Such punishments were rare, and after they were over the captain usually withdrew to his cabin and needed the help of the physician. I am noting this at this point because switches were cut for that purpose here, and they were myrtle switches.

We took on board (I have forgotten whether or not it was a gift of the governor) some wine from Concepción, which has a great similarity to the sweet Spanish wines. Our supply had suffered a great diminution here, and the substitution was welcome. Some sheep were taken on board. Everything was ready for departure. We climbed aboard, and a small ugly dog, that had become accustomed to us and bore or received the name Valet, followed us.

Before I leave this country I shall quote a few lines from a letter I wrote from Talcahuano to a friend at home, in which the mood of the fleeting hour left its lasting impression:

> Σύ μοί ἐσσι πατὴρ καὶ πότνια μήτηρ/'Ηδὲ κασίγνητος.[23] You know this, and through you Berlin has become for me the paternal city and umbilicus of my world, from where I departed on my circular trip in order to go back there and in due time rest my tired bones next to yours in easy repose. My good friend Eduard, life on a trip like this is like life at home. Much boredom during storms, when because of the pitching and rolling a person can't get himself to do anything except sleep, play *durak* (translated: sheepshead) and tell anecdotes, at which again I find I am more inexhaustible than even I had believed. Very unhappy and dejected when one has had some friction with the majority; happy when the sun shines; hopeful when land is spotted; and when one is on the land, again anxious to leave it. One is always looking ahead into the future here, which incessantly flies away above our heads as the present, and we become as inured to the change in the scenes of nature as at home we are to the change of the seasons. The polar star, τὸ τοῦ πόλου 'άστρον, has sunk, and we will do so too. The cold comes from the south and the midday sun is in the north. On Christmas Eve one dances in an orange grove, etc. What does all this mean except that your poets observe the world out of the neck of the bottle in which they happen to be enclosed. We have gotten away from that, too. Indeed, their south and north and all their natural philosophical and poetic apparatus stands out splendidly when the Southern Cross is at the zenith. There are times when I say to my poor heart, 'You are a fool to wander around so idly! Why didn't you stay home and study something sensible, as you maintain you love scholarship?' And that too is a deception, for I am breathing new experiences in through every pore at every moment; and quite apart from science, we will have material from my voyage to talk about for a long time when the old anecdotes begin to wilt. Farewell."

On March 8, 1816, we went under sail, after our friend Don Miguel de Rivas had tearfully extricated himself from our embraces.

# CHAPTER VI

## From Chile to Kamchatka.

*Salas y Gómez. Easter Island.*
*The Doubtful Island. Romanzov. Spirodov.*
*The Rurik Chain. The Dean Chain.*
*The Krusenstern Islands. The Penrhyn Islands.*
*The Northernmost Groups of Radak.*

HERE the *Rurik's* voyage of discovery begins. On March 8, 1816, we sailed out of Concepción Bay, and on June 19 we sailed into Avatcha Bay.[1] For three months and eleven days we had dropped anchor only once, for a few moments, at Easter Island, and only set foot briefly on land twice, on Easter Island and Romanzov Island, had had converse only with the inhabitants of Easter Island, the Penrhyn Islands, and of Radak [Ratak], and this only briefly, and had seen only the above-mentioned points of land.[2] Our glances had not rested upon a single European sail. Not until June 18, in sight of the coast of Kamchatka and about to sail into the Bay of Avatcha, did we see the first ship, the sight of which reunited us with people of our civilization.

The routes that cross this wide ocean basin are traveled much more sparsely than those of the Atlantic, and no shore borders them against which the seafarer could lean in imagination, but the flight of sea birds and other signs often let him suspect land, islands he doesn't see and doesn't seek, and still he is not lost in this unlimited space. Ships as a rule only encounter each other in the vicinity of harbors, which serve them as gathering places: the Sandwich Islands, etc. But on this long voyage we avoided all the paths of commerce, and on the lost trail of former seafarers we sought to clarify doubtful points of hydrography. This section of our voyage, which in respect to Mr. von Kotzebue's accomplishments is one of the most important ones and takes up much space in his account, will be compressed here into a few pages. Whatever I had to say about the islands that we saw and the people with whom we had concourse, I have said in my "Notes and Opinions." I discoursed extensively there, especially in the main section, "Survey" and in "Radak," on the geognostic nature of the low or coral islands, among which all the points of land mentioned here must be reckoned, except for Easter Island and Salas y Gómez [Sala-y-Gómez].[3] As far as nautical and geographical matters are concerned, I must refer the reader to Otto von Kotzebue and Krusenstern, who in the travel account itself and then in other works, critically evaluated the discoveries of the *Rurik* in the South Seas.[4]

It is regrettable that the original German edition of Mr. von Kotzebue's travel account is incorrect to the extent that the numbers cited in the text lack all reliability. If one compares the longitudinal and latitudinal determinations as they are given in the narrative and repeatedly are designated in the meteorological tables, one finds that in the narrative not only are the seconds most often left out but also that the numbers deviate. The table called "Aerometer Observations, III," which seems to be more correct than the text, will serve to correct the midday determinations from July 18, 1816, to April 13, 1818, from Kamchatka to the vicinity of Saint Helena and is especially important for a later segment of the voyage, from November 5 to 24, 1817, on the passage betwen Radak and the Marianas through the Caroline Sea.[5] Here, for example, the latitude of November 20, 1817, is given as 10°42′, which is obviously wrong, and in the table on page 226 it is given as 11°42′29″, which seems to be correct.[6] For the section of the voyage that concerns us here we must dispense with the help of such a table. It is regrettable that Mr. von Kotzebue did not include any extracts from his ship's log in his travel account. It is regrettable that he did not include in it, where one would expect to find them, many maps and charts that hydrography owe to him, and of which Krusenstern especially cites the chart of the harbor of Hana-ruru [Honolulu] and La Caldera de Apra on Guaján.[7] It is regrettable that he did not make known the instructions that were given him for the voyage, which both he and Krusenstern refer to at various places.[8] And finally, it is regrettable that he disdained preserving the barometer readings that were taken at various hours of the day over a long period of time at sea.

The figures communicated to me by the captain during the voyage (latitudes and longitudes, heights of mountains, etc.) never agree with those I find recorded in his work. Here I have followed the latter when I have found no reason to suspect a typographical error or a *lapsus calumni*.

Please excuse this digression. I shall now point with a casual finger to the course taken by the *Rurik* on the map and then add a little about the events of the voyage.

We sailed northward, leaving the island Juan Fernández to leeward, that is, in the west, until we reached the 27th degree of southern latitude, which we then followed westward.[9] On the 25th we saw the barren cliff of Salas y Gómez, 26°36′15″S latitude, 105°34′

28"W longitude, and on the 28th we touched at Easter Island. From there we headed somewhat more to the north, and on April 13 we reached 15°S latitude, at about 134°W longitude. We followed this parallel westward, on the trail of Lemaire and Schouten, through a very dangerous sea that is filled with low islands and banks on which there is the danger of going aground before they are visible.[10] At times we tacked about all night, partly to avoid danger, partly to leave no land unseen that lay within our range. On this passage we left untouched the Marquesas in the north and the Society Islands in the south. It is worthy of notice that since Easter Island and throughout this part of the voyage up to the Equator we mostly had north and northeast winds, where in this region of the southeast trades we counted on a southeast wind. We frequently encountered gusts of wind, squalls of rain, and lightning.

April 16 and 17. The doubtful island at 14°50'11"S latitude, 138°47'7"W longitude.[11] It is the only one of the islands listed here on which the coconut palm grows; the others have very little verdure. With their broad white beaches they all have the appearance of sandbanks, which is what the older seafarer thought they were, amazed that they could not sound the bottom with the lead in their immediate vicinity, a circumstance that they never fail to mention.

On April 22 Spirodov Island, at 14°51'00"S latitude, 144°59'20"W longitude.[12]

On the 23rd in the vicinity of Cook's Pallisers the Rurik chain, from which we traveled southward.[13] We saw them between 15°10'00" and 15°30'00"S latitude, 146°31'00" and 146°46'00"W longitude. Their greater extent toward the north was not investigated. To SSE land was seen but not investigated.

On April 24 and 25 the Dean chain, whose southern edge was sighted in the direction NW 76° and SE 76° between 15°22'30" and 15°00'00"S latitude, and 147°19'00" and 148°22'00"W longitude.[14]

From there we turned our course more toward the north, seeking various doubtful islands, which we did not find. We then headed for the Penrhyn Islands, which we saw on April 30, and with whose inhabitants we held concourse at sea on May 1. The center of the group, according to the captain's calculations, lies at 9°1'35"S latitude, 157°34'32"W longitude. A great storm raged over these islands as we left them.

We now frequently experienced calms and gusts of wind, often accompanied by squalls of rain. We crossed the Equator for the second time on May 11 at 175°27'55"W longitude.

On May 19 and 20 we sought the northern groups of the Mulgrave

Islands, and had already given up this search when as we headed north we rejoiced on May 21 in the first view of the northern groups of the island chain consisting of Radak, Udirik [Utirik], and Tegi [Taka].[15] These islands, whose amiable inhabitants we here perceived for the first time, will concern us later. The channel between both groups lies at 11°11′20″N latitude, 190°9′23″W longitude.

From Radak we directed our course almost due north toward Kamchatka. At 33°N latitude we entered the region of northern mists, and the sky and the sea lost their blueness. On June 13 at 47°N latitude we encountered storm and ice. At four o'clock in the afternoon of the 18th the mists parted, and the entrance to the Bay of Avatcha lay before us.

From Chile on the captain delegated the observation of the physical and meteorological instruments to Dr. Eschscholtz.

Before we turned into Concepción Bay the sea had already once appeared to us to be dyed a light reddish color in places and in strips. This phenomenon was repeated more clearly in the first few days of our passage northward along the coast. In any case the coloring agent must be very fine and widely dispersed, and not identical to the algae and infusoria of the Atlantic Ocean. I couldn't distinguish anything in the water drawn up on deck for this purpose and doubted that it had really come from one of the discolored areas.

On March 9, the day of the observation just mentioned, a dead whale floated past us on which innumerable flocks of birds (a small species of *Procellaria*?) were feeding.[16] Could the discoloration of the sea have been due to this putrefying mass of flesh?

Whales, which are often seen in Concepción Bay, where at that time only the Americans hunted them, accompanied us for some time. Only after the whales of the north have been suitably investigated and described will it be time to express the desire of comparing those of the south with them.

At six o'clock in the afternoon of the 10th the captain thought he detected a peculiar vibration in the air, at which time the ship also seemed to vibrate a little. The noise, which he compares to distant thunder, was renewed after about three minutes. After an hour he noticed nothing further. Others maintain they felt this same vibration repeatedly in the night preceding the 11th and on the 11th itself. I felt the apprehension rise up in me as to whether the land, which had been so hospitable to us, might be ravaged by an earthquake and thus the scene of terror and destruction. However, our fears were not confirmed.

In Chile we had taken an almost threatening number of fleas aboard. If they had proliferated we would have suffered considerably.

But as we traveled toward the sun they disappeared more and more, and we were soon completely free of them. In the Northern Hemisphere (on the passage from California to the Sandwich Islands) we had the same experience under similar circumstances.

On the other hand, another sort of vermin which we had not known up to this point appeared and increased perceptibly on this passage between the tropics. I mean the *tarakan* (*Blatta germanica*, the cockroach), which enjoys guest privileges among the Russians. Later they became a terrible plague for us. They not only devour the ship's biscuit entirely, but they gnaw on everything, including people when they are asleep. If they penetrate into a sleeper's ear they cause him indescribable pain. The doctor, who had often encountered this case, poured oil into the endangered ear with good success.

On March 16, at a distance of more than seventeen degrees (about 1,000 miles) from the nearest known land, the American coast, a bird was observed in flight that was taken to be a snipe.

On the 24th we saw the first tropic birds, these magnificent highfliers of the air, which I almost can't keep myself from calling birds of paradise.

On the morning of the 25th seafowl in great numbers, pelicans and frigate birds, were carried by the winds from Salas y Gómez to proclaim to us their breeding place, which we sailed past at noon.

March 28, 1816, was a day of joy. To make our first acquaintance with people of this charming race and to see the first marvelous promise of the voyage fulfilled! When the broad, deep green dome of Easter Island rose from the sea, the different colored divisions of the fields on the slopes testifying to their state of culture, and smoke rising from the hills; when getting closer we saw the people collecting on the beach of Cook's Bay; when two boats (they did not seem to possess any others) pushed forth from the beach and came toward us—then I was as happy as a child, old only in the fact that I was happy that I could be happy like this. The brief moments of our attempted landing went by as if in a delirium, surrounded by these noisy, childlike people. I had given away rather than traded all the iron, knives, scissors, everything that I had taken along, and received in return, I know not how, only a handsome, fine fishing net.

I tried to describe the suspicious reception accorded us in the "Notes and Opinions," and the reports of Kotzebue and Choris can be compared with what I said.[17] I did no more than hint at the probable cause of the half-threatening mood of the islanders. Mr. Kotzebue himself had written up the story, and it was up to him to make it known. I include it here by way of supplement in his original words.

The account can be found on page 116 of his travel account.

I believe that I must here communicate to the reader a piece of information which explains the hostile behavior of the islanders toward me, and which I received only later from Alexander Adams on the Sandwich Islands. This Adams, an Englishman by birth, in the year 1816 commanded the brig *Kahumanu*, belonging to the king of the Sandwich Islands, and had previously served as second officer on this same brig under Captain Piccort when it bore the name *Forester* of London and had not yet been sold to the king. The captain of the schooner *Nancy* from New London, America (Adams did not tell me his name), busied himself in the year 1805 on the island Más Afuero with catching a type of seal known to the Russians under the name *kotik* ("sea cats").[18] The pelts of these animals sell dearly on the market in China, so that the Americans search all over the world to locate them. On the still uninhabited island Más Afuero, lying to the west of Juan Fernández and the place they send the criminals from Chile, this animal was found by chance and hunted immediately. But as the island afforded no secure anchorage, for which reason the ship had to remain under sail, and as he did not possess a crew large enough to spare any of them for the hunt, he decided to sail to Easter Island, to steal men and women there, conduct his prey to Más Afuero, and there found a colony that would concentrate on catching kotiks on a regular basis. He carried out this cruel project in the year 1800,[19] and landed in Cook's Bay, where he attempted to gain ascendancy over a number of the inhabitants. The battle is said to have been a very bloody one, as the inhabitants defended themselves dauntlessly. However, they were forced to submit to the terrible European weapons, and twelve men and ten women fell alive into the hands of the heartless Americans. After the deed was accomplished, the unhappy captives were taken on board, kept fettered for the first three days, and only released from their chains when land was no longer in sight. The first use they made of their freedom was that the men jumped overboard, and the women, who attempted to follow them, were restrained only by force. The captain immediately hove to in the hope that they would again seek safety on board when the waves threatened to engulf them. However, he soon became aware how greatly mistaken he had been, for it did not seem impossible for these savages, who were familiar with the element, to reach their native land in spite of the fact that it was three days' journey distant, and at any rate they preferred death in the waves to a miserable life in captivity. After they had argued for some time as to which direction they should take, the little company divided up. Some headed straight for Easter Island, while the others turned toward the north. The captain, extremely outraged at this unexpected heroism, sent a boat out after them, which however returned after several fruitless attempts to rescue them, for they all dived below the surface when the boat approached them, and the sea received them compassionately in its protection. Finally the captain left the men to their fate, brought the women to Más Afuero, and is said to have made further attempts to steal people from Easter Island. Adams, who had this story from the man himself, and probably for that reason did not wish to name him, assured me he had been to Easter Island in the year 1806, where he could not land because of the hostile behavior of the inhabitants. According to his report, the ship *Albatross* under command of Captain Windship, had the same fate in 1809.

I seize this opportunity again to lodge a solemn protest against the designation "savages" in its application to the South Sea Islanders. As much as I can, I like to connect definite concepts with the words that I use. For me a savage is a person who, without a permanent domicile, agriculture and domesticated animals, knows no possessions but his weapons, with which he sustains himself by hunting. When the South Sea Islanders are accused of having perverted customs, it seems to me that these bear testimony not of savagery, but rather of overcivilization. The various inventions, coinage, writing, etc., that are suited to measure the various stages of civilization that people are at on our continent cease to provide a measure for these insularly separated human families, who live under this enraptured sky, without yesterday and tomorrow, for the moment and for pleasure.

The flying fish, at least two species of which seem to occur in the Great Ocean, seem to be more frequent in the vicinity of land. We saw many of them in the vicinity of Easter Island.

On the night of April 1 we crossed the southern tropic. On the 3rd we saw a frigate bird and were becalmed on the 7th and repeatedly on the 13th. It was here where, as we busied ourselves with the observation of the sea worm, Dr. Eschscholtz rejoiced in the discovery of the first true sea insect. It is comparable to our common water bug *(Hydrometra rivulorum F.)*, walks and jumps upon the surface of the water in the same manner, and is frequent in the tropics in all the seas.

On the 15th we saw many seafowl, frigate birds, and pelicans, suffered a few gusts of wind, and did not sail on during the night. The sky was thickly veiled with clouds, it rained violently, and there was lightning in all directions.

At noon of the 16th the cry "Land ho!" excited us to joy. Expectation is tense when voluntarily, I might say, and not at the behest of the seaman, land emerges from the surface of the sea and gradually unfolds before our eyes. Our gaze seeks eagerly for smoke, for the waving flag that identifies a man to the man who is seeking him. If smoke rises, one's heart beats strangely. But these sad reefs soon lost all interest for us except idle curiosity.

Still, there was a big celebration when on the 20th it was decided to attempt a landing on the little palm-fringed island Romanzov. The captain ordered Lieutenant Sakharin to investigate the landing place and me to accompany him. I climbed into the boat full of joy and hope. We cast off. We rowed quite close to the island, separated from the shore only by the foaming surf. A courageous sailor swam to land with a line. He walked along the shore, discovered human footprints, coconut shells, beaten paths; he listened through the bushes, plucked green twigs, and came back to the line. Sakharin pointed toward the island and spoke to me: "Adelbert Loginovich, how about you?" I do not believe that ever in my life before did I experience such a painful emotion. I write this in humiliation. What the seaman had done I was not able to do. He swam back to us, and we rowed back to the ship. After our report was made, a flat-bottomed boat *(pram)* was contructed out of all the wood on board that was not nailed down, and the next day we traveled toward the island on two boats. The boats anchored in considerable depth next to the surf. The seaman swam to shore with the line, and with the help of the flat-bottomed boat we could reach the shore one at a time, where the foaming wave broke over us. We now joyously wandered through the forest and explored the island. We collected all the signs of human beings, followed their paths, looked around in the abandoned huts that served them as shelter. I would like to compare the feeling with that we would have in the home of a highly regarded person whom we do not know personally. In this way I would have entered Goethe's summer home, would have looked around in his study. That this island has no permanent dwellings and is visited only from islands unknown to us I have said in the "Notes."

The day, which on top of this was the Russians' Easter holiday, was celebrated festively and with cannon fire onboard the *Rurik*. The crew received double rations. We brought a few coconuts back for those who had remained on the ship. To get them the ax had been used on the tree, a procedure that cut me to the quick. As recompense the ax had been left there.

In the vicinity of the low islands, the charting of which occupied us in the days following until April 25, the seabirds could be seen only rarely; on the other hand, the flying fish were frequent. Here I also once saw a water snake swimming in the sea.

We had been lacking all fresh food for some time. On April 28 water was rationed for the first time. However, the allotment was completely adequate, and I used only part of mine. I could have made do with seawater in an emergency. I have often drunk seawater on excursion without repugnance and without any disadvantage. Whether or not it quenched my thirst like sweet water is another question. The frequent showers that refreshed us, especially in the Southern Hemisphere, gave us the desired opportunity to collect fresh water, for which our tent was set up. Such fresh healthy water is a true refreshment, for unfortunately the supply on board never completely lacks "the nutritional parts," which are indeed sometimes present in an undesirable abundance. On May 4 it rained so hard that twelve casks of water were collected.

I really have nothing to add to what I said in the "Notes and Opinions" about the Penrhyn Islands, which we saw on April 30 and with whose inhabitants we conversed on the next morning. Such a day with its events is a point of light in the monotonous life on board ship, breaking through to enliven its monotonous dullness. If I would again describe the joy we felt, I would produce in the reader the same boredom it came to interrupt for us. I have never seen a more beautiful palm forest than I did on the Penrhyn Islands. Between the towering canopy of the crowns and the ground one could see the sky and the distant panorama between the trunks. The low undergrowth and the reef that usually encircle and protect islands of this formation toward the outside seemed to be at least partly lacking. The people who surrounded us were relatively numerous, strong and well-fed, peaceful and still confident in the power of their weapons, and unacquainted with the nature of ours. Every family seemed to have its own boat under the guidance of the elder. They traded with us for iron, the precious metal, and when we took leave again, they could scarcely be persuaded to leave us.

In the next few days we had frequent calms varying with gusts of wind, and on May 4 at about 7°30′S latitude we reached the real northeast trade wind. In the following days we saw many seabirds flying against the wind in the mornings and with the wind at sunset. The little sea swallow was repeatedly caught on board, and we released some we had decked out with a parchment collar bearing the name of the ship and the date. It could mean a great joy for a ship to recapture a messenger of this type in this wide ocean basin. In the China Sea a pelican was captured on board the *Rurik* that came from our supply ship the *Eglantine*, where he had already been taken captive.

On the 11th we crossed the Equator. On the 12th many seabirds could be seen. A porpoise was harpooned, the first we ever caught. It served us as a welcome change of diet. It is a black, bloody fish, earthy and not at all tasty, but not oily. I should like to praise porpoises for the table in the same way I did sharks. They come at times when they can't be criticized.

On May 19, as we sought out the Mulgrave Islands, a gust of wind unexpectedly blew in the opposite direction from that of the prevailing wind, brought the sails into confusion, and ripped apart some rigging. The captain was struck by a piece of dislodged rope that came hurtling through the air, and sank to the deck stunned. This incident, which spread terror among us, fortunately had no evil consequences.

On the 21st we discovered a reef that had sparse verdure only in a few points and from which only a few coconut trees raised their heads. On the 22nd two artfully constructed boats came toward us from this reef, tacking dexterously against the wind. The pleasant people, wearing their finery, invited us to their land but, feeling their weakness and our strength, did not dare to come any closer to us. A boat was launched, upon which Gleb Simonovich and Login Andrevich took their places, and we rowed toward them. But even this way we were unable to inspire confidence in them. They threw us presents, a decorative mat and a fruit of the pandanus, and quickly headed toward the island, inviting us to follow them. These were the Radakians. They gave us presents first and left without our returning the gifts at this first encounter.

Heading toward the north, we had the sun at the zenith on the 27th and on the 28th we crossed the Tropic of Cancer, after we had spent forty-two days south of the Equator and twelve days north of it in the Torrid Zone. We were returning to our familiar stars: before us rose the Big Dipper and behind us the Southern Cross sank below the horizon.

On June 2 and 3, somewhat farther to the south than the islands Rica de Plata and Rica de Oro are usually said to be located, at about the same latitude as Mearn we encountered a sign of land.[20] On the morning of the 3rd a small bird of the snipe family landed on the ship and was fed with cockroaches. Driftwood and seaweed floated on the sea, the water was extraordinarily murky; still the plummet found no bottom down to 100 fathoms.

The cold increased. We were in the northern fog, which often settled on our shrouds and trickled down the yards in drops as bitter as pitch. In the first days of June at the same latitude as Gibraltar we began to keep a fire for warmth, and toward the middle of the same month, before we had reached the latitude of Paris, we had ice on board. The sea, which in this same basin is deep ultramarine blue between the tropics, here is colored blackish green and is opaque. The depth at which a white object is visible was reduced from 16 fathoms to 2 fathoms. Toward the north the driftwood became more and more frequent.

On the 4th a second porpoise of a different species was harpooned. The species of this little known genus appear to be quite numerous. Indeed, almost every school that surrounds the ship seems to be different from all the others in color, design, and size.

On the 6th red spots appeared in the sea; they came from small crabs, with which the water was filled.

Ever since we headed north our wishes and thoughts rushed ahead of the ship toward the coast where we had hope of finding letters from home. We ourselves began to look through our journals, arrange our papers for sending them off, and to write letters to our loved ones. I, encouraged by a jest of the captain's, sent out an order from the north of the Great Ocean, dated according to the degree of latitude and longitude, for a basket of champagne to be sent to Councillor von Kotzebue, and the wine was actually sent and arrived safely.

On the 17th a small land bird (a *Fringilla*) announced the land that unveiled itself to us on the 18th.[21] A high land with jagged cliffs above which high volcanic cones rise in the interior. The snow does not cover the heights uniformly, as is the case in our Alps, but rather lies in spots and strips on the slopes of the disjointed mountains and continues along the slopes deep into the valleys. Still so much snow on the 18th of June!

On the 19th we sailed into the lovely wide basin known as Avatcha Bay. From the top of the mountain that forms the northern pillar of the outer gate we were announced telegraphically to St. Peter and Paul: a pilot boat came toward us.[22] We had sailed through the narrow channel of the entrance with a favorable wind, which suddenly failed us as soon as we arrived in the interior. It was night when we were towed into the harbor. An intolerable stench of fish announced to our nostrils the proximity of the town. The apparatus for drying the fish, the daily bread of these northern lands, lies on a tongue of land that seals off the inner harbor.

Here, at St. Peter and Paul, I first stepped on Russian soil; here I was to make my first acquaintance with Russia.

We had been announced here and were expected. We were all known by name—the newspapers had blared out our names, and what else does one have to do in St. Peter and Paul but study the newspaper? We were received in a way that was to be expected. We brought excitement to the dull life here, and a day dawned over this remote corner of the earth that was not like every other day. These were compatriots who met each other as hosts and guests in this remote place, so far from their real homeland.

The governor, Lieutenant Rudokov, took care of all the ship's needs, its copper being found in especially poor condition. He helped us out with the still usable copper plates of the *Diana*, the ship Golovnin had had to abandon in this harbor as unseaworthy after his voyage to Japan.[23] The captain went ashore, and a series of banquets and feasts now took place such as only could be provided in Kamchatka. In Kamchatka we had the pleasure of Russian baths. It is the first thing, and perhaps the most refreshing thing, Russian hospitality can offer. Our crew knew how to set up their bathing tent when it was desired, and only under happier, warmer skies is the practice not carried out, as being unnecessary.

On June 22 a festival of thanksgiving was celebrated on the *Rurik*, and dinner in the evening was at the residence of the governor. On Sunday, the 23rd, after church, the table was set on board our ship. On the 30th there was a banquet at the commandant's, at which toasts were made to the accompaniment of cannon fire. The wine was not the world's most select, but the guests, consisting of all the visible Russians, were numerous, and, according to English custom, which is more or less generally observed wherever salt water touches the land, every one of them wanted to drink a glass of wine to every one of us, which courtesy had to be returned, so that the glasses of wine consumed were many. After dinner we were to become acquainted with the local vehicle and drive down the slope of the hill on dogsleds on the green grass, as the snow in the valley had already melted. None of us could maintain his seat, which takes a bit of practice. When we were thrown off, each of us crept into the bushes, and everyone sought a quiet nook to terminate the festivities all by himself.

On July 4 we dined with Mr. Clark, an American who has made a new life for himself in this spot where he was stranded. He had only sailed around Cape Horn once, but had been in the Sandwich Islands six times, the last time six years ago. I found the information that he gave me of these islands, and the picture he drew of them for me, to be completely true and faithful. In Mr. Clark's residence I first saw a picture that afterwards I saw on many American ships and, distributed by their commerce, on the islands and the coasts of the Great

Ocean: painted delicately on glass by a Chinese hand, it was the portrait of Madame Récamier, the dear friend of Madame de Staël, at whose residence I enjoyed intimate contact with her over a long period of time.[24] When I observed this picture here, our whole voyage seemed an amusing anecdote, sometimes told in a tedious manner, and nothing else.

June 11 was the feast day of St. Peter and Paul. We contributed to a collection that was taken for the construction of a church. The first official of the Russian-American company played host to us on this day.

On the 12th Gleb Simonovich's birthday was celebrated on board, and the crew engaged in the celebration with especially boisterous merriment, for Gleb Simonovich was a general favorite. This celebration gives me occasion to report on a Russian custom that, in view of the strict discipline and the unconditional subordination of the subject to his superior, might seem strange. But it seems to me that the ordinary Russian places himself with regard to his master, whether captain, gentleman, or tsar, in a more childlike than servile relationship; and if he submits to the rod, he also asserts his childish freedoms. The crew first seized Otto Astavich, and, lining up in two rows facing each other and grasping each other's hands, they passed him mercilessly across their arms, this being a kind of tossing about that we would not consider an expression of honor or friendship. After Otto Astavich it was the turn of Gleb Simonovich and after him all of us that they could lay hands on. Those who were highest in their favor were tossed the highest and treated the most unmercifully. I learned afterwards that such action merits a gift in return, which the person tossed by tradition gives to the tossing parties.

On the 13th we were ready to sail, but the expected post from St. Petersburg had not yet arrived, and we had to commend patience to our deceived hopes until our return to Kamchatka, which was promised us for the fall of 1817. We were disappointed in this hope as well. During these three years we received no news from home that was addressed directly to us and no news of our relatives. If my longing for the mail had not kept me prisoner here I might have undertaken an excursion into the interior. However, it was still too early, as this year winter did not seem to want to yield its sway. There was still snow on the ground in St. Peter and Paul when we arrived, and only now did spring begin to bloom. When I wrote home from here, the dead letters falling on the paper not being an echo and evoking no echo, a painful feeling constricted my heart.

I must acknowledge a debt here. Books that travelers since Bering's times have left behind here or in Outer Siberia have accumulated to form a library in St. Peter and Paul in which to our surprise and pleasure we found works whose lack we had painfully felt.[25] Bosc could serve as a guide we completely lacked for the attractive study of sea worms, and I need scarcely say how desirable Pallas' *Journeys* and Gmelin's *Flora Sibirica* would be for us in the north.[26] The governor thought it the most natural thing in the world for these books to be used in a scientific expedition such as ours, and he allowed me to take the works I desired from the library under the condition (which I sacredly observed) of returning them to the St. Petersburg Academy upon our return home. Among other things, this library contained some books once left behind by Julius Klaproth on the Chinese border, stamped with his Chinese seal, the saying of Confucius, "Scholars are the light of darkness."[27] I possessed this very seal, a present from Julius Klaproth in the year 1804 or 1805, when I lived on familiar terms with him in Berlin and wished to learn Chinese from him. By chance I had taken this seal along on the voyage. I had it with me, and, presenting it, I could have claimed the books as my property.

A naturalist and collector, von Redovsky, whose life came to an unfortunate end in this corner of the earth, had left a few small chests containing dried plants and blotting paper, which Mr. Rudokov presented to me.[28] I was very glad to get the paper, too. How carefully I used every scrap in those days! Our transparency painting from Chile I used for seed capsules, and in a letter I wrote from St. Peter and Paul I find I mentioned with great gratitude a bunch of paper spills that the children of a friend in Copenhagen gave me just before I went aboard the ship.

In England I had acquired a good double-barreled musket. The captain himself had at that time directed us to provide ourselves with weapons. I had used it very little on the voyage; still, one lock was in poor condition and it was dirty, because I did not possess the tools needed to keep a gun clean and in good condition. Someone borrowed it from me in St. Peter and Paul, and I was exceedingly happy about this, expecting that it would get its due and it would look like new when it came back into my hands. In this I was wrong: I got it back in the same uncleaned state, and now its need was greater than before. The governor had seen my musket and wished to possess it. He commissioned the captain to bargain with me over the price that I wished to set on it. After I had ascertained that Mr. von Kotzebue, who wished to make himself agreeable to the governor, himself wished to see the transaction accomplished, I told him that, inasmuch as the musket, as he seemed to assume, was dispensable to me as a weapon of defense, I would gladly let Mr. Rudokov have it, but I did not know how to appraise its value in money and was not a business man. Let him take the animals and birds that he would shoot with it until the time of our return and have his people skin them and preserve the skins for me; that would be the price. This turn of the transaction seemed equally agreeable to all and would also have been greatly to the benefit of the Berlin museums if we had not neglected to return to Kamchatka.

Lieutenant Wormskiold remained in St. Peter and Paul. He would surrender the meteorological journal kept on board the *Rurik* according to the instruments of the expedition only under conditions that Mr. von Kotzebue was unwilling to grant. The latter, at whose disposal I had placed my entire supply of cash for the event that had transpired, did not make use of my money, thus allowing my offer to go unused. The ailing Lieutenant Sakharin also had to part with the expedition here, although unwillingly. We shook each other's hands cordially. He really should not have undertaken what he was physically unable to accomplish, for the duties of an officer at sea involve difficulties that remain unknown to the passenger.

The captain presented our jolly companion, the monkey, to the governor. One might think that monkeys, when they live on an intimate basis with human beings, as happens on board ship, clever and filled with curiosity and inquisitive as they are, would progress far in their education if they only had that most important appurtenance of the scholar, which nature has withheld from them, namely *Sitzfleisch*. They have no patience. This is all perhaps even more true of the East Indian monkeys, which we later took on board, than it is of this Brazilian species.

To augment the crew of the *Rurik* the captain obtained six seamen from the detachment here and an Aleut from the Russian-American trading company. The latter was a very experienced, very understanding man. These seven men Mr. von Kotzebue was supposed to give back upon his return to Kamchatka the next year. He also took on board a *baidare*, which he had had fashioned here: an open, shallow boat that consists of a light wooden frame covered with seal-skins and that is used as a tent or a windbreak when spending the night on land.[29]

We had all provided ourselves with parkas, and several had acquired bearskins for their beds. The parka is the usual fur garment of these northern peoples, a long seamless shirt made of reindeer skin with an attached hood or cowl. Some are of double thickness, having fur both inside and outside.

On July 14, 1816, we left the harbor of St. Peter and Paul but were not able to leave the Bay of Avatcha until the 17th.

# CHAPTER VII
## Northward from Kamchatka into the Bering Strait.

*St. Lawrence Island. Kotzebue Sound.*
*St. Lawrence Bay in the Land of the Chukchis.*
*Unalashka.*

"FOR the Discovery of a Northwest Passage" are words that the *Voyage of Discovery to the South Seas and to the Bering Strait,* by Otto von Kotzebue, bears on the title page. But now we are sailing toward the north, toward the Bering Strait, and it seems to me high time that you who have followed me blindly up until now without knowing where the voyage was headed and what its purpose was, should now belatedly be given the explanation of its chief purpose and the plan that was to be pursued, which I had obtained piecemeal. The summer campaign of 1816 was to be devoted solely to reconnaissance. A harbor, a secure anchorage for the ship, was to be sought in Norton Sound or, still better, in the northern part of the strait. The second summer campaign was to be reserved for proceeding from that harbor with baidares and Aleuts, the amphibians of these seas, to accomplish the real goal of the expedition. We were then to arrive in Unalashka early, where our equipment for the next year was to be provided by the officials of the Russian-American company, namely, baidares, crew, provisions for the latter, and interpreters who understood the language of the more northern Eskimos. These interpreters would have to be supplied from Kadiak, and the later in the year it was, the more dangerous and unreliable it was to send a messenger in a three-seater baidare along the coasts of the islands and the mainland. For that reason we could not lose any time now. The season of the northern winter we were to spend in sunny climes, partly to grant the crew some necessary recreation, partly to direct ourselves to geographic investigations elsewhere. Then, returning to Unalashka in the spring of 1817, we were to appropriate everything that had been prepared for our journey to the north and, as soon as the northern sea was open to shipping, sail the *Rurik* to the predetermined harbor, secure it and leave it behind there, and press forward with baidares and Aleuts to discover a northeastern passage as far to the north and east by land or water as good fortune allowed us. If the advanced season of the year or other circumstances made our goal unrealizable, we were to start our return journey by way of Kamchatka and on the way home investigate the dangerous Torres Sound.[1] Indeed, for discoveries in the Polar Sea it was expedient to make use of the sons of the north and their vessels. It was a mistake, however, to set all of the hopes of the enterprise upon a single cast of the die, upon one campaign, which an unfavorable year could bring to naught. But with tenacity, the last questions that the geography of these stretches of sea and coast still present might best be answered from Unalashka by Aleuts and a few hardy, toughened seamen who were qualified to undertake only the necessary place determinations.

The summer campaign of 1816, the results of which can be seen on the map Mr. von Kotzebue furnishes of the sound named after him, accomplished everything that could be expected of it in a most satisfactory manner. Kotzebue Sound, a deep inlet of the sea that penetrates into the American coast in the Arctic Circle, and whose inner shore lies about one degree farther north and at the same latitude as that of Norton Sound, offers ships the most secure anchorage and the most excellent harbor in the protection of Chamisso Island.[2] In the year 1817 Mr. von Kotzebue forbore to derive further advantage from his discovery, not advancing into the Polar Sea toward further discoveries. The task of the Romanzov expedition was later accomplished by the English, and Captain Beechey of the *Blossom* in the years 1826 and 1827 charted a part of the American coast in the Arctic Sea.[3]

Let me return to our northward journey. Its purpose was geography. We have, to be sure, had frequent contact with the natives, the inhabitants of St. Lawrence Island, the Eskimos of the American coast, and the Chukchis of the Asiatic, but we have never lived with and among them.[4] Mr. von Kotzebue's map and report, the painter's sketchbook, held open for us in his *Voyage pittoresque,* will be more informative than my scanty diary.[5] Moreover, what I had to say about these peoples of the Mongolian race I have compressed into a few words at the end of the essay that I devoted to the northern lands in my "Notes and Opinions."[6]

On July 17, 1816, we sailed out of the Bay of Avatcha and on the 20th caught sight of Bering Island, whose western end descends to the sea with gentle hills and clean lines. It appeared to us in the beautiful green of alpine meadows; there were only a few spots of snow.

From Bering Island we directed our course under a favorable wind toward the western tip of St. Lawrence Island. We were enveloped in extremely dense fog. On the 26th it lifted for a moment. A mountaintop became visible, and then the curtain dropped again. We tacked about in the dangerous vicinity of the unseen land.

On this day the appearance of a rat on deck was a worrisome event. Rats are extremely destructive guests on a ship, and their proliferation cannot be avoided. Up until then we had had no rats on the *Rurik*. If this one had come aboard in Kamchatka, several of them could have penetrated the lower hold. A rat hunt was arranged on deck as a very serious business, and three of them were caught. From then on no more were discovered.

On the 27th we headed toward the land, which appeared before us in the brightest sunshine just as we emerged from the sea's blanket of fog. Two boats were equipped for a landing. As we rowed toward shore we met a baidare with ten natives. We conversed with them, not without mutual wariness. "Tobacco! Tobacco!" was their loud desire. They obtained the savory weed from us, followed our boats in a friendly, joyous, yet cautious manner and gave us a helpful hand in landing in the vicinity of their tents. The tents of seal and walrus skins set up on the beach here seemed to be their summer dwellings, while the people's permanent dwellings seemed to be situated behind the foothills to the west. A second baidare came up from that direction. Our informed Aleut, who had spent some time on the American peninsula, found these people related in customs and language with those on the peninsula and served as a kind of interpreter. While the captain, who had been invited into a tent, was exposed to the embraces and caresses as well as the hospitality of these friendly fishy-smelling people, whom he presented with tobacco and knives, I, alone and undisturbed, climbed up the rocky bank and botanized. Seldom has a herborization appeared more joyous and stranger to me. It was our native flora, the flora of the High Alps of our Switzerland next to the edge of the snow belt, with the whole wealth, with the whole abundance and splendor of its dwarf plants pressing close to the earth, these joined by only a few distinctive ones, which blended in harmoniously with the others. On the height of the island, in the gravel that forms the ground, I found a human skull, which I took along carefully concealed under my plants. I had the good fortune of bestowing three not easily procured specimens upon the rich skull collection of the Berlin Anatomical Museum: this one from St. Lawrence Island, an Aleutian from an old gravesite on Unalashka, and an Eskimo from the graves in the Bay of Good Hope in Kotzebue Sound. Of the three only the latter was damaged. Only among warlike peoples who, like the Nukahiveans, count human skulls among their victory trophies, can such things be an object of trade.[7] Most people, like our northlanders, bury their dead and consider the graves to be sacred. Only through a rare happy accident can the traveler and collector gain possession of skulls, which are of the greatest importance for the history of the human races.

Toward two o'clock in the afternoon we reached the ship and, again submerged in deep fog, spent the 28th and the morning of the 29th in the vicinity of the island, around the western end of which we took our course. On the evening of the 28th the blanket of fog lifted, and we received a visit from a number of natives in three baidares, in whose leader the captain recognized his host of the day before. After a ritual embrace and nose-rubbing, gifts were exchanged and a lively trading session began. In a short time we and all of our crew were richly provided with kamleikas. The kamleika is the outer garment these northlanders wear for protection against rain and the splash of the waves, a shirt with a hood or cowl constructed of the fine intestinal skin of various seals and sea animals, the strips sewn together watertight in rings or spirals with a thread made of the sinews of sea animals, the seams sometimes decorated with feathers from seabirds or other things. The coarsest kamleika must have been the work of several, indeed, of many days even for the most accomplished seamstress, but they were exchanged joyfully for a few leaves of tobacco, the amount that a smoker could use up in a morning.

The strange custom of smoking tobacco, the origin of which is doubtful, came to us from America and began to become popular about a century and a half ago. Spread abroad by us, it has unexpectedly become the most widespread human custom. For every two who nourish themselves on bread, one could count five who owe the comfort and joy of life to this magic smoke. All the peoples of the earth have shown themselves equally eager to adopt this custom, the delicate, cleanly *lotophagi* of the South Seas and the dirty *ichthyophagi* of the Arctic Sea. Anyone who does not suspect its inherent magic should watch the Eskimo stuff his little stone pipe bowl with the valuable weed, which he has economically mixed with sawdust; should watch him carefully light it and then with closed eyes and a long deep breath greedily draw the smoke into his lungs and then blow it out toward the sky while all eyes are resting upon him, the next in line already stretching out his hand to receive the instrument and in the same way draw a joyous draft from it. For us tobacco is chiefly (and in some countries of Europe exclusively) the pleasure of the common man. I have always regarded with melancholy the fact that this small share of happiness, in which the needier classes are ahead of the more favored classes, is burdened with the most oppressive tax, and it has always seemed outrageous to me that, as is the case for example in France, the worst product that can be imagined is furnished in exchange for the money so painfully exacted.

On the 29th we caught sight of the northern cape of the island, a steep cliff to which was adjoined a settlement where *yurtas* of the natives appeared like molehills, surrounded by the hanging storage bins in which everything that is to be kept out of the reach of the dogs is preserved.[8] Immediately three baidares pushed out from the shore, each manned by about ten islanders, who, before they rowed up to the ship, performed religious observances. They sang a slow melody for some time; then one of them sacrificed a black dog, which he held up, slaughtered with a stab of the knife, then cast into the sea. Only after this solemn act did they come closer, and some of them come aboard.

On the 30th the weather cleared. In the morning we saw King's Island and soon afterward Cape Wales, the Gvozdev Islands (which are four pillars of rock standing alone in the middle of the strait), and even the coast of Asia.[9] Cook had seen only three of the aforementioned cliffs. The fourth, called Ratmanov Island by Kotzebue, is a discovery of his. We passed through the strait on the American side at a distance of about three miles from the shore in the afternoon toward two o'clock.

I must answer a question here that in the eyes of science demonstrates the irrepressible progress of time and history. You obstinate people, who deny its movement and wish to subvert it, you yourselves are progressing. Do you not open the heart of Europe in all directions to steamship travel, to railroads, telegraph lines, and bestow wings to thoughts that otherwise would but creep along? That is the Spirit of the Times, which is stronger than you are and seizes you. Gauss of Göttingen first asked me this question in Berlin in 1828, and since then the question has been repeatedly asked me: whether or not it would be possible to continue the geodetic survey and the triangulation from the Asiatic to the American coast beyond the strait.[10] This question I must simply answer in the affirmative. Both pillars of the sea gate are high mountains that are in sight of each other, rising sharply from the sea on the Asiatic side and on the American side having the foot surrounded by an extent of tide-swept beach. On the Asiatic side the sea has the greater depth, and the current, which passes from the south into the strait with a velocity of two to three knots, had the greater force. Only on the Asiatic side did we see numerous whales and innumerable herds of walruses.

The tops of the mountains may well tower above the blanket of fog, but there will also be days like July 30, 1816.

When the beach of the American coast began to rise into our field of vision, a magician seemed to have touched it with his wand. Heavily inhabited, it is covered with yurtas, which are surrounded by scaffolds and hanging storage bins whose pillars, whale bones or tide-washed tree trunks, rise above the bins they carry. These scaffolds first appeared on the horizon distended and altered through their mirror image in the play of the mirage. We had a view of an uncountable fleet, of a forest of masts.

Beyond the strait we followed the cost toward ENE as close as possible to the land at a depth of 5 to 7 fathoms. The land, except for a few points on the heights of the interior, was free of snow and covered with verdure. On the morning of the 31st we dropped anchor off a point where the low shore became lost to sight, as if there were the mouth of a river or the entrance of an inlet of the sea here. We landed opposite our anchorage and found ourselves on a low flat island that, like the sandbar of a river, half cut off the stream of water that poured through the low spots: Sarychev Island and Shishmarev Bay on Kotzebue's map.[11] The depth in the middle of the northwest entrance amounted to 8 fathoms, and at rising tide the current swept toward the land.

On Sarychev Island all the deceptions of the mirage surrounded us. I saw a surface of water before me in which a low hill was reflected that extended along the opposite shore. I went toward this water. It disappeared before me, and I reached the hill with dry feet. When I had covered about half the distance, I seemed to Eschscholtz, who had remained behind, to have been submerged up to my neck in the reflecting layer of air, and, shortened the way I was, he said I looked more like a dog than a human being. As I strode onward, toward the hill, I emerged more and more from the layer of air, and I appeared to him, lengthened by my reflection, to get taller and taller, gigantic, slender.

The phenomenon of the mirage can also be seen, for example, on the broad plains of our peat moors, for example at Linum, where I observed it myself.[12] It is seen in a vertical direction, and the conditions under which it occurs can be studied most conveniently on broad, sunlit wall surfaces (for example, on the walls encircling Berlin outside the city to the south and west), if one gradually brings his eye close to the wall. When land rises above the horizon, as seamen are wont to express it, the line that is taken to be the horizon is the edge of a reflecting surface formed by the lower layer of air and closer to the eye; a line that really lies below the visible horizon. I believe that this illusion in some cases can have an influence on astronomical observations and can cause an error in these of five and perhaps more minutes. Thus one ought to number the mirage along with the deviation of the declination of the magnetic needle observed on board among the causes that oppose exactness in astronomical calculations and coastal charting in the polar regions. This deviation (compare Flinders, Ross, Scoresby, etc.) had already been discussed at the time of our voyage.[13] I do not believe that Mr. von Kotzebue had considered the mirage or the deviation in this regard.

We had landed near yurtas that the people had deserted. Only a few dogs had remained behind. We took advantage of the opportunity to become acquainted with these people. Mr. von Kotzebue has described one of these yurtas.[14] A plan and sketch would have been more instructive.

A chamber of ten feet square, the walls six feet high, the ceiling arched, at the apex a square window closed with a bladder. The building constructed of beams flattened toward the inside. Opposite the door a cot for sleeping raised a foot and a half above the floor, taking up a third of the space. Along the wall various ladderlike hanging racks for storing tools. The door a round opening of a foot and a half in diameter in the center of the one wall. Passageways like mole tunnels but supported by wooden frames, only high enough to stand up in at a few places, connect the inner chamber door to the outer entrance, which, three feet high and square-shaped, opens out between two banks of earth toward the southeast. From the chief passageway a secondary passage leads to a pit where the provisions for winter, foot-square chunks of preserved meat, are kept, equipped with long-handled sieves to fish the meat out with. The exterior of the chief building and the entrances were covered with earth.

During our stay on the island a native baidare under sail came into the bay from the ocean through the southwestern entrance and was lost to our view in the east as it headed toward land. Two men, each in a one-passenger baidare, came from the mainland to observe us but could not be enticed to come close.

To these people the one-passenger baidare is what the horse is to the Cossack. This instrument is a long narrow tube of sealskins stretched onto a light wooden frame. In the center there is a round opening, and the man sits in it with his feet extended and his torso emerging out of the top. He is connected to the vessel with a tube of kamleika material the same width as the opening that encircles it and that he makes fast to his own body by tying it under his arms. His light paddle in his hand, his weapons in front of him, keeping his balance like a rider, he shoots like an arrow across the billowing surface of the sea. This vessel, which differs little among a number of different peoples, is well known from travel narratives and illustrations, and Eskimos have demonstrated them to us in the capitals of Europe. The large baidare, on the other hand, the women's boat, is analogous to the heavy vehicle that follows a procession of nomads.

When we returned to the ship toward evening, three baidares full of natives paddled after us, each furnished with ten men. They tied up alongside the one boat that had remained behind, manned only by the captain, Lieutenant Shishmarev, and four seamen. The Eskimos, who seemed not to be acquainted with firearms, took on a threatening attitude but refrained from open hostilities and followed the boat back to the ship but would not be induced to come aboard.

We followed the low-lying coast in the same direction, until toward noon on August 1 we found ourselves at the entrance of a wide bay. The land we were following continued eastward as far as could be seen, and a high promontory was visible far to the north. The wind left us. We dropped anchor. The current was strong through the opening into the bay. The view of things was promising. We could be at the entrance to a channel that separated the land in the north from the continent like an island and presented the questionable passage. Mr. von Kotzebue sent a party ashore so that at least a hill could be climbed and the land surveyed from a higher elevation. Here, on Cape Espenberg of his map, the natives visited us in great number.[15] They appeared, as is only right for brave men, equipped for war but ready for peace. I think that it was here where, before we had caught sight of them, I, alone and without weapons, botanizing on my own account, unexpectedly came upon a group of about twenty men. As they had no reason to be on their guard against me, an individual, we approached each other as friends right away. By way of currency that would be good here I had some three-edged needles with me such as can be found in Copenhagen for trade with Greenland, suitable for the needs of this same race of people. The eye of the needle is a useless adjunct. For use it is broken off and the thread of animal sinew is stuck to the steel. I pulled out my needle box and presented each of these strangers, who had grouped themselves in a semicircle around me, with two needles, starting at the left and going down the line. A valuable gift. I noted silently that one of the first, after he had received his allotment, stepped in line again farther along, where the others made room for him. When I came to him the second time and he stretched his hand out toward me for the second time, I gave him instead of the expected needles an unexpected resounding smack with all my strength. I had not miscalculated: everyone laughed uproariously along with me, and when people have laughed together they can go hand in hand without worry.

Several baidares followed us to the ship, and there we traded and joked with their occupants. They seemed to understand trade very well. They obtained tobacco and less-esteemed trifles from us, such as knives, mirrors, etc., but we were not able to offer them the long knives that they wanted for their valuable furs. From them we were able to obtain ivory articles, figurines of animals and men, various tools, ornaments, etc.

Toward evening the wind rose from the south, and we sailed toward the east into the strait. On the evening of the 2nd we still had high land to the north, a low coast to the south, and before us to the east open sea. Not until evening did individual points of land begin to emerge on the horizon and unite, forming a chain between both coasts: Only one spot seemed to leave any room for hope. The weather became unfavorable for us, and it was not until August 3 that we sailed through a channel between a narrow cape in the north and an island and cast anchor at a secure spot. The shores around us were primeval mountains; only in the north was our view not occluded. To investigate this spot on the 4th an excursion with longboat and baidare was undertaken, and soon we were enclosed by a bay that extended into alluvial tide toward the north and east, the shores precipitous and about eighty feet high, the ridges extending in gentle waves to an immeasurable bare plain scarred by spots of peat. We camped for the night underneath the baidare and returned to the ship on the 5th in unfavorable weather. We still had the hope of discovering the mouth of a river. On the 7th another excursion was undertaken toward the bay in the north. On the 8th a storm at our camp drove us back again. On this day Eschscholtz, who while the rest of us pressed forward went westward along the shore toward the anchorage, discovered the so-called icebergs, to which people who are not familiar with the north and traveling in the north seem to have attached almost too much attention. I have carefully read and tested Beechey on the subject of this ice bank, and I am unable to do anything else except adhere to the view I expressed in my "Notes and Opinions."[16] Either the destruction of the ice pack had progressed rapidly from 1816–1826 and had reached the border of ice formation and sand, or its effect had obscured the conditions, which were still clear to us. The quiet deposits in horizontal layers, which could be clearly seen on the wall of ice, in my opinion do not support Beechey's conception. Witnesses seem to agree that in Asia and

America at high latitudes the alluvial tideland nowhere thaws in the summer; that, where it is investigated, it has been found to be frozen solid at a great depth, and that in places the ice, often containing remains of primitive animals, occurs as a kind of mountain and as a part of the alluvial formation covered with fertile soil and verdure like any other soil.[17] (Estuary of the Lena and Mackenzie rivers, Kotzebue Sound.) But where the earth shows the old core, other temperature conditions may be present, and at the same latitude as the ice formation springs may be found.

I do not doubt that the mammoth teeth we collected here came from the ice. The truth is, however, that those that came into our hands had already been collected, tested, and discarded by the natives, on whose landing and camping places we ourselves camped. But if it is the ice that contains the remnants of primitive animals, it might be of older origin than the sand, in which I have found only reindeer horns and a good deal of driftwood quite identical with what is now cast up on the beach. That this bank of ice extends between the original rock and the sand must not be overlooked.

I had collected several fragments of fossil ivory and carefully laid them aside. One night the campfire was fed with them. I had to be happy afterwards to find the tusk, the molar, and the other fragment, which I bestowed upon the Berlin Mineralogical Museum. I had to stand guard over them and carry them into the boat myself. I was denied any help, even a protective word. The tusk, which seemed to me to be too thick and too little curved to belong to a mammoth, nonetheless was ascribed to this species on the basis of my sketch and description by Cuvier in his great work.[18]

The bay we were in received the name Eschscholtz; the island, in the lee of which the *Rurik* lay at anchor, received my name.[19] (It is unnamed in my "Notes and Opinions.")[20] Both on the sandy spit of land on which we camped and on the original rock of the island, the variation of the magnetic needle was completely irregular.

On excursions like this my watch with the second hand, made by Schunigk in Berlin, had the honor of doing service as chronometer. Not needing it myself, I had put it completely at the captain's disposal. After a two-day camp, during which the English patent meat (fresh meat and broth packed in tin boxes soldered together without any empty space) had served us in good stead, on the third day, the morning of August 9, we returned to the ship. During our absence the natives had sought to pay the ship a visit, but they had not been allowed on board, at the captain's command. The country behind Kotzebue Sound is uninhabited, and on its banks one finds only

landing places and camping places of the natives. One such can be
found, for example, on Chamisso Island and another near the icebergs of Eschscholtz Bay. They visit the latter, perhaps, just to collect ivory.

It rained on August 10. In the afternoon the weather cleared, and
we hoisted sail. A part of the southern coast remained to be explored. We dropped anchor when night fell and were visited by the
natives. On the 11th we approached a high cape (the Cape Deception of the map), from which several baidares paddled out toward
us.[21] Between this cape and Cape Espenberg to the north the low
coast encircled a broad bay. The depth of the water decreased. We
dropped anchor and immediately made preparations to go ashore.
There the estuary of a river could be expected. It was already late in
the afternoon. A dense fog enveloped us and forced us to return to
the ship. We accomplished the intended landing on the morning of
the 12th, but the greatly decreasing depth of the water permitted us
to row ashore only at a quite distant point, about six miles from the
ship. A channel that meandered through the flats, emptying into the
sea, and into which the inland stream seemed to empty, drew the
captain's attention. When I returned from a botanical excursion I
found him with a native, from whom he was endeavoring to obtain
some information as to the direction and nature of that stream. This
man, who had set up his tent here alone except for his family, had
advanced toward the captain with his boy, ready for battle, an arrow
in his bow, when the captain had appeared with an escort of four
men. He had comported himself in a decisive, brave, and clever
manner, as is fitting for a brave man in the presence of enemies who
are superior to him in strength and whose intentions he must suspect. The captain, by sending his escort away from them and
approaching him alone and without weapons, had conciliated the
man, and presents had sealed the peace. The Eskimo had received
him hospitably in his tent, where he had his wife and two children;
but he did not seem at ease with the intrusive strangers. Here again I
took over my old role of interpreter. In pantomime I pretended that I
was paddling inland and asked our friend with look and hand: Where
to? and When? He grasped the question immediately and answered
it in a very comprehensible fashion: Paddle for nine suns, sleep nine
nights, land on the right, land on the left; then open horizon, no
land in sight. A look at the map encourages us to the supposition
that this channel, with which the current of Shishmarev Bay may
unite, can lead to Norton Sound.

As soon as our friend succeeded in breaking away from us, he
struck his tent and moved himself and family over to the opposite

bank. But we established ourselves for the night, camping at the foot of a hill that was crowned with the graves of the natives. The dead lie above ground, covered with driftwood and protected from predatory animals. A few posts rise up, on which paddles and other signs hang. Our greedy curiosity rummaged through these grave-sites; the skulls were removed. What the naturalist collected, the painter and everybody else wanted to collect for himself, too. All the artifacts the survivors gave to their dead were sought and picked out. Finally, our seamen, to maintain our campfire, went there for wood and destroyed the monuments. What had better been left undone was not noticed until it was too late. I am not censuring us for that. Indeed, all of us were of a philanthropic bent, and I do not believe that Europeans could behave in a more model manner toward strange peoples, toward "savages" (Mr. von Kotzebue also calls the Eskimos savages) than we did everywhere we went. Our crew especially deserves in full measure the praise that the captain indeed gives them. But if this people had taken recourse to its arms because of the desecrated graves of their dead, who would bear the guilt of the bloodshed?

The arrival of a large group of Americans, who arrived on eight baidares from the vicinity of Cape Deception and set up their camp on the bank opposite, made us uneasy during the night. Their supe-riority in numbers dictated caution. We set out guards and loaded our guns. We took on the attitude toward them that one of them had shown toward us a short time before. To avoid a troublesome visit, the captain had us strike camp and take to the oars while it was still night. But it was ebb tide, and the sea broke across shallows we had not noticed at high tide. The captain seems to have considered our situation very dangerous. "I saw no way to avoid death," were his words. To be sure, I was on the baidare, which may have been exposed to slighter danger. In the meantime the breaking day put an end to our embarrassment, and we reached the ship in good condi-tion without any great exertion on the part of the crew.

We weighed anchor on August 13, after we had received the visit of two more baidares. We approached the high cape that on the north side marks the entrance to the sound. Well-inhabited flatland is sit-uated in front of the highlands, uniting the mountain masses that from the sea may seem like islands.

The chief purpose of our summer campaign was satisfactorily attained, and here we put an end to our discoveries. Plunging into the fogs again, we crossed the bay north of the strait over to the Asiatic coast, along which we wished to sail to enter St. Lawrence Bay in the land of the Chukchis. Perhaps we could have and should

have employed the time we spent in St. Lawrence Bay for a reconnaissance trip to the north, which under favorable conditions could
have turned out to be more successful than the intended second
campaign with more unfavorable ones.

The south wind blew continuously and slowed our progress, the
depth of the water increased, the temperature decreased, and even
the sea was found to be colder in the vicinity of the wintry Asiatic
coast. We tacked about on the night of the 18th to the 19th against
the wind and current in order to pass through the strait between the
East Cape and Ratmanov Island; and in the night, when we thought
we had reached the level of St. Lawrence Bay, we were still at the
East Cape, without having made any progress.[22] (Thirty fathoms is
the greatest depth of water that is marked on the map.) As a rift in
the fog let us catch sight of the cape, we headed in that direction and
immediately went ashore in two boats. The Chukchis received us
on the beach as if it were a state visit, in a friendly manner, but with
a solemnity that deprived us of all freedom. They invited us to sit
down on furs they had spread upon the ground but did not invite us
into their dwellings, situated farther back on the hill. After having
accepted our presents, some of them, among them the two most
prominent, followed us to the ship. The latter two, before they went
aboard, each presented the captain with a fox skin and then climbed
aboard fearlessly with their retinue. Mr. von Kotzebue, who drew
them into his cabin, where there was a large mirror, notes upon this
occasion "that the northern people fear the mirror, while on the
contrary the southern ones observe themselves in it with pleasure."[23]

We used a breath of air from the northeast, which could be felt in
the afternoon, to get under sail immediately. Walruses, of which we
had seen a few isolated ones the previous day when we sailed around
the East Cape, covered the sea in innumerable herds and filled the
air with their roars. Numerous whales sported about and shot high
streams of water into the air. In rain and fog we headed toward St.
Lawrence Bay. At noon of the 20th we were just at the entrance to it
when the weather cleared up, and at three o'clock we dropped
anchor behind the little sandy island that forms the harbor.

From the closest shore, on which the tents of the Chukchis covered the crest of a hill, two baidares shoved off, in each of which two
men were sitting. They approached us singing but stopped at some
distance from the ship until they were called over and then mounted
the deck without fear. We prepared to go ashore ourselves, and our
guests, satisfied with our liberality, followed us. They paddled their
light vessels a lot more rapidly than we could move our boats and

were amused at the vain efforts of our seamen to compete with them.

Moors and snowfields in the background, a few rare plants that bear the alpine character in great measure. The hills and slopes covered with gravel above which cliff walls and crags loom bare and bald, covered with snow wherever snow can lie. A stark winter landscape.

Twelve of the tents were of animal skins, large and roomy, unlike any we had yet seen. An old man had authority over the tribe. He received his guests with great honors, although their appearance may have seemed threatening to him. The Chukchis are an independent people in their mountains, subservient to no one. They recognize Russian sovereignty only inasmuch as they pay the tribute in the market places, where they trade with the Russians to their mutual advantage. One of the seamen whom we had brought from Kamchatka, who spoke a little Kariakish, could make himself understood on a very basic level.[24] The captain distributed presents and declined to accept any, which seemed strange to these people. All he wanted was fresh water and some reindeer. Reindeer were promised, but it would take a few days to procure them from the interior. We parted satisfied with each other.

I cannot refrain from citing an incident that seems to belong to the characterization of these northerners and from which the contrast in which they stand to the charming Polynesians can be seen. One of the participants at the above-mentioned important conference, while standing before the captain and speaking with him, without regard to respect spread his legs apart and relieved himself of his urine underneath his parka.

All preparations were made to undertake a trip in boats to the back of the bay on the next day. On the 21st the weather was unfavorable, and the party was postponed. The Chukchis from Nuniago [Nunivak] in Mechigmensk [Matchickma] Bay (where Cook once landed) came to visit us in six baidares. They paddled around the ship singing, after which they came aboard with confidence. They made friends with the crew, and a glass of brandy increased their merriment. They made camp on the beach, where we visited them in the afternoon and watched their dances, which had little charm for us.

On August 22 and 23 we carried out the excursion in longboat and baidare the results of which are incorporated into Mr. von Kotzebue's map.[25] The interior of the bay is uninhabited. On the shore where we took our noon rest on the first day we obtained several waterfowl and two freshly killed seals from Chukchi hunters, whose first impulse was to take to flight when they saw us but who became our friends as the result of our gifts. The birds supplied our table, while we let the seals lie to take them aboard the next day. But as they were partially eaten during the night, probably by foxes, we disdained them altogether. In the back of the bay where we set up our camp the view of the land and the vegetation had not changed. The willows rose barely a few inches above the ground. The cliffs above us were of white crystalline marble. Water froze to ice during the night.

When we arrived at the ship toward noon, we got the news that our reindeer had arrived. We went ashore to receive them. Some were already butchered, and we had them butcher the others before our eyes. Reindeer flesh is really a quite excellent dish, but how precious it tastes when for a long time one has tasted only fishy seafowl or something similar as a variation in a diet of old salted meat! I forgot our seals, the discarding of which because of the bite of a fox had seemed to me a prejudiced, punishable waste. In these days the Chukchis butchered a whale on the sandy island. They offered us some of the flesh, but we were satisfied with our reindeer flesh.

In the evening some more new arrivals visited us. On one of the baidares there was a boy whose amusing mimicry was rewarded with several tobacco leaves. Encouraged by his success, he was inexhaustible with his monkeyshines, which he did not tire in performing with original gaiety, desiring and garnering more and more rewards for his tricks. Under these skies, too, laughter is, as Rabelais so tellingly put it, the peculiar characteristic of mankind, when, that is, men, still independent, rejoice in their inborn freedom.[26] Soon we shall encounter on Unalashka the close relatives of these happy northerners, but these have completely forgotten how to laugh. I have come to know very different states of society and lived among different manifestations of it. I have seen neighboring peoples of the same race, of which some are free and some could be called servile; I have never found a reason for praising despotism. Of course, a letter of emancipation, a piece of paper alone, does not mean freedom and its benefits, and the hardest thing I know is the transition from accustomed servility to the enjoyment of independence and freedom.

We wished to go under sail on August 25. Unfavorable winds, calms, and storms held us in the harbor until the 29th. On the 28th it transpired that one of the strangers camping here used force against one of our seamen, seizing a scissors from him with drawn knife. One of the local Chukchis quickly sprang up and seized the perpetrator, who, when the matter came to be discussed, had already been punished by his chief. The captain was shown how in atonement he had to run incessantly in the same direction in a narrow circle like a circus horse, and the incident had no other consequences beyond showing us that a good police was maintained among these people.

We sailed out of St. Lawrence Bay early on the morning of August 29, 1816, and in the evening we experienced a very severe storm. We directed our course toward the eastern side of St. Lawrence Island, which the captain wished to chart. Fog frustrated his intent, and we sailed past on the 31st without catching a glimpse of the land. Shallows make sailing on the American side of this bay dangerous. We now headed toward Unalashka. On September 2 we had a sight rare in these stretches of the ocean: we beheld the rising sun. On the 3rd a small land bird (a *Fringilla*) came to the ship, and a waterfowl (a *Colymbus*) surrendered itself to us and allowed itself to be seized.[27] In the afternoon the island of St. Paul was seen far in the west from the crow's nest, and on the morning of the 4th we passed by St. George, which likewise remained in the west. On this day we unexpectedly rejoiced in the sight of a ship. We overtook it and spoke it. It was a schooner of the Russian-American company, which had taken aboard furs from St. Paul and St. George and was headed for Sitka.[28] We made our way toward Unalashka together. The night was stormy and dark, and at the same time the sea was phosphorescent to a degree that I have scarcely seen excelled in the tropics. The sparks of light adhered to the sails, which were splashed by the crest of the waves. On the morning of the 5th we were enveloped in fog, and the other ship was no longer visible. We knew ourselves to be in the vicinity of the land and could not see it and could not rely on our ship's calculations. In the afternoon the curtain of fog rose for an instant, and we saw a high land, which was immediately lost to sight again. We tacked about through the night.

On the morning of September 6 we enjoyed a glorious spectacle. A dark sky loomed over the sea, while the high, jagged, snow-capped crags of Unalashka, lit up by the sun's rays, were resplendent in a red glow. All day long we were forced to fight against an adverse wind in the sight of land. Endless flights of waterfowl, which hovered low above the surface of the water, resembled low floating islands from afar. Numerous whales played about our ship and shot tall jets of water into the air in all directions of our field of vision.

These whales remind me of something I once heard a naturalist of genius contribute to the conversation. The next step that must be made, which is much more obvious and will take us farther than the steam engine did with the steamship, this first warm-blooded animal that has proceeded from the hand of man—the next step is to domesticate the whale. Of what does this task consist? To get him to forget how to dive under the water! Have you ever seen a flight of wild geese moving along and then seen an old woman with a stick in her trembling hand drive a half thousand of these high-fliers onto a fallow field and control them? You have seen it and not been amazed at the miracle, so why are you startled by the suggestion of domesticating the whale? Bring up young whales in a fjord, put a spiked belt supported by air bladders under their pectoral fins, make experiments. Indeed, to unite both seas and to reduce the distance from Archangel [Arkhangelsk] to St. Peter and Paul to eight to fourteen days is well worth the effort. As to whether the whale should be a dray animal or a beast of burden, and how he could be hitched up or loaded down, how he could be bridled or otherwise controlled, and who should be the kornak of the water elephant—all that will take care of itself.[29]

On September 7, 1816, a favorable but weak wind brought us to the entrance of the bay, where it suddenly failed us between the high mountains of the island, so that we found ourselves in a rather helpless situation, as no anchor can reach the bottom there. But the agent of the company, Mr. Kriukov, came toward us with five twenty-paddle baidares and towed us into harbor. At one o'clock we dropped anchor before Illiuliuk, the chief settlement. The steam bath had been thoughtfully heated for us.

Mr. Kriukov, obliged by the command of the directors of the company in St. Petersburg to fulfill all of Mr. von Kotzebue's requests, exhibited a subservient obligingness toward him in everything. One of the few cattle on the island was immediately butchered for us, and our crew was provided with fresh meat, potatoes, and turnips, the only vegetables that are grown here.

Mr. von Kotzebue's requests consisted of the following: to construct one baidare of twenty-four paddles, two one-seater and two three-seater baidares; to keep fifteen healthy, strong Aleuts with all of their ammunition in readiness for the next spring; to procure kamleikas of sea lion necks for the entire crew for the same time; and to send a messenger immediately to Kadiak in order to obtain through the agent of the American company an interpreter who could understand and translate the language spoken on the northern coast of America.[30] Three resolute Aleuts were ready to undertake this dangerous mission.

The three-seater baidare is built according to the model of the one-seater, except that it is proportionately longer and equipped with three seat holes. In this a European who takes the middle seat in Aleut dress with kamleika and eye-shield (against spray from the waves) lets himself be propelled by two Aleuts. I myself on a beautiful Sunday morning had myself propelled in this fashion in such a baidare in the harbor of Portsmouth, to the infinite amusement of the English.

On the morning of September 8 the *Chirik*, the schooner that we had seen at sea, sailed into the harbor. A Prussian from the area around Danzig, Mr. Binzemann, was its captain. A Prussian who has become captain of a schooner of the Russian-American company traveling between Unalashka and Sitka has borne and experienced some things in the wide world not dreamed of by one who never got any farther in his life than, say, from the lower benches of the school up to the teacher's platform. Mr. Binzemann had only one leg. The other had been shattered on him by the explosion of a cannon on a ship that he commanded. He, who as captain was also ship's doctor on board, had a seaman cut off his limb, which was hanging together only by a small strip of flesh, with a knife and then bandaged the stump with a plaster of "Spanish flies."[31] This improvised cure of an amputated limb without tying up the arteries was crowned with the best success, and its healing left nothing to be desired. I have not been able to resist writing down this story because it, along with the reports that Mariner communicates to us of the surgical operations of the Tonga Islanders, has contributed to shaking the great faith I have always harbored toward surgery as the visible part of the healing arts.[32]

We were destined to have a fairly long sojourn on this melancholy island. After a fleeting glimpse of the misery of the servile impoverished Aleuts, and of their oppressors, themselves oppressed, the Russians here, I spent the days wandering about on the heights that crown the settlement and allowed the attractive gifts of the flora to divert my attention from the people. Eschscholtz was gathering plants on his own. We had found out that it was better for us to separate on land, as we had enough of each other on board ship.

On the 10th was the tsar's name day, and for this description I borrow Mr. von Kotzebue's words:

> September 11. To celebrate the tsar's name day, yesterday Mr. Kriukov gave the whole crew a dinner ashore at noon, and in the afternoon we entered a large subterranean dwelling where a number of Aleuts were gathered to dance. I certainly believe that their games and dances in former times, when they were still in possession of their freedom, were different from what they are now, when slavery has degraded them almost to the level of animals, and when this spectacle is neither enjoyable nor amusing.

The orchestra consisted of three Aleuts with tambourines,
with which they accompanied a simple sad melody containing only three notes. On all occasions only one female
dancer at a time appeared, who without any expression
gave a few jumps and then disappeared among the spectators. The sight of these people, who had to jump around in
front of me with sad gestures, pained me, and my crew,
who likewise felt oppressed, took up a gay song to cheer us
up, while two of them placed themselves in the center of
the circle and performed a national dance. This quick
transition pleased us all, and even in the eyes of the
Aleuts, who up until then had stood there with bowed
heads, a beam of joy sparkled. A servant of the American
company (Promishlenoi), who had left his Russian fatherland as a vigorous youth and had become old and gray in
this region, suddenly plunged into the room and cried out,
with his hands raised toward heaven, "These are Russians! These are Russians! Oh dear, beloved fatherland!"
On his venerable face at this moment lay the expression of
a blessed feeling. Tears of joy creased his pale, sunken
cheeks, and he hid, to devote himself to his melancholy.
This scene shook me up. I placed myself vividly into the
old man's position, whose youth, happily spent in the
fatherland, now passed before his mind's eye in painful
memory. He had come here with the hope of being able to
enjoy a carefree old age in the bosom of his family, and
now, like many others, he had to end his life in this wilderness.[33]

The Russian–American Trading Company, by loans of money to
those of an enterprising spirit who dedicate themselves to their service, knows how to keep them under its yoke. Care is taken that
they are never able to erase the debt, and, as Frederick is supposed to
have said of his army, "There is no redemption from hell."

We had taken on water, our work was done, and everything was
ready on September 13, 1816, to weigh anchor the next morning at
dawn. Night fell, and Eschscholtz, who had gone into the mountains to botanize, had not returned to the ship. I shall, even if I
expose myself to the danger of appearing silly, give a report here of
the only event of the entire voyage when I am conscious of having
been in danger. No one took any notice of it, no one thanked me for
it, and this is the first time I have mentioned it. The captain ordered
me and some crewmen and Aleuts to search for the doctor in the
mountains, where he must have gotten lost while botanizing. I
requested that we be given a few pistols to take along to fire signal
shots, but the request was not granted. I led my people to the declivity that led up to the gorge that I wished to search. The seamen
thought it was not possible to climb it. But when I, who knew this

pass well, had reached the top, they all followed me, and we reached the heights of the cliffs, the ridge of which I wished to follow by a more gentle slope from the inside. Then a cannon shot resounded from the *Rurik*, calling us back. I now left it up to our Aleuts to pick the best way down to the beach from the heights we had reached. I was led to a gorge that, worn by melting snow water, fell from the ridge on which we stood almost perpendicularly down to the sea. I took the lead, as was fitting, and one by one, as on a ladder, the others followed behind. It was unavoidable that some stones rolled; how my men and I ever got down in one piece in the pitch-black night I was unable to comprehend later when I looked up this gorge. When I came on board with the seamen the doctor had already been there for some time, and I could go to bed without worry. I was still sleeping when we got under sail on September 14, 1816.

# CHAPTER VIII
## From Unalashka to California.
## Sojourn in San Francisco.

EARLY on the morning of September 14, 1816, we sailed out of the harbor of Unalashka with a favorable wind. Some shots were taken at a whale that came too close to us in the bay; I was still lying in my bunk. The passage between the islands of Akun and Unimak had been praised to the captain as the safest to cross the chain of the Aleutian Islands from north to south.[1] He accordingly chose this route, which he also recommends to every seafarer. The weather was clear, and the lofty peak of Unimak, whose height Kotzebue estimates at 5,525 English feet, was cloudless.[2] The conditions that here delayed our voyage were favorable for the plotting of a chart that Mr. von Kotzebue refers to without supplying it.[3] The sea was especially bright between these islands. On the morning of the 16th we were in the open sea.

Our chief task now was to escape the northern winter. I do not consider that the stupidest thing I have done in my life is my escaping three winters on this voyage. Three winters! If I have endured winter again here at home, I think as a brave man I have done enough, but I cannot and will not praise it or honor it. We winterlanders, however, still praise the divine wisdom that in such an arrangement gives us the joy of spring. By analogy with this, should we not demand of our authorities that they put thumbscrews on us half of the day, so that we might look forward to the hour when they are taken off? This arrangement is a minor one on our terrestrial sphere, one of which the majority of speaking humanity know nothing. Our poets may boast of being favored by God above many, in that He gives them material for their spring songs, but it remains incomprehensible and like a lie to him who has crossed the line of the winter cycle that man, that fork-shaped naked animal, has had the audacity to settle at the 52nd, indeed at the 72nd degree of northern latitude, where he can eke out his miserable existence only by the power of his mind. Think how God created you, and go out on a winter day and observe the area, dead for a half a year, under its shroud of snow. Life exposed to the open sleeps in the seed and in the egg, in the bud and in the larva, deep under the earth, deep in the water under the ice. The birds have gone; amphibians and mammals sleep their winter sleep; only a few species of warm-blooded animals crowd parasitically around your dwellings; only a few of the larger independent species barely stay alive during the difficult time.[4]

But man is an intelligent animal, and with the fire he stole he knows no limits on earth. The Ostyak fishermen, whose native haunts lie at sixty degrees northern latitude, know of a lost paradise, Adolph Erman tells us, but they locate it toward the north beyond the Arctic Circle! The legend is quite readable.[5]

I have occasionally spoken of a preacher in Lappland. The man had spent seven years in this parish, which lay beyond the tree belt, during the warm summer months quite alone (during that time his parishioners and their reindeer herds moved to the cooler regions by the sea). During the winter night, when the moon was in the sky, he went around by sled, camped when the mercury was frozen solid, and visited his Lapps, whom he loved, in order to perform the duties of his office. Twice in these seven years he had enjoyed the company of members of his own race and language: once a brother of his had visited him, and once a botanist lost his way and came to his residence. He was well able to praise appreciatively the joy that man brings to man, but neither this joy nor any other in life, he assured me, can be compared to the rapture of seeing the disk of the sun rise in a circle over the horizon again after the long winter night.

For us spring is the awakening from a long debilitating illness, which, though less drastic than the hibernation of other animals, nonetheless corresponds to it. Man lives more fully and more rapidly under the direct rays of the sun, which, as in Brazil, draws forth the abundance of life from the womb of the earth. Under a sky without a radiant glow, on a land without fertility, he counts the days more, counts the years more.

In truth, I would like to live in the region of the palm trees and from there see the old demon (winter) banned to the tops of the mountains. I would also like to pay him a state visit along with Parry or Ross, but I find it hard to give him lodging for half of the year.[6] During the three years in two northern summers we had to bear only a few frosty nights, such as are not at all unknown even in our lands at this time of the year.

We had constant favorable north and northwest winds. The equinox and the full moon brought us only a strong wind, which almost increased to a storm, and before which we proceeded rapidly forward under full sail.

We headed for San Francisco in New California.[7] Mr. von Kotzebue had been instructed to head for the Sandwich Islands from
Unalashka and had obtained very good information about them
from the ships' captains of the Russian-American company. Kotzebue had preferred that port (San Francisco) to the islands, where the
frequency of shipping has increased the price of all necessities and
where payment can be made only with Spanish piasters or with copper plates, weapons, or the like, for the rest and recreation of his
crew and the provisioning of the *Rurik*.

As I have nothing to report of the journey itself, I shall interpose a
few things here that I have never before put down on paper. Because
of the ship's regulations, which I have described before, among
which also was the fact that the light was put out every evening at
ten o'clock, and because of our monotonous, quiet way of life,
which lacked any strenuous exercise, we could not fill all the hours
in which we were condemned to lying still with deep, unconscious
sleep, and a kind of half-sleep filled a large part of life with dreams,
with which I shall entertain you. I never dreamed of the present,
never of the voyage, never of the world to which I now belonged.
The cradle of the ship rocked me back to being a child again, the
years were rolled back, I was in my father's house again, and my
dead ones and other forgotten characters surrounded me, moving
about in their normal daily manner, as if I had never gone beyond
those years, as if death had never mown them down. I dreamed of
the regiment in which I had served, dreamed of the daily muster.
The drum rolled, I came running up, and my old colonel placed himself between me and my company and cried out, "My dear lieutenant, in the name of three devils!" Oh, this colonel! This terrifying
popinjay followed me incessantly across the seas of all five continents when I couldn't find my company, when I came to parade
without my sword, when—all sorts of things. And always his terrible cry: "My dear lieutenant, my dear lieutenant!" This old colonel
of mine was at the root an honest old war-horse and a good man, but
he believed, as a genuine product of the time, that being rude was a
necessary part of the business. After I returned from the voyage I
wished to see the man who for so long had disturbed my nights' rest.
I looked him up: I found an eighty-year-old, purblind man of almost
gigantic stature, much taller than the picture I had of him, who
lived in a little room off the courtyard in the house of a former noncommissioned officer of his company, lived from a few small charity
grants, as in the unfortunate war, more from obtuseness than from
guilt, he had ruined all claims for a pension. Almost astonished at
having been looked up by an officer of the regiment, in which he had

not been popular, and not knowing any moderation, he exhibited an exaggerated courtesy toward me that hurt me to the depths of my soul. When he shook hands with me he felt the cloth of my coat with two fingers, and what lay in this grasp—I don't know, but I shall never forget it. I sent him a few bottles of wine as a friendly gift, and when he passed away—I believe it was the next year—it turned out that he had decreed that I should be invited to his funeral. I followed him alone with an old major of his regiment and his subaltern—peace be unto his ashes!

I want to add something on the subject of the animals that enjoyed the hospitality of the *Rurik.* Our little dog from Concepción, our Valet, had remained true to us. He belonged to the main cabin, and at sea he demonstrated no small talent at enjoying a truly model indolence. He looked at us all beseechingly, and if one of us nodded his permission he was in his bunk with one leap, where he slept until the next meal. At every landing place, on the other hand, he had to be the first to go ashore, and if he was not taken on the boat he swam ashore. Like us, he sought others of his species, but when he found them, he usually came home in a sad, ragged state. Our Valet had found a rival in a young dog of the race serving the Eskimos, which the captain had brought along from his trip north. This new guest was called Big Valet on the *Rurik.* Third, we still had Shafekha, the sow, soon to meet the fate I have already described.

When we sailed north from Kamchatka, we had a last cock on board, which, having been released from the chicken coop, paraded back and forth on the deck as a proud fellow. I was curious to see how he would behave with regard to sleep when the sun no longer set for us at night. The observation was not carried out for two reasons: first, we did not get that far north, and second, the cock flew overboard, fell into the sea, and drowned before we reached St. Lawrence Island.

But let me return to our voyage. On October 2, 1816, at four o'clock in the afternoon we sail into San Francisco harbor. There is great activity in the fort on the southern entrance of the channel. They hoist their flag, we show ours, which does not seem to be known here, and salute the Spanish flag with seven guns, which, according to Spanish regulation, are returned with two fewer. We drop anchor in front of the *presidio,* and no boat pushes out from the shore to come to us, because Spain does not have a single boat on this bay.[8]

I was immediately ordered to accompany Lieutenant Shishmarev to the presidio. Lieutenant Don Luis de Argüello, after the death of the colonel the interim commandant, received us in an exceptionally friendly manner, immediately saw to the most pressing needs of the *Rurik* by sending fruit and vegetables on board, and on the same evening sent a messenger to the governor of New California in Monterey, to report our arrival to him.[9]

On the next morning (the 3rd) I met Artillery Officer Don Miguel de la Luz Gómez and a pater of the local mission, who came aboard ship just as I was about to go to the presidio on an errand of the captain's. I accompanied them on board; they were the bearers of the friendliest promises of assistance on the part of the commandant and the very powerful mission. The clerical gentleman also invited us to the mission of San Francisco on the following day, which was a saint's festival day, for which purpose we would find riding horses ready. At the express wish of the captain we were most abundantly supplied with beef cattle and vegetables. In the afternoon the tents were set up on the land, as were the observatory and the Russian bath. In the evening we paid the commandant a visit. Eight guns were fired from the presidio to receive the captain.

But it was not these superfluous courtesy guns that the captain desired, but rather the two that were still owed to the Russian flag, and he insisted tenaciously upon their delivery. There were long negotiations on this subject, and only against his will and under compulsion (I don't know but what it took a command from the governor) did Don Luis de Argüello finally agree to provide belatedly the two missing cannon shots. Also, one of our crew had to be sent to the fort to repair the line for hoisting the flag, for it had broken when last used, and there was no one among the inhabitants who could climb up the pole to fix it.

The feast of Saint Francis gave us the opportunity to observe the missionaries at their work, and the peoples to whom they are sent when these peoples are in a subjugated condition.[10] I shall have nothing to add to what I said in the "Notes and Opinions." One can refer to Choris with regard to the native tribes, as he has given us an estimable series of portraits in his *Voyage pittoresque*, except that Plates 10 and 12, which were painted later in Paris, should be excised: everyone knows that the bow is not used the way it is pictured there.[11] Choris even furnishes Californian music in his text.[12] I do not know who may have undertaken the task of putting notes onto paper in accordance with Choris' singing. Although I used to concede to this friend that he could sing better than I could, he still could not dispute the big advantage that my singing had over his, namely, that I almost never let it be heard.

Here, as in Chile, the captain was able to accustom the commandant and his officers to our table. We dined on land under the tent, and our friends of the presidio were usually not slow in arriving. This relationship occurred almost automatically. The misery in which they had been wallowing for six to seven years, forgotten and forsaken by Mexico, the motherland, did not permit them to be hosts, and the need to pour out their hearts in speech impelled them to approach us, as life was easy and pleasant with us. They spoke only with bitterness of the missionaries, who in the face of a deficiency in imported goods nonetheless enjoyed a superfluity of the products of the earth and would let them have nothing now that their money had run out except in return for a promissory note and, even so, only what is absolutely necessary to maintain life, among which things bread and flour are not included. For years they had lived on maize, without seeing bread. Even the detachments of soldiers who are placed in every mission for their protection were only provided with absolute essentials against promissory notes. "Our leaders are too good!" cried Don Miguel, meaning the commandant. "They should requisition, demand that they provide what we need!" One soldier went even further and complained to us that the commandant would not permit them to secure natives in order to get them to work for them as they did in the missions. It also caused dissatisfaction that the new governor of Monterey, Don Pablo Vicente de Solá, since he assumed office had wished to oppose smuggling, which is the only way they have of obtaining their most essential necessities.[13]

On October 8 the courier came back from Monterey. He brought the captain a letter from the governor, announcing his imminent arrival in San Francisco. In accordance with Mr. von Kotzebue's wish, Don Luis de Argüello had been empowered to send a messenger to Mr. Kuskov in Port Bodega, and the captain wrote to the latter in order to draw from his flourishing trading center some of the things that were beginning to be lacking on the *Rurik*.[14]

"Mr. Kuskov," says Mr. von Kotzebue, "Mr. Kuskov, agent of the Russian-American company, settled at Bodega at the command of Mr. Baranov, who is the head of all the possessions in America, in order to provide the possessions of the company with supplies."[15] But Bodega, situated about thirty miles, a half-day's journey, north of San Francisco, was counted by Spain, not without some appearance of justice, as part of its territory; and on Spanish territory, therefore, Mr. Kuskov, with twenty Russians and fifty Kadiakans [Kodiakans], had erected a fort in the midst of peace, a fort that was equipped with a dozen cannon, and there he practiced agriculture, possessed horses, cattle, sheep, a windmill, etc. He had a trading center there for smuggling with the Spanish harbors, and from there he sent out his Kadiakans each year to catch a few thousand sea otters along the California coast, the skins of which, according to Choris, who may have been well informed, were sold in Canton at an average price of 60 piasters, 35 piasters for the poorer skins and 75 for the better ones. It was only regrettable that the port of Bodega could only take ships that did not draw more than nine feet of water.

It does not seem incomprehensible to me that the governor, when he obtained late information about this settlement, was outraged about it. Different steps were taken to force Mr. Kuskov to vacate the premises. For everything they directed toward him he had referred the Spanish authorities to Mr. Baranov, who had sent him there and at whose command, in case they could get him to make it, he would very gladly withdraw again. This is the way matters stood when we entered San Francisco. The governor now placed his hopes in us. I, too, will have conferences and negotiations to talk about and shall reveal to the world the memorable events of my diplomatic career. But we haven't gotten to this point yet.

On October 9 some Spaniards were shipped to the northern shore to use the lasso to catch some horses for the courier to be sent to Mr. Kuskov, and I seized the opportunity to look around over there. The reddish brown cliffs there are, as is stated in my "Notes and Opinions," and as can be seen in the mineralogical museum in Berlin, silicious schist, but not a conglomerate, as Moritz von Engelhardt assumes in order to enlarge upon this assumption.[16]

The year was already old, and in the area, which in the spring months, the way Langsdorf saw it, should resemble a flower garden, now offered the botanist nothing but a dry, dead field.[17] In a swamp in the vicinity of our tents a water plant is said to have been green, and Eschscholtz asked me about its pedigree. I hadn't noticed it, but he had calculated that a water plant, my special fancy, would not have escaped me and so had not wanted to get his feet wet. That's the kind of thing you can expect from your closest friend.

On the naked plain that lies at the foot of the presidio, farther to the east a solitary oak tree stands in the midst of a shorter growth of brush. Recently my young friend Adolph Erman saw it, too; if he had observed it more closely he would have found my name carved in its bark.

On October 15 the courier dispatched to Kuskov returned, and on the evening of the 16th artillery salvos from the presidio and the fort announced the arrival of the governor from Monterey. Right after that a messenger came down from the presidio to request the help of our physician for two men who had been dangerously wounded firing off a cannon. Eschscholtz immediately acceded to the request.

On the morning of the 17th Mr. von Kotzebue waited on board

ship for the first visit of the governor of the province, and the governor in turn, an old man and an officer of higher rank, waited in the presidio for the first visit of Lieutenant von Kotzebue. The captain was notified by chance that he was expected in the presidio, whereupon he sent me to the presidio with the unpleasant talk of politely telling the governor that he, the captain, had been informed that he, the governor, wished to visit him on board this morning and that he expected him. I found the little man in dress uniform and all his decorations, except for a sleeping cap, which he still wore on his head, ready to take it off in time. I discharged my task to the best of my ability and saw the little man's face lengthen three times its normal size. He bit his lip and said he regretted that he could not bear the sea before eating and that he was sorry that for now he must forego the pleasure of meeting the captain. I saw it coming that the old man would mount his horse and start out again on his trip back through the wilderness to Monterey without having accomplished his mission, for it could not be assumed that Mr. von Kotzebue, once the rift had been expressed, could give in.

Pondering this I slunk down to the beach again, when a good genius intervened and, before unpleasantness could occur, sealed the prevailing peace with the fairest bonds of friendship. The morning had gone by, and the hour came when Mr. von Kotzebue had to go ashore to sight the noonday sun and wind his chronometers. The lookouts in the presidio reported that the captain was coming and when he stepped ashore the governor strode down the incline toward him. He in turn ascended the incline toward the governor's reception, and Spain and Russia fell into each other's open arms halfway toward each other.

A meal was served under our tent, and in the matter of Port Bodega, which was discussed, the captain had the opportunity to regret that he was without instructions to counter the wrong that had been imposed against Spain. From that port a large baidare arrived on this day and brought everything from Mr. Kuskov that the captain had requested. With this same baidare, which returned on the next day, the 18th, Mr. von Kotzebue, in the governor's name, requested Mr. Kuskov to appear in San Francisco for a conference.

On the 18th we did not see the governor, who perhaps expected a state visit in the presidio. On the 19th we dined in the presidio, and artillery salvos accompanied the toast to the alliance of the sovereigns and the friendship of the nations. On the 20th we were again the hosts at noon and danced in the presidio in the evening. When the eight o'clock bell sounded the music was silent for a while, and the evening prayer was read in the silence.

Mr. von Kotzebue was prepossessingly charming in social intercourse, and Don Pablo Vicente de Solá, who was very much a stickler for formalities, and had eschewed any deficiency of them, had been consoled in this respect and now devoted himself completely to us. The popular spectacle here of a fight between a bear and a bull was promised to us. On the 21st ten to twelve soldiers went over to the mission on the northern shore in the longboat in order to lasso bears there. Some claimed that in the late evening they heard cries from the direction of the sea, which were interpreted as coming from the bear-hunters on that coast; however, no campfire could be seen. The Indians are said to be able to raise a very piercing scream.

Not until the evening of the 22nd did the hunters bring in a very small she-bear. They had also caught a larger bear, but too far away from the sea for them to transport it to the shore. The animal, which was to fight the next day, stayed over night in the longboat; and contrary to custom, its head and mouth were kept free so that it would stay fresher. The governor spent the whole day, noon and evening, in our tents. At night on the land behind the harbor great fires burned. The natives are in the habit of burning the grass in order to further its growth.

On the 23rd the bear-baiting took place on the beach. Unwilling and bound as the animals were, the spectacle had nothing great or uplifting about it. One must pity the poor creatures that are so shamefully treated. I was in the presidio with Gleb Simonovich for the evening. The governor had just received the news that the ship from Acapulco, which had stayed away for so many years, had finally again sailed into Monterey to provide California with supplies. Along with this news he also received at the same time the latest newspapers from Mexico. He shared these papers with me, to whom he showed himself inclined and obliging at every opportunity. Edited under royal authority, they contained only short notices *de la pacificación de las provincias*, of the subjugation of the provinces, and a long, continuing article: the history of Johanna Krüger, noncommissioned officer in the Colberg regiment, which story was not new to me, as I had had the opportunity of meeting the brave soldier herself at the quarters of an officer of the regiment.[18]

Don Pablo Vicente, when he descended the hill to our tents, once brought a present *a su amigo don Adelberto*, a flower, which he had plucked by the wayside and which he solemnly handed to me, the botanist. By chance it was our cinquefoil or five-finger *(Pontentilla anserina)*, as beautiful as it could grow near Berlin.[19]

In Monterey at the time there were prisoners of various nations, whom smuggling and sea otter hunting had enticed to seek adventure on these coasts, and these few individuals were paying for the derelictions of others. Among them were a few Aleuts or Kadiakans, with whom seven years ago a American sea captain had engaged in otter hunting in the Spanish harbors of this coast. The Russians not only misuse these northern peoples, they also deliver them over to others for misuse. I have even encountered dislodged Kadiakans in the Sandwich Islands. Among the prisoners in Monterey was a certain Mr. John Elliot de Castro, of whom I shall have more to say further on. After many adventures as supercargo of a ship of the Russian-American company sent out to smuggle from Sitka by Mr. Baranov, he and others of the crew had fallen into the hands of the Spaniards. Besides the prisoners there were three other Russians there, former servants of the Russian-American company who had deserted the settlement at Port Bodega and now, missing the language and customs of home, regretted having taken the step.

Don Pablo Vicente de Solá offered to deliver the Russians, among whom the Aleuts and Kadiakans also were numbered, to the captain, while he refused them to Mr. Kuskov. It does not seem that the Spaniards asked any service of, or received any advantage from, these people, whom foreign greed had deprived of their homeland to profit from their strength here. The king of Spain gave recompense, or was supposed to give recompense, of one and one half reales a day for each prisoner of war. The captain, limited by circumstances, could take only the three Russian deserters on board and offer Mr. Elliot passage to the Sandwich Islands, from where he could easily get to Sitka or wherever else he chose. The governor sent for these Russians, and when they had arrived he handed them over to Mr. von Kotzebue after he had demanded and received from him his word of honor that they, who had sought and found protection in Spain, should not be punished in any way for this. I found his behavior on this occasion very noble.

Among these Russians there was one, Ivan Strogonov, an old man, who was sincerely happy to have come among his compatriots again. As he was hardly fit for duty as a seaman, the captain earmarked him for duty in the main cabin and made this known to us. On the last days we spent in port he was sent out to hunt. The poor wretch! On the eve of departure his powder horn exploded, and he was brought back mortally wounded. He wanted only to die among Russians. The captain kept him on board out of pity, and he died on the third day of the passage. He was quietly lowered into the sea, and with him went the last hope our boots had of ever being polished again. Peace be with you, Ivan Strogonov!

But I am getting ahead of myself; let me turn back.

On October 25 Mr. Kuskov arrived from Port Bodega with seven small baidares. A clever man, capable in every way of taking care of his affairs.

On the 26th the diplomatic conference took place in the presidio. Don Pablo Vicente de Solá, governor of New California, elucidated fully Spain's indisputable right to the territory occupied by the Russian settlement under Mr. Kuskov and called upon Mr. Kuskov to vacate the area occupied counter to international law. Mr. Kuskov, agent of the Russian–American Trading Company and supervisor of the settlement at Port Bodega, without going into the question of law, which was not his concern, manifested the greatest willingness to depart from Port Bodega as soon as he was empowered to do so by his superior, Mr. Baranov, who had ordered him here. Thereupon the governor called upon Mr. von Kotzebue to intervene in the name of the tsar and effect the evacuation of Bodega. Otto von Kotzebue, lieutenant in the Imperial Russian navy and captain of the *Rurik*, declared himself to be without jurisdiction to act in this case, even though the justice of the case seemed so clear that it merely had to be stated to be recognized. And so then we were as far as we had been before.

Hereupon it was decided to issue a statement about the day's negotiations and the state of affairs and to send it, *in duplo*, signed and sealed by all participants in said negotiations, to the two high sovereigns, His Majesty, the tsar of Russia through the captain of the *Rurik*, and His Majesty, the king of Spain, through the governor of New California.

The editing of this document I, as interpreter, had to supervise. I discarded the first draft, in which I felt that something was missing: "For," I said to Don Pablo Vicente, "by bringing this matter to the thrones of the high sovereigns, and expecting to secure an alleviation of this wrong and the punishment of the servants responsible for it from the tsar of Russia himself, you are divesting yourself of the right that you indisputably have of taking action into your own hands against the invader, and then must not anticipate the high decision of the monarchs."

Pablo Vicente de Solá had no objection to this. He praised my insight, had the statement rewritten, and when it was signed in the presidio on the evening of the 28th he gave his solemn word of honor not to undertake any act of force on his own initiative against the aforesaid Kuskov and the Russian settlement in Port Bodega and to leave affairs *in statu quo* until the decision of the high courts was made. I signed the document *en clase de intérprete*, as interpreter.[20]

I do not mean to boast about this turn of things. For even if the good Don Pablo Vicente de Solá had not sworn this oath, he would hardly have opened hostilities and undertaken a campaign against the Russian fort at Port Bodega.

I have heard that the said statement did not fail to reach its real destination in St. Petersburg and, without ever being acted upon, was consigned to the files in the appropriate ministry. But a Russian order of merit is said to have been sent to Don Pablo Vicente de Solá, gobernador de la Nueva California. I received a fine otter skin from Mr. Kuskov as a gift of recognition, and you can have it displayed to you in the Berlin Zoological Museum, to which I donated it.

An immediate consequence of the conference of October 26 was not a favorable one for the *Rurik*. The negotiations had stretched out beyond the noon hour, and someone else had wound up the chronometers for the captain. He confided to me that hereafter the large chronometer had changed its operation to such an extent that he must consider it ruined.

Spain's claims to the territory of this coast were not esteemed any more highly by the Americans and English than they were by the Russians. The mouth of the Columbia River was also counted by Spain as part of its territory. The history of the settlement there the Spaniards and Mr. Elliot both told in about the same way. The Americans from New York had gone there partly by land and partly by sea and founded a settlement. During the war between England and America the frigate *Racoon*, Captain Black, was sent out to take possession of this post. The English merchants from Canada went there by land, and when the warship that threatened the colony was in sight of the harbor, for the sake of a prize of money, 50,000 pounds sterling, they took possession of the colony and raised the English flag.[21] A land trade route is supposed to connect the Columbia with Canada. I merely report what I have heard.

The time of our stay in California had run out. On October 26, a Sunday, after a ride to the mission, there was a festive farewell dinner in our tents. The *Rurik's* artillery roared an accompaniment to the toast to the alliance of the monarchs and the peoples and to the health of the governor. A good missionary had dipped his cloak too deeply into the blood of the grapes and swayed visibly under the burden.

On the 28th camp was struck and the tents brought aboard ship again. While we sealed our statement in the presidio, Mr. Kuskov, with the foreknowledge of Mr. von Kotzebue, had sent two baidares out to catch otters at the rear of the bay.

On the 29th Mr. Kuskov left early in the morning with his flotilla of baidares for Bodega on the one hand, and on the other later in the day Don Pablo Vicente de Solá left for Monterey. The latter took our letters for transshipment to Europe, the last our friends received from us on our voyage. With them our trail vanished. For when in the fall of 1817 we did not return to Kamchatka, in Europe they gave us up for lost.

On the 30th all animals were aboard, and vegetables in great abundance. At the same time a terrible number of flies came aboard, thickening the air. We had taken on fresh water, which in this port, especially in the summer, is a difficult business. We were obliged to the governor for a cask of wine from Monterey. Our friends from the presidio dined with us at noon on the *Rurik*. We were ready to sail.

On the 31st our friends were still with us for a last farewell, and some of us rode to the mission in the afternoon. Late in the evening Mr. John Elliot de Castro arrived, still undecided whether he would take advantage of the captain's offer or not. He finally decided to accept.

On November 1, 1816, All Saints' Day, at nine o'clock in the morning, we weighed anchor while our friends were in church. We saw them arrive at the fort just as we sailed past. They hoisted the Spanish flag to the accompaniment of a one-gun salute, we did the same with ours. They saluted us first with seven guns, which we returned shot for shot.

The water of the harbor of San Francisco was highly phosphorescent from very fine particles of light, and even the surf on the beach of the coast outside of the bay unrolled with a perceptible shimmer. I examined the water of the harbor under the microscope and observed in it small amounts of exceptionally small infusoria, to which I however cannot ascribe the luminescence.

Here we daily observed the play of the banks of fog, which were blown across the sun-drenched land by the prevailing sea breeze, where they broke apart and became dissipated. The spectacle that they prepared for us upon departure was especially fine, as they first enshrouded and then unveiled various peaks and areas of the coast.

# CHAPTER IX

## From California to the Sandwich Islands.   Our First Sojourn There.

HARDLY had we left the harbor on November 1, 1816, when a mighty wind from the open sea took us in hand, rocking the ship to such an extent that old sailors and even the captain became seasick. I have never conquered this scourge; I have never gone back to the sea after even the shortest sojourn on land without suffering from it. I need not say that now I took to my bunk. The flies were blown away by the the wind—on the next day there were no longer any to be seen on the *Rurik*. On the second day we saw large clumps of seaweed, on the third dolphins, on the fourth at 31° north latitude the first tropic bird.

The sea was blue, the sky cloudy, everything empty of life as on no other stretch of the sea. No birds except tropic birds. Their flight is high, their cry is penetrating. They are often heard when they cannot be seen, and often their voice is heard at night.

In these latitudes we continued to have persistent south and southwest winds. In the evenings there was often lightning flickering in the south. Occasional periods of calm interrupted the south wind, which never failed to blow again. On the 9th porpoises frolicked and squealed around our keel. On the 12th a few whales *(Physeter?)* accompanied us in the morning and again in the evening.

On November 16 (22°34′N latitude, 104°25′W longitude) we finally reached the trade winds.

On the 21st the outlines of some of the mountains of O-Waihi [Hawai'i] became visible through the clouds.

Mr. John Elliot de Castro, of mixed English and Portuguese ancestry, was so small that I can only compare him to Jean Paul's little fellow who didn't reach up to his own knees let alone those of taller people.[1] He was a devoted Catholic and placed his hopes on a ribbon from the brotherhood of St. Francis he wore and by virtue of which he was to receive very special indulgence. He had been married in

Rio-Janeiro and employed as a surgeon in a hospital there. But he was also in love, and unhappily so, and this passion had driven him into the wide world and this misfortune. He was, it seems, in love with twenty thousand piasters, of which he could not gain possession and about which he spoke with such affecting desire, with such truth and depth of feeling, such enthusiasm as very few poets whose creations appear in literary journals can equal. His love was really poetic; it was touching to see him bending over the rail of the *Rurik* and fantasizing a sail in the blue distance—an American, loaded with piasters from the smuggling trade with the padres of the Spanish coast! We have more cannon than it does! We could seize it!—but there was no ship there at all. Once, when he had tried to smuggle tobacco into Buenos Aires, he had been put into jail there. Before seeking his fortune with Mr. Baranov, who helped him only to acquire a second captivity among the Spaniards, he had sought it for two years in the Sandwich Islands, where he had tried trading with the pearls of Pearl River.[2] However, the profit did not meet his expectations. In the meantime he had become Tameiameia's [Kamehameha's] personal physician and had been given some land by the latter. He was now returning home to his family there, expecting to find his possessions in good condition and trusting to return to his former position.

My discussions with our guest on the voyage across were incalculably instructive to me. To be sure, I had read what was written about the Sandwich Islands and had collected a good deal of data about their present condition, especially with regard to the commerce for which they have become a center. But there I had an O-Waihian (*Naja haore* [*nai'a haole*], porpoise of the white men) before me who had lived with and among the people, who had belonged to a definite caste and from whom I could hear the language and learn about the customs. I used the opportunity industriously, and I was really well prepared, and even not completely ignorant of the childlike language, to visit the residence of this engaging people, at that time still not deprived of its natural character. To his benevolent teacher, Mr. John Elliot de Castro, his willing pupil gladly and cordially extends his gratitude. But I also gave him great joy, for, once, when the conversation chanced to hit upon the gift of prophecy, with suitable seriousness and emphasis I prophesied that he would end his life in a monastery as a member of a monastic brotherhood, and judging by the emotion with which he received this word, I shouldn't be in the least surprised if the prophecy itself had laid the foundation for its realization.

On this voyage a word was spoken to me, too, which gave me

great pleasure, and which I shall here recount, albeit somewhat boastfully. The object of the conversation at table was, as usual, the country that we were about to see and the people with whom we were about to have dealings. Before now we had merely seen Polynesians fleetingly, while here we were to live among them. I remarked that my curiosity was greatly aroused this time and that I was looking forward very expectantly to the new impressions. Thereupon Mr. von Kotzebue, with the evident intention of saying something humiliating to me, observed that I could spare adding "this time" to what I had said, as I was always the one whose curiosity was most aroused and that no one was ever as expectant as I was. So I, the oldest in years, was rebuked for being the youngest in mind and heart.

I shall continue with my account of the voyage. No seabirds had announced land to us above the wind of the Sandwich Islands, and we saw none in periods of calm, either. Just the tropic bird high in the air and close to the surface of the waves the flying fish.

We directed our course toward the northwest corner of O-Waihi, in order to sail around this and, according to advice given us by Mr. Elliot, to speak with Haul Hanna ['Olohana], Mr. Jung [Young], in the Bay of Tokahai in the district of Kochala [Kohala], where the most famous man in the history of the Sandwich Islands was said to have his residence.[3] Mr. Jung would furnish us with the necessary information about the present state of affairs and the sojourn of the king. We would, however, have to present ourselves to the king before we ran into the harbor of Hana-ruru [Honolulu] in the island of O-Wahu [O'ahu], which is situated farther toward the west.

In the early hours of November 22, and continuing throughout the morning, the heights of the land mass revealed themselves to us, their smooth outline rising magnificently until it was covered by the clouds of midday and evening. We still saw only Mauna Kea, the small mountain, which, even if the smaller of the two, rises higher above the sea than does Mont Blanc above the valleys from which it can be seen. The northern coast at the foot of Mauna Kea is the most unfruitful of the island.

Toward noon we sailed around the northwestern headland of O-Waihi, sailed through the channel that separates this island from Mauwi [Maui], and lost the trade wind because of the wind from the high land. Along the western coast of O-Waihi we had very weak land and sea breezes and sometimes dead calm.

In the vicinity of the headland two islanders rowed up to the ship. The man who clambered on board answered the questions of the Naja, who was well known to him, so shyly and hesitantly that the latter began to worry about what might have happened on the islands. We soon learned that Haul Hanna was on O-Wahu with most of the princes and that Tameiameia was at Karakakoa [Keala-kekua].[4] The canoe, which was tied to the ship and in which the other O-Waihian still sat, capsized, and we had an opportunity to admire the power and skill of these fishlike people.

From the open sea we saw the European-type houses belonging to Mr. Jung towering above the straw roofs of the native houses. The whole beach is encircled by human dwellings, but without shade. Not until one gets farther south along the coast are there coconut palms intermingled with the houses. The forests, which occupy a high zone in the mountains, do not extend into the valley. Columns of smoke rose in various sections of the country.

Some other canoes came to the ship. We dickered with some of the natives and persuaded a widely traveled man, one of the king's men, who had been in Boston on the northwest [sic] coast of America and in China, to stay on board and pilot us to Karakakoa. We learned that two American ships were at anchor in Hana-ruru and that a third, which had lost its mast in a storm, was at Karaka-koa. We learned, finally, that Russians of the American trading company had threatened to overrun the kingdom with war and that Russian warships were expected that would carry out this threat.

Those were the conditions prevailing when we stood before O-Waihi, and we considered ourselves fortunate indeed to have Mr. Elliot, the king's personal physician, on board to vouch for us.

We lay to in a dead calm that night. On the morning of the 23rd we found out that the king had come northward from Karakakoa and was now at Tiutatua [Kaiakekua], at the foot of Wororai [Hualā-lai], and would not remain there very long.[5] Mr. Elliot sent a message announcing his and our presence and indicating the captain's desire not to miss seeing his majesty at Tiutatua.

We advanced very slowly. In the evening a dolphin was harpooned. During the night the breeze freshened, and on the morning of the 24th we lay to before Tiutatua. The American ship was just sailing into the bay under all sails. The captain sent out the dinghy, in which he sent Mr. Elliot ashore, accompanied by me, Esch-scholtz, and Choris. We met a European paddling a canoe. He transferred into our boat and accompanied us.

The village is pleasantly situated among palm trees by the beach. Behind it there is a view up a lava bed to the giant cone of Wororai. Two morais with their hideous idols were perched on an out-jutting of the lava flow.[6]

On the shore there stood a large crowd of armed men. The old

king, before whose residence we landed, sat on a raised terrace surrounded by his wives and dressed in his native costume, the red
maro [*malo*] (loincloth) and the black tapa [*kapa*] (a wide flowing
cloak of bark cloth).[7] His shoes and his light straw hat were the only
articles he had borrowed from the Europeans. (Only the nobles wear
the black cloak.) The resin used as a dye has the property of making
the cloth impervious to liquid. Before the king every subordinate
sits on a lower level than he does, and with bared shoulders. The old
gentleman received his physician well, but without excessive joy,
and allowed him to explain the peaceful purpose of our expedition.
Then he directed the salutation of peace toward us, shook hands
with us, and invited us to partake of roasted pig. (I am proud that I
had the honor of shaking hands with three of the outstanding men of
these old days, Tameiameia, Sir Joseph Banks, and Lafayette.)[8] We
postponed the meal until the arrival of our captain. Eschscholtz and
I requested permission to go looking for botanical specimens, while
Choris offered to draw the king's portrait. Tameiameia sent one of
his noblemen with us for our protection and warned us of the great
excitement among his people. He would sit for the painter only in
European clothes, that is in a red vest and shirt sleeves, as he cannot
tolerate the confinement of a coat.[9] He commissioned Mr. Elliot to
accompany the captain to shore, and he sent two of the noblest
chiefs along with him, one of whom was to stay on board the ship as
hostage until the captain had returned to his ship.

I shall now take a few words to report on the events that preceded
our arrival on the Sandwich Islands.

A certain Dr. Scheffer, who in the year 1815 arrived in Sitka as
ship's doctor on board the *Suvarov* [*Suvorov*], Lieutenant Lazarev,
captain, had remained there in the service of the American company.[10] Presumably sent out by Mr. Baranov, he had come to the
Sandwich Islands, apparently, for scientific purposes, and here he
had enjoyed the protection of the king. Dr. Scheffer had traveled
throughout the various islands. On O-Wahu, where two ships of the
Russian-American company were at anchor (the *Clementia* and the
*Entdeckung*), various offenses had been committed against the king
and the native religion. The Russians had desecrated a morai and
carried out the formality of taking possession of the island, hoisting
the Russian flag on land. Some Europeans had interceded to prevent
bloodshed, and the insolent foreigners, forced to take to their ships,
had threatened war and conquest. We must leave undecided the
question as to what share of the guilt should be ascribed to those
ships and what share to the doctor—the greatest bitterness was felt
toward the doctor.[11] At present the latter was in the western islands,

the king of which, Tamari [Kaumuali'i], he had persuaded to rebel under the Russian flag against his feudal lord, Tameiameia.[12]

It is generally known that at the time of Tameiameia's conquest the previously independent king of Atuai [Kaua'i] and the western islands had beaten the mighty king to the punch by voluntarily submitting to him.

That was the state of affairs at this time. When we returned to the Sandwich Islands in late 1817 Dr. Scheffer's role was already played out upon this stage: the king of Atuai, to whom he had become a nuisance, had sent him on his way and renewed his oath of allegiance to Tameiameia. Dr. Scheffer came to St. Petersburg, where he seems to have found no ear for his adventuresome plots and counsels. He later appears in Hamburg as the Imperial Brazilian recruiting officer.

As I went looking for botanical specimens with Eschscholtz, we were surrounded by a crowd that did more laughing than threatening. A chief, unmistakable from his demeanor and his almost gigantic stature, laughingly brandished his javelin at me as he came along the path toward us, then shook my hand, calling out the greeting of peace, "Arocha!" [Aloha]. What he then said might have meant, "Have you spoiled our fun again? We thought we were going to have a good fight, and now you are our good friends!"

The dry, sun-baked field behind the village offered the botanist only a scanty yield, and still it was a great joy to collect the first Sandwich Island plants here. "A Cyperacea!" I cried to the doctor, and showed him the plant from a distance.[13] "Küperake! Küperake!" our guide shouted, throwing a handful of grass above his head and dancing about like a puppet on a string. Such is the nature of these people, happy as children, and one becomes like them if he lives among them. After what I said about the O-Waihians in my "Notes and Opinions," I have only to let them appear before you in little anecdotes and sketches.

As we waited for the captain we were conducted to the queens, tall, stout, still almost beautiful women. Kahumanu [Ka'ahumanu] already appears in history in Vancouver's account.[14] They were all together, reclining on the floor of a straw hut, softly bolstered by fine mats. We had to find reclining places among them. The looks that my queenly neighbor cast upon me, the newcomer, made me feel uncomfortable. I followed Eschscholtz, who had already slunk out of the hut. I learned from him that his queen had expressed herself even more explicitly.

Our captain had arrived. The old warrior received him with cordiality. He understood protocol very well and knew how to act magnificently, impressively, and easily. Mr. Cook, a European who possessed his confidence, and who now had returned from the American ship to which he had been sent, served him as interpreter. He did not conceal his anger at the Russian who had rewarded his royal hospitality with such base ingratitude, but in us, who had nothing to do with them and had been sent out on an expedition of discovery, he would not see Russians, but sons and descendants of Cook and his friend Vancouver. We were not merchants, and he would not be one toward us. He would care for all our needs completely free of charge. We did not have to give the king a present, unless we wished. Thus was Tameiameia, king of the Sandwich Islands.

Our presents in return gave testimony of our peaceful intent. Two little mortars with the appropriate filled grenades and powder. Iron bars, which we had as ballast, and which seemed to please him, were unloaded for him at Hana-ruru. He himself inquired whether we might be able to leave him some wine. He received a cask of good Teneriffa from our supply. By chance the captain had brought a few apples from San Francisco. The king found them tasty, distributed them for tasting to the chiefs around him, and had the seeds carefully collected. At a wish that Mr. von Kotzebue expressed, Tameiameia immediately had a feather cloak fetched and handed it over for Tsar Alexander. With dignity and without fear he declined to come aboard our ship, as the present mood of his people, he said, did not permit it. We paid a visit to the heir to the throne, Lio-Lio [Liholiho].[15] I cannot add anything to what I said about him in my "Notes and Opinions," although the predictions made there, mostly according to Mr. Marini, were not fulfilled.[16] The table was set for us in the European manner in a house that was situated within the confines of the royal morai. The king accompanied us there with his chiefs, although neither he nor any of the others took part in the meal, which we alone consumed. Our crew was similarly treated after we were finished. We learned later that a religious significance was attached to the meal that had been given us. We, who had been announced as enemies and had come as friends, ate a consecrated pig at a consecrated place in the king's morai.

After we were through, Tameiameia dined alone in his house, and we observed him the way he had observed us. He ate according to ancient custom. Boiled fish and roasted fowl were the entrées, banana leaves the plates, and the beloved taro paste took the place of bread. The servants crept in with the food, which a man of greater nobility set in front of him. Mr. von Kotzebue speaks of the peculiar costume worn by Tameiameia's courtiers, claiming they all wore black frock coats on their bare bodies. I can only remember having seen this costume once on the Sandwich Islands, so that it was by no means common and did not attract the attention of our artist's eye. Compare Choris' *Voyage pittoresque.*

We had hoped to have Mr. Elliot accompany us to O-Wahu, but Tameiameia kept him with him. As a guide and transmitter of his commands with regard to us he gave us a noble of lesser rank, who enjoyed his complete confidence. He had this man, whose name was Manuja [Manuia], come a distance of ten miles, for which reason he was late in arriving.[17] The *Rurik* had stayed under sail. We had already fired signal shots, set off rockets, and hoisted lanterns when Mr. Cook brought our man on board at eight o'clock in the evening.

We set our course for O-Wahu under a weak land breeze. The rising sun found us on the 25th in sight of O-Waihi and Mauwi. The wind had died down. It was a beautiful morning. Immensity, calm, and clarity. Air and sea clear and calm; pure and cloudless the heights of both islands majestically delineated before us. Mr. von Kotzebue made use of the time to measure the heights of both islands.

At night the wind rose: we had caught the trade wind again. We saw fires burning on the island of Tauroa [Kahoʻolawe]. On the 26th we sailed rapidly forward along the island chain and to the south of them. A couple of whales *(Physeter)* spouted their columns of water into the air not far from us. Manuja lay seasick on the deck, and his servant was hardly in a condition to offer him any assistance. Manuja too had carefully collected and preserved the seeds of the apples that he had eaten with us. We lay to that night in sight of the island of O-Wahu.

On November 27 at midday we arrived before the harbor of Hanaruru. Manuja went ashore with the first canoe that appeared, and soon a royal pilot, an Englishman, name of Mr. Herbottel, came out and told us to cast anchor outside of the reef, as every entering ship must be towed into the harbor during the calm that here regularly sets in before sunrise.[18]

The captain went ashore as soon as the *Rurik* lay at anchor. An American schooner, the *Traveller* from Philadelphia, Captain Wilcoks, was just hoisting its sails. We looked across the surf at the pleasant city, which, shaded by coconut palms, consists of Hawaiian straw huts and European houses with white walls and red roofs. It interrupts the sunny plain that encircles the foot of the mountains. The forest that covers the heights extends far down its slopes. Two ships lay in the harbor; both belonged to the lord of the islands. A three-master, which was soon to receive the name of the wife of Kareimoku and which on the morning of the 29th, laden with taro, took sail for O-Waihi. The second, called the *Kahumanu* after Tameiameia's noblest consort, a small, elegant, fast-sailing brig, which, built in France to be a pirate ship and originally called *La Grande Guimbarde*, had been taken by the English and received the name *Forester*.[19] The *Kahumanu*, as a coast-guard ship, fired the usual shot at sundown to signal retreat.

The captain came back on board, not any too happy with the reception that he had received. The people were still upset about the Russians, and he had had to combat the same prejudice in the governor. Mr. Jung had been helpful to him. The governor, Kareimoku [Kalanimoku or Kālaimoku], whom the English called Pitt, the next in rank on the Sandwich Islands after the king, had promised the captain to carry out faithfully the commands he had received from Tameiameia with regard to him.[20]

On the 28th at six o'clock in the morning we fired a cannon shot to call forth the canoes that per agreement were to tow us into the harbor. The pilots and eight double canoes, each paddled by sixteen to twenty men under the guidance of the owner, came up. Mr. Jung was at their side in a small canoe. The anchor was weighed, and, while noisily laughing and joking, the Sandwich islanders in good order and with a power that our crew admired, moved the *Rurik* along. According to the log we traveled three knots. We dropped anchor before the walls of the fortress, and Mr. Jung came on board to collect payment for the service that had been rendered us by other than the king's people.

I cannot pass over in silence the first thing that we, like all other strangers, encountered in these islands: the general, importunate, greedy complaisance of the other sex; the propositions shouted at us by all the women round about and by all the men in the name of all the women.

Shame seems to be inborn in people, but chastity is only a virtue according to our precepts. In a condition closer to nature a woman is first bound in this respect by the will of the man whose property she has become. Man lives by the hunt. The male takes care of his weapons and his prey: he feeds the family. The arms-bearer reigns ruthlessly in the use of his superior force; woman serves and endures. He has no duty toward the stranger; wherever he meets him he may kill him and appropriate his property. Whether he uses the victim's flesh as food or not is of no consequence. If he grants the stranger his life, then he further owes him what is needed for life. The meal is prepared for all, and a man needs a woman.

At a higher level hospitality becomes a virtue, and the man of the house waits for the stranger by the wayside and takes him into his tent or under his roof, so that he might bring the blessing of the Highest One into his dwelling. Then he easily makes it his duty to offer him his wife, whom it would then be an insult to spurn.

Those are pure, unadulterated customs.

To this people of joy and pleasure (Oh, I wish I could teach you with a breath of this mild, spicy air, with a glance under this bright and colorful sky, what the joy of existence is!), to this people, I say, chastity as a virtue was unknown. We have grafted greed and avarice onto them and stripped the bark of shame off of them. On the northern coast of the island, separated by the mountains from the corrupted harbor town, I expected to find more patriarchal, less reproachable customs.

On this very first day I made the acquaintance of Mr. Marini (Don Francisco de Paulo Marini, called Manini by the natives). He was not overly anxious to oblige, but I always found him helpful and instructive, when I needed him, and, with good sense and acuity dealing with the point I was after, he taught me the best things I know about these islands. Marini was still very young when in a harbor of the Spanish-American coast, I think it was San Francisco in California, he was sent out with fruit and vegetables to a ship that was about to leave. The sailors plied the boy with drink, he fell asleep, and they hid him. The ship was on the high seas when he woke up and came out on deck. The die that decided his fate was cast. Put ashore on the Sandwich Islands, he here became a chief of high repute, who, as an active planter, continually extracts new sources of prosperity from the soil with the varieties of useful plants and animals that he has introduced and as an active merchant provides the numerous ships that dock here with all their needs. He is especially noteworthy for understanding how to salt down meat under this hot sky so that it will last for a long time, something that the Spaniards in the New World declare impossible. Marini as an independent man seemed to stay as far away from the king as possible and not to be in his favor. He rather lived for the world of commerce. I can be considered lucky that there were no ships here now to occupy him. In the first conversation I had with him he made one remark that I found noteworthy. We had been speaking of the latest historical events, and of Napoleon. *He*, he said, would have done well in Spanish America. I had never before heard a similar pronouncement from a Spaniard's mouth.

I made my first botanical excursion, climbed to the top of the extinct volcano behind the town, pushed up the mountain into the

forest, and came back through the valley, which is won for the cultivation of taro by artificial irrigation.[21] I became acquainted with the
coolness of the mountain valleys and the higher temperature that
hits one as soon as he steps out of them on to the sunny edge of the
island.

I shall not describe my daily wanderings through valley and
mountain in greater detail but rather collect here some of the small
adventures that occurred to me there.

Over brooks and rivers there are no bridges—indeed, people are
happy to have the opportunity for a fresh-water bath, as highly
prized and desired by those who dwell by the sea as is a sea-bath by
us inlanders. Everywhere such an opportunity presents itself it is
pointed out, and the question, "Do you wish to bathe?" is one that
one soon learns.

I had undressed in order to wade through the stream that empties
into the harbor behind Hana-ruru, and the water hardly extended
above my knees, when I heard a light canoe being paddled toward
me, along with peals of laughter. It was a lady, apparently of the
highest caste, who took delight in teasing me. I was like an innocent
maiden bothered in her bath by some rude bumpkin having his fun.

On another excursion, on which I was accompanied by a guide,
the path went through a wide, calm body of water. The O-Waihian
entered ahead of me and went across—the water did not reach his
chest. I hit upon the idea of swimming across, even though I can't
really swim. I tried it, and lo! the water bore me, and I made some
forward progress.

I was extremely satisfied with myself and thought, "It's good to
show these people that, although I'm not exactly a master in their
art, it is not completely strange to me." Then incessant peals of
laughter, that resounded more and more loudly from the shore,
woke me from my dream. When I could look around to see what was
going on, I perceived that the shore was densely packed with people
who had run up to laugh at the *kanaka haore* [*kanaka haole*] (the
white man) who, instead of walking through the water like a reasonable person, was taking great pains to display his awkwardness. But
laughter here does not contain anything hostile in it. Laughter is a
person's right; everybody laughs at everybody else, king or commoner, without detriment to their other relationships. More anecdotes will illustrate this pronouncement in their proper place.

"Arocha!" is the peaceful salutation that everyone offers to everyone else, and which is answered in kind. To every "Arocha!" that is
called out to you, you answer "Arocha!" and go your way without
looking around. Once when I went on a botany trip and had gone on

my way from Hana-ruru to the taro plantations, I was struck by the fact that, although the houses had come to an end, the salutations continued, and still no one could be seen on the open fields to right and left. "Arocha!" was called after me incessantly, and I answered every salutation faithfully. I looked around imperceptibly and perceived that a band of children was tripping along after me, amusing themselves by having the *kanaka haore* repeat his "Arocha!" Just wait, I thought, and with great patience returning all their greetings, I drew the band along after me into the narrow passes of the taro fields, over ditches, hedges, irrigation canals, and earthen walls. Then suddenly I turned around and ran toward them with uplifted arms, howling fearfully. In their first fright they took to flight and fell all over each other and into the inundated fields. I laughed at them, they laughed, and we parted as friends: "Arocha!"

On a walk through the fertile valley behind Hana-ruru I once found on the edge of one of the inundated patches in which taro is cultivated a kind of beautiful grass, which I didn't remember having seen before, so that I immediately pulled out a few samples. For this I was accosted and berailed by an O-Waihian, who berated me for this so emphatically that I had great trouble in appeasing him. I told Mr. Marini about the incident and showed him the grass. The man was his renter, the grass was rice, which, after several attempts to grow it had failed, this year had caught on for the first time on these islands. Many a botanist, who perhaps would not have fared better than I did, can have the laugh on me. I would not have mistaken *Oryza sativa* in the herbarium, either.

It may be characteristic for the plant world here, where the treelike gigantic lianas of Brazil are mostly represented only by weedlike varieties of morning glories and beans, spreading their nets out over the low brush, that once in the mountains at the side of the path I got entangled in such a net, and as I started to push forward, I finally perceived that I already had passed beyond the edge of the cliff and hovered in a kind of hammock above the precipice.

On November 29 we were first provided for in accordance with Tameiameia's command. All the roots and fruits that the land produced were extended to us in abundance, and the pigs that they delivered to us were so big that we could hardly consume half of them. The rest we took with us partly on the hoof and partly in brine.

The captain decided on this day to make a map of the harbor of Hana-ruru, and for this purpose had Khramchenko put in signal poles with flags at various points. These flags reminded the populace of the flag that had been hoisted when possession had been

taken, and now everyone seized his weapons, all promising themselves the festival of a battle, for this joyful people is fond of battle,
and it had not enjoyed this amusement for a long time. Haul Hanna,
who fortunately was informed in time, intervened, appeased Kareimoku, himself came aboard to warn the captain, and was our good
angel. Anything resembling a flag disappeared immediately, and the
war was called off.

On November 30, at the invitation of the captain, Kareimoku and
the noblest chiefs, Teimotu [Ke'eaumoku], brother of Queen Kahumanu, Haul Hanna, and others came aboard the *Rurik* for a midday
repast.²² Kareimoku was cordial and greeted the captain with the
salutation of peace. The native chiefs were all in European garb and,
if not strictly in accordance with the latest fashion, still very
respectably dressed. We sat down at the table, and their comportment could pass for a model of propriety and good manners. We, on
the other hand, we were the awkward ones, the oafs; for it is a social
duty to inquire about the customs and usages of those upon whom
one wishes to bestow hospitality and to govern oneself accordingly
in necessary matters. But the pig that we set before them had not
been consecrated in the morai and therefore (to express myself in
European terms) was not kosher, and nothing of all that had been
cooked and roasted on the same fire with it was kosher. A piece of
biscuit and a glass of wine were the only things they could touch.
They had to soberly watch us eat, without even being able to converse with us; that was our hospitality. But they behaved themselves better upon this occasion than we might have in their place,
and let our good will substitute for the act. Kareimoku drank an
Arocha! to the emperor of Russia, an Arocha! was offered to Tameiameia, and we were good friends.

The women, in the meantime, some of whom had also come
aboard (the taboo [*kapu*] is less severe on ships than on land, where
they may not enter the men's eating-house under pain of death)²³—
the women, I say, drank wine in the meantime, and got drunk,
something an O-Waihian of class will never do.

The excellent likeness of Tameiameia that Choris had painted
was a source of happiness to all. Everybody recognized it and took
pleasure in it. I shall not forget a detail that might be called characteristic of the customs of this people. In his sketchbook the painter
had drawn a woman of the middle class next to the king. Mr. Jung,
to whom the sheet was first shown, found this juxtaposition so dangerous that he advised our friend either to separate the two portraits
or not to allow them to be seen. Accordingly, the sheet was cut in
two before the picture of the king was shown to other O-Waihians.

Choris here distributed several copies of this very successful portrait. When we came to Manila the next year the American merchants had already gained possession of this picture and had had
many copies made for commerce in the Chinese painting factories.
Choris brought a copy of the Chinese edition back to Europe.

On November 30 at sunset the solemnity of a *tabu-pori* [*kapu
poli*] began, which ended at sunrise of the third day.[24] Desirous of
attending the most sacred mysteries of the O-Waihian cult, I addressed myself to Kareimoku, who without hesitancy invited me to
be his guest for the length of the festival in the sanctity of the morai.
He left the ship about four o'clock, and I joined him before sunset.

I did not note down the details of the liturgy and the holy customs, which can be found in the accounts of previous travelers anyway, but one thing I can say: compared with the gaiety with which it
was carried out, the gaiety of one of our masked balls seems like a
funeral service. The religious activities occupy only a few hours. As
is the case with the Catholic liturgy, at times the people join in the
song of the officiating priest. In the intervals the merriest conversation is carried out, and good meals are served, at which I alone was
served in the European manner, and given baked taro instead of the
usual paste. For both dining and conversing the people lie in two
rows on the mat-strewn floor, their heads pointed toward the central
aisle leading to the door. The food is served on banana leaves and is
conveyed to the mouth by the hands, the sticky taro paste being
licked off the fingers. Water for washing the hands is passed around
before and after the meal. At night torches of kukui nuts *(Aleurites
triloba)* strung on sticks give forth a very bright light.[25] All this in
the morai just as at home. Anyone wishing to leave the sacred confines is accompanied by a boy who carries a small white flag as a
warning to others. A woman, if touched, would have to be killed
right away, while a man would be subjected to the same sequestra-
tion only in the morai.

In his *Voyage pittoresque* Choris depicted the idols of a morai in
O-Wahu. The uniformly hieroglyphic type, which is repeated in figures 4 of Plate 6, 3 and 4 of Plate 7, and 1 and 3 of Plate 8, seems to
me to be the more ancient, popular one. The basket-weave figure
covered with red feathers, which, preserved in the inner sanctum of
the morai, appears during the customs of tabu-pori, belongs to this
same type.[26] The wide mouth is encircled by real teeth, dogs' teeth,
I believe. A couple of youths brought the figure to me during an
intermission so that I could examine it more closely. Desirous of
finding the limits of what was permitted me, I felt the teeth of the
idol, whereupon the one who was carrying the figure gave a sudden

twist to it so that he caused it to engulf my hand. Naturally I withdrew my hand in surprise, and they broke out in immoderate laughter.

These customs, which I still could see, are no longer carried out on these islands, and the language of the liturgy is destined to die away. No one appears to have thought of investigating and thus saving from oblivion that which could contribute to our understanding of the externals of the law of this people, perhaps shed light upon its history, and perhaps the history of mankind, and solve the great riddles that Polynesia presents to us. Indeed, the Romanzov expedition could have effected a praiseworthy achievement for scholarship if it had granted a year's stay on these islands to an earnest, energetic scholar. But one travels across the earth like a ball fired from a cannon, and when one comes home he is supposed to have investigated all its heights and depths. When I volunteered to the captain to stay here until the return of the *Rurik*, the answer I received was that he would not detain me: it was my privilege to withdraw from the expedition if I so chose.

On December 4 Kareimoku arranged a hurra-hurra [*hulahula*] or dance for us, and another on December 6.[27] Indeed, since I have repeatedly forced myself to view the repulsive gyrations that we admire in our danseuses under the name of ballet, what I said in my "Notes and Opinions" about the magnificence of that spectacle seems now pale and not equal to the subject. We barbarians! These people so endowed with a sense of beauty we call "savages," and we allow the ballet to crowd the shy poet and the mourning mime out of the halls that we boast we have consecrated to art! I have always regretted, and I must here repeatedly express my regret, that some good genius has never sent a painter, one called to be an artist and not just a sketcher by profession, to these isles. It is already becoming too late. In Tahiti and in O-Waihi the missionary shirts already veil the beautiful bodies, all artistic activity is becoming mute, and the taboo of the Sabbath is sinking quietly and sadly upon the children of joy.[28]

I must give some evidence that I am speaking the truth. On the 4th four men danced and on the 6th a group of girls, among them many of exceptional beauty. It was not the latter who made the lasting impression upon me; no, it was the men who were more artistic, and among them the foremost would not have been called handsome even by his own countrymen. Do not look at the two poor sheets that deface Choris' atlas.[29] Dancing cannot be painted, and may the genius of art pardon him for what he painted here.

I have never beheld any other audience on any other festive occasion so carried away and enraptured as the O-Waihians were by this spectacle. They tossed presents, cloth and jewels, to the dancers.

I shall here report a trifling matter, but in the child the character of the people can be seen. When the men were dancing under the coconut palms a boy in front of me annoyed me by continually stepping on my feet. I pushed him aside roughly, and when he turned around and looked at me fiercely I read in the dark expression on his face that I had hurt a human soul. I answered him with an angry face and the pantomime of hurling a javelin, as if he were my opponent and I was aiming at him. Then the boy was reconciled and smiled at me. As long as I considered him capable of bearing arms and my equal everything was all right, but he would not let himself be shoved or kicked.

Another spectacle was promised us—that of the popular contests at arms among chiefs and nobles, a mock battle, not without danger, and which, in view of the easily aroused passions of this people, can quickly turn into a real one. The weapon is, as everyone knows, the javelin, which is brandished, not with raised arm, as was the case with the ancient Greeks, but rather with arm lowered close to the ground, the back of the hand turned inward, the thumb toward the rear, and hurled upward from down low. The chiefs wear feather cloaks in these contests.

To have missed this spectacle is an irreplaceable loss in my life. It was to have taken place on the 7th and was postponed. On the 8th the captain organized a hunting party to the Pearl River area, on which he was to be gone for two days. I used this time to make an excursion directly across the island to the north coast. Kareimoku had given me two of his men to take along and had prepared a hospitable reception for me in the villages where I was to stop. I passed through the valley that lies behind Hana-ruru and mounted the ridge of the mountain range where it sinks to the lowest col. I clambered on bare feet down the steep declivity facing the northern coast, as one learns to do in Switzerland. I spent the night below, and on the evening of the 9th I came back to Hana-ruru by way of a much higher mountain pass farther to the west and a different valley. The fighting games, which took place on this day, were already over.

Manuja had punctually, industriously, and affectionately carried out his chief's commission, taking care of felling trees and transporting them, etc. He was further commissioned to bring back to the king that which was meant for him. He himself was amply rewarded.

On December 13 we were ready to leave. I note in passing that the

Europeans in the Sandwich Islands obtained their time-reckoning from west to east by way of Canton, so that we, who brought our time from east to west, reckoned the time a day ahead of them, as had been the case in Kamchatka and in the Russian settlements. This difference existed between neighbors, San Francisco and Port Bodega. When one has to cope with the old and the new calendar, the reckoning of time from the east and from the west, Greenwich time and ship's time, mean and real time, solar time and astral time, the astronomical day, etc., it is not easy to say what the time is. Until the circle is complete I reckon the longitude west of Greenwich and the days according to the new calendar and current ship's reckoning.

On December 14, 1816, at six o'clock in the morning, we called for the pilot with a volley from our cannon, and he came with two double canoes. We were towed out of the harbor. Kareimoku came on board. We saluted the royal Hawaiian flag, which flew above the fort, with seven shots, which were returned shot for shot. Then the royal coast-guard ship, the *Kahumanu*, saluted us with seven shots, which we again answered with the same number. At eight o'clock we were out of the harbor, and Kareimoku and his retinue took affectionate leave of us. When they had transferred themselves to their canoes and pushed away from us, they saluted us with a three-fold hurrah, which we returned in the same manner.

# CHAPTER X
## Departure from Hana-ruru.  Radak.

HAVING sailed out of the harbor of Hana-ruru on December 14, 1816, for three days long we had weak, playful winds and calms. Whales *(Physeter)* were seen in the distance. On the 16th a sea swallow *(Sterna stolida)* was caught on the ship.

The wind set in on the 17th and brought us rapidly forward. On the 19th we had rain. On the 21st and 22nd we vainly sought islands at 17°N latitude that had been seen by Captain Johnstone in the year 1807.[1] Pelicans and frigate birds hovered overhead in great droves. We continued our course to the southwest. We sailed very rapidly before the wind, but the ship rolled annoyingly. The seafowl accompanied us. The horizon did not have its usual clarity. From the 26th to the 28th we sought the island of San Pedro at 11°N latitude without discovering it.[2] Signs of land caused us to tack about during the night. On the 29th we saw porpoises, flying fish, driftwood. The number of birds decreased. From the 28th on we steered westward between 9° and 10°N latitude, to search for the Mulgrave Islands. We mostly tacked about during the night. In the night from the 30th to the 31st a land rain set in that lasted the whole day. A piece of wood on which a snipe had lit floated past the ship in the morning. Snipes had been heard during the previous night. The wind had become much more moderate. On January 1, 1817, we had already assumed a more northern course in order to locate the island groups seen in the previous year when land was seen in the afternoon hours.

At this time of the voyage the cockroaches *(Blatta germanica)* had increased terribly on the *Rurik* and took on the hue of one of the Egyptian plagues. There is something weird, something close to the miraculous about it when nature assists such a subordinate species, any individual member of which appears as a powerless nothing, through their swelling numbers, through the thriving of all of their cells, and through the transformation of all organic material into them, to attain an unexpected superiority. Concealed from man, the conditions that affect the increase and decrease of those species are beyond his control; they appear and disappear. He watches the play of nature powerless and astonished. When in the fall of 1817 we again headed south from Unalashka, the *Blatta* had almost entirely disappeared, and it never got the upper hand again.

Another unpleasant aspect of life at sea, which we had become acquainted with since California, was the stench of the rotting bilge water. On ships like the *Rurik,* which admit no water and on which the pumps are idle, one suffers more from this than on those where the penetration and pumping out of the water do not allow it to stagnate and putrefy. We had to pour water in ourselves in order to get the stagnant water out.

I have yet to mention a beneficent refreshment that we enjoyed in the Torrid Zone. I mean the shower, pouring seawater over ourselves, with which we refreshed ourselves in the evening in the bow of the ship. We were still not tired and in a humor for many a prank. Once, when Login Andrevich was bathing, Ivan Ivanovich sneaked away his shirt and made him believe the wind had blown it into the sea.

Login Andrevich was still sleeping on deck at night after the doctor and I had thought we had to renounce this pleasure. He pushed his mattress through the window onto the deck and then himself went up the hatch to bed down above. Once I waited for the moment when he was in the hatchway, pulled the mattress back into the cabin, and put it in its place on his bunk again. He searched all over for his missing bed except where it was, quarreled with everyone on deck, and fell into a very amusing state of despair.

Forgive me this amusing *entr'acte*. Now I will return to Radak and the Radakians.

After what I said in my "Notes and Opinions" there remains to be told here only the story of our appearance between those reefs and the report of how we made the acquaintance of that people whom I learned to love above all the other sons of the earth. The weakness of the Radakians removed our mistrust of them. Their own gentleness and goodness allowed them to have confidence in the more powerful strangers. We became friends without reservation. In them I found pure, uncorrupted customs, charm, grace, and the gracious bloom of modesty. In strength and manly self-confidence the O-Waihians are far superior to them. My friend Kadu, who, a stranger on these islands, joined our company, one of the finest characters I have met in my life, one of the people I have loved most, later became my teacher about Radak and the Caroline Islands. In my

essay "On Our Knowledge of the First Province of the Great Ocean"
I have had occasion to mention him as a scientific authority,[3] and I
have there attempted to put together his picture and his story from
the disparate features of our life together. Be indulgent, friends, if I
repeat myself sometimes; here I am speaking of my love.

The island chain of Radak lies between 6° and 12°, the groups
seen by us between 8° and 11°30′N latitude and 188° and 191°W
longitude. I note only that I mentioned a reef or shallows called
Limmosalülü to the north of Arno, which is missing on Mr. von Kotzebue's map, and refer for the rest, as far as geographical matters are
concerned, to Mr. von Kotzebue and Mr. von Krusenstern.[4]

I shall return to the day-by-day account of our voyage.

On January 1, 1817, the weather had cleared and the wind subsided. The high water showed that there was still no land behind the
wind. Bonito swarmed around us. In the afternoon land was discovered, just visible from the deck at sunset. A little low island: Mesid
[Mejit].[5] The bright moonlight kept us from danger during the
night. On the morning of the 2nd we approached the south side of
the island with a very weak wind. Seven small boats without mast
and rigging, each manned by five to six men, paddled up to us. We
recognized the ship design and the people of the island groups we
had sighted the previous year. The clean, attractive people behaved
well; when invited they came confidently closer to the ship without
anyone's daring to climb aboard. We began to barter with them, and
they acted with great honesty. We gave them iron; mostly, all they
had to offer us was their ornaments, their delicate shell wreaths.
The captain had the *yalik* and the baidare set out to try a landing.[6]
Lieutenant Shishmarev commanded the yalik, and I followed with
Eschscholtz and Choris in the baidare. The crew was armed. The
boats surrounding the ship followed us when they saw us rowing
toward shore. Others joined them from the island, so that as we
approached about eighteen similar vessels drew a circle around us,
and I counted six more of them on the beach. A number of men
stood on the shore; women and children were not to be seen. I estimated the number of those visible at about a hundred, Lieutenant
Shishmarev twice as many; at any event, a relatively much larger
population than on the other groups of the same island chain that
we had visited. In the face of our inferior number, which made the
islanders more forward, and in consideration of our superiority in
lethal weaponry, Gleb Simonovich decided not to step onto the
land. In fact, one of our people had already drawn a bead on a native
who while swimming had grasped a paddle of our baidare. The trading was continued in the vicinity of the beach. The people gave

everything they possessed for iron: coconuts, pandanus fruits, mats, delicate wreaths of shells, a triton horn, a short, two-bladed wooden sword set with shark's teeth. They also brought fresh water in coconut shells. They tried to get us to land; one of them tried to get into our boat. The scene was comparable to the one near the Penrhyn Islands. We let them have quite a lot of iron and drew back to the ship.

The length of Mesid Island from north to south may be about two miles. We approached it on the narrower southern side, where the people's dwellings are located. The coconut palms, irregularly distributed, rose only a little above the height of the low forest, whose chief constituent is the pandanus tree. Below the green foliage roof the white coral floor can be seen stretching into the distance. The view is comparable to that on Romanzov, but the latter is probably less barren in appearance.

We headed toward the west, and in the evening with a weak wind we had lost sight of the island.

On the 3rd we saw several snipes and sandpipers, a whale *(Physeter)* and some pelicans, one of which was shot. We changed course and headed for the SE.

On the 4th, toward noon, when we were about to give up any further search, we came upon a chain of islands that stretched from east to west as far as the eye could reach. On the green spots where reef and surf were joined no coconut trees rose, and nothing betrayed the presence of man. In the evening we reached the western tip of the group and found ourselves in their lee in a calm sea. The reef, denuded of land, took a southeasterly direction. We sailed along it and discovered gaps in it that gave us hope of penetrating into the inner lagoon, which presented a calm, mirrorlike surface. During the night the current drove us toward the northwest. On the morning of the 5th land had disappeared. Not until nine o'clock did we reach the point where night had befallen us.

Lieutenant Shishmarev was sent out to explore the entrances, and at the second one his signals announced that a gate had been found for the *Rurik*. Then a column of smoke arose from one of the distant islands. We greeted that sign of human habitation with exultation. No vessels of the islanders were to be seen.

The day was already declining. The boat was called back, and in order to be able to maintain ourselves throughout the night at our present stand, a tow anchor was carried out to the reef and fastened there, and the *Rurik* advanced under sail up close to the foaming surf in order to receive its rope. "Thus the mariner finally holds fast to the very rock against which he was to go aground." The blowing northeast trade wind kept us from destruction by the length of a rope.

Here around the reef and its openings we were surrounded by bonito, flying fish, and innumerable sharks, which followed our boat threateningly. Two were caught and eaten.

On the 6th the wind changed before daybreak and, going over to the east, drew us toward the foaming surf. Dropping the cable, we went under sail. A soon as the sun had risen we turned back. At ten o'clock in the morning, surf roaring on both sides of us, we passed under full sail with the wind and current behind us, through the Rurik Strait into the inner sea of the Otdia [Wotje] group of the island chain of Radak.[7]

As the lagoon empties and fills with ebb and flood, the current flows out at the gaps in its edge at ebb tide and in again when the tide rises.

Sent out with the boat, Lieutenant Shishmarev discovered a safe place for the *Rurik* to drop anchor at the westernmost island.

The bold and clever maneuvers that Mr. von Kotzebue executed at the entrance to this and other similar reefs must excite the interest even of those who have no knowledge of navigation. The European who, far from home, deals with peoples over whom he thinks he has an advantage, is tempted by many fits of conceit that he must not be overanxious to fall prey to. These sons of the sea, I said, will be surprised indeed when they see our giant ship with outspread wings like a seabird move contrary to the direction of the wind that carries it, penetrate the protecting walls of their reefs, and then move toward the east in the direction of their dwellings. And behold! I was the one who had to look on in surprise, as, while we laboriously tacked about and gained very little on the wind, they in their artfully constructed craft went sraight ahead on the same route we went in a zig-zag fashion, hurried on ahead of us, and dropped their sails to await us.

On Otdia, using the most experienced natives, Mr. von Kotzebue had had a large accurate model of one of these vessels fashioned and had devoted to the contrivance the attention that it demands from a seafarer. His narrative deceived me in my expectation of finding sufficient data in it about the Radakians' *oa*. Choris, in his *Voyage pittoresque*, gives three different views of it. The side view (Plate 11) is true, but the profile is incorrect. The foot of the mast always rests on the projection outside of the body of the vessel on the side of the outrigger, as can be seen on the outline in Plate 12. But on this outline the mast inclines further toward the outside and the outrigger beam than is consistent with reality. On the whole these drawings are inadequate. The boat of the Caroline Islands, on Plate 17 [Plate 18], which essentially corresponds to that of Radak, is better depicted.[8] No description can evoke a picture of the described object, and still I must attempt with a few swift words to give the reader some indication of the boat in question. It has two identical ends, both of which are equally adapted to become bow or stern when it is in motion, and two unequal sides, one of which remains before the wind, one away from the wind. Away from the wind bordered by a straight surface, before the wind a little curved, narrow, deep, with a sharp keel, somewhat turned up at the ends, is the ship's hull, which acts only as a floating body. Diagonally across the middle of it an elastic projection is fastened, which extends out over the water on both sides, shorter beneath the wind, longer on the wind side, where this light span toward its end is bent downward, and it is attached to a floating beam that runs parallel to the hull. On this projection, outside of the hull on the windward side, is the mast, which, fastened to several ropes, is inclined toward the end that is to be the bow, and to which a simple, three-cornered sail is hoisted, one corner of which is fastened to the bow of the ship. Steering is effected with a hand paddle from the rear of the ship. The sailors stand or lie on the outrigger and take their position closer to the beam when the wind is strong and closer to the hull when it is weak. On this same projecting part boxes are attached on both sides of the ship, in which provisions and other property are preserved. The largest of these vessels can carry up to thirty people.

I will here list the measurements of one of these vessels, which was scarcely of medium size:

| | |
|---|---|
| Length of the boat's hull | 17 feet  6 inches |
| Width | 1 foot 10 inches |
| Depth | 3 feet  7 inches |
| Distance of the beam from the boat's hull | 11 feet  0 inches |
| Length of the span beyond the hull to leeward | 3 feet  0 inches |
| Height of the mast | 19 feet  6 inches |
| Length of the yard arms | 23 feet  4 inches |

On Aur Mr. von Kotzebue measured two boats of 38 feet in length.[9]

I shall not endeavor to put the reader asleep with an extensive account of daily experiments and observations during our sojourn in this harbor. The intention was, after we had recovered the anchor left on the reef (which took place on the 7th), had made the astronomical observations considered necessary, and had reconnoitered

ahead with the boats, to penetrate more deeply into the group,
where we were justified in supposing the permanent dwellings of
the people to be.

This western part of the chain presented a sad sight. The islands
closest around us were bleak and without water, but man had left
his traces behind, and the recently planted coconut tree testified to
his concerned activity. It is really hard to foresee everything that can
happen in a little world like ours. Once our fatuous cook fell upon
this planting in order to consume the hope of future generations for
a dish for our table. I scarcely need say that it didn't happen again.

On the fourth island (counting from the west) there were, along
with a water hole, straw roofs that, resting on low posts, seemed to
be planned only as a protection for occasional visits to the area. The
breadfruit tree was also planted along with the coconut tree. On this
island a boatful of natives landed on the 6th and then went out to
sea again to observe us from a shy distance. We did not succeed in
enticing the natives to come near us, and they also took anxious
flight away from the boat in which we rowed toward them. They
threw a few fruits to us and invited us to land. It was the first act, as
in the previous year on the high seas near Udirik.

The boat showed up again on the next day, and then we followed
the people to their island. As we approached, the women stepped
back into the thicket. The men, at first only a few, came hesitantly
toward us with green branches. We also broke green branches. The
peaceful greeting "Eidara," already often heard, was called out to us,
and we returned it in the same way. No weapons were held in readiness toward us, the feared strangers. After we had cemented friendship with the first ones, the others came up, and the women were
called. The people seemed to us to be joyous, friendly, modest, generous, and not concerned with profit. Both men and women gave us
all the ornaments that they wore, their delicate shell and flower
wreaths, their necklaces etc., and it seemed to be more a charming
symbol of love than a gift.

The captain himself came to this island the next day but didn't
find our friends there anymore, they having probably gone on their
way to spread the joyous message of our peaceful disposition.

Of the animals that we had taken aboard at O-Wahu, only a few
goats were still on hand. Mr. von Kotzebue set them out on the
island, where they at first served to terrorize the islanders. With our
pious intent of introducing this useful species on the island it had
remained unobserved that in the tiny herd there was a he-goat (not,
let us hope, the only one) who—*horribile dictu!*—was castrated.
Whether from shame at not being up to his duties or from poison or

disease, he died immediately, and his bloated body was found on the beach the next day. Besides the goats, a cock and a chicken were left on the island, they immediately taking possession of a house. We later discovered that chickens are native to these reefs. Finally, a few roots and plants were planted and sown. A few small gifts were left behind in the houses.

Khramchenko found people on the island the next day, some men, different from those with whom we had made friends. At ebb tide the islanders walk along the reef to distant islands. He was received and treated in the friendliest fashion. The presents we had set out lay untouched wherever and however we had left them. They produced, when he distributed them, a lively joy. But the goats caused the utmost terror.

On January 10 Lieutenant Shishmarev was sent out with the longboat to reconnoiter. The wind gave him difficulties. He saw only uninhabited islands and returned in the evening. On the 12th we went under sail, the weather was unfavorable, and we soon had to return to our old anchorage.

On the 14th the captain himself undertook a second trip along the island chain with an officer and passengers.

A native vessel had landed on the goat island, and the people, when we went past, called to us and tried to entice us to land with fruits and gifts extended toward us. On the next island to the east we received the first visit from Rarik, the chieftain of this group. He came with two boats. In the first, in which he rode himself, Mr. von Kotzebue counted twenty-five men. Rarik, leaving his other men in the boats, came ashore with three and brought the commander of the foreign people his presents, perhaps his homage. In this manner did the princes of Europe once approach him who had power over them. However, Rarik did not stand before a conqueror, and found friendship rather than humiliation. The young man preserved a model bearing at this first meeting, which was so important for him, and his hesitant companions seemed to be more fearful for him than he was himself. We always found more self-confidence, more courage and magnanimity, among the leaders than among the people. It lies according to the nature of things, in the circumstances: in the Levant the Turk is also distinguished from the rajah. Rarik, who later became my very intimate friend, was especially distinguished by gentleness and good nature, but not by any special intellectual gifts.

Kotzebue and he sat down opposite each other, and around the two of them we and the other Radakians formed a circle. The young prince called out loudly to those remaining in the boats to give them information about everything that attracted his attention and was a new experience for him. "Jrio! Jrio!"—the cry of amazement—was frequently raised and echoed in a long, drawn-out fashion from everyone's mouth. We sought first mutually to discover each other's names. Kotzebue, Rarik, all of us were named. We asked the name of the Radakian who sat at the chief's left. "Jeridili?" the latter replied interrogatively, looking at the former. We picked up the word, and the youth let it pass for his name, in the way we took it; he is still known as Jeridili to us. The laughter that then arose we did not understand until later, when Kadu informed us that *jeridili* means "left" and is not a personal name. I think that it was already at this first encounter that Rarik offered the captain the friendly exchange of names. On a later occasion Jeridili offered this, his name, to Doctor Eschscholtz for his, which he did not yet know and about which he asked. Eschscholtz did not understand him, and I stepped in as interpreter between them. "Dein Name" ("Your name"), I cried out to my friend. "Deinnam," the Radakian repeated. "Yes, Deinnam," the Doctor affirmed; and so the two of them unabashedly exchanged their false names with each other.

Our friends had deprived themselves of all their ornaments for us. Now the captain had some ironware brought from the boats: knives, scissors, and other trifles. "Iron! Iron! *Mäl! Mäl!*"[10] Then one could see the real value of this precious metal. *Mäl! Mäl!* Even those left on the boats couldn't withstand this development; all the orderliness was gone. Everybody crowded about to look at the treasures, our excessive wealth! But no raw outbreak of cupidity, no display of bad manners.

During our long sojourn on Radak only a few attempts at theft were made upon us. Indeed, if foreigners had exposed so much gold carelessly to the greed of our lower classes, they would not have as good a report to give of the honesty of Europeans as we had of these people.

Everyone was amply rewarded. Mr. von Kotzebue made Rarik comprehend that he was seeking his dwelling place and invited him to enter our boat and pilot us there. Rarik understood him, all right, and climbed bravely into our boat, but the opinion of his companions, whose worries had not been entirely eliminated, seemed to be against this, and he too seemed to be powerfully drawn by another enticement: those animals of which he had heard, those wonderful, long-bearded animals, the seeing of which had been one of the goals of his journey. It occurs to me that on other islands of the South Seas where the Europeans have brought them goats are not unjustly numbered among the birds, for they are not hogs, dogs, or rats.

These have their names, and apart from them there are only birds or fish. Finally Rarik gave in to temptation. He leaped into the water and swam out to his boats, with which he set his course toward the goat island.

On the 15th we stayed overnight on the ninth island, where we found only deserted houses. It was richer in humus than the goat island, and the vegetation on it was more luxurious.

On the 16th we stopped at noon on the thirteenth island and had traveled a distance of only nine miles from the ship. Here we received the second visit from Rarik, who came walking along the reef with two companions and was glad to see us. His boats soon came after him, sailing against the wind, and put in to shore next to our boats. Now he invited the captain to climb aboard his boat and sail to his island. We promised to follow him, and he started off. In the afternoon we traveled another mile and a half to the fourteenth island, the one with the high forest line that I have mentioned especially in my "Notes and Opinions." From there the reef stretched to the northeast, away from any land for several miles; the next island could barely be seen on the horizon. A ship could anchor at the island we were on. The captain had the sails raised, and with a fresh breeze we reached the *Rurik* the same evening.

On the morning of January 18 the *Rurik* went under sail. The wind was favorable and did not compel us to tack until the afternoon; the weather was clear, and the bright sun, which lit up the depths, made the use of the lead unnecessary. At four o'clock we anchored at Oromed [Ormed], the seventeenth island, counting from the west, which, about twenty miles away from the westernmost one, forms the northern corner of the group.[11] From this well-protected anchorage we overlooked the northeastern part of the group, the bulwark, densely studded with smaller islands, which opposes the prevailing wind in a northeastern direction. We were in the more inhabited part of the group.

A boat, on which we recognized one of Rarik's companions, brought us a gift of fruit. But their fear was not yet conquered, and no one dared to board the ship.

On Oromed, the most fertile of the islands of this reef, upon which, however, the coconut tree still does not rise above the forest, a very old, worthy man, Chief Laergass, received us. He was magnanimous and unselfish beyond any other person I have known. He wished only to give, to bestow, and did it at a time when no counter gifts could be expected any more. By this characteristic he differed very much from Rarik, who lacked these virtues.

The population of the island seemed to consist of about thirty

people. Their permanent dwellings were no different from the roofs
that we had seen on the more westerly islands. As we were just
enjoying the hospitality of the old chief and decorated ourselves
with the ornaments that the daughters of the island handed to us, a
terror disturbed the comfortable atmosphere. Our little Valet, unconscious of his fearfulness, came running up cheerfully; and when
everyone fled from this unfamiliar monster, and he began to bark,
we had no small difficulty in restoring lost confidence.

The Radakians, who had known no mammal other than the rat,
bore a timidity toward our animals, dog, hog, and goat, that was difficult to overcome. But little Valet was the most frightening one of
all to them, running merrily and nimbly after everyone, and at
times barking. Big Valet, which the captain had brought with him
from the Bering Strait, was no such monster; he would not have
anything to do with anyone. He expired in Radak, in the Aur group.
Probably the warm climate was detrimental to him.

On January 20 we left this anchorage and, sailing along the reef,
after a short trip we came to Otdia, the chief island of the group of
the same name, which, the largest in circumference, makes up the
extreme eastern part of the circle. We found a good anchoring
ground in the lee of the island, and we lay secure, as in the best harbor. Beyond Otdia the reef curves to SSW and then away from land
toward the west and the Rurik Strait. The length of the group from
west to east amounts to nearly thirty miles, and its great breadth
from north to south about twelve miles. Mr. von Kotzebue counted
sixty-five islands in its area.

Otdia was, as they had indicated to us on Oromed, Rarik's dwelling place. I was sent ashore first. Soon, however, he, decorated very
elegantly, got into his boat, came up to the ship, and fearlessly
climbed aboard as the first of the Radakians to do so.

These clever mariners, whose skill compels our admiration, naturally devoted the most rapt attention to the gigantic structure of our
ship. Everything was observed, investigated, measured. It was an
easy thing to scramble up the masts to the flagpole, inspect the
yards, the sails, everything up there, and to rock back and forth joyfully in the breezy net of the rigging. But it was another thing to let
oneself down through the narrow hole and to follow the enigmatic
stranger from the joyous realm of air into the terror-provoking mysterious depths of his wooden world. At first only the bravest could
do that, as a rule the princes; I believe that our good Rarik had one of
his vassals precede him.

How could one entice one of these islanders, or an O-Waihian,
accustomed to enjoying the glories of his festivities outside in

nature under the canopy of his coconut palms, into the dark labyrinthine corridors of one of our theaters, only dimly lit in the daytime, and convince him that there would be festivities in this eerie locality, like unto a thieves' den. Indeed, sadness overwhelms me when I read that in Athens a theater of our type is being built to perform ballet in.

Down below in the cabin was the big mirror. Goethe says in the *Wander Years*: "Telescopes have something altogether magic about them. If we were not accustomed to looking through them since youth, we would shudder and quake every time we put them to our eye."[12] A brave and learned officer told me that with regard to the telescope he had what is generally called fear, and in order to look through it he had to really force himself with all his might. The mirror is another similar magic instrument that we have become used to but that still preserves its eerie reputation in the world of the fairy tale and of magic. The mirror generally gave rise to the most unbridled hilarity in our friends, once they were past their first astonishment. But there was one who was terror-stricken by it, left silently, and could not be brought in to it again.

In Hamburg I once came without warning into a house in the long foyer of which silver bars were stored on both sides as high as a man. I was affected curiously by the power slumbering in them, and it seemed to me as if I were walking through an overcrowded powder magazine. Naturally something similar must have transpired within our friends when they observed our iron cannons and anchors.

Our friends' treasures consisted of a few pieces of iron and a few hard stones that the sea had cast up upon their reefs and that were useful for whetting the iron. The former they had found in the wreckage of ships, the latter entangled in the roots of trees that had been torn from the ground. Their boats, their ornaments, and their drum: those were their possessions. Nowhere is the sky fairer, the temperature more uniform, than on the low islands. The sea and the wind keep a balance, and there is no lack of quickly passing showers to keep the forest a flowing, luxurious green. You dive into the dark blue flood to cool off when you are overheated from the sun directly overhead; and you dive into it to warm up when you feel the cool of the morning after a night spent outside. Why must the earth be so niggardly to those to whom the sun is so kind? The pandanus, whose sweet, spicy juice they suck out, on other islands serves only as a redolent decoration. Their food seems more appropriate for bees than for people. Almost nowhere is the soil adapted to the cultivation of edible roots and plants, which they are very intent upon. But everywhere, planted around their dwellings, a beautiful, sweet-smelling lily plant testifies to their industry and their sense of beauty.

Perhaps they could obtain more appropriate food from fishing and hunt the sharks that haunt the entrances to their reefs. We have seen them eat only very small fish, and we obtained only very small fishhooks from them.

We tried with love and persistence to open up new branches of food for them. According to Mr. von Kotzebue's narrative of his second voyage, of the animals and plants we brought them the yam root at least seems to have been maintained, so that our good intentions were not completely defeated.[13]

But, without being too terribly bound by the chronology, I must relate a few things about our friends, with whom, once they had overcome their first shyness, we lived on a most familiar footing.

On the island of Otdia, which is over two miles long, about sixty people had their usual dwelling places, but frequent moves took place, and our presence attracted guests from the most distant parts of the group. We wandered alone over the island every day, joined every family, and slept under their roofs without concern. They came aboard the ship, where they were equally welcome, and the chiefs and most distinguished among them were drawn to our table, where they learned to adapt to our customs easily and well-manneredly.

Among the inhabitants of Otdia a man soon stood out, who, though not of noble birth, distinguished himself above all the others by his quick perception and gift of communication. Lagediak, the man of our confidence, from whom we learned most and through whom we hoped to gain a reception for our teachings among the people, later exchanged names with me. It was from Lagediak that Mr. von Kotzebue first obtained important information about the geography of Radak. Through him he got knowledge of the navigable fords in the southern reef of Otdia, of the neighboring group of Erigup [Erikub], of the other groups of which the island chain consists.[14] Lagediak drew his map with stones on the beach, with slate pencil on the slate, and indicated the directions that could be marked according to the compass. With him Mr. von Kotzebue laid the foundation for the interesting work he has furnished about Radak and the more western island chain. The first step was taken; then it was a matter of going further.

Lagediak understood very well our intention of introducing species of useful plants still unknown here for the good of the people, of cultivating a garden and distributing seeds. On the 22nd a start was made at laying out the garden. The ground was cleared, the earth dug up, yam roots set in, melon and watermelon seeds planted. Our friends were gathered about us and watched our work sympathetically and attentively. Lagediak explained our enterprise and was incessantly at pains to distribute and impress upon the others the teachings he had learned from us. We distributed seeds, for which there was a pleasing demand, and in the next few days we had the pleasure of seeing several private gardens develop according to our model.

During this gardening work, that took place as detailed on the 22nd, something occurred that I shall narrate in order to illustrate a character trait of our dear friends. As I looked at the spectators I became aware of a pained wincing on several faces at once. I turned toward the seaman who to make space for the garden was digging up shrubs and clearing the woods. He had just used his ax on a fine sapling of the breadfruit tree, so rare and valuable here. The misfortune had occurred, the tree had been felled. Even if the man had sinned unknowingly, the commander had to openly remove from himself all responsibility for the deed. Thus the captain angrily upbraided the sailor, who had to give up his ax and retire from the scene. Then the good Radakians interceded for him appeasingly and propitiatingly. Some went after the sailor, whom they tried to comfort by caresses, and pressed gifts upon him.

Already on the next day the rats, which are present on this island in unbelievable numbers, had destroyed a lot, and pulled most of the seeds out of the ground. But when we left Otdia our garden was in a flourishing condition. Upon our second visit to Radak the next fall we left cats behind on the island. On his second voyage in the year 1824 Mr. von Kotzebue found that they had gone wild and multiplied, without any diminution in the number of rats.[15]

The forge was set up ashore on January 24. It with its tremendous wealth of iron was under the protection of a single seaman, who slept near it. On one of the following days an old man attempted to obtain a piece of iron by force, in which undertaking he was prevented by his outraged compatriots—also by force. That cannot be called a theft. But even when a real theft was committed the greatest displeasure was exhibited on the part of the Radakians and the loudest disapproval was expressed.

It is fairly obvious what an attractive spectacle the unsuspected treatment of the precious iron in the fire and under the hammer must have been for our friends. The entire population gathered around the forge. Friend Lagediak was one of the most attentive and courageous of those present. For it *does* demand courage to observe the unknown play of the bellows and the scattering sparks up close.

For him a harpoon was first forged, then a second one for Rarik, and a few trifles for others before the work for the *Rurik* was begun.

We still had a few O-Waihian swine, males and females, that could be disposed of and that we had destined for our friends. We had taken pains to accustom everyone to the sight of these animals on the Rurik and to impress upon them that it was their flesh that served us as food, which many had tasted and enjoyed at our table. The hogs were brought ashore and kept in a pen that had been prepared for them in the vicinity of Rarik's house. A seaman was placed in charge of the still-feared beasts. We counted most on Lagediak, who was impressed by the importance of our gift, for the success of the well-meant experiment, which in the end, as was to be expected, failed. The neglected animals later were set free and perished soon after our departure.

A few chickens, our last ones, we had also presented to Lagediak.

Living in pleasant community with the Radakians, I studied assiduously the constitution of their Neptunian dwellings and hoped to collect something more than useless evidence toward a better understanding of the coral reefs. The corals themselves and the madrepores would have demanded a whole lifetime of study. The bleached skeletons of those that are preserved in collections are only of slight value; still, I wanted to collect them and take them home with me. Eschscholtz had endeavored while swimming to make a complete collection of all the species occurring, had brought selected examples of them aboard ship, and had stacked them in the chicken coops for bleaching and drying. It is true that polyp bodies in this condition do not exude a very pleasant odor. When he went to see to his corals one morning they had all been thrown overboard, lock, stock, and barrel. On the southern end of Otdia where gaps in the upper stone layers of the reef allow little lagoons to form in which one can enjoy a bath in calm water and at the same time comfortably investigate and think about the puzzles of these formations in the midst of blooming coral gardens, I had staked out a space in the sand of the beach in which I exposed corals, sea urchins, and everything of that type that I wished to preserve to the drying sun. In my plot of ground I had set up a staff with a bunch of pandanus leaves tied to it, the sign of property. Under this protection my property had remained sacred to the good Radakians on whose path it lay, and no boy at play had ever touched the slightest thing in the designated area. But who can foresee everything? Our seamen obtained shore leave one Sunday and undertook a walk around the circumference of the island. They discovered my drying-place, completely destroyed my laboriously contrived collection, and then looked me up good-naturedly to tell me of their discovery and to give me fragments of my broken corals. Nonetheless, I put together another nice collection of the madrepores of Radak and presented them, filling an entire chest, to the Berlin Museum. But an evil fate seems to have reigned over this part of my endeavors. My Radak lithophytes, with the exception of *Millepora coerulea* and *Tubipora Chamissonis Ehrenb.*, were either set up in the royal collection without tags, or not set out at all, and sold for cash along with other doublets, so that Ehrenberg, in his monograph on the corals, could cite his interesting point of view only with respect to the two mentioned species.[16]

Rarik once accompanied me on a walk to my bathing-place and coral garden. When we had arrived there I indicated to him that I wished to bathe and began to undress. In view of the amazement that the whiteness of our skin occasioned to our brown friends, I, less sensitive than he, thought the occasion would be welcome to him to satisfy a very natural curiosity. But when, being ready to climb into my bath, I looked around for him, he had disappeared, and I thought he had deserted me. I bathed, made my observations, did my investigations, climbed out of the water, got dressed again, investigated my drying operation, and was just about to start out on the way home when the bushes parted, and out of the green foliage the good-natured face of my companion smiled out at me. In the meantime he had decorated his hair with the flowers of *Scaevola* in a most elegant manner and had also prepared a wreath of flowers for me, which he handed me.[17] We returned arm in arm to his dwelling.

A similar considerate modesty was general among the Radakians. No one ever hovered around us in our bath.

It was agreed that I should spend this night ashore, in order to observe the people in their domesticity. When we arrived the captain had already returned to the ship in his boat, and it seemed quite natural to everyone that I should join the family as guest. They were busy preparing the *mogan*, the pandanus dough.[18] We spent the evening under the coconut trees on the shore of the lagoon. The moon was in the first quarter, there was no fire burning, and I couldn't secure any to light my pipe. We ate and talked. The conversation, the subject of which was our splendors, was conducted happily and · in long sentences. My dear friends tried hard to entertain the foreign guest, singing songs that inspired them to the greatest joy themselves. Should one call the rhythm of this discourse song? Should the beautiful natural movements they made while they sat be termed a dance? When the Radakian drum had become silent, Rarik called upon me in turn to render a Russian song. I couldn't deny my friend this simple request, and now, with a voice that was infamous among us, I was to appear as a model of European musical skill. I acquiesced to this mockery of fate, stood up, and declaimed, strongly accentuating meter and rhyme, a German poem, namely Goethe's "Let today in this noble circle."[19] I hope that our immortal German Grandmaster will forgive me: the Frenchman on Radak presented that as Russian song and dance! They listened to me with great attention, imitated me in the most pleasing fashion, when I had finished, and I enjoyed hearing these words repeated, even with distorted pronunciation:

> "Und im Ganzen, Vollen, Schönen
> Resolut zu leben."

> ("And resolutely to live life completely, fully, beautifully.")

At night I slept at Rarik's side on the platform of his large house. Men and women lay above us and below us, and often conversation alternated with sleep. In the morning I went back to the ship, to return to land again immediately.

I have described one of my days on Radak; they passed by gently, with little variation—the one description may suffice. The delicacy, the elegance of the manners, the excessive cleanliness of this people was expressed in each slightest detail of their behavior, only the smallest number of which are suitable for being written down. Can the behavior of a family be described in which once in our presence a child behaved indecently? The way in which the delinquent was removed, and how in the face of the outrage that the incident excited the homage due the prestigious strangers was saved, and the child encouraged to a better way of life? In this connection, too, a denial is just as telling; and how can I speak of things that were always withdrawn from our eyes?

Our popular bringing-up, together with folktales, fairy tales, and proverbs, naturally work toward infusing us with great reverence for the dear divine gift of bread, to disparage which is a great sin. To throw the smallest piece of bread on the ground was a sin in my childhood that was punished unmercifully and inexorably by the rod. In the needy people of Radak a similar feeling can be expected with respect to the fruits on which its nourishment depends. One of our friends had handed the captain a coconut to drink from; the latter tossed the shell aside with the edible meat still adhering to it. The Radakian anxiously called his attention to the disdained food. His feelings seemed to be hurt, and in me the old teachings whipped into me by my governess were roused.

I note in passing that our friends did not learn of the potency of our weapons until the final days of our sojourn on Otdia, when the captain shot a bird in the presence of Rarik and Lagediak. That the shot frightened them terribly is readily understandable; that Rarik afterwards begged the captain not to shoot the musket when he saw him, lay in his character.

To the south of Otdia the reef bears, beside several smaller and desolate islands, only two fertile and inhabited ones. The first, Egmedio, differs from all the others through the fact that only on it does the coconut tree tower high above the forest, and only here are trunks and the roots of dead trees present. It was the dwelling place of Chief Langien, whose visit we had received on the *Rurik* already, when he had brought us a gift of coconuts and invited us to visit him on his island. The other island takes up the southeastern corner of the reef, which from there to the west bears only small uninhabitable islands.

On January 28 a trip was undertaken in two boats to investigate the fords Lagediak had told us about. We headed toward Egmedio, where Langien, who was sojourning on Otdia at the time, had hurried ahead to give us a friendly welcome as host at home, and he was a hospitable, cordial man, whom our visit greatly pleased. The island seemed to be inhabited only by him, his wife, and a few other people. I pleased him by putting in a little garden. On the same day we had investigated one of the gates, the Strait of Lagediak; the *Rurik* could not have managed this ford without danger.[20] Because of the unfavorable weather we gave up trying to reach the next strait and sought shelter for the night. The closest desolate islands were not adapted to this, and we had to go back to the one that made up the corner of the group. Here we had the unexpected pleasure of meeting an old friend coming toward us: jolly Labigar welcomed us on his own territory and brought us coconuts and pandanus fruits. Here he lived alone with his family. On the island of Otdia we had come to know the entire population of the group. I put in a little garden for the hospitable, friendly man (at this time the only seeds I had left were watermelon seeds). We had made camp on the beach, and when in the morning we roused ourselves from sleep, Labigar and his family were round about us, quietly and patiently waiting for us to awaken, in order to hand us a coconut for an early drink.

On this morning (January 29), we reached the ship. The other ford was reconnoitered later on February 3 by Gleb Simonovich in the longboat and called Shishmarev Strait after him.[21] Any ship can easily, safely, and without tacking pass in and out of this one with the prevailing trade wind.

On January 30 a bucket with an iron band on it was found to be missing by some of our people who had been sent out partly after water and partly after wood, an article with which we had to provide ourselves here for the entire length of our trip to the north. Rarik was seriously urged to recover the stolen property for us; but in this affair, about which all the others loudly expressed their disapproval, he was found to be in a state of lassitude that cast a shadow upon his character. Not until the next morning after a long conversation was held with the chief, did one of his people produce the bucket from the tangle of the woods. Thereupon it was announced that any further attempt at theft would be severely punished on our part. I shall not keep the only case secret when we had the opportunity of making good our threat.

Lagediak was dining with us on board ship. The thief of the bucket had accompanied him, but he was denied entrance to the cabin, and, lying on the deck, he watched us through the window. Lagediak handed him something to taste, and a shiny knife was also handed him to look at. The knife never came back to our table but rather found its way into the man's *mudirdir* (the male garment, a girdle of matting held in place like an apron by strips of bark). He was observed, and when he was about to leave the ship he was seized, searched, sentenced, stretched out, and whipped.

At the time our names had already been incorporated into short bits of song and thus rescued from oblivion. Deinnam, Chamisso, and others:

> Ae ni'gagit, ni mogit,
> Totjan Chamisso.

("—?— Chamisso drinks and eats the shelled coconut.")

Memorial coins, minted for us; memorial stones, set for us, and which, even though without inscription or shape, will be the bearers of the oral traditions and legends connected with them. In *Egil's Saga* the metrical memorial verses, which, recited at memorable events, are stamped in this manner and given permanent form through alliteration, assonance, and rhyme, often have no clear connection to the deed the memory of which is chained to it.[22]

Our intention of leaving Otdia in order to visit Erigup, Kaben [Maloelap], and other groups was announced and we desired and expected that the one or the other of our friends would accompany us on this trip.[23] Rarik was constructing a new boat, after which he promised to make the trip with us; but the work never seemed to get finished. Lagediak wished to travel with us on the *Rurik* but was detained because of Rarik's boat construction. Rarik, Langien, and

Labigar were going to accompany us on another boat, but that plan, too, was given up. We had to abandon our preconceived hope.

On February 7, 1817, we weighed anchor at dawn; our friends stood on the beach, but none of them came aboard. Only one boat followed us under sail from Oromed. Probably the old man Laergass. He had visited us a few days before. He was appreciative of our gifts and kind, like no one else. He probably wanted to be the last one to say goodbye to us. We lost sight of his boat when outside of the strait we doubled our sails before the favorable wind.

When we sailed away from Otdia the land of Erigup was already visible from the masthead. On the 7th and 8th of February we completed the charting of this poor, sparsely green group, which is said to be inhabited only by three people. We saw no more on the beach of the only island on which coconut trees were visible but did not rise above the woods.

On the windward side of the group a ford was investigated that probably could not be managed without danger. We left Erigup to search for Kaben. The group is about forty-five miles away from Otdia, and Lagediak had described its situation fairly correctly.

On the morning of the 11th we were before the ford on the windward side of the group that is situated most closely to its northwest corner. The wind was strong. Two boats came out of the gate toward us and observed us from afar. Seized by a gust of wind, the one vessel capsized. The other did not concern itself with the incident; here the boatmen are sufficient unto themselves. We saw them, now sitting on the keel, now swimming attached to lines, towing the boat toward the shore, from which they were over a half mile distant. Three other boats came up to us from the large island to the NW and invited us ashore.

The gate is broad, but the channel shallow in which we had to wend our way through banks of coral to enter. We executed the bold maneuver quickly and successfully. The transparency of the water allowed us to look down into the mysterious coral gardens at the bottom. We dropped anchor before one of the smallest and poorest islands of the group.

Kaben has about the size and the longish shape of Otdia, but from NW to SE it turns one of its long sides toward the trade wind, and the chief land, the island of Kaben, makes up the northwest tip of the group. On the windward side the reef is richly crowned with fertile islands. (Mr. von Kotzebue counted sixty-four of them in the whole circumference.)[24] The coconut palm rises with tall trunk above most of them. The breadfruit tree is common. Three species of *Arum* are cultivated, which, however, give only a poor yield, and we encountered the introduced banana plant on one of the islands.[25] The population is in keeping with the greater fertility of the soil. The people seemed to us to be more prosperous, more self-confident, more daring than on Otdia, and, animated by our presence, their boats, of which they possessed many, crisscrossed the lagoon at all times and in all directions, so that it resembled a busy harbor.

On Kaben we had more casual contacts with several people, and the images of the friendly figures are already confused in my memory; yet, some still stand out especially from the general run, and the friendly, merry, courageous prince's son on Airik, so full of life, I shall never forget.[26]

On the island before which we lay at anchor we found only young coconut plantings and deserted houses. On the 12th two large boats came from the east and approached us. We called out a peaceful greeting to them; they returned our greeting and came up fearlessly; we cast them a line, to which they fastened their vessels, and a chief, accompanied by a single man, ascended to the deck. He immediately sought out our chief, handed him a coconut, and placed his wreath of flowers upon his head. We were able to make ourselves understood well with the astonished people, and no mistrust reigned between us.

Mr. von Kotzebue, who had already lost his name to Rarik, here offered to exchange it with the enraptured Labadini, lord of Torua (an eastern island of this group).[27] The bonds of friendship were sealed.

The chief stayed overnight on the nearest island. The night was stormy; on the 13th we could neither go under sail nor go ashore.

On the 14th we left our anchorage, and by tacking about pressed more deeply into the interior of the group in the east. Our friend followed us in his boat, stuck to the wind more sharply than we did, and didn't sail much slower. In the afternoon we dropped anchor before a small island richly shaded with palm trees, and Labadini came on board. This island, called Tian, also belonged to him, but it was not his normal dwelling place, and he urged us to follow him to Torua, which we promised to do on the next day. We went ashore together, and when we landed he carried the captain through the water.

On this island, where the unfavorable weather still kept us on the 15th, we enjoyed the more comfortable prosperity of the charming people. We were hospitably invited under every roof, kindly received by every family. A cord of coconut fiber served instead of walls to enclose a few plantations and groups of fruit trees. We saw the white heron, tamed by cropping his wings, and a few tame chickens. Labadini regaled the captain with a cleanly prepared meal of fish and baked breadfruit. We sailed with as little worry on his boat as we did on ours, and on both days, when we returned to the ship, such a number of coconuts were brought us that they were enough for the entire crew for several days. In return we had iron distributed. We brought coconuts from Kaben to Unalashka.

On February 16 we went under sail again, and, following the chain of the islands, which took on a more southern direction, we surveyed their entire population, which the wonderful spectacle of the strange giant ship under sail brought down to the beach.

From a larger island, called, as we later learned, Olot [Ollot], a large boat pulled out, in which there might have been twenty to thirty people. They showed us coconuts and shouted and waved us toward them. We sailed on, and the vessel followed us. Labadini's boat, which was also following us, appeared in the distance. A large island, from which the chain headed toward the south, offered us a sheltered harbor, where we dropped anchor. It was Torua, Labadini's residence. The boat from Olot pulled up alongside, and the lord of the island, the young chief Langediu, immediately climbed aboard the *Rurik*. He was more richly tattooed and more elegantly decorated than Labadini. He offered Mr. von Kotzebue an exchange of names, which the latter, who always retained what he gave away, accepted without scruple. The procedure was calculated to cause a quarrel among the chiefs. Labadini, who soon appeared, turned away offended from us, and here, on his island, we had traffic only with Langediu. With this animated, clever, and mannerly young man the captain reviewed his geography of Radak and completed it.

Torua, twenty-four miles from Kaben as the crow flies, is twice as large and relatively less populous than Tian. Here we were regaled with the unpalatable dish that the Radakians make out of grated coconut shell. Here or on Tian we were also handed the sourdough prepared from the breadfruit, which is sufficiently well known from accounts of voyages to O-Taheiti and which Europeans cannot stomach. We remained at our anchorage for three days, secured many coconuts, and distributed a lot of iron. The sailor who handed out the iron was in especially high esteem with the natives, and he was flattered by all.

On the 19th we weighed anchor and headed southward along the reef, which here bears a green wreath of very small islands. After a distance of ten miles its direction changes, and the lagoon is drawn out in the shape of a sack toward the southeast, where the group ends in a final land mass. A larger island at the rear of this bay of the lagoon drew our attention, and we directed our course toward it. Before we reached it land was sighted from the masthead beyond the reef in the south. It was the Aur group. We anchored outside Airik, that large island.

We went ashore while the captain remained occupied aboard ship. A boat from Airik had already visited us at Torua. We were received with obliging cordiality. We were handed coconuts, and we seemed to be old, long-awaited friends. This island is the most populous and most fertile of all those we have seen. It alone possesses six or seven large boats. A youth or boy, who was still without the men's decoration of tattooing and who seemed to be paid more respect by the people than we had seen shown to other chiefs, seemed to us at first to be the lord of the island. But a young, likewise untattooed girl (his sister?) also shared the same honors, and a woman (their mother?) seemed to be elevated above them both and was enveloped in a nimbus of aristocracy of which I saw no other example in Radak. It is also the only case that I saw of a woman enjoying authority. That the different honor and power of the chiefs did not depend on their wealth and possessions alone was obvious; but I have never been able to garner any information about this inequality.

The youth, who embraced me cordially, came aboard ship with me immediately. An older man, who seemed to be assigned to guard him, accompanied him. Joyous, friendly, animated, curious, clever, brave, and mannerly: I have seldom seen a more charming creature. He impressed the captain, to whom he was immediately presented, the same way. With his companion he measured the dimensions of the ship and the heights of the masts. The cord, which was used for this purpose, was carefully preserved. To put on a show for him I brought out my rapiers and fenced a pass with Eschscholtz. Then he positively glowed for joy: he had to play this game, too. He courteously requested a rapier, and joyously, full of dignity, he took up a position before me, trusting himself and me, and presented his naked breast to the cold iron of the stranger. Think about it—it was beautiful.

In the afternoon we went ashore again, and the youth conducted the captain to his mother. She received the distinguished guest and his gifts in silence and in exchange ordered two rolls of mogan and coconuts to be handed to him. Mogan, the most valuable thing that a Radakian can give, cannot be purchased, even for iron. They then went to the sister, who had a band of girls around her, from whom, however, she sat apart. Here there were merriment and singing. During these visits and everywhere on the island a dense circle of spectators formed around the chiefs and their eminent guests.

At all hours the *Rurik* was surrounded by the natives' boats and overloaded with visitors. The islanders were here superior in number to us, and their familiarity became burdensome and disquieting.

On the 20th a large boat came from the west, in which we counted twenty-two people. It was Labeloa, the chief of Kaben, who had followed us here and presented the captain with a roll of mogan. He told us that it had been he whose boat had capsized before the entrance to the group.

A detail had been sent for water. In the evening, when it was getting dark, the boatswain's mate shouted from ashore that a seaman was missing. The captain fired a cannon and set off a rocket. The man, whom the islanders had not restrained for any hostile purpose, joined his fellows, and the boat rowed back to the ship.

On the 21st yesterday's terrible cannon fire was the general subject of discussion, and we found more respect and reserve among the people. On our part, we did not change our behavior. Eschscholtz indicated quite matter-of-factly to inquirers that our captain had traveled up into the sky, but was back again. We visited our friends here for the last time. Access to the old chiefess was denied the captain. We obtained a huge number of coconuts on this island.

We left Airik on February 21 and headed for Olot, Langediu's island, which the captain had promised to visit. Labeloa, who wished to accompany us to Aur, followed us in his boat, but when he saw that we were anchoring at Olot, he set his course for Kaben but did follow us to Aur.

Olot lags behind the other islands we saw in population and fertility. Still, taro was cultivated on Olot, and we also saw the banana here. Even as on all of the islands of Kaben at which we had landed I myself sowed watermelon seeds, exciting the most active interest of the islanders, and distributed their seeds to the chiefs, I did so here, too. While I was so occupied, my knife was pilfered. I addressed myself in this matter to Langediu's authority, and not in vain: my property was returned to me immediately. Labadini was here with Langediu, and good relations seemed to have been restored. Both chiefs were richly regaled with gifts.

On February 23, 1817, we left Olot and the island group of Kaben, from which we sailed out of the same strait through which we had entered. We headed for Aur, in whose precincts we entered under full sail through a narrow ford, skillfully steering between coral banks. The group, of slight expanse, could be surveyed from the lagoon. It is thirteen miles long, six wide, and consists of thirty-two islands. At five o'clock in the afternoon we dropped anchor before the principal island, which forms the southeastern tip of the group.

Immediately several boats of the natives surrounded us. We shouted "Eidara" to them, and the chiefs immediately climbed aboard and with them the strangers from Ulea [Woleia]: Kadu and Edok, whom fate had made his companion. My friend Kadu! I read over what I said about this man in the treatise "On Our Knowledge of the First Province of the Great Ocean," to which I must refer you, and memory warms my heart and dampens my eyes.[28]

The Radakians were horrified at Kadu's swiftly made decision to remain with the white men on the giant ship. They tried everything to change his mind. His friend Edok, deeply moved, tried himself to pull him down into the boat by force. Kadu, however, moved to tears, pulled away from him and pushed him, as he said farewell, back into the boat.

The anchorage here had disadvantages that moved the captain to seek a better one in the lee of the island of Tabual [Tabal], which, eight miles away from Aur, forms the northeastern tip of the group. He had indicated this decision to the chiefs, and on the morning of February 24 they followed us there in five large boats. The population was larger than it was even on Kaben and the number of large boats greater.

According to Mr. von Kotzebue, the high chiefs of the people with whom we here came into contact, who, gaining confidence, drew him into their council and importuned him to intercede with the superiority of our weapons in the prevailing war, of which they gave us the first indication, were as follows: Tigedien, a man with a snow-white beard and hair and bent with age, the lord of the Aur group, Kadu's patron, and in the absence of King Lamari the first of the chiefs; the second after him, Lebeuliet, an old man, the lord of the Kaben group, where the island of Airik was his usual dwelling place, the husband of that chiefess, the father of those children, whom we had met there; the third, youngest and most vigorous, Tiuraur, the lord of the Otdia group, the father of Rarik.

Lamari was the king of the whole north of Radak from Aur on. The king of the three southern groups, Meduro [Majuro], Arno, and Mille [Milli], was Lathethe, and there was war between the two of them.[29] Lamari was now traveling over his subject islands in order to call up his vassals and his war squadron to Aur and from here launch an expedition of war against his enemy.

Compare in this regard my essay about Radak. I will repeat here only because Mr. von Kotzebue, poorly informed, has reported differently: in these wars the islands attacked are plundered of all their fruits, but the trees themselves are not damaged.

Mr. von Kotzebue gave Tigedien weapons! Lances and grappling hooks! Tigedien had brought him a present of several rolls of mogan.

The circumstances and the impending war may have contributed to the high value that was placed upon mogan and to the difficulty we had in acquiring any. This delicious sweet confection is the only foodstuff that can be shipped for longer trips. It is the sea biscuit of these seafarers.

When our boats returned to the ship from the shore, they were loaded down with as many coconuts as they could carry.

At Tabual Kadu obtained permission from the captain to go ashore, from where he would return to the ship. We ourselves wandered across the island on this day and found it richer in humus than the most fertile of the islands of the Kaben group. We found taro and banana cultivations in a thriving state. When we returned from our walk we found our Kadu, surrounded by a large circle of Radakians, talking animatedly, emotionally, deeply moved, while all around him listened to his talk tensely—captivated, touched—and several broke out in tears. Kadu was loved in Radak, even as he came to be loved among us.

Various vessels from the Kaben group arrived, the one from Airik, another two or three with Labeloa from the island of Kaben, the latter with a very violent wind. From our anchorage the land of Kaben could be seen from the masthead.

On Tabual I made a last attempt to obtain a tattoo. At that time I would gladly have purchased that beautiful covering with all the pain that everyone knows it costs. I spent the night in the chief's house, who seemed to have promised to undertake the operation the next morning. The next morning, however, the operation was not undertaken, and only later could I make sense out of the refusal from Kadu's remarks.

In spite of the war being waged between the south and north of Radak and the passionate hatred that often burst forth when these unhappy conditions were mentioned, a chief of Arno lived on Tabual without danger, beloved and honored.

On the 26th we went ashore on Tabual for the last time and took leave of our friends. All night long the Radak drum and song resounded under the palms on the beach of the lagoon.

On February 27, 1817, early in the morning, we sailed out of the bay of Aur through the very gate through which we had entered. We headed north, all day long under the wind from Kaben, on the 28th across the wind from Otdia, and before nightfall we caught sight of the Eilu [Ailuk] group, which lay to windward.[30] Kadu recognized the group. He had already been there, and likewise on Udirik, and, well versed in the geography of Radak, he told us the directions in which Temo [Jemo] and Ligiep [Likiep] lay.[31]

On the morning of March 1, 1817, we were at the southern tip of

Eilu, which is formed by the island of the same name. We followed the south and east side of the enclosure, where the reef is devoid of any land, and sought a passage through. Three boats came toward us into the open sea, and our companion Kadu carried on a lively conversation with his astonished old acquaintances. The latter showed us the broader gates of their reef fortification more to the north. Of the three only one appeared to be navigable for the *Rurik*. Evening was already coming on.

On March 2 we again sought the reef, which the current had drawn us away from. The wind blew toward us through the narrow channel, and it seemed scarcely possible that we could squeeze through. Lieutenant Shishmarev explored the passage. Between two perpendicular walls the strait was fifty fathoms wide and of sufficient depth. The ship had to be turned into the strait and at the same time conducted in by the strong current. If it obeyed the helm sluggishly, it would be ripped apart on the coral wall. The bold maneuver was executed swiftly and successfully—it was a fine moment. All sails were stretched to the wind. Deep silence prevailed on the *Rurik*, where everyone harkened to the word of command. On both sides of us the surf roared. The word is called out, and we are in the lagoon. In the passage itself a bonito had taken the hook, so that we exacted a gate toll.

The Eilu group is fifteen miles long from north to south and only five miles wide. All land is on the windward side. It is covered with scant amounts of verdure; the coconut palm rises above the forest only on Eilu to the south and Kapeniur [Kapen] in the north.[32] The lagoon is shallow and filled with banks of coral and shoals that threatened us with danger. Toward noon we went to anchor in the vicinity of Eilu.

Three boats surrounded us immediately, and Kadu had enough to say for himself and for us. Lamari, whom we hoped to meet here, was already on Udirik, and the chief of Eilu, Langemui, resided on Kapeniur. Kadu went ashore with the Radakians, where we later followed him. Here we saw the pandanus being eaten when it was still quite green, and the breadfruit was entirely lacking. A few plants of the taro species cultivated on Kaben testified to human assiduity and the reluctance of nature. These good, needy people regaled us with a number of coconuts, with which we perhaps were more richly provided than they. They expected no reward for it. We distributed iron, and I sowed watermelon seeds, as I had done all over on the other groups.

At dawn of the 4th we got under way, and after a difficult journey did not arrive at Kapeniur until late in the day and there dropped anchor. We lay securely and comfortably in the vicinity of the land, which sheltered us from the wind, and it was decided to tarry here for a few days to get sails and rigging in shape for the journey to the north that awaited us.

Langemui first visited us on board ship and brought the captain some coconuts. He was a very old, gaunt man with a pleasant, lively spirit, even as old age seems to retain a youthful state of mind on these islands. According to our unreliable estimate, he may have been about eighty years old. He bore several scars on his body. These, when he was asked about them, caused him to give us the first information we had about Ralik, the island chain farther to the west, with whose geography every woman, every child on Radak is familiar.[33] People are a lot like nature: what you already know you can easily find repeated examples of; but to find out what you don't know you need skill, you need luck. After Langemui's description, he having obtained his wounds on Ralik, Mr. von Kotzebue drew up a chart of these islands that can be seen in his account of the voyage. At Udirik he had a second point where he had himself told the direction of the northern group, and in the late fall he had the opportunity to test and correct his work on Otdia. In my "Notes" I have included Kadu's statements about Ralik.[34] According to him Sauraur, whom we had known in Aur, had been in Ralik after Langemui, had there acquired by exchange the name he now bears, and had established friendship with the natives.[35] Ralik belongs to the same cultural world as Radak and seemed at the time, like Radak, to be divided into two hostile kingdoms.

On Eilu there was a young chief from Mesid who had arrived here after he and his little fishing boat had been carried away from his island by a storm. He was thinking of joining Lamari for the journey back, as he was about to travel to Mesid to fetch reinforcements. Our seafarers consider it daring to seek a point of land that is not visible for more than six miles, over a distance of fifty-six miles, without a compass and fighting against wind and current, a journey that must take the Radakians about two days and a night. They wouldn't dare to undertake such a risky affair. We learned in the fall that Lamari had missed Mesid this time, and, giving up on the help that he expected from this island, had turned to the other groups of Radak.

On Kapeniur there was another chief, who, apparently much older than Langemui, was possessed of the same active and merry disposition.

On March 7 the wind changed about from north to west, and a constant rain interrupted the work on the *Rurik*. The 9th and 10th were likewise rainy days. On the 11th the work begun was quickly finished. We were ready to sail.

In spite of the devastation that the rats had wrought, several watermelon plants had grown most satisfactorily from the seeds I had sown on Kapeniur, and their propagation seemed assured.

Speaking only of this one plant species: I carefully entrusted an unbelievable amount of watermelon seeds to the ground at suitable spots on the reefs of Radak. The entire yield of seeds of all the watermelons that were consumed on the *Rurik* in California and in the Sandwich Islands ended up in Radak, either planted by me or entrusted to the hands of industrious natives. Upon our second visit to Radak I conducted a second sowing on Otdia and consigned another considerable amount of seeds to Kadu's loving care. According to Mr. von Kotzebue's last voyage and last visit to Otdia in the year 1824, this most willing of plants, which has followed Europeans wherever there is no lack of a mild sun, seems not to have maintained itself on Radak.[36] Indeed, it is easier to do evil than to do good!

In the middle of the Eilu group two sharks were caught from the ship on different days. I was told that the one had three living young in her body, each three spans long; two in an egg, the third alone. Normally in lagoons that are encircled by coral reefs there is no danger from sharks.

The water in these inner seas had little luminescence.

When the good Langemui learned of our intention of leaving Eilu the next day, he became saddened. During the night we saw lights moving along the reef. Quite early in the morning our friend came aboard and brought us a last present: flying fish, which he had had caught by torchlight, and coconuts.

We left Eilu on March 12, 1817. The wind, which was favorable for our exit, permitted us to pass through a narrower gate farther toward the north. A shark was caught right in the passage. At three o'clock in the afternoon we sighted Udirik and Tegi, which, as we had already confidently recognized, were the groups we had sighted the previous year. Approaching nightfall compelled us to avoid the vicinity of the land. On the morning of the 13th we found we had been driven eight miles to the west. We soon reached the channel that separates the two groups, sailed through it, and before noon found ourselves in calm water sheltered from the wind by Udirik. No gate in the encircling reef permitted the *Rurik* to enter the inner lagoon of the group. Lamari had to be here, and we wished to meet the powerful potentate of this Neptunian kingdom, who, proceeding from his cradle, the Arno group, had united the northern part of Radak forcefully under his sole rule.

Several sails could be seen, and, after crossing the reef, they came out into the open sea. Two boats first approached the *Rurik*, and the occupants recognized our friend immediately and called to him loudly by name, prefixing a particle to it: "La Kadu!"[37] All timidity was overcome. They came alongside, they climbed on deck. Among these men was the companion who shared Kadu's fate whom I mentioned in my "Notes and Opinions," the old chief from Eap [Yap], who immediately resolved to stay with us and could be dissuaded only by the threat of force.[38] Kadu harbored a gentle pity for this man who tried to force him off the *Rurik* and later tried to work out some scheme that would allow news of him and his present whereabouts to get to Eap.[39]

I boarded one of the natives' boats together with Kadu with the intention of landing on the island. Soon after we pushed off from the ship Lamari arrived there on another boat and climbed on deck immediately: a stately, corpulent gentleman with a long black beard and with one larger and one smaller eye. No external signs of subjugation on the part of his companions toward him were seen to be given.

In the meantime we tacked about before the reef, which even these boats did not seem to dare to cross at high water. We finally approached the island, to which two men swam over through the surf. Lamari followed us and conversed with us. Of all the boats I saw only a single one penetrate into the lagoon from the open sea at this time, even though all of them had easily sailed out from it. The one I was on had been recently repaired. It carried fourteen people, and it was not one of the largest. We returned to the ship with some coconuts. It was noon. Kadu, who was again earnestly told that we were now leaving Radak never to return there, stuck unmoved to his decision. He distributed his last possessions among his hosts. We did not wait for the other fruits these islanders promised us. We set our course for Bigar [Bikar].[40]

The uninhabited reef Bigar, which, according to the reports of the Radakians, is situated to the northeast of Udirik and is visited by the seafarers of this group for the purpose of catching birds and turtles, was inaccessible to us. We fought two days against the wind. The western current of the ocean, which is exceptionally strong to the north of Radak, drove us back twenty-six miles to the west on March 14, and twenty miles on the 15th. We lost against the wind instead of winning, and, defeated in our own art by these seafarers whom we call savages, we gave up any further attempt to reach Bigar.

One might suppose that the Radakians had given us the direction in which they steer to get to Bigar as the one in which this reef really lies, and that it therefore lay to the west of us while we sought it to the east. But then on the other hand the same geographers would have had to indicate a much more eastern situation for the Udirik group when approached from Bigar. In any event, the trip over and back presupposes a sufficient knowledge of the current and a reliable estimate of its effect.

We set our course for the islands seen by Captain Johnstone on the frigate *Cornwallis* in the year 1807. Frequent seafowl, whose flights Kadu observed in the evening, seemed to be conducting us there. We sighted these islands on March 19, 1817. The sickle-shaped, desolate group has a length of thirteen and a half miles from north to south. On his chart Mr. von Kotzebue sets their center at 14°40′N latitude, 190°57′W longitude. Lieutenant Shishmarev, sent out in a boat, could find no passage in the wall-like naked reef that borders them to leeward.

In the meantime a shark of extraordinary size took the hook. Excited by the hope of securing this valuable prey for us, Kadu undressed, ready to plunge into the sea to give assistance. The monster broke away, hook and all, and escaped.

We continued our journey northward.

# CHAPTER XI
## From Radak to Unalashka.

*The Journey Northward.*
*The Islands of St. Paul, St. George,*
*and St. Lawrence.*
*The Purpose of the Voyage Is Abandoned.*
*Sojourn in Unalashka.*

ON March 13, 1817, we had seen Udirik of Radak and on the 19th the last reef belonging to the domain of Polynesia; now we turned from a pleasant world to the gloomy north. The days became longer, the cold became noticeable, a foggy gray sky lowered itself above our heads, and the sea exchanged its deep azure color for a dirty green. On April 13, 1817, we caught sight of the Aleutian Islands. The real purpose of the journey now lay before us: beyond Unalashka our thoughts raced toward the Arctic Sea. With fresh minds and full of energy we all promised each other, officers and men, that now that we had had pleasure from nature, we would find joy within ourselves during this more serious segment of our voyage and our life.

The present was not without charm for me. The result of Kadu's statements about his known world, from the Pelew [Palau] Islands to Radak, can be perused by the reader in my "Notes and Opinions."[1] But to get what was written down there into words, to determine these facts, that was the task, that was the pleasurable torture of this period. First the medium of understanding had to be expanded, developed, and practiced. The language was composed of the dialects of Polynesia that Kadu spoke and a few European words and expressions. Kadu had to become accustomed to understanding, and, which was harder, to making himself understood. Concrete and historical things could soon be negotiated, and the narration was without difficulty. But what else did the curtain conceal? His answer never went beyond the question. Natural history books with illustrations settled many doubts about questionable objects. Further inquiries were made on the basis of the letter of Pater Cantova about the Carolines in the *Lettres édifiantes*.[2] Then Kadu's joyous astonishment was great when he heard so much about his native islands from our mouths. He confirmed, corrected; many a new connecting point presented itself, and every new path was diligently followed. But our friend also often caused us similar astonishment.

Once I was talking with Eschscholtz while Kadu seemed to be doz-
ing in his chair, and, as many strange expressions had become mixed
in our shipboard language, we were counting in Spanish. Then Kadu
began of his own accord to count in Spanish, very correctly and with
good pronunciation, from one to ten. That brought us to Mogemug
[Mogmog] and the last traces of Cantova's mission.[3] The land of
Waghal, which Kadu's songs told about, the land of iron, with rivers
and high mountains, a larger land inhabited by Europeans and visited by Caroline Islanders, long remained an enigma for us, and we
did not receive its certain solution until we were on Waghal itself,
that is, Guaján [Guam], where we immediately greeted Don Luis de
Torres with the song that glorifies his name on Ulea, which we
had learned from Kadu, who had sung it often on the heights of
Unalashka.

I beg the pardon of those whom I must contradict. My friend Kadu
was no anthropophagus, as fine as the word might sound, nor did he
ever regard us as cannibals who had taken him along as part of the
ship's provisions. He was a very understandable man, who, if he had
harbored this understandable suspicion, would never have so stubbornly insisted on traveling with us. Nor did he ever construe people
on horseback as centaurs. In both cases he can only have gone along
with a joke or have made a joke himself.

It is true that when he saw us fail to find the much closer Bigar,
toward the end of such a long-lasting voyage he began to wonder if
perhaps we had also lost the promised land of Unalashka. *"Emo
Bigar!"* ("No Bigar!") remained proverbial on the *Rurik*. Kadu observed the change of the stars in the sky attentively; the way some
stars rose in the north and others sank into the sea in the south; he
saw us observe the sun every midday and saw us steer according to
the compass. Repeatedly the land rose before us when, where, and
as we had predicted it; and then he learned to trust confidently in
our superior science and skill. These were naturally immeasurable
for him: How could he have been able to value and compare their
accomplishments and how judge what lay on the edge of their
domain? The information I gave him about balloons and travel by
airship did not seem any more incredible and fabulous to him than
that of a horse-drawn coach. But do we ourselves have any yardstick
for this judgment other than what we are accustomed to and not
accustomed to? Does not that which has become commonplace to
us seem by that very token to be unworthy of attention, and for the
very same reason does not that which has never been attained seem
unattainable? Does it not seem quite natural to us that a boy should
drive geese, and fabulous to talk about domesticating the whale?

In Unalashka and everywhere that we landed Kadu saw us pay attention to all the products of nature, investigate them, and collect them, and he understood much better than ignorant members of our own people the connection of this unlimited intellectual curiosity with the knowledge upon which our superiority rested. Once in the course of the voyage I happened to pull a human skull out from under my bunk. He looked at me questioningly, and in order to amuse themselves with his surprise, Eschscholtz and Choris did the same thing and moved toward him with skulls in their hands. "What is this?" he asked me, as was his custom. I had no trouble at all in getting across to him that we were interested in comparing the skulls of the variously formed human races and peoples with each other, and he promised me right off of his own volition to procure a skull from his tribe in Radak for me. The short time of our last stay on Otdia was filled with other cares, and there could be no question of his keeping his promise.

I shall give a short report of our voyage to Unalashka.

We headed toward the north and a little more to the west in order to reach the point where the previous year we had seen indications of land. On March 21 Waker's [Wake] Island seemed to lie to the northeast of us, but the wind was unfavorable for our reaching it. Many seafowl were seen whose flight in the evening, against the wind, crossed our course somewhat to the east. "They are going to the land to sleep," said Kadu. However, I noticed that not all the birds followed the same direction, and the deviating flight of others brought unreliability into our observations. The seafowl still accompanied us the next day.

On March 23 we lost the trade wind at 20°15'N latitude, 195°5'W longitude. In the next few days it was forced upon us that we were outside of the tropics. The unsteady wind increased to a gale one minute and the next died away to a complete calm. The cold at 15° Reaumur was perceptible.

On March 29 we were at 31°39'N latitude, 198°52'W longitude in the stretch of ocean where according to our former experience we supposed land to lie. Now nothing pointed in that direction. We now headed straight for Unalashka. From here until April 5, 35°35'N latitude, 191°49'W longitude, we had an exceptionally strong current against us, which drove us to the southwest twenty to thirty-five miles a day.

On the 30th we caught a pelican on the ship. We tacked about from March 31 to April 2, between 34° and 35°N latitude and 194° and 195°W longitude, against the north wind and the current in a dark green sea. Few seafowl and many whales were seen. These, although not unfamiliar to Kadu (we even saw a *Physeter* near the reefs of Radak), had an exceptional charm for him.

On April 3 we were becalmed. A "swimming head" (a fish, *Tetrodon mola* L., but which is no *Tetrodon*),[4] which seemed to rest motionless on the surface of the water, was harpooned by a boat sent out and provided the whole crew with very precious fresh food for several days. Its flesh is firm and very similar to crab in taste. As a precaution, because of the ambiguous relationship of this fish to *Tetrodon* species believed poisonous, we fed the liver and intestines to a hog. Numerous whales played around the ship. When they spume out water, a smooth mirrorlike surface remains on the water from the oil ejected.

On the 4th we headed eastward with a north wind. A heron circled over the ship and followed us for some time. Numerous flights of seafowl were seen. Driftwood and a cross of bamboo lashed together with cords drifted past us. Three swimming heads were seen.

On the morning of the 5th a second swimming head was harpooned. All of the flesh, cartilage, and skin were exceptionally strong in phosophorescence. After some days I could still tell the time on the clock at night in the glow of the maxillary bone that I had preserved. We had near calm all day long.

On the 9th, after we had sailed four days with varying winds without a midday observation, we found that we had been driven about one degree to the north of our ship's calculation by the current, which by then had shifted to the south.

The great storm at Unalashka of infamous memory became proverbial, and its memory lasted beyond the years of the voyage, at least in my family. Strangely, this storm seems to have brought some confusion in our chronology, which otherwise agrees.

Mr. von Kotzebue says:

> The 13th of April was the terrible day that destroyed my fondest hopes. On this day we were at 44°30′N latitude and 181°8′W longitude. On the 11th and 12th there was already a violent storm with snow and hail. In the night of the 12th to the 13th a hurricane broke loose. The waves, which had already been high enough, now towered up in gigantic masses, the like of which I have never seen. The *Rurik* suffered unbelievably. Right after midnight the fury of the hurricane increased to such a degree that it separated the tips of the waves from the sea and swept them across the surface of the sea in the form of a thick rain. I had just relieved Lieutenant Shishmarev: apart from me there were four seamen on deck, two of whom held the

wheel. The rest of the watch I had sent below for safety's sake. At 4:00 A.M. I was gazing in astonishment at the height of a raging wave when it suddenly came in the direction of the *Rurik* and knocked me down senseless at the same moment. The extreme pain I felt when I came to was deadened by the sad sight of my ship, which was close to destruction, which seemed inevitable if the hurricane lasted another hour; for not a corner of it had escaped that horrible wave. The first thing that struck my eye was the broken foremast (bowsprit), and you can imagine the force of the water, which broke in two a beam two feet in diameter with one blow. This loss was all the more important because the other two masts could not long withstand the way the ship was being hurled to and fro, and then no salvation was conceivable. The giant wave had broken a leg of one of my seamen; a boatswain's mate was hurled into the sea, but saved himself with great presence of mind by grasping a line that was dragging along next to the ship. The steering wheel was smashed, the two seamen who had held it were very badly hurt, and I myself had been hurled so that my chest struck a corner; I suffered very severe pains and had to stay in bed for several days. In this terrible storm I had the opportunity to admire the undismayed courage of our seamen; but no human power could provide help if it were not that, fortunately for seafarers, hurricanes never last long.[5]

In this part of the voyage, until the arrival in Unalashka, Choris is a day behind. I noted myself under date of April 15: "Friday, the 11th of April, the most violent storm we ever experienced began.— Extraordinary size of the waves.—On Saturday night (from the 11th to the 12th) one smashed the bowsprit. The storm lasted through Sunday. Not until Monday, the 14th, did the cabin become bright again. In the evening the wind again took on the force of a tempest. —On the 15th still very strong; but we do enjoy daylight. Today the first snow. In these days we got a lot out of Kadu."

After the wave had struck, the captain had the bilge water measured, lest the ship had suffered a leak from the great shaking-up it had received. This is done by lowering a plummet through one of the pipes of the pumps. The young boatswain's mate who had received the command, a man who did not stand out from our brave seamen by greater fearlessness, reported as pale as death that the ship was all full of water. The matter was too interesting not to be explored more carefully: it turned out that no water at all had penetrated into the ship; the line or the pipe had been wet.

I have lost among my papers a few stanzas that idleness inspired in me. I can only remember the first one, which may claim a place here for the sake of curiosity. Not many German verses are made on or in the vicinity of Unalashka.

> So wüthe Sturm, vollbringe nur dein Thun,
> Zerstreue diese Planken, wie den Mast,
> Den wohlgefügten, mächt'gen, eben nun
> Du leichten Spieles schon zersplittert hast!
> Da unten, mein' ich, wird ein Mensch doch ruhn;
> Da findet er von allen Stürmen Rast.
> Was kracht noch? Gut! die Welle schlug schon ein?
> Fahr' hin! es ist geschehn, wir sinken.—Nein,
>
> Wir sinken nicht! Geschaukelt wird annoch,
> Getragen himmelan der enge Sarg. . . .
>
> So rage, storm, complete your work,
> strew these planks about, even as
> you so easily split the mast,
> so well-fitted and mighty!
> Down below, I think, a man can find peace;
> there he will find rest from all storms.
> What is cracking now? Good! The wave has struck?
> Go away! It has happened, we are sinking.—No,
>
> We are not sinking! We are still being rocked about,
> our narrow coffin carried toward the sky. . . .

Kadu, who, another Odysseus, had led a very active and adventuresome life in the tropics on a stretch of ocean whose extent is approximately equal to the width of the Atlantic Ocean and had never seen the liquid azure of the water congeal, had never seen the luxuriant green of the forest wither, Kadu in these days first saw the water become a solid body and fall as snow. I believe that I had never before told him the gruesome tale of our winter so that he would not consider me a liar, at least until the sad fulfillment of my words.

On April 17 we promised our friend sight of land the next day, which we described to him with its high, craggy, and whitely gleaming peaks.[6] The wind abated, and the chain of the Aleutian Islands became visible for the first time on the evening of the 18th.

We found ourselves to the west of Unalashka. The snow had melted on the southern slopes. The whales that spend the summer here had still not arrived, the same ones, probably, that we had encountered between 45° and 47°N latitude. In this early season of the year in the north of the Great Ocean we had had much less prevailing fog than in the preceding year, when we had traversed the same extent of ocean in May and June.

On April 21 at sunset the snow-white peaks of Umnak afforded us a remarkably magnificent sight at sunset in a blood-red glow against a background of dark clouds. On this day we essayed the passage between Umnak and Unalashka. The wind changed and we lost all visibility in the thick snowfall. Our situation, it is said, was not without danger. "We could already calculate the hour of our destruction, when the wind suddenly changed and saved us," says Mr. von Kotzebue. During the night we reached the high seas south of Unalashka.

On the 22nd and 23rd, with bright weather and a weak breeze, which often left us entirely, we tried to reach the passage east of Unalashka. On the 24th we sailed before the wind, which began to pick up, through the strait between Unalashka and Unalga.[7] We had the current against us, which was rapid and comparable to surf. By a cannon shot we called a fourteen-paddle baidare that became visible. It reached us as we lay in calm around the edge of the cliff. The wind swelled to a gale, with never-ending thick snow. We dropped anchor in the bay and on the 25th were towed into the inner harbor where, close to the settlement of Illiuliuk, we dropped four anchors near the shore.

The past winter had distinguished itself from others by the extraordinary amount of snow that had fallen. It still lay deep on the slopes; nature had not yet awakened, not a plant was blooming except the cranberry *(Empterum nigrum)*, with wintry, dark, almost purple leaves.[8] Toward the middle of May the snow gradually drew back to the hills. Toward the 24th the sun lured out the first flowers, the anemones, the orchids. Toward the end of May fresh snow fell, which stayed on the mountains for some time, and the nights were freezing. With July the time of blossoming began.

The ship, its bowsprit broken close to the foot, its other masts damaged, its rigging rotting, its copper sheathing torn away so as to hinder its progress, had to be unloaded, re-rigged, and its keel resheathed. The old bowsprit, shortened and spliced together, had to be put into condition to carry out its service. There was a lot to be done, and the work was started without delay.

What the captain had requested as equipment on our second northern journey was partly ready, partly being taken care of, and soon was finished. On May 27 two interpreters arrived from Kadiak who spoke the dialects of the more northern coastal tribes of America, with whom they had lived, and seemed to be understanding, useful people in other respects as well.

The captain had gone ashore to reside with Mr. Kriukov, the agent of the company, and we maintained our table there. We ourselves resided on board the ship. Every Saturday the pleasurable steam bath is heated.

We lived mostly on fish (salmon and a giant flounder). Indeed, indeed! the worst food you can find. A large crab *(Maja vulgaris)* was the best thing that came to our table, and really good.[9] We craved vegetable nourishment. The only vegetable we had enough of was a large turnip. When it was thoroughly boiled in water we thought it tasted fine. Otherwise we seek out wild plants: a few umbrella plants, a few cross flowers, some varieties of sorrel, and the young shoots of *Uvullaria amplexifolia*, which taste like cucumbers.[10] Later in the year we had various berries, especially an exceptionally fine-looking but not very tasty raspberry *(Rubus spectabilis).*[11] The Russians and Aleuts eat the stems of *Heracleum*, which grows in abundance in the mountain valleys, wherever they find it.[12] Mr. Kriukov had a head of cattle butchered for us from his little herd. We tasted preserved whale meat a few times. For us it was a poor, yet edible food. But what could not be eaten, and was really carried away from our table uneaten, seems to me worthy of mention.

We had saved a pregnant sow from our O-Waihian animals as a gift for Unalashka, where to be sure there already were hogs, and meant it for another part of the island, Makushkin. The beast, which gave birth in the first days of our sojourn here, was fed with fish. One of the little pigs came onto our table. The mother's food had imparted a more intolerable fish stench to the flesh than we had ever experienced in seafowl or sea mammals.

We had discussed the fact that with respect to our table and our provisions the arrangements left things to be desired. Pantry and cellar were not in the condition they should have been in. In order to get things straightened out the office of stewardess was awarded to our own Choris, who had inclination and talent for this role, and subsequently we were quite pleased with this agreement. When we left Unalashka in August Choris provided us with a supply of seafowl eggs and salted sorrel that we continued to enjoy in the tropics. In Hana-ruru and Manila he obtained from other benevolent ship captains many a spice and adjunct to our meals that previously had been lacking. From time to time he had fresh bread baked on the *Rurik*, etc. All things that are more pleasant at sea than one can believe on land. At the same time he was very economical with his expenditures. But friend Login Andrevich began the reforms he was introducing with an all-pervasive zeal, manifesting the importance of his new position in a way that did not entirely strike my fancy. That is, I found when I came down from the mountains in the evening, where I, in pursuance of my duties, had been botanizing, and had missed the dinner hour, that the cupboards were all locked, and orders had been issued that a piece of biscuit and a swallow of brandy, which was the extent of my modest request, should be made inaccessible to me. And that is the way it was to stay. There are no inns and restaurants on Unalashka. I could not be satisfied with the new order. I believe that our good Sikov, who was also an authority on board ship, interceded for me and bent the reformer's intractability in my favor. The affair improved by itself, and I no longer had to fear hunger.

Mr. Kriukov proved to be of an exceedingly obliging subservience toward the captain both in official and unofficial matters. He had served him, the more powerful of the two, to the detriment of Choris' claims, and the latter did not forget this and gladly seized the opportunities that presented themselves to step on his corns. My memories of Unalashka are as depressing as those of Radak are happy. I should like to draw the curtain over this dirty material.

The customary gift that is made to a ship's captain here—other notables probably never go astray on this island—consists of a very finely made kamleika, the trimmings of which are really worthy of admiration. This gift costs the managers only the labor of the poor Aleutian girls, who get nothing for it but a few sewing needles and— held in as high esteem as gold and jewels—a piece of red frieze the size of a hand. However, half of it is used up on the kamleika itself. The seams are elegantly trimmed with a very fine frieze fringe.

Kriukov had not failed to promise a kamleika to the captain and his lieutenant and finally to each of his passengers. It later occurred to him that there was no good reason to undergo expenses for my sake. The others received their gifts, but I was passed over. Login Andrevich perceived the situation and told him with a certain authority that he knew how to put on, that he shouldn't forget Adelbert Loginovich. I afterwards received my kamleika, and Login Andrevich received my thanks for it.

Kriukov told Mr. von Kotzebue of a hundred-year-old Aleut who lived on the island. At the wish of the Russian captain the old man was invited to visit us and came before him from his distant dwelling place. An almost mythical figure from the time when they had their freedom, towering above the fate of his people, now blind and broken from old age. The captain, a powerful commander on this Russian island, let him be assured of his favor; whatever was in his power he would do for him. He should take courage and express his boldest wish that had remained unfulfilled all his long life. The old man asked for a shirt—he had never possessed one.

During our sojourn on Unalashka the Aleuts shot birds and stuffed them for us. The Berlin Museum owes to Mr. von Kotzebue and his zeal for science the considerable collection of northern seafowl and predatory birds that it received from me. Without the help of the captain and the command he issued I would have been able to do and collect little for ornithology, especially as I had given up my double-barreled musket to the governor of Kamchatka. (Incidentally, I was prevented from collecting the agreed price for the gun because of the changed plan of the voyage.) A few large boxes of stuffed birds were packed in Unalashka. Whenever during the voyage my bunk was filled to the brim with what I had collected, the captain had packing boxes made that he stored away well-packed, nailed shut, and sealed with pitch.

I had the most experienced Aleuts construct and explain the whale models that I presented to the Berlin Museum and depicted, described, and discussed in the *Transactions of the Academy of Natural Scientists.*[13] For this area of zoology every bit of information is valuable. After our return to Unalashka a whale of the species *Aliomoch* was dissected in our vicinity by the Aleuts. This unappetizing work is carried out so busily by so many people that the natural scientist feels no obligation to interfere. We brought the beast's skull to St. Petersburg.

Firewood is sadly lacking on Unalashka. No trees grow there and no great amount of driftwood is washed ashore. Peat would replace this deficiency, but the people do not know how to find and use it. It is more a lack of technology than of nature. At the time I had not yet investigated a peat bog and had yet to write about peat.[14] I would now know how to find the peat under the grass and moss with more certainty and would counter with emphatic advice the prejudice that makes it so hard for people to do what they have never done before.

I shall add a *feuilleton* to the natural history newspaper above. A son of Kriukov's, a good-natured boy, had come from Unalashka to Unimak—that was the world for him. He had seen trees there; why, he had even clambered up on a tree and had swayed on its branches. He told us this with great pride but also with no little fear of being thought a liar because of the strange story, and he took great pains to explain to us in a credible manner what a tree is.

On the Aleutian islands there are no amphibians, and the natural history of Unalashka knows nothing of frogs. Nevertheless, once in the Chinese sugar syrup, which is used there, a well-preserved large frog appeared. This had happened many years ago, but it was still talked about, and people still were at odds as to whether it had been a little human being, a kind of savage, a young forest demon, or some other creature.

I spent my days in the mountains. Kadu, after he had ceased to regard the sea-kale of these latitudes *(Fucus esculentus)* as banana leaves and had reluctantly allowed himself to be convinced that it would be a vain effort to plant coconuts on this inhospitable strand, collected nails and discarded iron in the harbor for his friends in Radak, carefully selected from the tide-washed rubble those stones that were best adapted for whetstones, followed the cattle in the meadow, and sat down on the closest hills and sang himself songs of Ulea and Radak.

He asked to learn how to handle our firearms, and Eschscholtz undertook the instruction. For this purpose an old musket in poor condition was provided by the ship. When our friend took his first shot, the powder slowly burned out of the vent, while he remained in firing position, not knowing what he had done wrong so as not to get the same loud report that the captain had obtained. I do not know whether or not the instruction was again undertaken with a better gun; but at least our peaceful friend Kadu never did become a marksman.

We had taken aboard a son of Mr. Kriukov's and fifteen Aleuts; baidares, large and small; salted and dried fish (cod). The *Rurik* was ready to sail. We had waited in vain for the arrival of a ship from Sitka to provide us a number of things we were lacking. Contrary winds kept us back in the harbor a few days, at the entrance of which we lay at anchor in calm on the dividing line between two opposite winds. Before us the wind blew from the sea, behind us on the other hand, in the inner harbor between the little island and the mainland, toward the sea. On Sunday, June 29, 1817, according to ship's reckoning (a day later according to the island's reckoning), we got under way.

On our northern journey we were to be provided with many things we lacked on the islands of St. George and St. Paul by the agents of the company who manage the settlements there under Mr. Kriukov, at his direction. On both islands, which lie isolated in the bay to the north of the Aleutian chain and were otherwise uninhabited, the herds of sea lions and ursine seals that occupy the shore are exploited by a few Russians and several transferred Aleuts, and the company extracts a considerable and sure yield from them. Both islands are without harbor or anchorage.

With bright weather and a favorable wind on the afternoon of June 30 we caught sight of the island of St. George, approached it, made our presence known by a cannon shot, and tacked about through the night. On the morning of July 1 the settlement's large baidare took us ashore. We observed the very strange sight of an extensive herd of sea lions *(Leo marinus Stelleri)*, which, as far as the eye could see, encircling the island up to the settlement, covered a broad, rocky, bare, fat-blackened belt of the beach.[15] Shapeless, gigantic masses of fat and flesh, awkward and ponderous on land. The males guard their females and fight each other furiously for their possession: they follow the victor. Their roar is heard six miles out to sea. One can walk up to within a few steps of them. They merely turn toward people and roar at them. During the time that Kadu spent with us, nothing so captivated him and made a deeper impression upon him than the sight of these animals. He joined me when I went to view them but always kept a few paces behind me. Old males are killed, mostly for their hides, which are used for covering baidares. Their entrails are also used for kamleikas. The young are slaughtered for their flesh, which we found not to be at all bad tasting. A few people armed with sticks drive the old animals off, and the young, cut off from the sea, are driven inland to the spot where they are to be dispatched. A child drives a herd of twelve to twenty before him. Old animals are shot with a gun: there is only one spot on the head where the shot is deadly. St. George and St. Paul are called the islands of the ursine seals by the Russians, because this animal yields them the greater profit. But St. George is the island of the sea lion. Only a few families of the ursine seals occupy separate spots on the beach. A few young sea lions were slaughtered for us and our crew, and we also increased our larder by a few kegs of eggs, which stay fresh for a long time when packed in oil. The nests for the seafowl that have their breeding places here are regularly plundered, and the people deal in seals and birds as if they owned them.

On that same evening we had sight first of Bober Island, a cliff in the vicinity of St. Paul, and then of this island itself. St. George and St. Paul lie in such proximity to each other that one can be seen from the other. On July 2 in a calm with fog and rain we lay to in the vicinity of Bober Island. The sea was dark and dirty. Frequent blobs of fat on it shone with the colors of the rainbow. The baidares of St. Paul came and went between the land and the ship. From the *Rurik* not a boat, not a baidare, was loaded into the sea. In the afternoon a weak breath of air came up; we sailed past the crag and approached the main island. Early in the morning of the 3rd a cannon shot announced to the settlement that we were in its vicinity. A baidare paddled out right away, and we went ashore on it. Choris and Kadu missed their chance this time and stayed behind on the *Rurik*.

The island of St. Paul maintains its greatest importance from the ursine seals *(Ursus marinus Stelleri)* and at the time when the females bear their young has its beach covered with endless herds. The skin of the young seals is prized as fur and finds a sure market and fixed prices in Canton. The male is twice the size of the female, which also is differentiated by shape and color. Male and young are darker, the young paler. I have brought back skulls of both sexes: they deviate very much from each other in shape, yet the difference in size seems less than that of the animals themselves. The skull of the male is more rounded, that of the female flatter, with greater prominence of the apophyses and edges that form the cavities of the eyes. The ursine seal is more supple than the sea lion and moves rapidly and with greater ease than the former. The male surveys the circle of his family from a raised seat and jealously guards his mates. Some possess only one or a few, while others rule over half a hundred, more or less. The female bears two young, which come into the world with teeth in both jaws. The mother does not bite the umbilical cord off, and the young animals are seen dragging the afterbirth along after them for a long time. I observed and petted such a newborn calf: he opened his eyes and took up an attitude of defense toward me, rising on his hind legs and showing me very pretty teeth. At the same time the *pater familias* took notice of me and started out toward me:

"*Et qui vous a chargé du soin de ma famille!*"[16] I assured him that I had no evil intent, but took leave and walked on.

The seafowl *(Uria)* take up the open spaces between the families of seals.[17] Without any timidity they fly right through the herd and right up to the jaws of the males on guard, without heeding their roar. They nest in innumerable droves in the caves of the tide-swept walls of the cliffs and under the rolled stones that build a dam along the beach. The crest of this dam is colored white from their ordure.

Once an American ship is said to have appeared before St. Paul, whose captain went ashore with a large detail, bringing brandy, with which he was not at all stingy. Russians and Aleuts drank all they wanted, but the generous friend used the time afterwards, when they slept, to slaughter and skin; in this way he acquired his cargo. In such cases, when there is no time to dry the hides, they are salted down, from which they are said to lose none of their value.

Our captain had brought a compass ashore in order to be informed of the exact direction in which it was thought that volcanic phenomena and land could be seen on the high seas both from St. George and from here. The magnetic needle was found to be very unstable on this soil of volcanic iron slag. But there was a point where it remained stable and from where the direction of those phenomena was determined as SW by W. In this very direction at noon on July 4 we were sixty miles distant from St. Paul with bright weather and a clear horizon, and no land was to be seen. Then we headed north in order to reach the eastern tip of St. Lawrence Island.

The days were mostly overcast with alternating winds and calms. On July 9 we had crossed the latitude of St. Matwey Island, without desiring to see it, and the next day, when the wind became more favorable, we were to catch sight of St. Lawrence Island. We informed our friend Kadu of this. We had seen whales, and quite a few seals, while on this evening some sea lions seemed to be following the course of our ship. In this sea without depth, where we often cast the plummet, several codfish *(Gadus)* took the hook, providing us with fresh sustenance.

On the morning of July 10 we saw land and headed toward the southern cape of St. Lawrence Island. The view is of a group of moderately high islands bounded by unpretentious ridges and having a precipitous coastline. But low-lying lands unite all these rocky islands, and in some places they stretch away from them far out to sea. On these flats are the human settlements, where the people drink the snow water that collects in standing puddles and lakes. We dropped anchor, and in the afternoon we went to a settlement ashore. We had armed ourselves. Kadu, outraged at this, asked us what we were thinking of. But when he had perceived that our intentions were peaceful, and that we were just providing for our safety among strangers, he got himself a saber and joined the captain.

Only men of fighting age came toward us self-confidently, while the women and children were taken away. Our interpreters made themselves understood. They spoke words of peace, and tobacco and beads formed the basis for a friendly relationship. The men had tattooed lines around the face, along with some symbols on forehead and cheeks. The "mouth buttons" were rare, and often replaced by a tattooed spot.[18] They were shaven on the crown of the head and wore a wreath of longish hair around their heads (the Aleuts do not cut their hair off). They do not possess the reindeer. For coastal journeys their dogs are hitched to their baidares. They obtain their wares from the Chukchis, with whom they have trading connections.

We did not enter their dwellings. We saw their earthen yurtas along the beach, surrounded by the usual scaffolding, and the holes for their dogs are underneath. Skin tents were their summer dwellings.

We learned that the ice had broken up only three days ago (five days, according to my own notes) and was floating northward with the current.

We went back to the ship and went under way, in order to sail around the island from the eastern side.

On the morning of July 11 we tacked about in bright weather and a southern wind. I learned that during the night ice had been encountered near the eastern tip of the island and that the captain was suffering from a chest ailment and had taken to his bed.

On the 12th the captain told us and the crew in writing that he was abandoning the purpose of the voyage because of his impaired health and must use what remained of it to lead us back home. Accordingly we had only to do in reverse what we had already done. Here are Mr. von Kotzebue's words in his narrative:

> At twelve o'clock at night, just as we were about to cast anchor by the northern cape, to our horror we saw standing ice that, as far as the eye could reach, stretched out toward the northeast and covered the whole surface of the sea. My sorry condition, which became worse daily since we left Unalashka, here suffered the final blow. The cold air attacked my ailing chest in such a way that I could not catch my breath, and finally chest cramps, loss of consciousness, and spitting-up of blood took place. I now understood for the first time that my condition was more dangerous than I had wanted to believe up until now, and the physician declared earnestly that I could not remain in the vicinity of the ice. It cost me a long painful struggle. More than once I was resolved to defy death and carry out my mission, but when I considered that we still faced a difficult return voyage to our homeland, that the preservation of the *Rurik* and the lives of my companions were perhaps dependent on my preserving mine: then I felt that I had to suppress my ambition. The only thing that kept me on an even keel in this struggle was the calming conviction of having honestly fulfilled my duty. I informed the crew in writing that my illness forced me to return to Unalashka. The moment in which I signed the paper was one of the most painful of my life; for with this stroke of the pen I gave up an ardent, heartfelt wish that I had long cherished.[19]

And I myself cannot touch upon this unhappy event without the most painful feeling. Event, yes, more than a deed! Mr. von Kotzebue was in a state of ill health, that is the truth, and this condition perfectly explains the command that he signed. Explains, I say, but whether it justifies it or not, is a question that must be discussed. A competent judge says this about it in the *Quarterly Review* for January 1822:

> We have little more to offer on this unsuccessful Voyage, but it appears to us that its abrupt abandonment was hardly justified under the circumstances stated. It would not be tolerated in England, that the ill health of the commanding officer should be urged as a plea for giving up an enterprise of moment, while there remained an other officer on board fit to succeed him. But we rather suspect that when the physician warned him against approaching the ice, the caution was not wholly disinterested on his part, and that the officers and men, like the successors of the immortal Cook, had come to the conclusion that the longest way about was the nearest way home.[20]

This is also my opinion. However, the same judge's suspicions are unwarranted that officers and men encouraged the command because of discouragement. For my part, I received Mr. von Kotzebue's command with painful outrage and wrapped myself up in my instructions: "A passenger on board a warship, where it is not usual to have any, must make no demands."

I also thought I saw the same thing that was going on inside of me in the silent, downcast faces around me under the veil of their customary subordination. As far as Dr. Eschscholtz's medical opinion is concerned, the latter has taken the responsibility for it; more cannot be said.

At that time I deeply pitied Mr. von Kotzebue in his infirmity because a procedure that I seem to have observed under similar circumstances in ships of other nations presumably was not part of Russian naval custom, so that the decision he made was not discussed, was not acknowledged to be necessary and justified by a council of war to which everyone entitled to vote should be drawn. For a while I hoped that Mr. von Kotzebue, controlling the onslaught of his illness, would change his mind and rescind the command he had given. In so doing he would have demonstrated strength of character, and I would have bowed before him in humility.

But let us not forget that, although the *Rurik* flew the Imperial Navy's flag, ship, captain, and crew acknowledged only Count Romanzov as authority; that Count Romanzov had equipped the expedition; and that to him alone was it necessary to give an accounting. Mr. von Kotzebue did give an accounting to Count Romanzov, from whom his instructions were issued, and gave him complete satisfaction. Consequently, what Count Romanzov has called good is good, and the question as to what might have been is purely academic.

But now you demand (and after what I have said you have the

right to demand) that I answer the question for you out of my own wisdom and tell you what else I think might have been done. Frankly, not much. With a single serviceable officer and two petty officers (the third could not be counted on at the time for reasons that are here irrelevant), we were very weak, and if in the night of July 10 to July 11 the ice was found to be still standing between St. Lawrence Island and the American coast, then this summer might have been more unfavorable than the preceding one.

We could have spent the next few days in the vicinity of St. Matwey Island. The ice that was drifting northward with the current did not threaten us with any danger. We could have followed it on the Asiatic side of St. Lawrence Island and here collected anticipatory results of what we were destined to encounter in the north. St. Lawrence Bay offered us a safe harbor and valuable provisions. We could have lived on reindeer meat there, stocked up on reindeer meat, and awaited the time when Kotzebue Sound, freed of ice, could have become accessible to the *Rurik*. Here near the ship the ill captain could have rested just as well as he could in Unalashka, while he could have transferred the command of the northern journey by baidares to Lieutenant Shishmarev. I am of the firm opinion that in the worst conceivable case a petty officer would have sufficed perfectly to sail the ship into the harbor of St. Peter and Paul. I hope that I will be spared any further elucidation, which is outside of my sphere, anyway.

With varying winds, and mostly wrapped in fog, we made our way to Unalashka. We went past the islands of St. Matwey, St. Paul, and St. George without seeing them. On July 20 in the vicinity of Unalashka we ran over two whales of the species *Kuliomoch*. They were of very different size; their skin was smooth; only the protuberance on the front of the head and the outer edge of the flap of the very large and only slightly separated spout-holes were spongy. They were hit by three spears from our Aleuts without paying much attention to them. They spouted little water, and I could perceive no odor, even though I was looking for it. The jolt from the collision, which was felt below, was not perceptible on deck.

On the morning of the 21st a few sea lions appeared around the ship. In the afternoon we discovered Unalashka a slight distance away under the cloak of fog. We lay becalmed. We had our boats tow us in. We arrived at night, and on the morning of July 22, 1817, we lay at anchor in the harbor of Unalashka.

This time the ship stayed far off shore. The captain moved in with the agent Kriukov again. We dined aboard the *Rurik* and drank tea ashore.

The captain informed us of our itinerary: the Sandwich Islands, Radak, Ralik and the Carolines, Manila, the Sunda Strait, the Cape of Good Hope, and Europe. "The lack of fresh stores and the poor condition of the *Rurik*, which was in need of thorough repairs, did not permit me to return home through the Torres Strait, in accordance with my instructions," wrote Mr. von Kotzebue.[21] The Sandwich Islands provided us with a surplus of fresh foodstuffs.

We were supposed to find letters from home at St. Peter and Paul and again have the opportunity to write home. We entrenched ourselves in Unalashka, lost to the world, unloaded what we had taken aboard as equipment for our trip north, baked the flour we had taken aboard in San Francisco into biscuits, which were threatening to run out on us, and spent the time as if we were in a den of corruption.

I shall describe a small trip that I had the chance to take into the interior of the island. A hog that had been butchered for the *Rurik* in Makushkin played the chief role in this expedition and was the important personage whose retinue I was allowed to join. The whole mountain mass over which the volcano of Unalashka, Makushkeia Sobka, arises lies between Illiuliuk and Makushkin. Two inlets of the sea of fjords come toward each other in different directions and make a peninsula out of that section of the mountain range. But to cross the tongue of land from one fjord to the other by way of mountain valleys and passes that extend into the snow region takes at least eight hours. I started out at six in the morning on August 1 with two Aleuts and a Russian boy. At eight o'clock we reached the back of Captain's Bay, the fjord on which Illiuliuk lies, and from there started on foot up the valley. There is no real path; the mountain stream to whose source one ascends leads one through the wilderness. One must often cross it, and undress for a cold bath in churning snow water that reaches up to above the waist. The customary covering for feet and legs, the *tarbassi*, which, although always damp, allows no water to penetrate, allows one to wade through more shallow waters without undressing.[22] In the lower valley the grass is luxurious and handicaps the walker. At the snow border many a plant attracted my attention, and, not realizing the length of the way, I did not accelerate the march as I should have. The valley on the other side leads through deep swamps to the sea. Night fell when we reached the beach. I thought I was already at Makushkin, but the path follows the beach in a part of the circumference of the island, and behind every point of land one reaches in the hope of arriving at Makushkin one sees another tongue of land extending, which arouses a similar deceptive hope. It was eleven o'clock at night when we arrived. I was known as a vigorous hiker, and what I have achieved as such hardly anyone will be able to imitate; but I have never endured a more fatiguing day's march than the one just described. Everyone was asleep. The Russian in command here, to whose house I turned, received me in a most hospitable manner. But it was too late to heat the bath, and he had nothing to set before me but tea without brandy, without sugar, and without milk, which drink he urged me to imbibe as if it were malmsey. Good Sanin, as my host was called, gave me his bed, and that was the best thing that he could give me.

On the 2nd I enjoyed the steam bath, rested, and leisurely explored the hills around the settlement and the hot spring that there on the beach bubbled forth from the rock below the level of the water at high tide. A valley lies between the settlement and the foot of the snow-capped mountain range that forms the foundation for the peak of Makushkin. This wintry wilderness affords one a terrifying sight. A secondary peak constantly gives off smoke, but you only perceive it when the wind drives it to the side on which you are standing.

Sanin himself provided a caravan of bearers to bring the butchered hog to the harbor. The bad weather delayed the departure a day, which I used to wander around the area. We started out early in the morning of the 4th. The large baidare of the settlement brought us to the rear of the fjord, from where the way by land is shorter across the narrowest part of the peninsula than the one that I took on the way out. I believe I have said that these large baidares are called "women's boats": Aleutian girls were our paddlers. Poor creatures! Misery, disease, dirt, vermin, and ugliness do not exclude a certain tender elegance of manners, and a gift that I possess from them touched me more than testimonials from kings could do. At the place where we landed in good time in the afternoon we immediately set up our camp. Lying under the baidare I observed my cap, which was torn, and perceiving a chance to have the damage repaired, I stuck three sewing needles in it and handed it to the closest girl and called her attention to what I wanted from her. Three sewing needles! Such a treasure for nothing! An inexpressible joy shone in her eyes. All the girls came up to admire the needles, to congratulate the favored one, and some seemed to contemplate their own misery with sadness. Then I made them all joyful, and gave each one three needles. We started out early the next morning and were in Illiuliuk at three o'clock. Here Sanin handed me the return present of the grateful girls, which he was commissioned to hand me only after we had arrived at our destination. A ball of animal sinew twine they had made.

I have seen Aleutian girls examine a brocade shirt button, consult among themselves about it, and finally imitate the delicate thing in such a way that their imitation was found worthy of being fastened to the captain's shirt.

I have seen Radak women consult about a fabric of our manufacture, about a straw hat, seen them observe and discuss the material and workmanship and debate the question as to whether it would be possible for them to produce such a thing.

I have seen my wife and her companions endeavor to solve the riddle of the decorative knots on English suspenders. Everywhere I have seen women busy themselves with finery in order to deck out the works of their hands without sparing time, effort, and thought and to deal with ornaments for men as well as for themselves. However, whenever I have seen this abroad, I have always drawn a good deal of pleasure from it.

To strengthen the crew of the *Rurik* Mr. von Kotzebue retained some, I think four, of the Aleuts we had taken on our northward journey. Among these there was a young alert fellow of cheerful disposition and good intellect with whom Eschscholtz got along well and with whose help he had undertaken to shed light on the language of the Aleuts, which he had already identified as a dialect of the Eskimo language family. I took pleasure in his investigation, with the results of which he made me acquainted. But to complete the work he had begun, a work that would have filled a recognized need of linguistics, and to derive profit from what he had already determined, one thing was necessary: Dr. Eschscholtz in Europe, where grammars and lexica could be compared, without losing the assistance of his language instructor.

I have often had occasion to lament that after profligate amounts have been spent to obtain data, no thought is ever given to making the data useful, and that even the slightest contribution for preserving them is stingily denied. Ostentation purchases the most expensive materials; it equips collectors and sends out travelers; but that which is so expensively obtained and carefully stored is carelessly left to destruction. The ostentation that equipped the traveler sometimes provides for the publication of a book; everyone can make demands according to the measure of what it cost; but if someone or something is volunteered gratis, he or it is disdained. I once heard a young woman in Berlin say that artificial roses were much more beautiful than the real ones, because they cost much more. That is a great chapter in the history of mankind.

But I was about to speak of the Aleutian language. As soon as we arrived in St. Petersburg the young man was again, together with the other Aleuts, handed over to the Russian–American Trading Company, and there was no further mention of the worthwhile work that Eschscholtz wanted to take on and that scholarship would gratefully reckon to the fame of the Romanzov expedition.

Perhaps it will be characteristic in more than one respect to confess that I myself have learned and remembered only a single word of the Aleutian language: *kitung* (i.e., *pediculus*). And, with respect to the word *kitung*, casting a last look at the gloomy north in parting, I shall note for the sake of completeness that during our northern journey in the years 1816 and 1817 the above-mentioned was nothing rare on the *Rurik*, to combat which Ivan Ivanovich secretly dispensed something from a small pitcher that did good service.

On August 18, 1817, we left Unalashka for the third and last time.

# CHAPTER XII

## From Unalashka to the Sandwich Islands. Second Sojourn There.

LEAVING the harbor of Unalashka on August 18, 1817, we again sought to reach the channel between Unimak and Akun as the most convenient strait to gain access to the Great Ocean through the chain of the Aleutian Islands. Calms and headwinds held us up; we did not effect our passage until the 20th. Two whales of the species *Aliomoch* came very close to the ship. On the morning of the 21st we lay in a dead calm and looked toward the North for the last time at the chain of volcanic mountains that comprise the Aleutian Islands. The two peaks of the Alaskan Peninsula rose high above the clouds into the clear sky and seemed incomparably higher to us than the peak of Unimak, which was much closer to us. In the evening the wind came up and conveyed us toward the south. The gloomy rainy sky of this stretch of ocean closed in on us.

We, however, were tired. The hopes of our journey lay behind us as memories. We were not proceeding onward with any new hopes. It only remained for us to reread some of the known chapters, and home was the goal of our long journey. The captain's ill health and the irritable mood that this imposed upon him often deprived the little world in which we lived of its everyday cheer.

From August 23 until September 10 we struggled against prevailing and often stormy south winds without seeing the sun. The temperature gradually became milder, and we stopped maintaining a fire, which was necessary at all times in Unalashka. A porpoise of a magnificent species that we hadn't seen before, and which our Aleuts said was not native to their seas, was harpooned in the vicinity of the 44th degree of north latitude. The skull, like that of all the porpoises we caught, is now the property of the zootomic museum in Berlin. Choris kept the drawing he made; my notations were never used. A little farther south, with a strong wind and a restless sea, we noticed a number of spots where the surface of the water was as smooth as a mirror, the way it is in a dead calm. Our very experienced Aleut Afzenikov interpreted this phenomenon as the result of the oil from a whale decomposing on the bottom of the sea, which was in agreement with my own supposition.

On September 10 the wind shifted to the north and the weather cleared. At noon we were at 40°10′N latitude, 147°18′W longitude, and in eighteen days the current had borne us five degrees to the east of our calculations. We had varying and often recurring calms until the 23rd, when the trade wind set in (26°41′N latitude, 152°32′W longitude). Two days earlier, about one degree farther toward the north, snipes had flown around the ship.

On September 25 we expected to see O-Waihi, but it was shrouded in clouds. On the morning of the 26th Mauna Kea became visible, first through the clouds, then above them. Not until after nightfall did we come close to land. A thick layer of clouds rested above the heights of the island and even above Mauna Puoray.[1] A chain of signal fires was ignited, extending from Puoray toward Mauna Kea. We sailed pass the northwest tip of the island during the night. The clouds dissolved, and on the morning of the 27th the weather was extremely fair. We now enjoyed calm or light, playful breezes. Only two canoes paddled toward us. In the first a woman sat all alone, and it was turned away. In the second were some male natives. We discovered only that Tameiameia was in O-Waihi. The captain busied himself repeatedly with the measurement of the heights of the mountains.

On the morning of the 28th we were sailing past the foot of Wororai when at ten o'clock Mr. Elliot de Castro came after us in his canoe and overtook us. We had already left Powarua behind us, the place where the king was sojourning and amusing himself with catching bonito.[2] Mr. Elliot took the captain and us passengers of the *Rurik*, among whom Kadu was numbered, aboard his canoe, and we paddled toward land.

Kadu, whose curiosity was greatly aroused by everything he saw and heard, now for the first and only time saw us show respect to someone more powerful than ourselves, and this mighty one was a man of his race and his color. He was presented to the king, who showed him some attention and had him tell him about the islands that he had left to follow us. On this occasion our friend was shy, but quite poised and well-mannered. The O-Waihians were kind and obliging to him, and he mixed happily with the people.

Powarua lies at the foot of Wororai in the middle of the lava flow that the mountain last spewed forth. Round about, the glassy, shiny ground is bare and unscarred. To the side on the beach a few red-flowered *Cordia sebestena* have taken root—the only vegetation.[3]

Everything for sustaining life must be brought here from afar. The king seems to have made a strange choice in this place to set up his pleasure camp for bonito fishing. He himself, his wives, and his most powerful subjects, whom he likes to have gathered around him, live here, unseemingly deprived of all luxury, under low straw roofs.

When we landed the king had not as yet returned from bonito fishing. This form of fishing, like our upper-class hunts, is a royal pleasure. It has often been described. The canoe is maintained at its greatest speed by the full force of the paddles. At the rear the fisher sits and causes the mother-of-pearl hook to hover on the surface of the sea, at the same time sprinkling it with water. The fish must be deceived and himself jump out of the water to swallow the hook, which seems alive to him.

We visited the queen, who lounged under a linen canopy and divided some watermelons with us. The taboos that apply to eating do not extend to the eating of fruits, which are considered to be like drinks.

The king came, naked except for his maro. He welcomed us cordially as old acquaintances. The latest events on Atuai and O-Wahu, of which we heard more on the latter island, had changed the state of affairs in our favor.

Two bonitos were carried along behind the king. In a fine gesture he gave the captain the fish that he himself had caught, just as one of our hunters would give away the game that he shot. He donned the red vest we had seen him wear the year before, breakfasted, and conversed with the captain as he did so. Mr. Elliot was the interpreter—at this time Mr. Cook was no longer in the king's favor. As in the previous year, Tameiameia sent a noble along with us. His name was Kareimoku, but one must not confuse him with the powerful Kareimoku who is the king's representative on O-Wahu.[4] Birth is certainly important here, and one could speak of families, but there are no family names yet. Even in our land the name was not attached to the coat of arms until late, and the latter, the sign of the family, is of a later origin than the family itself. Kareimoku was the transmitter of the royal command: we should be received as we were in the preceding year, and given as many supplies as in the preceding year. The king asked only iron from us, a commodity he needed for ship construction.

We took ship again on September 28, and, as on the previous occasion, we took our way southward to O-Wahu along the beautiful chain of islands. We were becalmed below Ranai [Lana'i]. On October 1 we beheld O-Wahu at daybreak. An American brig came from the north between Morotai [Moloka'i] and O-Wahu and sailed along with us toward the harbor. Many canoes paddled toward us. At 5:00 P.M. we cast anchor outside of the harbor and the captain went ashore, having been preceded by our escort.

Seven ships were anchored in the harbor, the eighth came right along with us, and they were all American. Only one old ship of the Russian-American company, the *Kadiak*, lay on the beach.[5] Kareimoku was expecting yet another ship, a handsome schooner, which, under the command of Mr. Bekley, commandant of the fortress here, was transporting sandalwood from Atuai.[6] Most ships were after sandalwood. For the sake of this trade the chiefs were burdening the people with feudal service that is detrimental to agriculture and industry. There was a bustling activity in Hana-ruru.

Dr. Scheffer had left Atuai, and Tamari was again paying homage to his feudal lord. I heard conflicting accounts of the incident. The one I am noting here I have borrowed from Mr. von Kotzebue.[7] He reports that Kareimoku told him that the king and the people of Atuai had driven Dr. Scheffer out and that he and his crew, consisting of a hundred Aleuts and a few Russians, had recently arrived in Hana-ruru on the *Kadiak*. The ship was leaking badly, and the refugees had had to beach it as soon as they reached the harbor, which they had barely been able to do. He had not returned evil for the evil tendered him, but rather received the Aleuts and the Russians kindly and even allowed Scheffer to depart unhindered on an American ship that sailed away to Canton a few days ago. Mr. von Kotzebue adds:

> Mr. Tarakanov, agent of the Russian-American company, came aboard with several officials of that company. Tarakanov, who, by Baranov's order, was completely under Scheffer's command, expressed his disapproval of the proceedings at Atuai, by which they had all been subjected to the greatest danger, and he considered it a miracle that on their flight from Atuai only three Aleuts had been shot, as Tamari, who considered them all his worst enemies, could easily have deprived many of them of their lives. He also mentioned the dangerous trip here, and he and his men were now in a very serious situation, as the natives naturally did not wish to provide them with provisions without cost. Fortunately I had taken aboard such a quantity of dried codfish at Unalashka that I could supply these poor souls with a month's supply of provisions. Tarakanov, who seemed to me to be a very sensible man, had signed a contract with Mr. Hebet, the owner of two of the ships at anchor here, according to which the latter contracted to feed and clothe the Aleuts for an entire year on condition

that he might take them to California, where he wished to employ them in catching sea otters on the coastal islands. At the end of this year Mr. Hebet will bring them back to Sitka and give the company half of the pelts they acquire. This contract was advantageous to the company, which often rents out the Aleuts in this manner, for these unfortunates will remain the victims of their oppressors as long as the company is subject to the wilfulness of a monster who gains all of his profits with the blood of his fellow man.[8]

An alleged attempt of the Russian-American company to take possession of the Sandwich Islands seems to me fantastic. It is not inconceivable to me that the people in Sitka might misjudge this people, dependent for their protection upon naked soldiers who go on guard with a gun in their hand and the cartridge box strapped to their naked bodies. But how could they not know that this kingdom is under the direct protection of England, to which Tameiameia has done homage? In the year 1816 we saw a letter from the Prince Regent of England to Tameiameia in which he lauds His Majesty's conduct during the war between England and America, thanks him for it, and announces that, in addition to the gifts already transmitted, a ship would come, which he was having built in Port Jackson.[9]

As soon as we had cast anchor on October 1, 1817, the captain, as I said, went ashore. We had left behind us a good repute in Hanaruru, so that Kareimoku [Kalanimoku, governor of O'ahu] received him in a most friendly fashion and caused him to be saluted with three shots from the fort. The American merchants likewise honored the commandant of the Imperial Russian Exploration Expedition and greeted him with their cannon. When the matter of towing the *Rurik* into the harbor was discussed, they offered their boats for this task and really did perform this service for us at dawn of the next day. When we entered the harbor we exchanged salutatory volleys with the fort and received Kareimoku with a volley of three shots when he came aboard to bring us fruits, roots, and pigs. The ceremonious behavior of yesterday was repeated.

The Americans proved to be very helpful to us with their obliging courtesy. We obtained many things from them that they let us have from their own stores without profit: English beer, biscuit from a ship that had arrived from Sitka on the 6th, and other things. Nevertheless, an unpleasant friction was not avoided. When several merchant ships of various nations are together in a foreign harbor, the oldest captain generally takes precedence, and, where it is possible to do so, fires off the shot at retreat each sunset; but when there is a warship among the merchant ships the honor is bestowed upon its captain. Now it is claimed that the American captain fired the retreat shot thoughtlessly, and the complaint Mr. von Kotzebue lodged about it was of such a nature that it incited him to defiance. The affair lay out of my sphere, to be sure, and I only heard about it secondhand.

The foreign merchant captains gathered at Mr. Marini's and held their table there. I dined at their board one evening. They drank tea instead of wine with the hot meat dishes. The gentlemen were exceedingly courteous toward me. An older captain asked me how often I had made this journey. I answered modestly that this was the first time and naturally felt compelled to direct the same question to him. This was the tenth time he had undertaken such a commercial journey to the South Seas and around the world; but now, he said, he had become tired, and this would be his last trip. He was now heading home and would retire. Choris, who was better acquainted with him, met him and spoke with him again in Manila and finally again in Portsmouth, where he had arrived ahead of us. He had found letters from home: there a ship awaited him ready to sail, and in this he would make the journey for the eleventh time, but the eleventh time would be the last.

It was our custom to repay every slight service the O-Waihians rendered us, such as transporting us between ship and shore, and things of that nature, with a string of beads. Such shiny light wares were always happily received, even though no real money value was attached to them. Among his supply Choris had some strings of an unusual type and color that he distributed along with the others without making any distinction. But fashion, as we found out later, placed a most extraordinary value upon this particular color, a peculiarly dark red, and upon this particular kind of bead. Some like this, which Vancouver had first brought to the Islands, and no other mariner since him, were among the adornments of the queens. Now they had appeared again, and some strings of them had come into circulation. The source was investigated and soon found to be Choris, whom rich chiefs offered several hogs for a string of them. The American merchants on their part made him handsome offers—all too late. Our friend Login Andrevich, usually a careful trader and not the man to disdain profit, had this time exchanged his doubloons for maravedíes.[10]

With so many ships at anchor in the harbor, the press of affairs claimed Mr. Marini's time and energy, so that I could enjoy but little of his edifying society. A year ago he had promised me to write down a number of things for me and had not secured the leisure to do so. Now there was no longer time to make up the deficiency. I spent my

days mostly on botanical excursions in the mountains, while Eschscholtz, at least during the first days, was constrained by a foot
injury to remain on board and saw to the plants I laid in. Standing
guard over the bundles of plants spread out in the sun was a time-
consuming and annoying occupation that nonetheless could not be
avoided. Once Eschscholtz was missing one of his own packets,
which he had had on deck, and was conversing with me about the
loss. The captain came up to me and asked me what had happened. I
told him calmly, without any inkling of the storm that then burst
upon me. He dealt out to me a superfluous rebuke and repeated
something I very well knew, that it was my affair and not that of his
crewmen, whom he would not see beaten because of my plants. I
had done nothing but listen to Eschscholtz's complaint.

Choris spent a great deal of time with the American merchants.
Kadu disappeared among the natives, who liked him, and with
whom he soon learned to make himself understood. He traded what
he possessed and what we gave him for various artifacts of theirs and
made presents from among them to each of us according to his
notions.

In Hana-ruru there were newspapers of fairly recent date, Russian
and English. Peace was abroad in the world, at least apparently. To
read everything of interest in a newspaper is an occupation for
which one never has leisure on land. With regard to friends and
acquaintances, I learned only of Madame de Staël's journey to
Italy.[11] On my trips through the island there were only a few times
that I was offered newspapers by O-Waihians—probably old issues.

In the Sandwich Islands trading brings together the most varied
assortment of all the peoples of the earth. Among the servants of
upper-class women I saw a young Negro and a Flathead Indian from
the northwest coast of America. Here I saw Chinese for the first
time. Under this magnificent sky I saw these living caricatures
walking among the beautiful O-Waihians in their national costume,
and I can find no expression for the indescribably ridiculous nature
of the sight. (Often in these seas Chinese, who are docile and easy to
feed, are used as sailors.)

Once on a long hike, after I had been speaking German and Russian on the ship, and also the languages of the Caroline Islands with
Kadu, and a little Danish in the way of greetings with the cook; after
having spoken in Hana-ruru with Englishmen and Americans, Spaniards, Frenchmen, and O-Waihians, with each one in his own language; after I had seen Chinese on the Island, with whom, however,
I had not spoken; in a remote valley I was introduced to a compatriot
with whom I could not speak at all. He was a Kadiakan, a Russian

subject. I acknowledged that we were compatriots, shook hands with him to affirm it, and went on my way. That seemed to me to be proper, and quite natural. Only later in retrospect did it occur to me that this compatriotism and my seriousness were ludicrous.

I had determined to visit the western mountain chain on the island. Mr. Marini furnished me with his advice and Kareimoku with his assistance. I completed the planned trip from October 7 to 10, 1817. One of Kareimoku's canoes carried me, my guide, and a boy who accompanied him along the coral reef, sometimes inside of the surf, sometimes outside it, into Pearl River and into the interior on this river up to the foot of the mountain I desired to traverse. A ship was just entering the harbor as we shoved off from Hana-ruru. On this trip I had the opportunity of examining the nature of the reef. Once, heading more or less seaward, we passed over a mass of coral over which our vessel had to be carried. Several canoes were engaged in catching fish outside of the surf in a depth of 10 to 15 feet. Very many different kinds of fish were caught in the long nets they dragged along, especially magnificently colored species of *Chaetodon*.[12] Here my people took what they needed in the name of Kareimoku. They consumed these fish raw and, unhygienically enough, some after they had kept them for three days, when they had started to rot and were full of insect larvae. When we again passed through the surf on our way toward land there was some clumsy steering, and a wave filled the boat. The fish we had just received swam around my feet, my people swam in the sea around the canoe, but everything was soon back in order. We now passed between surf and shore in shallow water, which suddenly became darker: we were in Pearl River. In the midday hours I tried the effect of the vertical rays of the sun upon my arm, bare and wetted with seawater, which I exposed to it for a time. The result was a slight inflammation and the renewal of the epidermis.

I once had reason to be dissatisfied with my guide, who, as we went into the mountains and I needed him most, had me go ahead with the boy and didn't follow along after us at all, so that I had to turn around and find him. I shot up the whole quiver of my O-Waihian vocabulary in an angry address in which I reminded him of his duty and threatened him with Kareimoku, who had put him under my orders. The man, as is the right of an O-Waihian, laughed immoderately at my clumsy speech, which, however, he very well understood, and he gave me no further opportunity to pour out my eloquence in the course of the trip.

We encountered a heavy rain, a kind of cloudburst, on the heights of the mountains. The O-Waihian bark cloth reacts to water like

unglued paper. To preserve their clothes my people used the top of
the *Dracaena terminalis.*[13] Maro and kapa (loincloth and cloak)
were wound tightly around the trunk and over them the broad
leaves were turned down and fastened with a piece of twine. In this
way they carried their clothes in the trunk of the little tree in a form
somewhat like that of a turban. For my part I took off all of my thoroughly drenched light clothing, and we descended the mountain in
the "national costume of savages." The fact that the O-Waihians are
much more sensitive to cold and rain than we are has been remarked
so often and is so little remarkable that I scarcely need to repeat it. I
will merely observe that the conditions were not favorable to me in
my capacity as collector. When we again crossed the mountains
through a higher pass it rained repeatedly, so that there was no view
at all of the surrounding country. When we descended to the inhabited plain and were about to enter the village where we were to spend
the night I made myself a garment for decency's sake out of two
handkerchiefs. A tinier one was sufficient for my guide—his entire
garb consisted of an end of twine three inches in length, *quo pene ad
scrotum represso cutem protractam ligavit* ["with which he tied the
penis to the scrotum"].

On this trip I never used tin botanical boxes, but rather handkerchiefs instead. You spread out the cloth, put the collected plants
down with the stems pointing toward one corner, press them
together with one hand and with the other hand and your mouth tie
the two side ends of the cloth together. The lower end is also connected to these two, and the upper fourth end serves as a handle. On
larger excursions, when you have a guide and bearers, you take a
bound book of blotting paper along, and the more delicate flowers
can be preserved in this right away. Here my supply of plants was
soaked by rain, and rotting had to be avoided. When we reached our
billet for the night one side of the house was put under taboo, and
there the plants were spread out for the night. Such a taboo is considered sacred and faithfully observed. But on shipboard no taboo
gives any protection, and the whole harvest of four days whether
wet or dry must be "made to disappear" in the shortest possible
time. That was our official expression. In our sealed-off, moving
world a cant language had developed out of all the languages that
were spoken on board or on land, out of all the anecdotes that were
told, and out of all the social happenings, a language that the non-
initiate would scarcely understand. As this narration places me on
board the *Rurik* again the expressions we used there impress themselves upon me again, and I may scarcely hope to keep these pages
free of them.

Having returned from my trip on October 10, on the 12th I made a last excursion into the mountains, on which Eschscholtz accompanied me for the first time. Everything was ready for our departure, which was to take place on the 13th, but Kareimoku, who together with the chief members of the nobility was confined to land because of the celebration of a taboo, asked us to stay a day longer so that he could take leave of us, and his friendly request was not denied.

People have been surprised to hear me speak of nobility among the Polynesians. To be sure, I find nobility there the way I imagine it used to exist among us, where, already discarded, it lives on only in faint memories. In our states under the name of nobility only privilege is recognized, and it is against privilege that the spirit of the times is blowing and is almost taking on the force of a storm. A nobility that is given and taken away, that is sold, is no nobility. Nobility lies deeper; it lies in one's creed, it lies in faith. I find words in the French language, such as it was in my childhood, that are lacking in German, and I shall make use of them here. *Le gentilhomme*, that is the true nobility, such as exists in Polynesia, such as no king can bestow, and no Napoleon can stamp out from the face of the earth. *Le noble*, this is the last dart that kings have victoriously shot off against the nobility, out of whose womb they themselves emerged, and whom it was their task to suppress. Indeed, changes occur that could amaze a person! Now it is "the king and his nobility," after the third estate, which the kings built up as an ally against the nobility, has become overpowerful. Now it is also "Throne and Altar!" after "Throne *or* Altar" had long been the catchword.

I shall not recall with vanity the past of our history when a nobility existed to which my forefathers belonged. I believe in a God, and consequently in His presence in history, consequently in progress in the course of history. I am a man of the future, as Béranger described the poet to me.[14] Learn to look fearlessly and trustingly into the future toward which the Almighty is leading us, and let the past go, since it is past. And what was that better time that your heart clings to? The time of the religious wars, with their burnings of heretics at the stake, with their St. Bartholomew nights, their *auto da fe*?[15] The time of Damiens' execution?[16] Really, really, this one horror story! Read the documents! In the bloody time of the Revolution that followed there was a prevailing gentleness in comparison with this. Wherever there was, is, or will be a civil war, people are killed, torn apart, corpses are mutilated. But Damiens' execution, thanks be to God, will never, never recur: the time has completely run out.

But I am straying away from my goal. I merely wished by way of addendum to put more emphasis here upon what I said in my "Notes and Opinions" about the social order, the division into castes, and the nobility as they are on the islands that I was called upon to discuss. I believed and assumed that it was obvious that there could be no mobility possible from one caste to another, and these castes, like species of animals, are differentiated by nature, and that, just as it is only a fable that the ass wanted to be changed into a dog and the frog into an ox, it is also beyond all belief that a common man would ever dream of becoming a noble. Therefore envy and pride have no place in these relationships. But, one might ask, what is obvious?

I read with dismay in Mr. Kotzebue's *Reise* about pilots of the Caroline Islands "who, although from a low class, are often raised into the nobility for their services, . . . and the pilot was raised to the *tamon* because of his service."[17]

When an irreproachable man who is called upon to testify gives such testimony, what will we not have to expect from those whose business it is to excerpt, copy, or collect the reports of eye-witnesses without having seen anything themselves? Malte Brun, in a short review of Choris' *Voyage pittoresque*, calls my dear friend Kadu *un anthropophage de la mer du Sud* and has long nights devoted to drinking on Eap, where only water is drunk.[18] Once something palpably tasteless is put down on paper, it rolls on incessantly from book to book, and it is the first thing the professional writers of such books reach for. As long as books are written, in each one that there is room for it, the nonsense will be found that the natives of the Marianas or the Ladrones first became acquainted with the use of fire through the Europeans.

But should I depart for the second and last time from the Sandwich Islands without letting the word slip from my pen that, dear reader, you have sought here, turning these pages with quick curious glances? The missions that have become so controversial did not set foot on these islands until after my time, and I do not take any side in this matter. Look at the documents and don't listen to those who without having seen for themselves raise their voices in the controversy. I myself have not read all of them. The native culture, which must perish in the wake of rising Christianity, I have seen and found worthy. That I mourn for it I am frank to confess. But that I am a man of progress and that the spirit of Christianity with all its blessings means more to me, I believe I demonstrated when I published my poem "A Day of Judgment on Huahine."[19] Even in pious Ellis *(Polynesian Researches)* I have failed to find two things: it seems to me he should have become an O-Taheitian [Tahi-

tian] himself before he undertook to alter O-Taheitians, and he
could have conceived and carried out his work in a more spiritual
manner. Mariners who have sought women and pleasure in the
Sandwich Islands may have become inimical toward the missions,
but, dropping more serious accusations, it still seems to me to be
plain from all the reports that the missionary work is carried out in
-an uninspired way in O-Waihi, where no progress in the social order
bears testimony to an uplifting of the spirit. The quiet observation
of the Sabbath and the forced attendance at church and school still
do not amount to Christianity.

Be that as it may, in accordance with the progress of history, the
main isles of the Great Ocean will sooner or later join the world of
our way of life: already a newspaper is appearing in the native language and mostly written by natives in O-Taheiti! Imagine! A newspaper in O-Taheiti! You who support the press, the periodical press
there, stop being outraged by it and stop fighting it at home! There is
freedom of the press in Europe! The Tory Walter Scott says in his life
of Napoleon: "Germany has always owed the blessing of the freedom of the press to the political diversity of its territory."[20] What he
says of Germany goes for the entire world as well. The press is only
an echo, powerless when it is not. Public opinion—that is the power
that has become great. Thank the press and learn from it.

But these trivialities are not in the right place here. When we
were about to set sail I remembered that after two sojourns on the
island and frequent dealings with the natives, I had still not gotten
to taste dog meat, for on O-Waihi the European is received and
treated according to his customs and prejudices, and for the foreign
guest a hog, which he appreciates, and not a dog, which he disdains,
is prepared in the bake-oven. Then I learned, when it was already
too late, that I had missed this long-sought opportunity every day,
on board ship, where our royal guide had been in the habit of dining
on baked dog every day. That's the way it goes with many joys in
this life.

On October 14, 1817, we weighed anchor at dawn, and the boats
of the American ships towed us out of the harbor. Kareimoku came
out of the morai to visit us and brought us fish and fruit. We
exchanged the usual salutes with the fort, we took cordial leave of
our friends, and set our sail to the wind.

# CHAPTER XIII
## From the Sandwich Islands to Radak.
## Farewell to the Radakians.

ON October 14, 1817, the islands of the O-Waihian kingdom lay behind us, and with banners flying our hearts and minds turned toward Radak. We had made a special effort to supply gifts of lasting value to our dear and valued friends. With our last farewell to them we would also take leave from those foreign parts that, when they were still far away from us, drew us on with such tremendous attraction and now still held us back enticingly. Beyond Radak there were only well-known European colonies to retard us on our way homeward, and the rest of our trip resembled the evening walk of the tired pilgrim through the lengthy suburbs of his native city.

In order to delay my imminent separation from the Polynesians that the last few lines have made real to me, I should like to concern myself with them some more; I'd like to find something else to say about them. I would compose many more chapters if you would listen to me as long as I could talk. For example, I should like to furnish the author of *Sartor resartus* with an article for his "Philosophy of Clothes."[1]

We do not desist from boasting in an aesthetically vain manner of having given up the hoopskirt with *paniers*, the high heels, the *frisure à la grecque*, the powder, the rouge, the *ailes de pigeon* tresses, etc., in which at the time of my youth we still saw beauty,[2] but we do not look down with shame at the cut of our dinner jacket and all the repulsive distortions of the human body with which we take such pains to adorn ourselves. I have seen the celebrated beauty after whom one might name the days of our history that preceded Polignac's ordinances—I have seen Mademoiselle Sonntag so disfigure herself in natural roles, where nothing compelled her to do so, that the artist saw himself compelled to turn away in disgust from the idol of the times.[3]

But you smile and ask me if I am speaking of Polynesians here? I find beauty in simple, unadulterated nature, and I know of no other way of praising it, as is my intention, than to contrast the unnatural with it.

I find that everywhere beauty is coupled with expediency. For man the most beautiful thing is the human form; it cannot be otherwise. Its healthy uniform development in all of its parts alone determines its beauty. The larger angle of vision determines the beauty of the face because man as a thinking being rises above animals and finds the expression of his humanity reflected in the increase of that angle.

On the one hand clothing serves our sense of shame, which wants to clothe the body partially, and on the other hand fills our need of seeking protection from external influences. Only the barbarian invokes its help for disfigurements, in which he takes pleasure. The Polynesians' clothing satisfies our sense of shame without cloaking the noble build of these powerful, healthy, handsome people. The O-Waihians' cloak, which is put on and discarded according to need and whim, and which respect compels them to remove when in the presence of a superior—especially the wider, more flowing variety that the rich wear—is just as beautiful as it is practical.

But tattooing? Tattooing is a very general practice; Californians and Eskimos both engage in it more or less, and the Mosaic prohibition indicates that the peoples from whom the children of Israel were to keep themselves separated also were devoted to it. Tattooing, very differently applied on different islands of the Great Ocean, on Radak forms an artistic whole. It neither covers nor disfigures the body but rather blends in with it in graceful adornment and seems to enhance its beauty. We must criticize the way the O-Waihian women wear their hair, because it deprives them of their natural adornment. Among the Radakians, however, both sexes take great pains with their hair, and the attractive strings of shells with which they garland themselves enhance very effectively the shine of their black curls and the brown of their delicate skin. Their ear adornments, which are held in place by their enlarged earlobes, may put one off, but I must confess that I have found them to have a pleasant effect.

When we force ourselves into our hideous clothes we renounce the expression of body and arms; mime fades in importance among us North Europeans, and we hardly glance at the face of the speaker. The volatile, talkative Polynesian speaks with mouth, face, and arms and with the greatest economy of words and gestures, so that expeditiously the shortest and fastest expression is chosen, and a gesture takes the place of speech. Thus, affirmation is expressed by a movement of the eyebrows, and it is only the foreigner, who repeats his question several times because of his slow understanding, who forces the word *inga* [?] out of the mouth of the O-Waihian.[4]

Our shoes and boots have restricted our use of the feet to walking. They render other quite different services to the four-handed Polynesian. He holds and directs with his feet the object on which he is working with his hands, the mat he is weaving, the cord he is twisting, the piece of wood on which he is attempting to bring forth fire through friction. How clumsily, slowly, and awkwardly we must bend down in order to pick up something that lies at our feet. The Polynesian grasps it with his foot, which passes it to the hand on the same side, and he has neither moved from the spot on which he was standing nor ceased to speak. If something is to be removed that lies on the deck of a ship, one of them grasps it with his foot and passes it to another. It passes from foot to foot and overboard, and the watch, which has its attention focused on their hands, notices nothing.

The Master's words come to mind and lead me even farther from my goal: "Charm proceeds only from perfect power."[5] Perfect power does not merely seek what is right, it finds it with certainty, and what is right is beautiful. Every attempted arbitrary adornment is disfigurement and deformity. I know of no more charming sight than that of the Indian juggler who plays with a cannonball that is astoundingly obedient to him. My artist's eye revels at the sight of the development of the human form in all of its beauty, while at the same time I enjoy myself like a child with this childlike man who is just playing and enjoying himself. Indisputably, I have seen the European juggler perform much more difficult tricks, but the silly, repulsive person spoiled my pleasure in his artistic performance because he quite seriously demanded the kind of admiration for his empty playing that I reserve for heroic deeds alone. There is the same difference between the gay, amusing magicians such as I saw in my youth and today's boring *professeurs de physique amusante*.[6] Their refinement has broken their necks. But to return to my Polynesians: I compare them to the Indian juggler, who belongs to the same ethnic stem as they do.

We caught the trade wind and sailed before it. On the morning of October 20 we saw many snipe and seafowl. At two o'clock in the afternoon those bare cliffs hove into sight that are so dangerous to navigation and that had first been sighted by Captain Johnstone in the frigate *Cornwallis* in the year 1807. The previous year we had sought them in vain. Their highest, most visible point lies, according to Mr. von Kotzebue, at 16°45′36″N latitude, 169°39′21″W longitude. Hidden reefs stretch out around them for a considerable distance. Snipe and seafowl were often seen on this stretch of our trip. To the north of Radak we found the strong western current we were already acquainted with. On the 21st a flight of ducks passed us headed southeast. On the 24th a snipe landed on the ship. On the 30th we had a view of Otdia, and as we were about to enter the Strait of Shishmarev, a storm overtook us from the southeast, something that was not without danger in the vicinity of these reefs. The rain came down in buckets, and a small *Physeter* (whale) swam around our ship.

The wind, which shifted over to the east again, blew violently through the night, and we tacked about in sight of land.

We arrived at Otdia at ten o'clock in the morning on October 31, 1817. A sail hove in sight from the west; we overtook it. We recognized our friend Lagediak, who greeted us enthusiastically. At five o'clock in the afternoon we arrived at our old anchoring place before Otdia. Lagediak came aboard the ship immediately and brought us some coconuts. His joy was indescribable: he could hardly keep it in check enough to give us a report of our friends and of the state of the islands in general.

Kadu, for whom as a child of nature distant things were remote on luxuriant O-Wahu, who did not collect his thoughts enough to think about the old dear friends to whom we were taking him until he was in the close quarters of our house of boards; Kadu, I say, from the moment he had caught sight of and recognized the reefs of Otdia, belonging to the present and seizing it firmly, was a complete Radakian among the Radakians. He brought them presents, stories, fairy tales, joy and exulted with them in rapturous pleasure. But always in control of himself, as he was when action was involved, he was incessantly active and started a job while others still hesitated. He did this with all his heart in the way we desired. He was our right hand among the Radakians, and up to the last day he was one of us without reservation.

I myself, after I had through my earnest endeavors convinced Kadu to talk about Radak, had collected, compared, and studied his statements and had only to compose the more abstract chapters on their beliefs and their language, etc. After I had become more familiar with the customs, mores, and conditions of this people, I now had a clearer view of them and could read and get an overview of what before I could only write down laboriously.

The Radakians, too, were much closer to us now. Kadu's connection with them and with us was the bond that united us. With respect to us our friend became for them what he was for us much more easily and rapidly. We were now one family.

But we were to spend only three days on Radak, and it was necessary to work and get things done, not study in idleness.

The greatest part of the population of the group had left with Lamari's war squadron. Of our friends only Lagediak and the old man of Oromed, Laergass, had remained behind, the latter the only chief and for the time being the ruler of Otdia. Only twelve men and a few women and children were present at all. Shortly after our departure Chief Labeuliet from Aur had come there and had appropriated a part of the iron we had given them. At the time the goats were still alive—he had also taken those with him. Later Lamari had arrived and had appropriated the rest of our iron and our other gifts. He had remained some time to carry out the preparation of mogan and at his departure had left only a few fruits for the scanty maintenance of those who had remained behind. A few yam roots were still alive in our garden, and he had had them dug out and taken them along to transplant in Aur.

On November 1, 1817, we first went ashore. The desolate spot where we had cultivated the soil was a depressing sight. Not a miserable weed, not even the chickweed, remained to bear witness to our pious intention. We set to vigorously, not discouraged because, not entirely unexpectedly, our first efforts had remained fruitless. The garden was renewed and cultivated more extensively, but of all our seeds and seedlings a part was set aside so that we could make a similar attempt on Oromed. Some, which were in greater supply, were also distributed among our friends. Kadu, spade in hand, spoke very forcibly to the spectators, instructing them and supplying them with many goodly bits of useful information. We ate and slept on land that night. We had saved up a few watermelons for this day, and these, together with a few roots, which the captain had had prepared, were distributed among the Radakians, thus serving to illustrate Kadu's remarks. In the evening our friends sang us several of the songs that had been composed in order to preserve our names and the memory of our coming.

On the second day the dogs and cats were brought ashore. The former ran off into the woods, while the latter joined the humans. However, they immediately threw themselves upon the rats and devoured several of them, and I saw that I could put my mind at rest, assured that they would be preserved at the expense of a troublesome parasite that must be combatted.

Goats and pigs, to keep them away from our planted areas, were to be taken to another island. The Radakians were still hesitant to deal with these animals that were still unfamiliar to them. Kadu took on the task right away and carried it out. From that island he was to travel on to Oromed in order to take care of the garden spot there. When he had finished his trip he met the arriving Laergass and came back to the ship with him. This old friend, kind and generous, brought us breadfruit and coconuts and complained because we hadn't cast anchor before his island. After a short stay both boats went back to Oromed under sail. I quickly resolved to go along and climbed into the old man's boat. Kadu, who headed for Otdia first, was to follow us. On this same evening I planted the sugar cane, which was already suffering from lack of moisture, and began with the work of the garden. Kadu arrived. The one day I spent with these charming children on Oromed, completely in accordance with their habits, without reservation, without any foreign intervention, has left me with the gayest, freshest memory that I brought home from my entire trip. The population of the island, three men and numerous women and children, were gathered with us on the beach around a socially blazing fire. Kadu told his stories, into which he wove roguishly amusing fairy tales, and the girls joyously sang the numerous songs that had been composed for us. The older people withdrew and went to their rest. We drew farther apart, and by turns there was wise conversation and gay singing far into the night.

I have spoken of the innocence of customs and unrestrained relations, of a gentle feeling of shame and moral decency. Did the Saint Simonians have a dream of these sea-engirdled gardens when they failed in their task of doing what cannot be done and thought that they could turn time forward until in a circle it came to where it once might have been?[7] Now a slight example of Radakian propriety. In the circle I sat next to a young girl on whose arm I observed a delicately tattooed drawing that, even as it was perceptible to the eye because of its dark-blue color, seemed perceptible to touch through the slight swelling of the delicate skin, and I allowed myself to succumb to the attempt, gently allowing my hand to pass across it. That should not have taken place; but how could the young girl censure this harmlessly meant breach of etiquette on the part of the respected and esteemed guest who was a stranger to their customs and also did not understand the language well? How could she put an end to this and at the same time protect herself from it? I did not notice at first that my actions had been improper, but when the song that had just been sung was over, the girl stood up, found something to do somewhere else, and when she returned she sat down, as friendly and joyous as ever, not in her old place next to me, but in another, among her companions.

The next morning the planting and seeding were accomplished, at which tasks Kadu exhibited the greatest industry. On this occasion I discovered taro and *Rhizophora gymnorhiza* on Oromed, a few examples of which I had seen cultivated even on the inhospitable reef Eilu, but which I had not previously perceived on the Otdia group.[8] As soon as the task was finished, Kadu cried, "To the ship!" We parted from our friends and set our sail to the wind.

What follows in the course of events I have narrated in another place (see "Notes and Opinions," "On Our Knowledge of the First Province of the Great Ocean," at the beginning, and "Radak" at the end).[9] I have nothing to add to what can be read there.

You, my friend Kadu, made the better choice: you parted from us in love, and we also have a right to your love, having harbored the intention of lavishing good works upon your second fatherland and having exerted ourselves in that direction. You have learned the good that we had to offer, and it took possession of you; you have undertaken to continue the good work in accord with our pious intent; may He Who guides the fates of men bless your work and protect you in your dangerous mission! May He keep Europeans away for a while from your bleak reefs, which offer them no temptations. At first they would only bring you the filth from O-Waihi. But what would you have done in our old Europe? We would have played a vanity-satisfying game with you, we would have exhibited you to princes and potentates; they would have hung medals and tinsel around your neck and then forgotten you. The loving guide whom you would have needed, my good fellow, would not have stood at your side. We would not have remained together; you would have found yourself forsaken in a cold world. No position among us would have been suitable for you, and if we had finally prepared the way for you to return to your fatherland, what would we have made of you before?

With Mr. von Kotzebue's second journey and his visit to Otdia in April and May 1824, the history of Radak comes to an end for us.[10]

His arrival in Otdia spread a terrified panic among the natives. After he had been recognized, the old friends appeared again: Lagediak, Rarik, Laergass, Langien, Labigar appeared, but Kadu was missing. The friends showed signs of great shyness and hesitancy. This was explained by the fact that the copper plate, which had been fastened to a coconut palm in the year 1817, had disappeared.[11] Of everything that we had brought to Radak, Mr. von Kotzebue saw only the cat, gone wild, and the yam. The grapevine, which had grown up to the top of the highest trees, had dried up.[12]

Allegedly, Kadu was on Aur with Lamari, with whom he had reached an agreement, and under his care the animals and the plants that had been transferred and planted there were said to have increased to an extraordinary extent. Allegedly only the grapevine had perished. Mr. von Kotzebue adds that the size of his ship had unfortunately prevented him from looking up Kadu on Aur.

We receive these unsatisfactory reports with a doubtful heart.

Kadu had gone along with the war party for which Lamari was preparing in the year 1817. He had fought in a European shirt and a red cap with the saber in his hand, and the iron, all the iron, had given Lamari the upper hand. He had returned home victorious.

The men of Odia [Wotho?], the island chain of Ralik, had recently attacked Kaben under their chief Lavadok, and to avenge this incursion Lamari was now preparing to carry the war to Odia.[13]

So the friends said.

Lagediak secretly urged Mr. von Kotzebue to assume sovereignty over Radak and offered him his support in this undertaking. When the latter, not concurring in this plan, made ready to depart, he begged him to take his son along with him to Russia but could not bear to part with the child when he learned that Mr. von Kotzebue had visited Radak for the last time. But when the ship was about to set sail, Lagediak brought his friend a final gift: young coconut trees, which he wanted to see planted in Russia, as, as he had heard, there were no coconut trees there.

On November 4, 1817, we left the reef of Otdia and sailed out into the Strait of Shishmarev. The weather was fair, the wind faint. We sailed past Erigup and steered, according to the directions given us by Lagediak and our other friends, in search of Ligiep. At four o'clock in the afternoon we were in sight of this group, but the wind failed us completely as we drew closer. Finally a weak breath of air from the north pulled us out of what was becoming an embarrassing situation. A boat came toward us and observed us from a distance. We identified ourselves, at which point all shyness disappeared from these people. They drew close, fastened the boat to the ship, and climbed confidently on deck. Lamari on his expedition had given us a good testimonial. They brought us the usual gifts, coconuts and their delicate strings of shells, and dealt without suspicion or reservation with their people's old, well-known friends. They urged us to visit their islands and praised the beauty of the daughters of Ligiep to us. This is the first time that this kind of talk struck our ears at Radak. Their gifts were not extended without being returned. They were astonished at our liberality and at our wealth of iron. We gave them, as well as we could, news of Otdia and their friends.

Without Kadu it was hard for us to communicate with one another on Radak, and so we learned little from the inhabitants of the island of Ligiep. The Radakians, I might say, like the English are very unobliging when it comes to understanding their language in the mouth of a foreigner. They fail to recognize the words of their language that we endeavor to reproduce. Their way then is to repeat what they hear from us, and thus they deceive us, as we can't help construing such a repetition as an affirmation.

We saw only the most inhospitable part of the group. The more opulent islands, over which the coconut palms raise their fronds on high, Mr. von Kotzebue did not see until the year 1824. The breaks in the reef seem to promise convenient gates even for larger ships to enter and leave with the prevailing trades. The people seemed to us to be better nourished and more prosperous than those on the other· groups of Radak, and we were prepared to find them so.

On Otdia Mr. von Kotzebue had repeatedly gone over the geography of the other island chain with Lagediak, who, it turned out, himself had often been on Ralik. Here, at the point of departure of Radak's seafarers when they travel there, he again had himself told the direction of the Kwadelen [Kwajalein] group belonging to this chain, and, in accordance with previous information garnered, the west was indicated to him.

In the evening the breeze freshened, we took leave of our friends and steered toward the west. But we were not destined to discover this or any other group of Ralik. In the year 1825, to the west at the longitude of Udirik, where according to our information the northernmost reefs of Ralik were supposed to be situated, Mr. von Kotzebue discovered three different island groups that were overgrown with tall coconut palms but were uninhabited.[14]

# CHAPTER XIV
## From Radak to Guaján.

ON November 5, 1817, we had lost sight of Ligiep, the last island group of Radak. The captain had decided to set his course for Guaján in the Marianas. We first caught sight of Sarpane [Sarpana] or Rota and soon after of Guaján on November 23.[1] (I preserve the Spanish orthography, Guaján; the name can be found as *Guaham*, *Guam*, and otherwise.) The purely negative result of this passage, on which we traversed the chain of Ralik and the stretch of ocean that the Caroline Islands take up on some maps, is not without importance in a hydrographic respect. The seafarer who is to travel this sea for purposes of exploration should be referred to the table labeled Aerometer Observations, so that he may avoid the course that we followed.[2]

Mr. von Kotzebue notes that the sea to the west of Radak and in the stretch where the Carolines were sought (between the 9th and 10th, and in the last three days up to the 11th degree north latitude) had a paler blue color, had a greater salt content, and deep under the surface had a noticeably lower temperature than elsewhere at the same latitude in the Great Ocean, and concludes from this that it might be less deep there. When we steered in a more northerly direction to reach Guaján, the sea again took on its usual dark-blue color, its usual salt content, and its usual temperature beneath the surface.

Up until then we had frequently been becalmed and once experienced a nocturnal storm with violent gusts of wind. A porpoise was harpooned. A fabulous occurrence delighted our crew exceedingly.

One of our seamen wore an old cap of sealskin, which, almost unrecognizable as such because of tar, fish oil, and old age, had become an object of derision. Fed up with it all, he one morning cast it into the sea. On the same day a shark was caught in whose stomach the fateful cap was found, still well preserved.

On the afternoon of November 23 we had approached the northern tip of Guaján. We had no map that we could direct our course by, and the city of Agaña was known to us only through inadequate descriptions.[3] We left the land. On the 24th we sought out the land again and followed its west coast toward the south, to seek out the city and an anchorage.

The trade wind blew with increasing velocity. After we had sailed around the northern tip of the island, we found a calm sea in its lee, and a light breeze, which swelled out our sails, blew pleasant scents toward us from the nicely wooded shore, the likes of which I have experienced near no other shore. This green, scent-laden island seemed to be a garden of desires, but it was a desert. No joyous populace animated the beach, no vessel came toward us from the *Isla de las velas latinas*.[4] The Roman missionaries have planted their cross here. To it 44,000 people have been sacrificed, and their residue, mixed with the Tagals who were brought to settle here from Luzón, have become a silent, sad, submissive little people that Mother Earth feeds without effort and invites to multiply.[5] In my "Notes and Opinions" I have let the Spaniards themselves report about this.[6]

We had been noticed. As we searched for an anchorage in the bays so charmingly surrounded by green, the pilot of the governor, Mr. Robert Wilson, came toward us in a European boat to lead us into the harbor. In view of the city, Artillery Lieutenant Don Ignacio Martínez came to reconnoiter us. He rode up in a proa, a boat similar to the vessels of the Radakians, such as used to be common on these islands, which bestowed the first name on them by which Europeans have called them. The more southern natives of the Carolines now build these vessels for the Spaniards and bring them here to be sold.

The harbor called La Caldera de Apra, [Apra Harbor], formed by a coral reef, is exceptionally safe, but difficult of access. We had not yet dropped anchor when we received a message from the governor, who invited us to Agaña, having sent us horses and mules for the trip, which was about four miles.

The ship was put under the command of Lieutenant Shishmarev, and we went ashore with Mr. Wilson. In the harbor there lay at anchor only the small brig of the governor, which Mr. Wilson had been commissioned to use. To get to the village of Massu, where the horses awaited us, and to which we could not head directly because of the shoals, we had to row about two miles. Night came on us as we landed. The Tagals have brought the architecture of the Philippines with them. The people's houses are neat cages of bamboo set on posts and having roofs covered with palm leaves.

The road, which was illuminated for us by the moon, led us through the most pleasant of areas: palm groves and forests, the hills to our right, the sea to our left. We dismounted in Agaña at Mr. Wilson's residence, and then immediately introduced ourselves to the captain-general of the Marianas. Don José de Medinilla y Pineda received us in full uniform in all formality but also in a most hospitable manner.[7] The captain and I stayed with him, while the other gentlemen were quartered with other Spaniards. His table was profligately laden several times a day with a plethora of meat dishes; but as for fruits, the green products of the earth for which the seafarer when he comes ashore is especially hungry, nothing was served, except an orange drink that constituted an in-between-meals snack, that gave any indication of the spicy green land. Bread was served only to the host and the foreign guests; the Spaniards received maize cakes instead.

In the meantime, on the *Rurik* there was a great abundance of the fruit I felt the lack of in Agaña. The governor provided the ship profligately with fresh meat and all the roots and fruits the earth produces. In addition, the seamen who were sent ashore were allowed to take as many oranges and lemons from the forest as they could carry. This soil, these fruit trees once nourished a strong, flourishing people. The small number of its present-day inhabitants bears no relationship to the rich gifts of the willing earth.

One might ask how this food suited our northern ichthyophagi. The oranges tasted better to them than whale blubber. Indeed, it is such a joy to see Aleuts eat oranges that on the passage to Manila we preferred seeing them gulp down the last of our store to eating them ourselves. At least, Eschscholtz gave the ones allotted to him to his language teacher.

In my "Notes and Opinions" I have spoken of Don Luis de Torres, with whom character similarities soon connected me intimately. I think of him with heartfelt affection and sincere gratitude. Don Luis de Torres, who on Ulea itself had become familiar with the ways and customs, history and legends of these wonderful people, who had had their most experienced seafarers, with whom he had lived on familiar terms, show him the map of their Neptunian world, and who had remained in uninterrupted contact with his friends there through the Lamurek [Lamotrek] commercial fleet that comes to Guaján annually;[8] this Don Luis de Torres opened for me the treasure chest of his knowledge, laid his cards down before me, and spoke willingly and lovingly to me about his hosts and that people for whom I had conceived a great preference through my friend Kadu. All my moments in Agaña were devoted to the instructive and cordial company of this kind Don Luis de Torres, from whose mouth I wrote down the items that I preserved in the "Notes and Opinions." Mr. von Kotzebue, to whom I communicated the results of my studies, anticipated my desire, and added a third day to the two he had intended to stay in Guaján, a sacrifice for which I am most gratefully indebted to him. While he himself divided his time between the harbor and the city, I remained in Agaña and followed my goal.

I have spoken of a vigorous married couple on Guaján, the ancestors of the sixth coeval generation. Don Luis de Torres was their grandson, himself a grandfather; another line descended to the sixth generation.

Don José de Medinilla y Pineda had known Alexander von Humboldt in Peru, from where he had come to these islands, and was proud of having once lent him his own hat when he had sought one to wear to the viceroy's court. Later in Manila, which capital has long had lively connections with the New World, we often heard the world-famous name of our fellow countryman mentioned with veneration and met a number, especially clergymen, who boasted of having seen or known him.

Incidentally, I have narrated how Don José de Medinilla y Pineda put on an operatic ballet by torchlight for our captain, who expressed the desire of seeing the popular dances and festive games of the natives. I heard him consult with others in this difficult case where he was requested to show something that didn't exist and repeatedly answer their objections by saying "But he wants to see a dance!" So we were shown a dance.

Choris, who had a special talent for quickly and easily dashing off a well-executed portrait in watercolors, one morning offered to paint the governor's portrait. The latter went immediately to attire himself in full-dress and came back in gala attire with silk stockings, shoes, and buckles. Choris made only a bust, upon which only his epaulets could be pictured. These epaulets were the target of vicious tongues, which asserted that Don José would not be able to send the picture thus ornamented to his family, for which it was intended, as he had the right to wear them only from himself.

November 28, when we were to embark, had come around. I wanted to present a few piasters to the Spaniard who had served me in the governor's house when we left but found a man who, foreign to our customs, did not seem to understand what I was driving at. Fearful of having insulted him, I told him it was *para los muchachos*, for the lower servants, and so he accepted the money. Neither the captain nor another of the gentlemen had been able to leave a tip. Any object such as a bright cloth, of the kind they wear around their heads or the like, would have been accepted with many thanks. For piasters one can only obtain here what the only businessman, the governor, may give for them.

I was the witness to a painfully comic incident between the governor and our captain. The former had magnanimously refused to accept payment for the provisioning of the *Rurik*. The captain had brought along for presents a few copies of a Russian medal that he was in the habit of bestowing as if it were struck for the present expedition of the *Rurik*. In Agaña and many other places Russian is not read fluently. He wished to give this medal to our noble host with the usual conventional words, "of sentimental value only," etc. Don José de Medinilla y Pineda completely misunderstood the affair. What he may have imagined, I do not know; in short, he pushed back the proffered medal and stubbornly refused to accept it, to the outrageous indignation of the captain. I finally convinced him with great effort to accept the thing, which he appeared to look upon as something dangerous, and we won the battle after all.

It was here I first became acquainted with trepang.[9] The governor, who had this precious commodity collected and prepared for the Canton market, had given me the information about the various species of *Holothuria* in commerce, their occurrence, their preparation, and about the important trade itself of which they are the subject, which information I have published partly in my "Notes and Opinions," partly in the *Transactions of the Academy of Naturalists*.[10] He had procured a few of these animals for me, those that were at hand, alive; others smoked and in the condition in which they were brought to market. (They can now all be seen in the Berlin Zoological Museum.) He performed the exceptional courtesy of acceding to my wishes and having this food, so much in demand by Chinese voluptuaries, prepared for us. But I had the same experience with this as did that German scholar who collected learned information from the mouth of the cicerone in a picture gallery and wrote it down assiduously, but at home read over his notebook and afterwards belatedly asked his travel companion how the pictures had actually looked.

Trepang must simmer over a slow fire for forty-eight hours. Accordingly, the enjoyment of this food had to be saved for the last meal Don José de Medinilla y Pineda gave us before our departure from Agaña. But in daylight I had seen the green spicy forest of Guaján only from a distance, and I wished to cast at least a fleeting glance at this flora. I renounced the noon meal and used the time to follow the path back to the harbor on foot, botanizing the while and being accompanied by Don Luis. As far as collecting plants was concerned, Eschscholtz could rely on me, but I couldn't rely on him.

On the evening of November 28 most of the Spanish officers came aboard the *Rurik*. We spent some more happy hours together, and they stayed overnight with us. What I had left of small commodities, beads and the like, I handed over to Don Luis de Torres and left him, the friend of the Indians, as my heir. I bought some large knives from Choris, who had been unable to sell them, and directed that they should be distributed on Ulea to Kadu's friends and relatives as presents from him.

On the morning of November 29, 1817, Don José de Medinilla y Pineda came and handed our captain dispatches for the governor of Manila. We took leave of our friends, saluted the captain-general, when he left our ship, with five guns and three rousing hurrahs, and unfurled our sails to the wind.

# CHAPTER XV
## From Guaján to Manila.
## Sojourn There.

LEAVING the harbor of Guaján on November 29, 1817, we directed our course toward the north of Luzón, in order to penetrate into the China Sea through the volcanic islands and cliffs there situated.

On December 1 (16°31′N latitude, 219°6′W longitude) seafowl heralded cliffs that according to Arrowsmith's map should have been to the west of us.[1] On the 6th a predatory bird was caught on the *Rurik*.

"A few days ago," says Mr. von Kotzebue, "a considerable leak was discovered in the ship. Probably a copper plate loosened, and the worms, which are so frequent among the coral reefs, bored through the wood." He continued under the dateline of December 12th: "The water in the ship increased considerably." I borrow this condition, which I either did not learn about at the time or neglected to note down, from his travel account.[2]

On the 10th we sailed around the northern tip of Luzón between the Bashees [Bashi] Islands in the north and the Richmond Cliffs and the Babuyanes [Babuyan] Islands in the south.[3] On the 11th we caught sight of the mainland, along the western coast of which we sailed toward the south. The current was strong and against us, but the wind was powerful and we hastened toward our destination. On this day a bonito was caught. Flying fish were frequent.

The wind subsided. We did not reach the entrance to the Bay of Manila until noon of the 15th. The telegrapher of the island of Corregidor set about announcing our arrival.[4] This island, which defends the gate of the beautiful bay, seemed to me to be formed from the edge of a partially submerged crater. Along the coast of Luzón we had already seen a few craft under sails. Here several more appeared.

As night fell we were tacking against the east wind to sail into the bay when an officer of the guard drew up to us on a twenty-oared boat to reconnoiter us. He left us a pilot to guide us to Manila.

We made only slow progress. The lively amount of shipping in the interior of the bay announced the proximity of an important com-

mercial city. The wind failed us; we dropped anchor on the 17th.
Two officers came to welcome the captain from the governor-general
of the Philippines, Don Fernando Mariana de Fulgeras. He utilized
this opportunity to go ashore, and took me along. Eight merchant
ships, American and English, were at the wharf. The governor
received us most kindly and promised to tender us all possible assistance. The same boat brought us back to the ship. We weighed
anchor the same evening to sail to Cavite, the port and the arsenal of
Manila where the governor's commands were to anticipate us. Calm
delayed us and forced us to drop anchor again. Fishing boats brought
us their catch for sale; not until the noon of the 18th did we reach
Cavite. The commandant of the arsenal, Don Tobías, did not receive
the commands pertaining to us until the 19th. Then the *Rurik* was
immediately taken into the interior of the arsenal, an empty galleon
was designated to receive cargo and crew, and a spacious house was
emptied for the captain's quarters. We moved into this house on the
20th. The captain would have liked to see a sentinel before his door,
and as he himself could not request a guard of honor, he requested a
security guard. We were no longer in Chile, and here it was known
what was the custom in Europe and what was not. Instead of the
requested sentinel an orderly appeared, who was placed at the captain's disposal and reported to him. Mr. von Kotzebue dismissed the
man, scarcely repressing his annoyance.

In the meantime Don Tobías inspected the *Rurik* with a master
shipbuilder and immediately put a hundred workmen on the job,
which, vigorously attacked and industriously carried out, was finished before the end of the two-month stay that the duration of the
northeast monsoon permitted us to have in this port. With all dam-
ages repaired or renewed; with new rigging; equipped with a new
copper sheathing, which had always been troublesome, as it had
never been of excellent quality; with an improved rudder, which
perceptibly increased its speed, the *Rurik* sailed out of the arsenal of
Cavite completely rejuvenated. In this way it could have undertaken a voyage around the world, could have defied the storms of
the north. But all that remained for us was the voyage home.

After the repairs to the ship our next concern was to have our
Aleuts inoculated against smallpox, which Dr. Eschscholtz saw to
without delay.

On the wharf of Cavite we had met up with the *Eglantine* from
Bordeaux, Captain Guerin, Supercargo Du Sumier; Mr. Guerin, an
officer of the royal navy, had visited us on board before we were
taken into the arsenal. We remained on the most friendly terms
with these gentlemen, as well as with the Spanish authorities, but

regrettably here again made the observation that two authorities are not feasible on one ship.

I passed as a Russian everywhere: the flag labels the commodity. Besides this, however, Germans and Frenchmen recognized me as their compatriot. Thus here, besides the gentlemen from the *Eglantine*, I met an amiable compatriot whom I must mention with heartfelt gratitude. Don San Iago de Echaparre was one of the French *émigrés* who had wandered to Spain, where he had continued the career in naval service that he had started in his homeland. He had been on Luzón for many years, and was now an elderly man, but was still completely the *gentilhomme françois* and was here not among the people or the conditions of his choice. His heart was still in his old homeland. Don Iago possessed and lived in a country house in Tierra Alta. Cavite, on the extreme tip of a three-mile-long sandy tongue of land, is no suitable domicile for a traveling naturalist. I moved to Tierra Alta, a village situated on the high bank of Manila Bay at the place where Cavite Point joins it, and there I spent most of the time that the *Rurik* spent in the port. I was the guest of my compatriot, even if I did not reside in his house, and spent the hours with this kind, good-natured firebrand that I did not spend wandering through ravines and across fields. As in our houses, the same opportunities were afforded him daily to excite himself. His servant Pepe had forgotten to bring radishes, one of his favorite foods, back from the market. He raged about this for a time but soon added mollifyingly that he would not become angry for a mere radish. Then we sat down at the table, and it turned out that Pepe had again placed the broken chair that he didn't like to sit on in readiness for him. He jumped up in a rage, shoved the chair away, and took another, already smiling again. Then the two of us dined together and talked about the Philippine Islands and France.

A large tortoise had taken up quarters in Don San Iago de Echaparre's yard and garden; honeysuckers *(Nectarinia)* nested in a branch of a tree that almost extended into the window of his room;[5] and every time we drank coffee a small gecko (a house lizard) appeared on the table to lick the sugar. He offered me these various animals. But how could I have laid hands on these companions and guests of this man who was already so deprived of friends and relatives? To do this I would have to be a different person than I am.

The enclosures in which the houses stand are generally guarded by dogs that are not chained down and know their business quite well. I found this out the first evening, when I came home unexpectedly. Dogs were barking round about, which didn't bother me much, but a powerful mastiff stepped in front of me, ready to do battle. We stood still and measured each other with our eyes. I understood very well that retreat was out of the question and thought that the smartest thing would be to walk bravely toward the animal, which would then perhaps become fearful and retreat. That's what I did, and now we were right close to each other. Just in time voices were heard in the house, where I had supposed everyone was asleep, and the dog was called off before a fight developed in which I certainly could have come off second best.

This dog reminds me of another one I once encountered at home. It was a dog that was chained up and that, when I passed him, fell into such an exceptional rage that I had to think, "What would happen if the chain broke?" And behold, the chain did break! But the result was this: the dog rolled head over heels to my feet, stood up again, looked at me, wagged his tail, and went back to his doghouse as meek as a lamb. I have often thought of this dog when reading the newspapers. For example, when the Tories upon the occasion of the Reform Bill overthrew Gray's government and then meekly requested that the broken chain be restored.[6]

In Tierra Alta I experienced the only illness to strike me on the entire voyage. I had an exceedingly high temperature and feared an intestinal inflammation. My bed, which in the local manner consisted of a wooden bench and a straw mat, seemed quite hard to me in my indisposition. Don San Iago saw to it that I got "a good, soft bed," sending me a bench woven from reeds. Eschscholtz visited me, and the malady subsided, without disappearing entirely. Under such conditions, not quite free of worry, I had to embark on the journey to the interior of the island and the Taal volcano for which I had already made arrangements, because the days of our sojourn on Luzón were already drawing to a close.[7]

I had had to see to it that the necessary passes that had been offered me were made out and was really not yet properly equipped in this respect, as I was to enter an area where I would have needed other papers and signatures, which could not be obtained without more loss of time. I had had to deal with the Spanish love of pomp and ceremony, which wished to burden me with a military escort of thirty horses when all I needed was a guide. I alone bore the cost of all my scientific excursions and undertakings and did not wish to leave services rendered me unrewarded. On January 12, 1818, I left Tierra Alta with an honor guard of six Tagals of the mounted militia, whose commander, Sergeant Don Pepe, was both my guide and interpreter.

Don San Iago de Echaparre had lifted one of Don Pepe's children out of the baptismal font. The spiritual bond of godparenthood, which in Germany has lost all importance and power, is honored to a high degree in Catholic countries in general, and here most especially. Don San Iago, who had selected his godchild's father as my companion, sent for him the evening before and gave him his orders in approximately the following words: "Your grace will serve this nobleman on a trip to Taal as his bodyguard and guide. I will decide with your grace what villages you will stop at, at which of our kinfolk's houses you will stay. Above all your grace will be careful to ride only in daylight, because this nobleman wishes to see everything. Your grace will often have to ride at a slow pace and often order a halt according to the desire of this nobleman, who will look at every plant and every stone by the wayside, and every worm; in short, every damned thing that I don't know anything about, and about which your grace doesn't have to know anything, either," etc.

Don Pepe was a useful, handy, understanding man, with whose service I had every reason to be satisfied. Except that he tried to keep me, for whose safety he was responsible, on the beaten path and under his eyes by threatening me with crocodiles and snakes, the way you lead a child. However, I soon saw through him. Never in my life, hardly, did I hear a more fearful shout than the one with which he once called out to me to look down in front of me: across the path a little snake was slithering, which I killed, and which, as it turned out, was a quite innocent creature. In the same way he once warned me about a tree, which I immediately investigated with excited curiosity: it was a stinging nettle, which I tried and found not to be any more dangerous than our common variety.

In all the villages, in the way I had grown accustomed to, the people came to the Russian doctor, to complain about their ailments to him and to seek his help. I had to explain the difference between *doctor naturalista* and *facultativo* to them, and they had to be satisfied with that.[8] Let any one who has the yen to travel note this: the name and reputation of a physician will be the safest passport and letter of recommendation for him as far as the earth is inhabited and, if he should need it, assure him the most reliable and most abundant reward. Everywhere frail humanity, feeling itself helpless, believes in a stranger's help and sets its hopes on the one who promises this help. The person in need of help longs for the most distant, the most unknown person, and the stranger awakens the confidence in him that he has lost toward his neighbor. In the learned physician's family the advice that the old washerwoman secretly dispenses is valued more than his skill.

For the person who needs it, medicine is an eerie, almost magic art. A good part of its power always rests in faith. Witchcraft and magic, which, in a thousand forms and with a thousand names, are as widespread and old as the human race, were the first of the healing arts and probably will be the last. They constantly are rejuvenated under new names and contemporary forms, for us under scientific names, such as mesmerism, and . . . I do not wish to offend anyone.[9] But who will deny that today in an enlightened city, such as Berlin, more illnesses are treated with magic spells, or by sympathetic or marvelous remedies, than are entrusted to the care of the scientific physician?

I have only wished to advise the person who desires to see the world to equip himself with a doctor's hat as a convenient travel-cap, and young friends have already tried this advice and found it to be sound. Next to the physician the portrait-painter is best equipped for a trip to foreign lands. Everyone has a face that he prizes and knows fellowmen to whom he would like to grant a copy. But this art is rare and has still to penetrate to many corners of the world.

While I turned away others who requested my help, I had enough to keep myself occupied with in the state of my own health. I treated myself with coconut milk and oranges, with which I kept myself fed, but I could not break my Don Pepe of his habit of over-spicing the chicken, which was usually boiled into a soup, with ginger and other spices according to the local custom. This seemed to be the extent of his medical art, and he meant well in persisting in it. Only in bathing did I find any relief.

In the evening the horses were driven onto the meadow without restraint and rounded up again early in the morning for the continuation of the trip. That is the local custom. But in this process not only time but also a horse was lost, which was not found again.

It is widely known that in all the Spanish colonies the monopoly on tobacco forms the chief income of the Crown, which in this way imposes a head tax instead of a property tax or an income tax; for rich and poor alike have the same need for tobacco. On Guaján this hated tax still does not oppress the population. But here the poor Tagal cannot pay the king for what the earth desires to give him for nothing. Usually, if you meet him in the highways or byways he asks you for the butt of the cigar you have in your mouth, which you generally do not smoke up so completely as necessity has taught him to do. Don Pepe had me give him my cigar butts, and he distributed them among his command with great justness.

On the third day we reached the ridge, the edge of the cone of the crater, from where one can gaze down into the Lagoon of Bonghong and the Taal volcano, which forms a sad, bare circus in its center. From there we came down westward through the forest to the present fortified village of Taal on the China Sea. It was here that the horse was lost. I spent a part of the morning of the 15th in my bath, and in the afternoon I went up the outlet of the lagoon by a light boat, accompanied by Don Pepe and one of my Tagals, until we reached the lagoon itself. We rested in a miserable fishing hut and at night again embarked to paddle across it to the volcano. It was here that Don Pepe conjured me to be on my guard, to look around, but to keep silent. The volcano, which was not, he said, hostile to the Indians, was provoked to new eruptions by Spaniards visiting it. I responded to the good Tagal that I was not a Spaniard, but an Indian from a foreign land, a Russian—a bit of sophistry that did not seem to appease his concern. I decided not to defy his opinion, but rather to comply completely with his prescripts. But he forgot them before I did. We landed to windward on the island. The first rays of the sun struck us on the edge of the hellish caldera. As I followed this edge to reach a point of the circuit from which it seemed possible to descend into the interior, Don Pepe had lost all caution. He was enraptured at completing a daring deed that, he said, no one had ever carried out before us, and no one would ever carry out after us. We would probably be the only people ever to tread on this path. I showed him in all modesty that cattle had trod on it before us. On the banks of the island a little grass grows here and there, so that a few cattle have been brought there to graze it off. I do not understand what can impel these animals to ascend the steep bare cone of ash and make a path around the sharp edge of the defile.

I have described the Taal volcano in my "Notes and Opinions," and again in Choris' *Voyage pittoresque,* who depicted it after a sketch of mine.[10] In the evening we returned to Taal, and on January 19, 1818, we again entered Tierra Alta.

I have not yet spoken of Manila itself, to which I made several small trips by water and by land along the well-developed shore of the bay, and where I always met with the most accommodating, friendliest reception. In Manila, where there are no inns, Dr. Don José Amador, to whom we had been recommended by the governoı of the Marianas, was our host. His nice wife was a ward of Don San Iago de Echaparre, who when her father died lost a friend, compatriot, and long-time associate. The charming *señora* spoke only Spanish. In the absence of Don José Amador, the adjutant of the governor, Don Juan de la Cuesta, received us on our first trip to Manila. The governor himself observed the most obliging politeness toward the captain and all of us. An easy, charming sociability reigned in his house. Here you could divest yourself of the garb in which you had been presented to the governor-general of the Philippines and don a light jacket such as was appropriate to the climate. When we weighed anchor he sent me several months of the last French and English newspapers he had received. In the China Sea that provided me with a very enticing occupation. Here I obtained the first news of my relatives to come to me since our departure and owed it to Don Antonio Mariana de Fulgeras. The prefect of the Department of Lot was my brother, etc.[11] Only in the China Sea or under similar circumstances can one have any idea of the number of things that can be read out of a European newspaper like that.

My chief occupation in Manila was ransacking libraries and monasteries for books and people that might be able to provide me information about the peoples and languages of the Philippines and the Marianas. In the proper place I have given an accounting of my successes and failures in this regard.[12] In a very short time I collected a fine library of Tagalists and historians of Manila. A few things could be purchased, several things were given to me, in return for which I sometimes was able to give other books. Everywhere I found the most humane attitude, the greatest willingness to be helpful to me, and the most courteous manners. Only in the monastery where the *Vocabulario de la lengua tagala* could be obtained did the brother who handed me the copy I had paid for form an exception to the rule, in that he told me to leave and closed the door behind me.[13] His behavior annoyed the Spaniards who heard it more than it did me, who knew that monks and women *no hacen agravio*, cannot insult you in a way that impugns your honor.

When in the night of July 3–4, 1822, the house that I occupied in Neuschönberg, near Berlin, was reduced to ashes, the first thing that I took pains to save, after the lives of my family, was this Tagalog library, and I immediately saw to it that it became a part of the royal library in Berlin, where the learned scholar of languages of the Malayan family will find some things that most libraries do not contain.

We were not on Luzón in the season for mangoes, a fruit that is highly praised and, present in great abundance, seems to make up a large share of the average person's food. A single prematurely ripe mango was secured and at a meal divided among the crew of the *Rurik*. After this insufficient test I can't say anything about it. In general we consumed only those fruits of the Torrid Zone that are available at all times and that it was not possible to miss. No mango! No pineapple! No eugenia![14] Etc.

The Chinese suburb is an attraction for someone who has never set foot in the Middle Kingdom. "Non cuivis homini contigit adire Corinthum" ("Not every traveler succeeds in going to Corinth").[15]

It is, nonetheless, no matter how much we think we are superior to the Chinese, the normal realm of conservative politics, and any one among us who follows this banner would certainly find a lot to learn in that model. I don't engage in mean attempts to turn the clock backwards, which are always unsuccessful, in things where we really have progressed farther than the Chinese but rather to determine what should be conserved and how one conserves in general. But here I am out of my province. Look for illumination in the *Mémoires pour servir à l'histoire de la Chine.*[16] I enjoyed looking at the Chinese faces only as a dilettante.

On January 19, 1818, I had again returned to Tierra Alta. Eschscholtz visited me on the 21st. On the same day the captain also came on his way to Manila. I returned to Cavite on the 22nd. The captain arrived from Manila on the 25th. The *Rurik* was ready to sail, the chronometers had been put aboard. Early on the morning of the 26th I traveled to Manila in a light boat, breakfasted on the *Eglantine*, which waited for us outside of the reef, made my last round in search of Tagalog books, and entrusted myself not in vain to Don José Amador's hospitality. The *Rurik* arrived before the reef on the 27th. I shipped aboard on the 28th, and this day was the last that we spent at Manila. The governor came aboard and was honored with fifteen guns. Our friends joined us, and our last hours, embellished by the charming presence of Señora Amador, became a happy and cordial farewell party.

I have not named one of our friends, who had often mentioned Free Masonry in conversations with me, and in such a way as to attract my attention, and still had not returned the signs of initiation that his behavior had caused me to cull forth from my treasure trove of half-forgotten youthful memories. This evening he sought me out and clasped my hand. I was astonished. "But why did you deny . . . ?" "You are going away, but I am remaining here." That was his answer, which I have not forgotten.

Our sailors' choir sang Russian national songs to the accompaniment of janissary music, and Señora Amador, who moved among us in the happiest of moods like a charming fairy, threw them a handful of piasters in accordance with Spanish custom. Mr. von Kotzebue construed this as an insult. After our guests had left he had this money collected and sent it back to the well-meaning donor with a note that, addressed to a beautiful woman, could have given no more favorable concept of the sensitivity of Russian customs than the generosity, which he rejected, had given of the Spanish way.

On January 29, 1818, we went under sail along with the *Eglantine* and left Manila Bay.

# CHAPTER XVI
## From Manila to the Cape of Good Hope.

AFTER we had sailed out of Manila Bay on January 20, 1818, we crossed the China Sea in consort with the *Eglantine* with a favorable northeast wind in a WSW direction on a well-traveled route, and on February 3 we were in sight of Pulo Sopata.[1] From here with a southwestern and more southerly course we caught sight of Pulo Teoman, Pulo Pambeelau and Pulo Arve on the 6th (names according to Arrowsmith, whom I follow, in order to have something to go by for the variant spelling of Malayan names. According to others, Pulo Timon, Pisang, and Aora).[2] The *Eglantine*, which sailed less rapidly than we did, held us up.

From this westernmost point of our trip in the China Sea we steered toward the south and a little more easterly in order to reach the Gaspar [Kelasa] Strait, between the island of the same name and Banca [Bangka].[3]

On the early morning of February 8, 1818, we crossed the Equator for the third time. It was the first time for the Russians and Aleuts whom we had taken on board in St. Peter and Paul, San Francisco, and Unalashka. Our veteran crew members had terrified the Aleuts especially with fantastic tales about the terrible line and the dangers and terrors encountered in crossing it. We let it go at this teasing. Nobody was baptized and no solemnities were undertaken.

On this day the captain sent me at noon to the *Eglantine* in order to inform Captain Guerin what the night signals were, as they had not yet been agreed upon. I dined on board the *Eglantine*. Such a visit on the high seas has a special charm. When you see the ship you are traveling on under sail from these changed surroundings, it is as if you are standing at the window and seeing yourself going by on the street. I returned to the *Rurik* in the afternoon.

All day long a Malay sail had been seen from both ships, which, with only its tip emerging above the horizon, seemed to hold the same course as we did. In the evening at nine o'clock, a light—a boat, perhaps that sail—appeared in the vicinity of the *Rurik*. The captain immediately ordered one of our guns to be shot at it, the light disappeared, and a few more volleys of canister were fired into the night—without, it is to be hoped, causing any damage. Indeed, in these seas, which are not kept quite free of Malayan pirate rabble, it might have been quite smart to show at the first suspicious events that we had cannon and were not asleep. The *Eglantine*, which was half a mile behind us, thought our shots were distress signals. Captain Guerin thought we had struck a shoal and smartly turned his ship so as not to run aground himself. We hove to, called him to us by a signal, told him of the event through a megaphone, and continued on our way in his company.

A more detailed description of the whole episode can be seen in Mr. von Kotzebue's *Voyage*, where he says, "Firmly determined to be victorious or to die, I commanded . . . ," etc. I refer you to this account.[4]

On the morning of the 9th the island of Gaspar was discovered from the masthead. In the evening we sailed southward along its west coast and at midnight, when it lay to the north of us, we dropped anchor. At dawn we set sail again, and in the morning we were already passing through the Gaspar Strait.

The coast of Banca and that of Sumatra, along which we sailed on the days following, are lowlands. The jungle, which clothes the plain luxuriantly, stretched down to the beach. The palms are not predominant in it.

On the 11th we dropped anchor at midnight and lifted it again at half past four. On the morning of the 12th we sailed through green meadows formed by blooming plants floating freely in the sea, probably a species of tree. The plants had already cast off their seed pods. Wind and current formed these floating crops into rivers that twisted along for great distances. Soon the Two Brothers appeared. These islands, situated close to the low-lying coast of Sumatra, resemble the low islands of the South Seas, except one does not see the surf pounding against them. At first we thought that bushes of rhizophores rose straight out of the water.[5] We sailed through between these islands and the mainland and dropped anchor at seven o'clock in the evening.

On the 13th there was only a weak land breeze blowing, and it failed us several times. We went under sail and cast anchor repeatedly, at length very close to the coast of Sumatra. We were in the vicinity of the Zupflen Islands[?]. The northern island lay behind us. Three small jungle-covered islands were missing on the map. Java could be well descried, and close to its coast a large ship. In our vicinity two fishermen had their lines in the water from a light skiff. We gave them small gifts when they approached us. They immediately rowed toward land, waving to us in a friendly fashion, and soon came back to bring us a huge turtle. Another boat brought us several of them and also chickens, monkeys, and parrots. The people wanted pistols and powder or piasters for them. Turtles were provided for all on board for several days, and besides, some of the ship's company bought monkeys of various genera and species.

Among these monkeys, all of which took sick and none of which reached the Cape of Good Hope, there was a young one that was ugly, mangy, and very small. Because of the latter circumstance the crew had named him Elliot. All the adult monkeys, both male and female, wanted to take this monkey child under their wing; they all wanted to pull him close to them, have him, caress him, and not a one belonged to the same species. The second mate, Petrov, to whom said Elliot belonged, was begged beseechingly for him by the masters of the other monkeys. He distributed his favor around and made a different person happy every day. In his travel narrative Eschscholtz described one of these monkeys as belonging to a new genus.[6]

We had brought along from Manila a pair of the species common in Luzón. These were thriving admirably; they enlivened our rigging, as they did their native jungles, and remained our happy comrades all the way to St. Petersburg, where they arrived sound and happy.

I find contact with monkeys very instructive, "for," as Calderón says of donkeys, "they are almost human." They are the quite natural animal that is the foundation of man. Masurier knew that well: he played Jocko the way Kean did Othello.[7] The difference in character among individuals of the same species is as striking among monkeys as it is among humans. As in most of our homes, the more cunning female ran things, and the male acquiesced.

With regard to turtles I shall note that in the last one that was butchered, and after it had been dissected, I perceived phosphorescent light. It was especially apparent on the shoulder joint of the one foreleg. But several parts of the dissected neck also glowed—the nerves, perhaps? The glowing material could be picked up with the finger and spread out on it, where it retained its light.

In the China Sea, which we were about to leave, a sea swallow and a pelican had let themselves be caught on the *Rurik*, the latter after it had been a captive on the *Eglantine*. Insects and butterflies came aboard our ship when we were close to land. The calm in the Sunda Strait provided us with a large yield of sea worms, nor was the insect of the high seas Eschscholtz had discovered lacking here.

I return to our anchorage of February 13, 1818. In the evening the masters of the *Eglantine* visited us. We took leave of each other. The *Rurik* would probably arrive in Europe before the *Eglantine;* nonetheless I handed Captain Guerin a few lines for my relatives.

The current moved at a speed of two knots, alternately into the China Sea at high tide, out of it into the Indian Ocean at ebb tide.

On the 14th we weighed anchor very early and sailed with a very strong current and in nice proximity to the land through the channel between the Zupflen Islands, of which we counted eight, and the heart of the current into the Indian Ocean. At twelve o'clock noon we had lost sight of the *Eglantine*. We saw her once more at four o'clock, when the wind forced us to tack, lying at anchor before the island of Crocotoa [Krakatoa].[8] By the evening of the 15th we had the strait and the islands behind us. On the 16th we caught the constant east wind. Up to that point we had counted three or four ships every day, now sailing around us alone, and now together. On the 18th no more sails were to be seen.

On the 21st we had the sun at the zenith. On the evening of March 2 a fireball of exceptional brilliance was seen in the northern sky. In the Atlantic Ocean and in other seas I have observed some meteors of the type with some exactness. But science demands coinciding simultaneous observations of the same phenomenon, and my observations were not supported by any others.

On March 3 we were pleased that a bonito was caught. On the 4th we crossed the southern tropic. On the morning of this day a large ship was cutting across our course in NNE direction. In the evening a sea swallow flew into our hands.

On March 12, 29°19'S latitude, 313°26'W longitude, south of Madagascar, we had lost the constant wind. Squalls with lightning and thunder, calms and tempests alternated. In the night of the 18th, which was exceptionally dark, we unexpectedly found ourselves in the vicinity of a very large ship and in danger of being run down. We still saw tropic birds at this latitude.

The equinox (March 20) brought us storms. From the 14th, the first quarter of the moon, till the 21st, full moon, we constantly had a stormy sea, varying with the most violent gusts of wind we had ever suffered. (About 31°S latitude between 318° and 325°W longitude.) The nicest weather was on Easter, the 22nd. In the morning a porpoise of an excellent species, which we had not encountered before, was harpooned.

On the 23rd, when the wind was very weak, a sail was discovered in the north from the masthead. In the evening we reached the meridian of St. Petersburg. On the 27th we were already on the bank that surrounds the southern tip of Africa, and the current quickly drove us westward toward our goal. On the 29th we caught sight of land, to the west of Cape Agulhas.[9] In the night of the 30th–31st we sailed into Table Bay.

There old Adamastor had played a trick on us and enticed us into the greatest danger, perhaps, that we had met on the voyage.[10] Mr. von Kotzebue was not familiar with Table Bay and must not have had a chart of it. He himself says, "Led astray by various fires on shore, I had not reached the place where ships customarily lie at anchor.—At daybreak we first noticed that we were not anchored before Cape Town, but rather in the eastern part of the bay, three miles away from the city."[11] On the beach before us, which we had steered toward in the night and from which the wind had held us back, lay the wrecks of different ships as a warning.

A stormy wind blew from the south. A pilot directed us away from the dangerous place that we had taken and brought us to the safe anchorage before the city, where there was calm, or at most a light breeze from the north. The captain went to the city and I had to await his return on the *Rurik*. I was all afire with anticipation. Cape Town is an outpost of home. Here in a German world I would again find traces of people dear to me; here, perhaps, letters were awaiting me from my relatives; here I counted on a friend, Karl Heinrich Bergius of Berlin, Knight of the Iron Cross, naturalist, who before my departure had gone to the Cape as a pharmaceutist.[12] And as I looked across at the city, which on this morning gradually emerged from the mist that enveloped it and lay clear before me, crowned by the familiar mountain group, a small boat rowed out from the forest of masts toward the *Rurik*, and Leopoldt Mundt, another botanist friend from Berlin, climbed aboard and embraced me.

The first news that he gave me was a death notice. Good Bergius, generally loved, respected, and honored, had ended his life on January 4, 1818. Mundt himself had been sent to the Cape by the Prussian government as a naturalist and collector.

As soon as the captain came on board again, I went off with Mundt, and first of all we went aboard the *Uranie*, Captain Freycinet.[13] Even as the *Rurik* was returning tired and disappointed from its voyage of discovery, the *Uranie* was just about to embark from this port with hope in full bloom on a similar voyage. We did not find Captain Freycinet on board. His officers, who were also his scholars, kept us at table. I was pleased with the favorable accident, which allowed me to make their acquaintance, even if it was only fleeting. It had been promised them that they should stop at Guaján, and for this port of call I had some things to tell them as to what remained to be done and could send greetings to my friend Don Luis de Torres. One of the gentlemen had served with a Chamisso and had been commissioned to wish me good luck from him and the family, in case he should meet me anywhere in the world. Here I met my good friend and rival, the botanist Gaudichaud, for the first time.[14]

After the meal we returned to the *Rurik,* and there I packed up a few things and moved in with Mundt for the duration of our stay at the Cape. You are surprised yourself at the increased activity that you put yourself to as soon as you set foot on land, waking from the indolent sleep that you feel fettered by under sail. To write a page, to read ten pages, that was an occupation for which you painfully sought the time, and before you had found it the leaden hours of the day had gone their empty way. Now the full hours are spent in a felicitous fashion, and you have time for everything and energy for everything; you have no interest in sleep, no feeling of fatigue. "The body has subordinated itself to the mind so far as to forget its needs."[15]

We stayed at the Cape for only eight days. During three of these days a NE storm raged with such intensity that it broke the connection between the land and the ship. The storm didn't bother me any; during the daytime hours I was out in the open, while at night I was busy with my collected materials and my books. Mundt, Krebs, a pharmaceutist and naturalist there, and others, mostly friends of my departed friend Bergius, were my guides and companions.[16]

We made a great excursion to Table Mountain. We climbed it before daybreak from the side of Lion Mountain and came down again in the dark of night by the more beaten path to the ravine behind the city. My companions immediately retired, exhausted and drunk from sleep, not to wake up until late the following day. However, I, after I had taken care of my plants, studied a Dutch-Malayan grammmar all night long, the first Malay language text that had come into my hands, and obtained the first glimpse of this language, the knowledge of which was essential to me for comparison with the dialects of the Philippines and the South Sea Islands.[17] Early in the morning I was already at the beach collecting seaweeds.

Among the oceanic plants that I brought home from the Cape one, or in my view two, have played a great role in science, in that they are said to bear witness to the change of genera and species into other genera and species. I have written fairy tales in my lifetime, but I am careful never to let my imagination zoom beyond the perceived facts in scientific matters. I cannot find any intellectual peace in a nature that is the way the metamorphosists would have it. The genera and species must have constancy or there are no genera and species. What separates me, *Homo sapiens*, from the beast, the more and the less perfect one, and from every plant, more or less perfect, if every individual can transfer from one state to another, both progressively and retrogressively? In my algae I see only a *Sphaerococcus* that has grown upon a *Conserva*, not for instance the way mistletoe grows on a tree; no, like a moss or a lichen.[18]

In order to become familiar with the Cape of Good Hope, Cape Town, and its surroundings, you have your choice among many travel narratives. I am glad to leave superfluous works unwritten, and shall make no attempt to give another portrait of this marvelously unique landscape, but will just add a few touches to the well-known picture. Nowhere can the floral garb of the earth be more attractive and convenient than it is at the Cape. Nature unfolds its gifts in inexhaustible abundance and variety before his eyes and hands; everything is within reach. The fields and groves of the Cape seem to have been created for his pleasure, even as the jungles of Brazil with the gardens borne on the tops of trees seem to have been put there for his despair.

In the city and for a considerable distance along the road that winds around the foot of the mountains you find to your annoyance only European pines, silver poplars, and oaks. Wherever he goes, man takes a bit of home along with him, as much as he can. But if you leave the road and climb up the mountain, no expression can do justice to the concentrated variety and variegated mixture of the plants. With Mundt I found many plants on Table Mountain that had escaped him until then, and, passing traveler as I was, I brought home several undescribed species of plants from this most frequented of botanical gardens. And every season develops its own peculiar flora.

The range containing Table Mountain, which is separated by plains from the ranges of the interior and which could be looked upon as the northernmost cape left standing of the southern land that sank into the sea with all its mountains, Table Mountain range differs from the closest ranges by its flora, in which genera and species are mixed in a different proportion in a characteristic way, and which apparently possesses several plants exclusively peculiar to this area. For instance, *Protea argentea*, common in our botanical gardens, has been found only on Table Mountain, and it is easily conceivable that a whim of accident or of people could destroy it in its limited home soil, so that this species would be maintained only in our hothouses.[19]

Some of the planters from the interior came to the city during my stay here. When they heard that a new "flower-hunter" was here, they offered to take me to their estates. Any traveling naturalist can count on being received in the interior of the colony in a very hospitable manner.

Islamism and Christianity have been preached on the East Indian islands at the same time, and the missionaries of both faiths have competed on the same field. I was surprised to hear talk of Mohammedan missionaries at the Cape. Under pretext of trade, they told me, those who dedicate themselves to this work come and try to penetrate into the interior of the colony. They direct themselves by preference to the slaves, of whom they convert more than a few. But it is also not unheard of that freemen and whites turn to their confession. I repeat only what I have heard and cannot vouch for its truth.

I had received the command to go aboard ship on April 6. When I came aboard a day was added, and I went ashore again. On the 7th I took another long excursion with Mundt and Krebs. In the evening both of them accompanied me on board. Mundt slept on the *Rurik* that night. When we woke up on the morning of April 8, 1818, the *Rurik* was already under sail and had left the ships on the wharf behind. The captain wanted to send our shanghaied passenger back by the next ship. Then a boat appeared and was called alongside. The owner demanded a cash payment immediately. It turned out that Mundt was not only without his hat but also without any money. I quickly ransomed my friend, we embraced, he sprang into the boat. The *Rurik* glided into the open sea under full sails.

# CHAPTER XVII

## From the Cape of Good Hope
## to Home. London. St. Petersburg.

AFTER we had left Table Bay on April 8, 1818 (according to ship's reckoning), on the usual route for returning ships we caught the trade wind on the 16th, crossed the southern tropic on the 18th, and on the 21st reached the meridian of Greenwich. Here we corrected our time calculations and wrote, accepting that of Greenwich, Wednesday the 22nd instead of Tuesday the 21st.

On April 24, 1818, we caught sight of St. Helena. Our captain cherished the notion of anchoring at the cliff of Prometheus Bound;[1] that is understandable. The high powers had commissars on the island. It could not appear unnatural that a Russian man-of-war should offer to transport dispatches for the Russian commisar (Count Balleman). The English brig of war that sailed across to windward of the island visited us. The officer who came aboard stepped into the captain's cabin with a cocked pistol. After examining our papers he directed us to remain in the vicinity of the island during the night, which was beginning to fall, and to head for Jamestown the next morning.[2] The brig signaled, the telegraph ashore became active; night fell.

In the morning we sailed toward the town and the anchorage. A battery gave us to understand by means of a cannonball that whistled across our bow that we might go no farther. The telegraph was active. A bark pushed off from the admiral's ship and rowed toward us. We thought we should be allowed to sail toward this bark, started up our old course again, and received another cannonball across the bow when we arrived at the same point. The officer who had come aboard offered to guide us to the wharf: the battery, he said, had no authority to fire at us and would not do so again. With our guide we headed toward the harbor again and immediately took a third cannonball. Thereupon the officer got into his boat again and rowed back to his ship to put an end to misunderstandings, which could have arisen only because of the absence of the governor, who was not in town but in his country residence. In the meantime, all the warships at the wharf weighed anchor and hoisted their sails. We waited until after twelve o'clock; as at this time we were still without news, we lowered our flag to the accompaniment of a cannonball, and after a delay of about eighteen hours we set our course northward again.

I note in passing that according to naval custom for the kind of conversation that the battery conducted with us, the first ball is generally sent across the bow, the second through the rigging, and the third into the captain's cabin. The battery had really fired the first shot three times but never fired a second one at us. Moreover, it is illuminating that in the procedures of the guard brig, the admiral's ship, and the land battery there was no agreement; and the fault for the confusion that prevailed with regard to us can only be attributed to the governor.

In these days I was called on the carpet by the captain because of a misunderstanding. We had a discussion in which the kind sense of justice of this sensitive, easily irritated man appeared in the finest light. He acknowledged that he had been wrong about me, offered me his hand, and agreed to assume half the blame, and I should assume the other half. And indeed, I may have exhibited pride and defiance in the face of his sensitivity at the wrong time. Everything I had had to bear was forgotten, and all our grudges sank into the sea.

On April 30 we saw Ascension Island, which we left unvisited, to our west. The turtles that one can hope to find on its beach did not impel us to try a landing. Clouds rested on the mountains. Many birds could be seen.

On May 6 before daybreak we crossed the Equator for the fourth and last time. The day was celebrated festively. I no longer have any remembrance of the comedy the crew performed. I couldn't have had my heart with it completely.

We had lost the trade wind and had light playful breezes and calms. We had seen a ship on the 5th, and another appeared on the 8th. On the evening of this day there was rain like a cloudburst, and heavy thunder.

On May 12 we caught the northerly trade wind, kept it until the 26th, when the wind shifted to the southeast, and from about the 22nd to May 30, between 20° and 36°N latitude and 35° and 37°W longitude we passed through the Sargasso Sea. This is the name given to a broad meadow of floating seaweed, mostly of the same species, torn away from the unknown rocky strand where it must have been produced, and driven together by the wide vortex of the oceanic current into the middle of its circuit.

Since we had crossed the line the number of ships that we saw almost daily increased. We often showed each other our flags. On May 29 we saw a bottle floating in the sea, which, however, we did not take up. What might the letter have said, which it probably contained? On June 1 an American schooner hailed us and obtained ship's biscuit from us, of which it was short.

On June 3, 1818, we saw the island of Flores, the westernmost island of the Azores, and from there we headed toward the Channel.

On the 5th a derelict ship came into sight. It was not further investigated. The number of ships increased; several maintained the same course as we did; we conversed with some of them.

On the 15th we were at the entrance of the Channel, without yet being in sight of land. An English fleet could be seen. A pilot climbed aboard. The first news I obtained was a death notice: in a newspaper that the pilot brought aboard an edition of the works of the late Madame de Staël was announced![3]

On the evening of June 16, 1818, we lay at anchor at the wharf of Portsmouth at Cowes next to an American we had already met in Hana-ruru and Manila.[4] On the evening of the 17th we were in the harbor.

My first concern was to distribute to all four winds the letters that I had foresightedly written at sea. I was on European home soil and could not immediately obtain news of those through whom a definite point of the all-nourishing earth had become home for me. Friends, as an interlude I should like to invite you to accompany me on a quick excursion to London. But my soul thirsted for only one thing, for letters from my friends, and I couldn't rest until I arrived in my Berlin home.

In a letter of mine dated from the Channel I find the following words: I am returning to you the same person I always was—completely so—somewhat fatigued, not surfeited from this voyage, still ready under the right circumstances to go forth into the world again, and "with my mantle wrapped around me."[5]

On the morning of the 18th I stopped at the first best house in Portsmouth to inquire about tailor, shoemaker, etc. I was held fast: "What do you need?" "Everything, and I wish to ride on the coach that leaves for London tomorrow afternoon at four o'clock."— Cloths, materials, calico, linen were presented for my selection. Workers took measurements. Hats, boots were tried on, stockings selected, the order carefully noted down. I was finished in ten minutes. On the 19th at half past three I got my packed trunk on the *Rurik*, everything according to plan and instruction, the linen newly sewn, labeled, washed, and ironed. The only thing that annoyed me was the anxiety with which money was demanded before the goods were allowed to leave their hands.

In England the work day begins at ten o'clock in the morning, as a rule, and ends in the afternoon at four. A coach between Portsmouth and London leaves at four o'clock in the afternoon and arrives the next morning at ten o'clock: the businessman has not lost an hour's time on the journey. Another coach travels during the day for other people.

At four o'clock I sat in the coach and watched out the window as the milestones passed by with incredible rapidity. On the fly I recognized some plants of our home flora, and the purple foxglove with its long clusters of blossoms seemed to beckon to me in friendly welcome.

On the roof of the coach—I almost said on the deck—several vacationing pupils of a nautical school had taken seats. The young fellows were amusing as they practiced their climbing arts on this vehicle that was speeding along like an arrow, and they were everywhere except where they were supposed to be.

I had revealed myself as the titular scholar of the Russian exploring expedition. The companions on my trip showered attentions on me, the stranger, which I was far from expecting.

I was awakened in the middle of the night from the soundest, healthiest sleep. Dinner was to be served. Everyone tried his best to be of service to me in my sleep-drugged awkwardness. My eyes half-open, in a Babel-*Rurik* confusion of tongues I tried one after another all the tongues of human speakers that I knew and didn't know before I hit upon the right one and found myself in old England again.

Among the pupils in our traveling company there was a Russian by birth. He was presented to me, and I was supposed to converse with him. With all the best will in the world, this I was unable to do.

What a happy find, what a gem, for a well-trained police! A person, who without a passport, and without papers of any kind, is on his way to the Capital; who, in order to hide himself quickly, passes himself off as a Russian, when a special turn of fortune immediately demonstrates that he does not understand the language. However, the poor English do not possess this charitable institution. The embarrassment that betrayed me wasn't even noticed. They took me at my word, and I was as safe as a rascal would be in our country who had forged his own papers.

Out of ignorance of London I got off in the City, at the Belle Sauvage Inn in Fleet Street. The world in which I wanted to move was in Westminster, Piccadilly. Seven days in London encompass more experiences, more sights than three years on board ship on the high seas and in view of strange coasts—in London, which along with and alternating with Paris makes and announces history for the rest of the world. I shall not give an account here of every bird that I saw flying around.

In London I lived exclusively with scholars and in museums, herbariums, gardens, and menageries. Just to enumerate the names of the men to whom I feel deeply obliged would take too long. Sir Joseph Banks' library became a sort of headquarters for me. Sir Robert Brown, who directed it, was exceedingly obliging to me.[6] I had the honor of being presented to Sir Joseph Banks. At his residence I saw, among others, Captain James Burney, Captain Cook's companion on his third voyage and author of the *Chronological History of the Discoveries in the South Sea*, a masterpiece of thorough scholarship and rare healthy criticism.[7] To have dared to stand up against a man like James Burney in the question as to "whether Asia and America are connected or separated by the sea" and to have been right where he was wrong is one of the things that honor me in my eyes.

One day I was wandering around in a museum, notebook in hand, and making notes about objects that especially caught my attention. A quick, lively man was doing the same thing with great zeal. Accident brought us together, and he addressed me. He must have soon noticed by my answers that I was not a native Englishman, and he asked me in French, if he should use this language. But in the joy of my heart I burst forth in German, "Why, that's my native tongue!" "Then we will speak German," Sir Hamilton Smith continued in German, and from that time forward he became my obliging and learned guide to the various museums, which we agreed to visit together.

I first met Cuvier in London and also met Professor Otto of Breslau there, who gave me a lot of news from home.[8]

The well-known Mr. Hunnemann was obliging and helpful to me in all things. He was my adviser, my guide, my interpreter. He devoted a large part of his valuable time to helping me. He helped me to collect everything belatedly that I had been lacking on the voyage in the way of instruments, books, charts, in order for me to equip myself for the trip home with everything I should have had on the trip out. Would anyone who is smiling at this have been any smarter about it? For my part, for every new chapter of my life that I simply live through as well as I can, I am modestly prepared for the fact that it will not bring me the wisdom I needed at the beginning until it is over, and that on my deathbed I will find the missing wisdom of my life. And I have no regrets, because I have not failed knowingly and on purpose, and because I am of the opinion that other people do not do much better than I have done.—But I was speaking of my purchases, for which I had earmarked about £100. In Arrowsmith I found a nice liberal scholar. He said that we had worked for him and gave me the chart I had wished to purchase from him.

Having lived in nature the last few years, I now felt an inexpressible, irresistible attraction to art, which nature has intellectualized according to the need of intellectual man, and I had to devote some of the numbered hours that I could spend in London to seeking calm in the contemplation of the paintings of Raphael or of Antiquity.

The French Restoration, which took pains to deny recent history, hastened to topple statues and scratch out inscriptions and names, in the traditional fashion. But public opinion in Europe forbade it to destroy works of art which it took into its custody. It had chosen the middle road, at least removing these bearers of hated memories from their roots and showering them upon strangers as gifts. I knew that Canova's *Napoleon* had been awarded to Lord Wellington and had to be in London.[9] I had been curious about this statue for some time, and I wished very much to see how Canova had idealized the emperor in order to clarify for myself whether the *vieux Sergeant de la garde*, to whom I believed this statue was addressed, could recognize his idolized *petit Caporal* in the naked Greek demigod.[10]

"Here," Robert Brown told me on the way to Kew, whither he had the goodness to accompany me, "here, in this house, behind this door stands the statue of which we speak." And I in response, "Then, let us go up, knock or ring; the door will open and we'll look in." "If you wish to see the statue," answered Robert Brown, familiar with the custom, "I will write to Sir Joseph Banks. At his request the permission will doubtless be granted you. Or the Russian or Prussian envoy could make the request." I cannot use great measures to achieve small gains and employ block and tackle to move a feather. I shook my head, and we went on.

Mr. von Kotzebue was in London the same time I was. I saw him only briefly. He had attached himself to the Russian envoy, had been presented to Grand Duke Nikolai Pavlovich, and complained that his time was filled up differently from the way he desired and that he was getting to see only little of that which interested him.[11]

But I am in London and haven't spoken of London yet. You can find natural history collections elsewhere, and scholars helpful to the stranger, too. A number of cities are richer in art treasures than this one.

Indeed, I did not wander like a blind man through this admirable world that, excited by the parliamentary elections, unveiled its essence to me. In England the public life moves on the public market with parliamentary elections, popular meetings, processions, speeches of all types. What is spoken behind closed doors echoes in the streets, which are crowded at all times by hawkers, by distributors of broadsides and newspapers, at night by transparent pictures and slogans. The walls of London, with their political placards, are for the foreigner, who cannot believe his eyes, the most fabulously wonderful, the most incredible book that he can ever get to see. And it is these sacred freedoms that make the building safe, in that they concede free play to every force, even destructive ones, into the open air. It is these sacred freedoms that will, it is to be hoped, shape the long-postponed and overdue revolution, which England is now busy effecting, as a peaceful evolution. This revolution would have long ago flooded any other soil with a muck mixed of blood and dust.

The Duke of Wellington began this revolution with the untimely resistance of his word "No reform."[12] He gave the ship over to the wind and current that pull it along irresistibly. The same duke has presumed to take over the helm and now promises himself to steer it past the rocks under reefed sails, but downstream, always downstream toward his goal.

Inclined to comparisons, I cast my glance aside from London to Paris first. There *las narices del volcán*,[13] the safety valves of the steam boiler, are to be closed off and soldered over. Public life is being forced bodily into the inner building and can only force itself into the marketplace as an *émeute* or revolt. On the walls of Paris only private affairs are transacted next to the theater posters, bookshop advertisements, and the like. Here the merchant praises his goods above those of his neighbor, here the petty rivalry of tradesmen carries out petty quarrels, etc.

Across the Rhine people have still not awakened to any public life. That in spite of that there are sentiments, capable and dynamic, was proved by the year 1813 and will be demonstrated further by every like stellar year that dawns upon Germany.[14] In Berlin on the street corners you still read comedy and concert notices, the advertisement of the big elephant, of the strong man, and of those things in general that can be seen there; and, finally, announcements of auctions.

In St. Petersburg no product of the press can be exposed to the eyes of the people. The walls are kept clean, and the comedy notice is sneaked surreptitiously into the houses of those who desire them.

I shall return to my point of departure. On the walls of London I read the placard with which Lord Thomas Cochrane took leave of his constituents, the voters of Westminster.[15] After many defamatory remarks against the ministers he came to speak of the hero whom they illegally and illicitly held captive on St. Helena. They, not Napoleon, belonged in this dungeon. It would be fitting to free him and imprison them in his stead. If no one else would take it upon himself to do this, he, Lord Thomas Cochrane, was the man to do it.

This war manifesto was not found more repugnant in London than the notice of the opera *Alcidor* in Berlin.[16] It was under the protection of custom.

I came to the election platform for Westminster in Covent Garden a half hour too late to see the prime minister get hit by mud-balls as punishment for his unpopular acts as he exercised his rights as a voter; a truly popular amusement, to have attended which the wisdom-seeking traveler would have to regard as a special favor of fate.

We know from tradition that in days gone by among the academic freedoms belonging to the youths studying at German universities there was the right (bought, to be sure, for the price of a few days room-arrest) to throw stones through the windows of a disliked teacher without any accusation of a conspiracy against church and state. Upon such an occasion a stone as big as a fist once landed on the desk of old Johann Reinhold Forster.[17] He angrily picked the stone up, and, throwing open the window, he threw it back at the students, crying out, "A freshman threw that!"

Similar things happened, translated into English, at the elections mentioned above. The people had made use of their undeniable right toward a ministerial candidate and had thrown mud at him. But a stone had also flown through the air; at least the mistreated individual claimed to have been hit by one, and took to his bed. Bulletins were issued, and it seemed as if the fateful stone was to be outweighed by the votes that flowed in the direction of the wounded man. As I stopped before the platform his opponent made a speech in which he discussed the incident. He declared: "The person who threw that stone could not have been an Englishman." Then the thunderous applause of the assemblage drowned out the speaker's voice.

On June 26, 1818, at four o'clock in the afternoon, Mr. Hunnemann brought me to the coach that was leaving for Portsmouth. My purchases, which he had seen to having packed, filled a medium-sized chest, which I took along on the coach. I embraced my unforgettable compatriot and took leave of the metropolis of London.

I was in Portsmouth on June 27. I found no letters waiting for me.

No return greetings from my dear ones reached me in England, no news of them. The *Rurik* came to the wharf on the 29th and went under sail on the 30th. On July 1 we went through the Straits of Dover, lost sight of land on the 2nd, saw Jutland on the 10th, went through the Sound on the 11th, and were at Copenhagen on the 12th. We were to sail by without stopping, but the wind, which failed us, decided otherwise. I was allowed to go ashore for a brief hour. I received my first greeting from home and embraced my old friends.

We weighed anchor on the 13th. On the 23rd we ran into the harbor of Reval, where the captain wished to speak with Mr. von Krusenstern. He was not in town and did not arrive until two days later. On the 27th we set sail again and on July 31 were at Kronshtadt. On August 3, 1818, the *Rurik* lay at anchor in St. Petersburg in the Neva before Count Romanzov's house.

The count was on his estates in Little Russia, and we had to wait for him to come and dissolve the little world that had held together so long in his name. Mr. von Krusenstern did not appear until about two weeks after we did. Some upper rooms in Count Romanzov's house were opened up to Mr. von Kotzebue and his crew. A Prussian resident here, a university friend, drew me hospitably to his fireside. I left the *Rurik*.

But I had no passport, and here the police were much better equipped to deal with foreigners than they were in England. However, I happened to have a protector in the Prussian Embassy, and what cannot be arranged, if one has friends?

I had only one task in St. Petersburg: to get myself released from St. Petersburg as soon as possible. I turned away from every prospect that was to be opened to me in Russia and stubbornly avoided every proposal that would tie me down under any circumstances. Another land was calling me home. I will not mix any high names into this chatter. My heart belonged to Prussia, and I wanted to return to Berlin.

St. Petersburg is a marvelously planned and magnificently executed decoration. The shipping that animates the sea between Kronshtadt and the mouth of the Neva points to a place that is rich in population and commerce! You step into the city and the people disappear in the broad, unsurveyably long streets, and grass grows everywhere among the cobblestones.

Decoration in big as well as little things: appearance has been made the essence of everything. The finest materials are used for decorating: cast iron and granite. But occasionally one finds, to restore the interrupted monotony, that granite is painted black like cast iron, and the cast iron is painted to resemble granite. The city is painted anew every three years, and in the colors prescribed by the police to the houseowners, also specially on special occasions, for the reception of a royal guest, etc. Then the grass is also pulled out of the street. The ruler once remarked on the pleasure with which he had seen massive houses on a trip, in which all the woodwork, doors and window frames, were of oak. Thereupon painters were trained by the police, and doors and window frames of all the houses of the city were painted like oak at the cost of the owners. Then the painters came into the quarter where the rich English merchants live, and where the luxury of oaken doors and window frames is not rare, and they began to paint the real oak like oak. The property-owners protested against it and argued that it was already oak. In vain! The order of the high police had to be satisfied.

The same procedure and game is played with monuments, for which popular piety ought to be solicited, as is the case with mere decorations. The Romanzov pillar is brought from one bank of the Neva to the other to favor a new point of view, and the order has been given to move the statue of Tsar Peter the Great from the place it now occupies, for the purpose of a similar embellishment.

It is painful to me to have to express a sharp criticism here, which also concerns impiety, of which people at home are also guilty. But just what is a monument? A piece of ground is dedicated to the memory of a man or a deed; then a stone is placed upon it and children are whipped past the stone and told at the same time: Remember this and that! In this manner legend, oral tradition, is attached to a definite external matter among people. That is the essence of a monument. That you later learned to carve letters into the stone, and to chisel the stone itself into the likeness of a person, those are inessential additions. If you move the stone away from its place, you have only a stone, like many others in the field. If you move the statue from its place, then you reduce it to its artistic value, then you have only an image, like many others you have in your museums, which once were gods in temples. Do not lay a hand on a national monument of the people, do not lay a hand on the statue of one of your heroes: the place where it stands belongs to it, you no longer have any right to it. Erect monuments in places where they can be seen, but not for mere embellishment, and choose the place thoughtfully, as you mustn't change it arbitrarily.

Count Romanzov arrived in St. Petersburg in the first days of September.

All the books and instruments that had been provided for me at the cost of the expedition were demanded back from me, as they

were from each one of us. On the other hand, I remained in possession of what I had collected. I was released so that I could finish the
writings expected of me in Berlin. The *Rurik* was sold.

Now the police, who had had such a hard time deciding to tolerate my presence in St. Petersburg, detained me there. The lengthy
formalities to which one must submit before he can obtain a passport are well known. (The announcement of one's intention to
travel published three times in the weekly paper, etc.) I was finally
back: the world to which I had belonged had already disintegrated.

I hope I may be permitted, now that I am soon to depart from this
earth, to seek out once more the men in whose company I endured
and learned so much. Mr. von Kotzebue's *New Journey Around the
World in the Years 1823–1826* (the second, which he commanded,
the third he made) has been mentioned in these pages. It has
attracted attention, especially because of the unfavorable reports
about the missions in the South Seas. Khramchenko commanded a
ship in the northern part of the South Seas and sent friendly greetings to me from Rio-Janeiro in the year 1830. My eye can no longer
catch sight of the other mariners in their ever-changing element. Of
those who were in circumstances similar to mine, I, the oldest, am
the only one who has not departed from the scene. Eschscholtz, professor in Dorpat, again accompanied Mr. von Kotzebue on his new
journey. He visited me in Berlin in the year 1829, where he published his most important work: *The System of the Acalephae.*[18]
After a few months he was no more.[19] In the year 1825 I saw Choris
in Paris, where he was living for art. Soon afterwards he undertook a
trip to Mexico: between Santa Cruz and Mexico City he was
attacked by robbers and murdered. Lieutenant Wormskiold in Copenhagen, sunk in deep melancholia, left the world behind him.

On September 27, 1818, my chests were put aboard the *Asträa*
from Stettin, Captain Breslack. Various circumstances delayed our
departure. I had to wait in Kronshtadt a few more days for a favorable wind.

The metamorphoses of insects can also be perceived in a human
being, only in reverse order. In the period of his youth he has wings
that he later casts off in order as a larva to live off the leaf to which
he is restricted. I was at the turning point. Before my fortieth year (I
had only two and a quarter years left until then) I wished to strip off
my wings, take root, and found a family; or spread my wings again
and on another journey away from Europe, more mature and better
prepared, make up what I had neglected to do for science on my first
journey. These democratic times, in which, in science and art as
well as in history, the masses are stepping forth instead of individual

princes, grant each mortal the hope of playing a role of some importance in the nation where formerly homage was paid only to outstanding heads to whom God had given it.

On October 17 the *Asträa* lay at the wharf in Swinemünde.[20]

Here this period of my life ends. As a sequel, my friends, I am
going to give you the book of my poems.[21] In this for my own pleasure I have carefully folded and preserved the blossoms of my life,
while the branches on which they grew withered away.

But let the lines that I wrote on the wharf at Swinemünde con-
clude the present book as they also serve as an introduction to the
next.

> As homeward turns at last from foreign shores
> The wanderer, deeply moved within his heart,
> He casts aside his staff, falls on his knees,
> Bedewing with his silent tears thy breast,
> O German homeland! Pray do not deny
> His one request as payment for his love:
> May he at nightfall when his eyelids droop
> Find shelter on thy soil beneath a stone
> Where he can rest his weary head in peace.

Written in the winter of 1834–1835.

# PART II
## Notes and Opinions

Kadu, native of the Carolines, who accompanied the *Rurik* to the Aleutian Islands. Detail of a watercolor by Louis Choris. Honolulu Academy of Arts. Gift of the Honolulu Art Society, 1944.

# Table of Contents.

# CHAPTER I
## California.

A low mountain range enclosed the coast of California, wherever we saw it, and obstructed our view into the interior.[1] It does not have a volcanic appearance.[2] San Francisco Bay, in which Burney as the result of learned investigation recognizes Sir Francis Drake's harbor, passes through a narrow gate, absorbs rivers from the interior and makes a peninsula out of the land situated south of the entrance.[3] The presidio and the mission of San Francisco are built on this neck of land, which, with its hills and dunes, was the not very favorable field that was first open to our investigations.

The heights on the northern side of the harbor are mountains of silicious schist. The hill opposite them on the southern side is of serpentine. If you follow the beach southward toward the Punta de los Lobos, the serpentine comes to an end, and you come to some almost perpendicular layers of slate that lie like a shield against coarse-grained sandstone with veins of calcareous spar, and this sandstone, of which the southern hills as far as Punta de los Lobos consist, seems to be the deeper-lying mountain type.[4] Drifting sand is present to a considerable height above the stone in some places, and in places a new sandstone has been produced.

The region around San Francisco in the Northern Hemisphere exhibits a far sparser nature than does the coast of Chile at the same latitude in the Southern Hemisphere. In the spring, after the winter has granted the earth some moisture, it is true, the hills and meadows are adorned with brilliant irises and other flowers, but the drought soon destroys them.

The fogs that the prevailing sea breezes spread over the coast dissolve again in the summer above a heated and thirsting earth, and in the fall the land shows only a vista of bare areas burned brown, alternating with bushes pressed pitifully against the soil, and in places with blinding deserts of drifted sand. Forests of dark firs can be seen here and there on the ridges of the mountains between Punta de los

Reyes and San Francisco Bay.[5] An oak with acuminate leaves *(Quercus agrifolia)* is the commonest and strongest tree. With jaggedly bent branches, their closely compacted twigs thickly covered with usnea, like the other growth they are bent inland, and the leafy surfaces that the sea breezes touch seem to be smoothed by the gardener's shears. The flora here is meager and is adorned by none of the plant forms that a warmer sun produces. But it offers the botanist much that is new. Known American genera associate with those strange to us, and most species are still undescribed.[6] Only Archibald Menzies and Langsdorff have made collections here, and the fruits of their endeavors have yet to be presented to the world.[7] The season was not the most favorable one for us. However, we collected the seeds of many plants and may promise ourselves that we shall be able to enrich our gardens.

These deserts serve as the dwelling place for many animals, some of which may still be undescribed. Here they bear the names of known species: little lion, wolf and fox, stag, goats, and rabbits. Their most fearful visitor, however, is the bear, which according to the reports of the hunters is of extraordinary size, strength, savagery, and tenacity of life. He attacks humans and animals even if he is not lacking vegetable forage and gathers in countless packs when dead whales are cast onto the shore. His coat varies from brown to very light and often displays different colors in spots. It does not seem to be the white bear described by Lewis and Clark, nor is it the known American black bear. From the specimen we saw, a young female, we cannot distinguish it from the European brown bear, and the skull, which Professor Rudolphi has examined, also seemed to him to belong to this species.[8] The Spaniard is quite used to catching this dangerous beast with a lasso and takes pleasure from watching him do battle with a bull. The whales and seals of the north visit this coast. The sea lion is common, the sea otter now nowhere more numerous than here.

Birds are present in great variety and amounts, the *Oriolus phoeniceus* being especially plentiful in endless flights.[9] We did not note a single species of the family of climbers, and a brilliantly feathered hummingbird seemed like a stranger from the south who had gone astray in this region.

With a feeling of sadness we set about writing a word about the Spanish settlements on this coast.[10] With envious greed Spain here expands merely in order not to allow others to have the territory. It maintains its presidios at great expense and seeks by the prohibition of all trade to force the currency back to its source. However, a little freedom would soon make California into the granary and market of the northern coasts of these seas and the ships sailing them. Grain, cattle, salt (in St. Quentin, Old California), wine, the manufacture of which would increase demand, in many respects give it an advantage over the Sandwich Islands, whose situation on the route of trade between China and the northwest coast is, to be sure, the more advantageous one. And who, with industry and shipping, daughters of freedom, could have a more advantageous share of this trade than this very California, that now possesses the sea otter more than any other coast?[11]

But without industry, trade, and shipping California remains desolate and unpopulated.[12] For six to seven years during the internal wars between Spain and its colonies it has languished forgotten, without any imports from Mexico. Just now, during our stay in Monterey, the ship from San Blas arrived that used to provide necessities to the settlements annually.[13] In San Francisco harbor the missions possess several poor longboats, which foreign prisoners built. The presidio itself has no boat, and other harbors are no better equipped. Foreigners catch the sea otter even inside Spanish harbors, and a smuggling trade, which the present governor of New California has been trying to oppose since his appointment (fourteen months ago), is all that provides this province with the most indispensable necessities. Spain gave in in the Nootka affair;[14] now, without regard for its vain territorial claims, England and the Free States of America are negotiating over the settlements at the mouth of the Columbia, and the Russian-American company still has a trading post a few miles north of San Francisco.

However, a reason other than a political one is pretended for the retention of these settlements: namely, the pious purpose of spreading the belief in Christ and the conversion of the heathen peoples. Even the governor of the province advanced this point of view as the correct one. Well then, here a good work was begun injudiciously and poorly executed.

The pious Franciscans who maintain the missions in new California are not trained in any of the arts and crafts that they are supposed to practice and teach here nor in any of the languages that the peoples to which they are sent speak. They are monks like those in the monasteries of Europe.[15] In each mission every two of them manage a considerable amount of farmland, conduct the religious services, and converse through interpreters, who themselves are Indians, with their charges. All property belongs to the congregation of the mission and is administered by the fathers. The Indian himself does not draw any direct profit from his labor and no wages if, for instance, he is rented out as a day laborer to the presidio. The mission, this rational being, draws the penny that he earns. He does not come to know property and is not bound by it. We do not deny the gentleness, the paternal care of the missionaries, of which we have been witnesses at various times.[16] But the relationship remains the one described and would, it seems to us, be different only in name if a slaveholder kept them for labor and rented them out at will; he too would feed them.

The savage comes to the mission thoughtlessly, accepts the food that is gladly handed to him, listens to the doctrine.[17] He is still free. But once he has received baptism and belongs to the Church, he looks back to his home mountains with vain longing. The Church has an irrevocable right to its children and here vindicates this right with force. Can this be a surprise when the motherland still harbors the Inquisition? The savage is thoughtless; he is as inconstant as a child. Unaccustomed labor becomes too hard for him; he regrets the step that has fettered him; he longs for his inborn freedom. The love for his native soil is powerful in him. The fathers generally grant their charges a few weeks' leave twice a year to visit their relatives and the place of their birth.[18] Upon the occasion of these trips, which are undertaken in droves, apostates depart and neophytes come in. The former, from among whom the Spaniards' worst enemies arise, the missionaries try to win back by kindness on their official tours, and if they are unable to do so, armed force is requisitioned against them. Several of the hostile incidents between the Spaniards and the Indians proceeded from this cause.

The Indians are dying out in the missions at a rate that is increasing terribly. Their tribe is vanishing. San Francisco contains about a thousand Indians; the number of deaths in the preceding year surpassed 300, while this year it already amounts to 270 (to October), of which 40 occurred in the last month. The number of proselytes, however, must surpass that of the apostates and the excess of the dying. We heard of five missions that were founded in this province since Vancouver's time. On the other hand, some of the missions of the Dominicans in Old California have already perished, and the peoples there won to the Faith can already almost be regarded as extinct.

There is no medical help to be found here, except that a ship's doctor is said to have once taught them blood-letting, and since then this expedient, being applied at every opportunity, hastens death. One disease especially, which, although opinions vary on the subject, the Europeans may well have spread abroad here, claimed its victims without opposition.[19] It likewise prevailed among savage tribes, but these do not disappear from the earth with the same terrible swiftness. Conversely, the number of whites increases.

The contempt that the missionaries feel toward the peoples to whom they are sent seems to us to be an unhappy circumstance in view of their pious purpose. None of them seem to have concerned themselves with their history, customs, beliefs, or languages. "They are unreasoning savages, and there is no more to be said about them! Who paid any attention to their ignorance, who wasted time with it?"

Indeed, these tribes are far beneath those that inhabit the northern coast and the interior of America. As a whole they are similar in appearance, except perhaps the Cholovones, whom we soon learned to differentiate by their splendid physiognomies, something the fathers themselves could not do.[20] They are all of a very savage appearance, of a very dark color. Their flat, broad faces, from which large, savage eyes blaze forth, are surrounded by long, straight hair, black and thick. The gradation in color, the languages, when the roots are alien to each other, their way of life, arts, weapons, differently tattooed lines on the chin and neck of some of them, the way in which they paint their bodies for war or for the dance, differentiate the various tribes. They live among themselves and with the Spaniards in differing relationships, friendly or hostile. Among many of them the weapons are the bow and arrow. Among some of them these are of extraordinary elegance, the bow light and strong, the outer arch covered with animal sinews; among others they are of wood alone and crude. Some possess the art (a woman's task) of plaiting attractive watertight vessels out of colored straw, but the Indian generally forgets his industry in the mission. They all go naked, all are without horses or boats of any kind. They know only how to join bundles of reeds together, which because of their specific lightness carry them over the water. Those who live by rivers live chiefly on salmon, which they catch in basket traps; those in the mountains on wild fruits and grains. No one plants or sows; they just burn the meadows off from time to time to increase their fertility.

The South Sea islanders, differing greatly from each other, and distributed over almost a third of the Torrid Zone of the earth, speak one language. In America, especially here in New California, tribes of one race living near each other often speak completely different tongues. Every fraction of the history of mankind has importance. We must leave it up to our successors, as our predecessors left it up to us, to gather satisfactory information about the natives of California and their languages.[21] We had set ourselves this goal on a projected trip to some of the closest missions. Business of another type kept us in San Francisco, and the day of our departure drew near without our being able to find time for this trip.

We refer for further details to the reports of Lapérouse and Vancouver, which we have found reliable. Very little has changed in California since their day.[22] The presidio has been rebuilt of adobe, its roof covered with tile. The structure of the chapel, still unstarted in their day, has been constructed in the same manner, and the barracks of the Indians in San Francisco are of the same construction. An artilleryman set up mills activated by horsepower in the missions, but now they are mostly out of use and cannot be repaired again. In San Francisco a stone that a horse draws across another stone without any mechanism is the only mill still functioning. For a hurried need the Indian women grind the grain between two stones. A windmill of the Russian-American settlement arouses admiration but finds no imitation. When some years ago artisans were brought here at great expense to teach the various crafts needed here, the Indians utilized the instruction better than the gente racional ("rational people"), the expression with which the Spaniards designate themselves. It was the latter who gave the former this testimony.

We noted with regret that the best relationship did not exist between the missions and the presidios. The fathers looked upon themselves as the highest in this land, for whose protection alone the presidios are established. A military unit that carries weapons and often uses them does not willingly bear the guardianship of the church. The presidios, living from their salaries alone, are dependent for their needs upon the missions, from which they purchase them for cash. They have suffered privations lately, and they accused the missions of having allowed them to suffer.

Finally, we must mention the noble hospitality with which military and missions alike strove to anticipate our needs, and the willingly granted unlimited freedom we enjoyed on Spanish soil. We dedicate these lines of memory and gratitude to our friends in California.

The following tribes of Californians have been mentioned to us as those that reside in the realm of the San Francisco mission:

The Guymen, Utschiun, Olumpali, Soclan, and Sonomi: all speak one language; they form the majority in the San Francisco mission.

The Chulpun, Umpin, Kosmitas, Bolbones, Chalabones, Pitemen, Lamames, Apalamnes, and Cholovones: live by the Rio del

Sacramento and all speak one language. They bear the best weapons. The Cholovones, a warlike tribe, are allied with the Spaniards against the other Indians.

The Suysum, Numpali, Tamal: they tattoo themselves, speak the same language, and live toward the north, the Tamal toward the northwest.

The Ululato: live farther north than the Suysum, and only a few of them come to the mission.[23]

# CHAPTER II
## Pacific Languages.

THE language of the Papuas, who live among other peoples in isolated tribes without any communication and connection, must have split into many greatly deviating dialects. The Malays of the Malacca Peninsula consider the dialects of the Negroes of the mountains as mere chirping, comparable only to the voice of the larger birds, and on some of the islands the idea prevailing about it is no more favorable.[1] The language of the Haraforas also is considered to be quite unique, having nothing in common with the languages of the other peoples.[2] On the other hand, the Spaniards say of the Aetas of the Philippines that in general their idiom exhibits a great similarity with that of the inhabitants of the coast (Fra Juan de la Concepción), and that they speak dialects of the same language as the Indians (Zúñiga).[3]

According to Forster the languages of the peoples of his second race are not only quite different from the common language of the southlanders, but also completely alien and dissimilar to each other.[4] The samples he furnishes, however, besides numerals, also contain a few other roots that are common, and the same remark is also applicable to the vocabularies that Lemaire and Schouten collected in New Guinea and the Isle de Moise.

The languages in New Holland seem to be quite divergent among themselves and compared with the dialects of the other race; however, the word collections we have of them are inadequate for making a judgment. Sir Robert Brown has assured us that the peoples with whom he has had connections are unable to count beyond four, and that "five" and "many" converge for them.

We come now to the prevailing race of handsome facial formation, long, curly hair, and white in color, although tanned more or less brown by the effect of the climate, that is distributed from Madagascar in the west to Easter Island in the east.

With Marsden we must acknowledge the identity of the language family to which all the dialects belong that are spoken by the various peoples distributed over such an immeasurable space.[5] The agreement of the numerals in all the dialects from Madagascar to Easter Island can, strictly speaking, demonstrate only common contact, not the same derivation.[6] The numbers are easily borrowed from a foreign language. We find them in some dialects of the Papuas, whose relationship remains doubtful, and the inhabitants of the Marianas have forgotten how to count in their own language, having accustomed themselves to the Spanish numerals.

In all the dialects, besides the same numerals, there is a considerable number of common roots that generally designate the closest, simplest things and concepts and that seem to have been inherited from a proto stage, not learned from a foreign people. We can demonstrate these roots in the vocabularies of Madagascar and in those of the islands of the Great Ocean.

Finally, the grammar in the better-known dialects, Malayu, Tagalog, Tonga, developed to varying degrees, remains essentially the same, and nothing justifies our assuming that the situation is any different in the less-known ones. The very simple language system is approximately the same when the roots are polysyllabic as it is for monosyllabic languages. There are no inflections, the roots either standing abruptly next to each other as in Chinese, and obtaining their value by their position, or, in the more developed dialects, being determined by particles that are variously affixed or interpolated.

Many different and different-speaking peoples of this race inhabit the islands of the East Indian archipelago. Leyden represents the purer dialect of Javanese spoken in the interior as being closely and intimately connected with Sanskrit.[7] The simplest objects and concepts seem to differ from Sanskrit only in pronunciation, which the use of a less perfect alphabet necessarily causes. Language, monuments, and history point back to India.

History first shows us one of these peoples in the twelfth century, the Malays, proceeding from the region of Manangkabau [Minangkabau] in the southwest of Sumatra, their first residence, spreading their conquests and the law of Mohammed, which they had received from Arab merchants, expanding both on the continent on the peninsula of Malacca and to the coasts of the other islands. The converted peoples are often confused with them, and the terms Malays, Moors, and Mohammedans used synonymously without criticism.

In the third book of Marco Polo we find a picture of what this archipelago was like at the end of the thirteenth century, and this picture is still applicable today.[8] This traveler's remarks are always true in the realm of his own experiences, and the fabulous tales he spins on someone else's authority have still not been forgotten in the places where he gathered them. Pigafetta deserves similar praise. Marco Polo found that the people who live by the sea in the kingdom of Felech on the island of Little Java were Mohammedans who learned the law of Mohammed from the merchants who traveled there. Pigafetta, who was in Tidori [Tidore] in the year 1521, reports that the Moors had conquered the Moluccas about fifty years before and had transplanted their faith there.[9] The collection of words he made there agrees with present-day Malay.

Malay has become the common language of communication in this part of the world, the language of all commerce and intercourse, and it is spoken inside the houses of Europeans as far as the Cape of Good Hope. This language is completely known to us—Marsden's dictionary and grammar (London, 1812) fulfill all our needs in this regard. In the Introduction to the grammar there is a history of the language and the literature regarding the sources for learning it.

Malay is a later-blooming branch of the general language family. Along with a number of common roots it contains a considerable number of Indian words, and Islam had a later effect, which remained more superficial. The Arabic system of writing has displaced the Indian system, to which the heathen peoples, with the training peculiar to them, still adhere. The four types of style and expression in the common Malayan language, which are adapted to the station and conditions of those who speak them—the language of the court, of the nobles, the common people, and the market place—have been examined only by those inexpert in dialects. In Malay grammar we have been given a random point of comparison for the other less-known tongues of this language family.

We owe our increasing knowledge of the peoples and languages of the East Indian islands to the research zeal of the English and refer to the works already cited for their study: Marsden's *Sumatra*, Raffles' *Java*, the *Asiatick Researches*, the *Asiatic Journal*, etc.[10] Their scholarship will succeed in deciphering the monuments of forgotten history in Java, in elucidating languages and customs in their connections with those of other peoples, in tracing the original people we are concerned with from Asia proper, and in tracing the path by which they wandered to their present sea-splashed habitats.

The Philippines present to us a peculiar family of the same people and the same mother language. Here we find the language at the highest point of its peculiar independent development, and the grammars of the various dialects, which we owe to the Spanish missionaries, reveal to us a linguistic treasure at which we shall try to take a look.[11]

The coastal inhabitants of these islands, who can be regarded as their first conquerors, *los indios* of the Spaniards, according to their tribal affiliations speak seven different main dialects, namely: in the north of Luzón the Pampangos, Zambales, Pangasinanes, Ylocos, and Cayayanes; in the Manila area the Tagalos; and on all the southern islands the Bisayas, along with some unrelated tribes. [12]

The Spaniards are foreigners on the Philippine Islands. Many tribes of the Indians, even in the interior of Luzón, have maintained their independence, and those of the coasts, who have taken on the foreign yoke along with Christianity, have not learned the foreign language. The orders of monks who completed the spiritual conquest of the peoples and assure political power, have adopted their language. Tagalog especially, which, through the circumstance that it is spoken round the capital, has become the chief language, has obtained through them not only textbooks for learning it but also considerable literature both in prose and verse of edifying works of all kinds. Father Francisco de San Joseph is called *el Cicerón*, and Father Pedro de Herrera *el Horacio Tagalo*, and even a tragedian to translate Dionysius Areopagita has not failed to appear. [13] *Artes* and *vocabularios* of the Pampango, Bisayan, and Yloco languages have appeared in print. The textbooks of the other dialects are in manuscript, and the copies by which they are disseminated are generally to be found only in the provinces in the hands of the padres.

According to the testimony of all Tagalists the seven dialects cited agree essentially both in grammatical forms and roots. We ourselves have compared the grammars of the Tagala, Pampango, and Bisayan languages and noted only insignificant deviations. If differences in pronunciation at first hamper understanding for the native of one province when he is in another, a short time is sufficient to level out the differences, and he soon learns to recognize his own language. What has been said of Tagalog is likewise true for the other dialects.

Leyden in his *Asiatick Researches* presented Tagalog, Malayan, Bugis, and Javanese as sister languages, traced the more artful structure of Tagalog to the elements of Malay, and demonstrated the identity of the particles in both, particles upon which all the grammar rests in a linguistic system free of all inflections. [14]

Leyden does not seem to us to value highly enough the meritorious zeal with which the Tagalists have put the verb with simple, reduplicated, and half-reduplicated root, together with all the particles with which it can be variously connected, and which modify it, into a conjugation table, which at least affords one an easy survey. It cannot be denied that with this advantage their presentation of the Tagalog verb does not conform to the original simplicity of the language and strives to present our linguistic system where a different one is really present.

By article and preposition generally, not more than a direct and indirect (object) case are indicated for the noun. The plural and not, as in Malay, the singular, is especially designated by a separate particle. The pronouns are the same as in Malay, only more complete. Beside the two plurals of the first person, one of which includes the person addressed, and the other excludes him, there is also a dual for each person.[15] The pronouns have different forms in the direct and indirect cases. Particles, which correspond to the prepositions of our languages, are prefixed, suffixed, and infixed to the root that expresses the action and designate toward it the time and the relationships that we are accustomed to express in nouns and pronouns either by inflecting them or by accompanying prepositions; hence the three passives, to teach the meaning and use of which is the Tagalist's hardest task. In a sentence we can put only the subject or the object of an action in the nominative and designate the relationship in the verb itself, active and passive, *amo et amor,* Danish *jeg elsker og elskes.* The Tagals can put the subject, the object, the purpose or the instrument, and the place of the action in the direct case and express the relationship with the verb. The meaning decides what is emphasized as the nominative of the phrase and should be put first, and the form of the verb is adjusted accordingly. In this way, in the sentence "Petrus cut off Malchus' ear with the sword," the emphasis can be placed at will on "Petrus (the subject), who cuts" (active form), "the ear (the object) that is cut" (first passive form with *y*), "the sword (the instrument), with which is cut" (second passive with *in*), and "on Malchus (the place) upon whom is cut" (third passive form with *an*). All the niceties and difficulties of the language reside in usage. The same particles that modify the roots as verbs also modify them in similar combinations as nouns and adjectives. The already compounded word is treated like a simple one, and further compounded. Wealth accrues from wealth, but there are no real inflections.

The Tagals in their poetry use verses that, although distinctive, by the number of syllables and a kind of rhyme or half-rhyme are reminiscent of Spanish syllabic meters. They have, however, refused to accept the artificial canzones and sonnets that Padre Francisco de San Joseph tried to give them. We have endeavored in vain to have samples of their original heathen songs, some of which still exist, brought to us. Who values history, art, and relics of a suppressed people in the country itself?

In the Appendix we furnish the Tagal alphabet from three separate sources. It is connected with the older writing system on the East Indian islands, and we refer to the observations with which it is accompanied.[16]

The coastal inhabitants of the island of Formosa to the north of the Philippines seem to us to belong to the same race, their language to the same family.

We come to the islands situated to the east of the Philippines, which we have considered the First Province of Polynesia. In their inhabitants we find a racial family that is united to a large extent by the same customs and highly developed skills, shipping and commerce. A peaceful, charming people worshipping no images, without domestic animals, they live from the gifts of the earth and sacrifice to invisible gods only the first of the fruits from which they derive nourishment. They construct the most artistic seagoing vessels and complete large sea voyages with the help of their great knowledge of the monsoons, the currents, and the stars. In the western islands, the Pelew Islands, Eap, the Marianas, customs of the East Indian islanders, like the chewing of betel nuts, have been introduced.

In spite of the great similarity of most of the tribes (others, like those of the Pelew Islands, which are distinguished by shamelessness of morals and less knowledge of seafaring, might have joined the family from abroad), and in spite of the frequent connections that link them to each other, a great variety of tongues exists among them. We were in a position to collect samples of their dialects because we had enjoyed a more intimate connection with them than other scientific travelers before us, and in the Appendix we furnish a comparative word list of the Marianas, Eap, Ulea, and Radak.

According to Fra Juan de la Concepción the peoples of the Marianas resemble the Bisayans in appearance and in language, which latter, however, deviate in a few particulars *(in algunas cosas alterado)*. This Chamori [Chamorro] or Mariana language, however, has almost disappeared with the people that spoke it.[17] The new generation speaks the language of the conquerors and their own only deformed through an admixture. It can be noted that counting is done only in Spanish, and it cost us trouble to obtain the numerals of the Mariana language. On the other hand, designations from the Philippine languages seem to have won out for some of the foreign animals and objects that have been introduced. In the same way, in the Pelew Islands animals that the English introduced have received Malay names. (The goat *gaming*, Malay *kambing*.)

A *Vocabulario de la lengua Mariana* in the form of the vocabularies that we have of the languages of the Philippines, especially the

*Vocabulario Tagalog* of Fr. Domingo de los Santos, still remains, coming from the Jesuits, in Agaña; one *arte* seems to be missing. This manuscript is moldering away unused, as the Spanish language suffices for the office of the present-day pastors. We have endeavored to investigate the grammatical structure of the Chamori language and in Manila sought out the padres who presided over the missions in Guaján. Some had really not learned the language, and one old man was incapable of giving an account of it. Place names in the Marianas, as in the Philippines, mostly end in -*an*, a particle that in the languages of the Philippines has locative function and also forms the third passive; and we find still other characteristics of analogy, all of which disappear in the dialects of the Carolines. Don Luis de Torres has assured us that in the language of the Marianas and in that of Ulea there are no inflections. We note that the words of the language of the Marianas that we furnish for comparison were not derived from the *Vocabulario*, for which we had no time, but were written down with our own orthography according to Don Luis's pronunciation.[18]

A vocabulary of the dialect spoken in the Pelew Islands is furnished us by Wilson, which only causes us to wish that the same effort had been applied to elucidating the grammar; or that only a few samples, a few songs, had been furnished that would have enabled us to take a look at it.[19]

This work has more authority for us than a slight collection of words, hastily thrown together, that a Spaniard in Manila furnished us and that for this reason we suppress. It would only illustrate how the same sound is differently construed and differently designated by different nations.

We must excuse ourselves for the inadequacy of the word collections from Eap, Ulea, and Radak, which we likewise furnish without going into the structure of the language. You must consider how suddenly and unexpectedly our friend and teacher Kadu departed from us. As these collections grew, a means of understanding had developed between us that improved gradually, and we had postponed reviewing our work, correcting it and completing it, conversing about abstract concepts, and dealing with grammar, to a time that we then did not spend together.

The natives of Radak, like the English, along with a pronunciation difficult to acquire, have no skill in understanding foreigners easily and in turn making themselves understood to them. We believe these dialects to be less simple in construction than the dialect of eastern Polynesia. In various sentences the roots, which one expects in them, are no longer recognizable, and the difficulty of mutual understanding seems to point to this. The dialect of the

Pelew Islands seems to us to be the more deviant, that of Radak, however, to approach the common language most closely, and we also first find there a numerical system based on the scale of twenty, as in New Zealand and the Sandwich Islands, while the western Caroline Islanders, the Malayans, and the Tagals use the pure decimal scale that is customary in Tonga.

Within the boundaries assigned to these provinces, in the southwest closest to the habitats of the Papuas and the Moluccas, we already find some islands, namely the Mavils Islands, whose inhabitants were understood by natives of the Sandwich Islands and whose boats were similar to those of the O-Waihians.[20] A phenomenon that seems to deserve our attention.

In New Zealand, the islands of the Second Province as far east as the remote Easter Island, and in the isolated group of the Sandwich Islands, there is, as we know, only one people, which everywhere is at the same level of culture, has similar customs and morals, and speaks a common language, the dialects of which are affected almost solely by local deviations in pronunciation, so that travelers often can make themselves understood on one island with words they have collected on another one quite remote from it, the natives of the Sandwich Islands being able to converse with those of the Friendly Islands [Tonga], and Tupeia, an islander of this latter group, with the New Zealanders.

We owe a complete grammar of the dialect of Tonga to Messrs. Mariner and T. Martin, which enables us to illuminate the language of eastern Polynesia.[21] In this we recognize the Malayan language system in its greatest possible simplicity and, in our view, at the level of undeveloped childhood. It is a pleasant childish babble that can hardly be called a language.

The Tongan language is more directly related to the infinitely more artful Tagalog than to Malay. It has a frequent use of the article and prefers to express the plural through particles. The pronouns are unmistakably the same, and it still has the dual along with the two plurals of the first person. The roots are used without distinction for the noun, the property, or the action. In the action the three tenses are designated by mere separate particles (adverbs). When two roots stand next to each other, as in other dialects the first is the noun and the second its quality.

For all this simplicity, the dialect of Tonga could nonetheless well be not only a deviant, but one of the most developed dialects of eastern Polynesia. Tonga lies on the western boundary, closest to the motherlands, and the numerical system, as we have already seen, is not that of New Zealand and the Sandwich Islands.

The language of the Sandwich Islands really did seem much more childlike to us than the dialect of Tonga appears in its grammar.[22] We have discovered only two pronouns in it, *wau* for the first person, *hoe* ['oe] for the second, and only two adverbs for determining the time of an action, *mamure* [*mamuli*] for the future, *mamoa* [*mamua*] for past time. The interrogative or doubting particle *paha*, which is a postpositive enclitic, is of frequent use. *Nue* [*nui*] and *nue nue* [*nui nui*] "very" and "large" form the comparative and superlative. Some particles designate the relationships of nouns as prepositions.[23]

Words formed the way that children do by the repetition of a sound, in which the root now has the same sense, now a different one, now no sense at all, which occur much more frequently in the common language of the eastern islands than in the more developed western dialects, where, however, they are not lacking, bestow a peculiar, pleasant character to it.[24]

The O-Waihians have already adopted many words from the foreign nations with which they have dealings, words that are often difficult to recognize by their pronunciation in view of the lack of some letters and the falling-together of others. Their number increases daily, and they are displacing the native words.[25]

The liturgical language on the Sandwich Islands is a peculiar one, deviating from the one now spoken, and which the common man does not understand. Probably the older, unchanged language of the people, it should be one of the first objects of the scientific researches of the scholar whom fate might grant a longer sojourn on these islands. The reports from O-Taheiti agree with this, and it may well be that it was through this older liturgical language that the scholar Tupeia made himself understood with the New Zealanders, as other common people of his nation did not have the same success he had.[26]

It is well known that in O-Taheiti, upon the advent of a new regent and on similar occasions, words from the common language are completely banned and replaced by new ones. Such arbitrary changes in recent times have very much estranged the language of this island from that of O-Waihi, which used to deviate little from it, and the natives of these two islands no longer understand each other.

The following fact from the history of O-Waihi, which we owe to the communication of a trustworthy witness, a thinking and well-instructed man, Mr. Marini, a Spaniard settled there, and which the natives have confirmed for us, unexpectedly allows us to find this strange custom on the Sandwich Islands as well and, indeed, in the most surprising manner.

Toward the year 1800 Tameiameia, upon the occasion of the birth of a son, devised a completely new language and began to introduce it. The newly devised words were not related to any of the roots of the current language, nor derived from any of them; even the particles that replace the forms of grammar were recreated in the same manner. It is said that mighty chiefs, whom this change displeased, sent the child who had given cause to it, on his way with poison. Upon his death that was then given up which had been undertaken upon his birth. The old language was again accepted and the new forgotten. The innovations went from Hana-ruru out to O-Waihi, where Tameiameia sojourned at the time. Mr. Marini was in O-Waihi when they barely began to penetrate. When we asked Mr. Marini how one or another word was said in the new language, he discussed the matter with natives of Hana-ruru who were present, all of whom were well acquainted with the matter but had forgotten most of the words.[27] Mr. Marini knew no other example of arbitrary linguistic change in these islands. Kadu on the Carolines had formed no idea of such a possibility.[28]

Man has emigrated from the larger land masses situated between Asia and New Holland from west to east against the force of the wind and has taken possession of all the bits of earth that bob up out of the Great Ocean as far as the remote island of Pascha [Easter Island], which stands alone and isolated in the east. His language testifies to its origin. His morals, customs, and crafts point in this direction, his domestic animals and useful plants, which have followed him everywhere and all of which belong to the Old World, tell us the coast from which he brought them.[29]

Sugar cane, the banana, the paper mulberry tree, the *Hibiscus populneus*,[30] turmeric, the bottle gourd, arum species, yams, and sweet potatoes and, among animals, finally, the chicken are found on Easter Island; the breadfruit tree and other plants, the pig, and the dog as far as the Society, Marquesas, and Sandwich Islands. Swine seem not to have been able to maintain themselves on the low-lying islands. New Zealand had only the dog, the Friendly Islands only swine, but the dog was known by name (*ghuri* according to Forster, *gooli* according to Mariner) there too, and we believe that in the word *giru* in Radak we found the same name and a similar passed-down knowledge of this animal.[31] Pig and dog are lacking on all the islands of the first province.

The preparation of the bark cloth customary on all of the islands was first described by Pigafetta on Tidori (Molucca Islands), and this same author depicts the Bisayans of his time with the pierced and elongated earlobes such as those found by Forster on the inhabitants of Easter Island,[32] a fashion the latter had already abandoned in our time and which we still found prevalent in Radak and the Caroline Islands.

The attempts to trace the sacred, largely prohibiting customs and laws of the taboo—which segregate the sexes, raise unbreakable walls between the classes of the people, and differ in the different peoples, although they are always in the same spirit the foundations of social order—back to one principle and one source and to understand these human statutes in their context or to derive them from the religious and civil system of other known nations will probably always be in vain. Here writing is unknown, and if we did not have the written document at hand, who would have been able to detect the gentle spirit of the Mosaic Law in the similar prohibitions and customs of the Jews, a law that even gives animals well-measured rights and in which, moreover, the idea of pure and impure seems unfounded to us?[33] Also, we are far from assuming that that civil or religious order proceeded as a complete whole from one mind: such a structure is often built up by history, which receives the stones for it by accident. And do we not ourselves see silly man turn from a purely spiritual religion back to polytheism, and put his vain, earthly trust in a material object, stone and wood? Is it not easier for us ourselves, like other peoples of the world, to believe magic, lies, and the word than to adhere to the spirit?

The deeply rooted inequality of the classes of people among the islanders of the South Seas, the special sacredness of some families and persons, independent of fortune and civil power, remind us involuntarily of India. The objection is invalid that the special castes of India are devoted to special trades, ways of life, etc. Such a distinction cannot prevail on these islands.

The voluntary death of the wife at the funeral of her husband on the Fiji Islands and the similar custom in the family of Tooitonga in Tonga also point toward India.[34]

If the question is posed as to how and at what time an originally Asiatic people distributed itself against the prevailing winds, bringing domestic animals and useful plants along, to the remotest islands of the Great Ocean; how in their isolation the different peoples still preserve similar customs and identical crafts and, lacking a writing system, which alone seems able to retard the language in its mutability, and in spite of the custom of arbitrary linguistic innovations, still speak a common dialect: then we stand exposed in our ignorance. The circumstances mentioned demonstrate a simultaneous emigration from one point and seem to point to a new epoch; but the childlike quality of the language and in many respects of the people themselves seem to plunge this point of time into gray antiquity. Our first seafarers found the peoples of the South Seas in the condition in which they still live.

Monsoons and storms drive the seafarers of the Carolines both to east and west and frequently as far as Radak, about 180° longitude from Greenwich. We can easily give an account of the population of these islands. But in this province we find differently speaking peoples characterized by a more highly developed type of navigation, but possessing no domestic animals. Only on Radak is the name of the dog known in the eastern dialect.[35] For all the other similarity and perhaps demonstrated transition of the languages, the eastern islands of the Great Ocean seem more to isolate the peoples from the western lands than to connect them.

The opinion of Zúñiga and those who have tried to derive and explain the population of the islands of the Great Ocean according to the direction of the trade winds from east to west from America toward Asia, is refuted.[36]

In case research should indicate that there are really sufficient reasons at hand to recognize the same proto-people in the inhabitants of South America and the islanders of the Great Ocean, or the peoples of East Asia, and the same language family in their languages, then in Molina's opinion the inhabitants of the New World should rather be derived from the Old World across the sea, either across the island chain of the Second Province and against the prevailing trade winds, or by way of New Zealand and in the realm of the changing winds.[37]

First of all we eliminate the comparison that has been attempted between the colossal statues of the island of Pascha and the monuments of Peruvian architecture. In the former figures, which are carved from light volcanic stone, we recognize only the usual idols that are to be found in the morais of most of the islands and that on the Sandwich Islands are called *akua* "gods," and in the Society Islands *tighi* "spirits, souls."[38]

We note that the islands situated closest to the American coast, the Galepagos [Galapagos], Juan Fernández, etc., like all of the dots of land situated in the Atlantic and Indian oceans far from the land mass, were without inhabitants; no American people was a seafaring one.

Zúñiga proposes the supposition that the language of the Araucanians and the Patagonians must agree essentially with the languages of the Philippine Islands and, devoid of any means of investigating the problem, builds upon this presupposition.[39] However, such is not the case.[40]

We have found no agreement between the roots of the Araucanian language and those of the language family with which we have been concerned. The numerals, the pronouns, are different. One could probably trace the conjugation of the verb and the declension of the noun back to the root, which always remains unchanged and to which only particles can be attached, the latter, however, only post-clitics; and in the nature and spirit of compounding a completely unique spirit prevails, which has nothing in common with the Malay and Tagalog one. The person is indicated in the ending of the verb, the personal endings remain completely identical through all the tenses and essentially the same through all the modes. By infixation of various particles after the root (only a few prepositions are placed before it) a number of conjugations are formed in which the meaning appears variously modified. Thus negative, frequentative, etc. In the transitive conjugations (*transiciones* of the Spanish grammarians) the object of the action, the accusative pronoun, is absorbed by the verb. A sentence is often treated as the root of a verb and equipped with the particle of time, the person, etc., so that the meaning is forced into a single word. From such compound verbs, as from simple ones, derived words are formed by various endings. Araucanian has a dual in declension and conjugation, but it does not have the double plural of the first person that the Quichua language in Peru has in common with the languages of East India. This coincidence, however, is also merely accidental in Quichua and not based on any inner relationship. Quichua is as foreign to the language family that has concerned us as is Chilidugu, with which, although there is a striking dissimilarity of the roots, it agrees essentially in grammar, and belongs unmistakably to the same language system.

The complete regularity of the Araucanian language, which without any anomala follows inexorable rules, gives testimony of a calm, undisturbed independent development, which has not been impinged upon by any foreign admixture or influence. The ending -*an*, which is often heard in the Araucanian language and contributed to deceiving Zúñiga, is completely different from the same ending in Tagalog.

Both the languages and the people seem completely different to us, and we believe that they should rightly be counted as different races. Common features unite the Araucanians with the other American peoples, as they do the islanders of the Great Ocean with the other peoples of the East Indian islands, and with the differences in social order, morals, and customs only two points remain to be considered, which to be sure are likely to excite attention and about which we communicate what we have heard, in order not to distort the matter.

Pig and dog have their own names in the Araucanian language, where the other animals introduced by the Spaniards are designated by foreign words. The pig is called *chancho* with Spanish orthography, *ciancio* in the Italian fashion, two different kinds of dogs *quiltho* and *thega*; and Molina is inclined to assume that they were autonomous before the incursion of the Spaniards, and brought across the sea from the west by the original inhabitants. P. Acosta, who wrote soon after the Conquest, does not dare decide whether swine were previously present in Peru or brought there by the Europeans.[41] We note only that the names cited are completely foreign to the languages of the South Seas and East India.[42]

Burney in his *Chronological History of the Discoveries in the South Sea* mentions a passage in Hendrik Brouwer's *Voyagie naar de Custen van Chili* where a drink of the Chileans in Valdivia is mentioned, *cawau* or *schitie*, and called by others *cici* with Italian orthography, which is prepared like the *kava* or *ava* of the South Seas, but needing a longer fermentation.[43] The root from which it is prepared is called *inilie*. The drinking of kava is a custom peculiar to the inhabitants of the eastern islands that is completely unknown in the East Indian islands, even though the plant itself occurs there. We have collected *Piper methysticum* in Guaján and the very similar *Piper latifolium* on Luzón.[44] It cannot be assumed that this noxious plant could grow in Chile, but others might replace it, and we confess that the agreement of the name is striking. We find nothing at all in Molina about this drink.

Burney in the same work looks for a similarity that we do not find between the Araucanian poncho and the clothing of the islanders of the Great Ocean, and we can attach no greater importance to a varying legend of the Araucanians, according to which they come from the west, while another has them immigrating from the north, and yet another depicts them as natives of the earth that they inhabit.

The result of our study of both history and nature is to picture man as being very young on this old earth. In the layers of the mountains the ruins of an older world lie buried like hieroglyphics. The waters recede, animals and plants spread out in different directions over the surface of the earth, and the mountains separate the lands. Man rises from his cradle and climbs down the back of Asia and, proceeding in all directions, takes possession of the solid land. He spreads across Africa to the west, where the sun colors the Negro, and across Europe, where tribes that immigrate there later in threefold tongues unmistakably speak the language of India.[45] The Papuan in the eastern lands situated at the Equator undergoes the same change as the African under the same influence, or perhaps belongs to the same race. The Chinese remain unchanged in East Asia. In the north other tribes spread out from Asia; the northeastern tip of the Old World paves the way to the new. Here the peoples spread out and become foreign to each other. A certain similarity lets us assume a common race, but the languages have become completely separated from each other. History shows us still in living memory a stream of people that flows from north to south across the plain of Mexico, pushes other tribes before it, leaves monuments of its passage behind, and, faithfully preserves memories of its motherland, high Asia.[46] Another tribe, the Eskimo, whose facial formation betrays to us the Mongolian and Chinese race, pours from North Asia across the northern edge of America to Greenland and preserves in both parts of the world an identical language, the same way of life, and the same crafts. Finally, from the southeastern tip of Asia a bold seafaring folk, the Malay race, pours forth across the habitations of the Papuans to the easternmost, most remote islands of the Great Ocean, and the question is posed: Did man make the passage from the Old to the New World on ships south of the line (Equator) as well?

We suspect that if someone equipped with the requisite knowledge could survey and compare all of the languages spoken by men he would recognize in them only different dialects derived from one source and could trace roots and forms back to one race.

# CHAPTER III
## Kadu. Don Luis de Torres.

A T the beginning of 1817, in the extreme east of this province, in the Otdia and Kaben group of the island chain of Radak, we had made the acquaintance of and formed a friendship with the attractive people that inhabits it. When we then sailed into the Aur group of the same island chain, and the natives came toward us in their boats and, as soon as we had cast anchor, climbed aboard, one man stood out from the rest, distinguished from them in many respects. He was not regularly tattooed like the Radakians, but bore faint figures of fishes and birds individually and in rows around his knees, on his arms and shoulders. He was more thick-set in stature, was of a lighter color and had curlier hair than they did. He addressed us in a language, which, different from that of Radak, seemed completely foreign to us, and we immediately tried, in vain, to speak the language of the Sandwich Islands with him. He made us understand that he was inclined to stay on board our ship and accompany us on our journeys. His request was gladly granted. He remained on board from that time forth, went ashore at Aur just once (with permission), and remained with us, our true companion, treated like the officers, and loved by all, until our return to Radak, where with swiftly altered decision he chose to settle and be the preserver and distributor of our gifts among our needy former hosts. No one could have been more permeated with the humane spirit of our mission than he.

Kadu, a native of the Ulea island group in the south of Guaján, not of noble birth but a confidant of the king, Toua, who had him take care of his errands on other islands, on former journeys had become familiar with the chain of islands with which Ulea has contact, in the west as far as the Pelew Islands, in the east as far as Setoan [Satawal]. On his last journey from Ulea to Feis [Fais] with two of his compatriots and a chief from Eap, the latter wishing to return to his homeland, he was afflicted by storms that drove the boat from its course.[1] The seafarers, if we can give credence to their unreliable time calculations, were lost for eight moons on the open sea. Their niggardly doled-out provisions lasted for three moons; for five moons, without any sweet water, they sustained themselves only by the fish they caught. To quench their thirst Kadu, diving into the depths of the sea, brought up cooler and, in their opinion, less salty water in a coconut shell. The northeast trade finally drove them to the Aur group of the Radak chain, when they thought they were to the west of Ulea. Kadu had heard tell of Radak and Ralik from an old man on Eap: seafarers from Eap are said to have once been shipwrecked on Radak, the Aur group specifically, and from there found their way back to Eap by way of Nugor [Nukuoro] and Ulea.[2] The names Radak and Ralik were also known to a native from Lamurek whom we met on Guaján. Boats from Ulea and the surrounding islands are often driven ashore in the eastern island chains, and in the southern Arno group of the Radak chain five natives from Lamurek still live, led onto the same track by an identical fate.

The chieftains of Radak protected the strangers against low-minded members of their people, whose greed had been aroused by the iron they possessed. The more noble-minded views are always found among the chiefs.

The inhabitants of Ulea, who live in greater prosperity and have more widespread contacts than the Radakians, are superior to them in many respects. Kadu enjoyed a certain esteem in Radak. When we visited these islands, he probably had arrived there about four years before. He had two wives on Aur, and from one of them a daughter who already was beginning to talk.

Our appearance in Aur, where the news about us had not yet penetrated, spread terror and confusion abroad. The much-traveled, very experienced Kadu, who at the time was on a remote island of the group, was immediately sent for and his advice sought as to how they should approach the powerful strangers, whom they were inclined to look upon as evil cannibals.

Kadu had learned a lot about Europeans, without ever having seen one of their ships. He infused them with courage, warned them against thievery, and accompanied them to our ship with the firm intent of staying with us and in the hope of coming to his beloved homeland again through us, as a European ship had once been in Ulea at a time when he himself was absent.

One of his compatriots and companions in misfortune, who was with him, endeavored in vain to dissuade him from his intention, and his friends assailed him in vain with fearful talk: at the time he was unshakable. Another companion of Kadu's, the chief from Eap, whom we encountered in the retinue of King Lamari at Udirik, made the same decision, had the same hope as our friend. He was a weak old man; his request fell on deaf ears. It was hard to get him to leave our ship, where he remained in tears in the calm position with which he had tried to symbolize his resolution. We remonstrated with him, citing his age and the difficulties of our journey, but he remained determined. We protested that our provisions were calculated only for a certain number of people. He suggested that we should set our friend Kadu ashore and take him on instead.

We must praise the easy, appropriate way in which Kadu was able to fit into our world. The new conditions into which he found himself transplanted were hard to judge and to deal with. He, a man of the people among these foreigners so superior in power and wealth, was unexpectedly looked upon as one of their nobles, and the lowly band of sailors served him as they did the supreme chief. We shall not conceal the mistakes that he was incited to commit at first, but that he too quickly and easily rectified to deserve a severe reprimand. When shortly after his admission among us, chiefs of Radak came aboard, he rose to meet them and he took on the bearing that is appropriate only to them. A guileless mockery on their part was his well-deserved reward. It did not happen a second time. At first he tried to imitate the walk and the manners of the captain, but desisted from this of his own volition. It should not come as a surprise that at first he regarded the sailors as slaves. He once commanded the attendant to bring him a glass of water. The latter quietly took him by the arm, led him to the water cask, and put the vessel in his hand that others drank from. He retreated within himself and studied the conditions and the spirit of our customs, into which he easily and quickly learned how to transport himself, and to be at home in, even as he learned to adapt himself to our outer manners in living and at the table.

Kadu learned the power of our alcoholic beverages only slowly. It was claimed that he at first induced the sailors to give him brandy. When a sailor was punished after this incident it was indicated to him that this had occurred because of his secret drinking of fire (the name by which he designated brandy). He never drank brandy again, and wine, which he was very fond of, only in moderation. The sight of drunken people, which he had in Unalashka, made him cautious about himself in his self-esteem. At first he conjured the wind in our favor, according to the custom in Eap. We smiled, and he soon smiled over these adjurations, which thenceforth he repeated only in jest and to entertain us.

Kadu had heart, understanding, wit; the better we got to know each other, the more we came to like him. For all his pleasant character we found we had to combat a certain indolence in him that opposed our intentions. He liked only to sing or sleep. When we endeavored to get information from him about the islands he had visited or of which he had knowledge, he answered only the questions that we asked him and did not like to answer the same question twice, referring to what he had already answered. When in the course of the conversation new information was brought to light, which we reproached him for having suppressed, he would calmly return, "You didn't ask me that before." And along with that his memory was not reliable. Memories revived within him gradually, as events evoked them, and we thought we could notice immediately that the number and variety of objects that attracted his attention extinguished earlier impressions within him. The songs he sang in various languages, and had learned from the peoples among whom he had lived, were also the book in which he sought information or substantiation for his data.

While he was with us Kadu kept his journal according to moons, for which purpose he tied knots in a string. But it seemed to us that he kept this journal in a very disorderly manner, and we could make nothing of his calculations.

He was not unteachable, not without intellectual curiosity. He seemed to understand well what we endeavored to make him understand about the shape of the earth and our nautical arts, but he had no tenacity, became exhausted through the effort, and returned to his songs to avoid it. He took some pains to learn writing, the secret of which he had comprehended, but he was without talent for this difficult attempt. What he was told with the intention of encouraging him might have completely deprived him of courage. He suspended his study, took it up again, and finally put it aside entirely.

He seemed to grasp with an open mind everything that we told him about the social order in Europe, of our customs, morals, arts. But he was most receptive for the peaceful adventure purpose of our journey, with which he connected the intention of telling newly discovered peoples what was good and useful for them, and by this he understood chiefly what goes toward sustenance; but he also recognized that our superiority rested on our greater knowledge, and he honored and served our research efforts as much as possible, even when it would have seemed very idle to many a more educated person among us.

When we had arrived in Unalashka, and he had surveyed this desolate earth, devoid of all trees, he hurried busily to request that we sow some coconuts, which we had on board and to which he would add some of his own, in appropriate spots here. He insisted on the attempt, pointing to the misery of the inhabitants, and it was hard to convince him that it would be completely superfluous.

Nature most attracted his attention and curiosity. The cattle in Unalashka, which first reminded him that he had earlier seen some on the Pelew Islands, constantly attracted his attention, and every day he followed them in the pasture to observe them. Nothing on the whole trip excited his joy more than the herds of sea lions and ursine seals on the island of St. George.[3]

Even as during the voyage Kadu had carefully picked up and preserved discarded pieces of iron and glass and anything else overlooked by us that might have value for his compatriots, on Unalashka he searched among the rocks of the shore for stones that were especially suited for whetstones. Only once did we see this gentle man in a state of repressed anger, in a fury. This happened when in the course of the voyage he sought these stones in vain in the place on the ship where he had left them, and the complaint he made about them got little attention. His sense of justice was offended.

Kadu was generous in his poverty and grateful in his heart. He served all of us who had given him gifts, and on O-Wahu he used the opportunity furnished him by the trade that he carried out with the small wares with which we had enriched him to bring gifts in return, bestowing on us and the sailors who had waited on him such as would be welcome to each one according to his taste. For himself he put nothing aside except things with which he hoped to enrich or please his compatriots. Thus he had left everything he possessed behind for his friends on Radak and retained only a single ornament, a necklace, which he wore among us for a long time. Once with moist eyes he confided to us smilingly the secret of this necklace. He fought in the battle on Tabual (an island of the Aur group of Radak) in the ranks of his hosts against the enemy invading from Meduro and Arno. There he obtained the advantage over his opponent and was about to pierce the body of his enemy on the ground at his feet when the latter's daughter sprang forward and held back his arm. She obtained from him the life of her father. This girl promised him her love; he, the man, secretly carried worthy presents over to her, and in memory of her he wore the pledge of love with which she had regaled him on the field of battle.

We must emphasize two of the chief features of Kadu's character: his deeply rooted repugnance toward war, the murder of human beings, and the delicate sense of modesty that marked him, and which he never denied among us.

Kadu abhorred the shedding of blood, and he was not cowardly.

On the front of his chest he bore the scars of wounds he had received
in the defensive war on Radak, and when we armed ourselves for a
landing on St. Lawrence Island and he was instructed that this was
taking place not for a hostile attack but for self-defense in case of
emergency among a people whose disposition was unknown to us
and with whom we merely wished to trade to our mutual benefit, he
asked for a weapon—a saber with which he could assist us in case of
necessity, as he had not practiced shooting enough in Unalashka. He
firmly maintained the opinion that he had impressed upon himself
on Eap that gray hair grew only from the fact that people had participated in battle in all its horror.

With regard to the other sex Kadu was a model of considerate delicacy. He stayed away from a woman who was in the possession of
another man. He always had the correct measure for what was
proper. What he discovered on O-Wahu repelled him, and he spoke
freely about it as well as about the immorality he had found prevalent in the Pelew Islands. When drawn into free and open conversation among men, he could participate in such a way that he always
remained within the bounds indicated to him.

One finds the most active sense and the greatest talent for fun
among peoples who are least estranged from nature and especially
where the mildness of the climate grants the people an easy, enjoy-
able life. Kadu was especially prone to having fun but also understood how to observe proper bounds in innocent jokes: he had great
skill in knowing how to reconcile those he had made superlative fun
of by performing small services for them or giving them small
presents.

Our friend vowed repeatedly in the course of our journey that he
was inclined to stay with us until we had reached our goal, and even
if we were to come across his beloved Ulea not to desert us, but
rather to accompany us to Europe, from where we could promise
him the return to Ulea, as commerce regularly takes our ships to the
Pelew Islands, where boats from Ulea regularly ply their way. We
ourselves were still ignorant of the other route by way of Guaján.
But he cherished the desire, and this would have been fulfilled for
him on Guaján, to find a chance on one of the islands known to him
to send a message to Eap about the fate of the chief of this island, his
companion in misfortune on Radak, so that, he thought, his kins-
men would build a ship and look him up there. He concerned himself busily with this thought.

On O-Wahu we took pains to gather useful animals, plants, seedlings, and seeds of the species we wished to try to introduce on
Radak. Kadu knew that we intended to land there, and stuck to his

resolution. We urged him to inform us here about everything that could be of use on Radak, as he could instruct our friends and teach them what advantage would accrue to them from our gifts and how they should care for them. He agreed with our intentions, but the goal was too distant for him, and frivolity and indolence caused him to use fitfully a time for apprenticeship, the neglect of which he later regretted.[4]

We came to Radak and landed at Otdia, to the delight of the few of our friends who had not gone off to the war. From that moment on Kadu was busy, indefatigably and quite assiduously, in helping us in word and deed with planting, sowing, and caring for the animals, as well as explaining and impressing what was necessary on the natives. He was still firmly resolved to stay with us.

When everything necessary was taken care of on Otdia, Kadu went to Oromed, the island of the old chief Laergass, to lay out a garden there. On this excursion, which was carried out in boats of the Radakians, he was accompanied only by the author of these essays. On Oromed the daylight hours passed in work, those of the evening in pleasant company. The women sang for us the many songs that had been composed about us during our absence, preserving the memory of our names. Kadu reported to them on his travels, and mixed amusing tall tales into his narrative. He distributed presents he had prepared for his friends in the course of the voyage. As soon as the boat that was to convey us to our ship was under sail the next day, the last of our stay in Radak, Kadu, whose happy mood had changed to calm seriousness, declared that he was going to stay on Otdia and not go any farther with the *Rurik*. He expressly commissioned his friend to announce this new irrevocable decision to the captain, and, rejecting counter-arguments, he explained the reasons that impelled him. He would remain on Otdia as the protector and caretaker of the animals and planted areas that without him would perish with neglect without being of any use for these non-comprehending people. He would see to it that our gifts would extend sufficient nourishment to the needy Radakians, so that they would no longer have to kill their children out of dire need and would cease to do so. He would work toward establishing peace once more between the northern and southern groups of Radak, so that people would no longer murder people. He would, if animals and plants were sufficiently increased, build a boat and cross over to Ralik in order to distribute our gifts there as well. He would ask the captain, after giving him back everything that he had received from him, for only a shovel to work the earth, and this and that useful tool. His iron he would keep secret from the powerful Lamari and, if necessary, defend against him. In this undertaking he reckoned on the cooperation of his compatriot and companion in misfortune, whom he would call to join him from Aur, where he was now residing. He would tell him to also bring his child, his daughter along, who, as he had now learned, had been sad since his departure, had asked for him, cried for him, and would not sleep. His wives had taken other men, and he was concerned only about his child, and in a very tender way.

At this time Kadu regretted having neglected learning many useful things—the preparation of bark cloth on O-Wahu, etc.—and in these last moments he desired advice about many things, and he listened to it with rapt attention.

The boat in which we completed this trip against the wind was a poor sailer. The sun was already inclining toward the horizon when we came to the ship, the captain fortunately being on board. When Kadu's decision became known, he soon and unexpectedly found himself in the possession of endless treasures, those that in this part of the world excite the greed of princes and nations.[5] The love he enjoyed among us became manifest, and soon everyone could be seen busy, quietly increasing from his own supply the pile of iron, tools, and useful things that were gathered for him. (Samples of mats and cloth from O-Wahu, samples of straw hats, etc., were not forgotten.)

When Kadu busied himself tying together his bed, his clothes, his linen, which he now kept, into a bundle, he carefully separated his winter clothing from the rest and brought them as a gift to the sailor who had waited on him, the latter, however, refusing to accept them.

The sun had already set when Kadu was put ashore with his treasure. Time did not permit us to fashion and leave behind any written testimony for him. Just one inscription on a copper plate, fastened to a coconut tree on Otdia, contains the name of the ship and the date.

Kadu was established before the collected inhabitants of Otdia as *our man*, to whom our animals and gardens were entrusted, and who was also commissioned to bestow our gifts upon Lamari. The promise was given that we, who had already come to Radak three times, would return after some time to look for him and to demand an accounting. To reinforce this promise and as a sign of our power (up until then we had given signs only of our gentleness and friendship), when we had returned to the ship in the dead of night two cannon and a rocket were fired.

When we weighed anchor the next morning, our friend and companion was busy on shore with the animals, and he often looked across at us.

One of the songs that Kadu often sang among us glorified in the language of Ulea the names of Samuel, Bormann (he pronounced it Moremal), and Luis. This song had reference to the European ship that visited Ulea at a time when Kadu himself was on a journey. Waghal appeared in Kadu's narratives as a large country where cattle existed, where there was a great supply of iron and other riches, where King Toua had once visited, and from where he had brought back three two-pound cannonballs, especially.

As soon as we had landed on Guaján, we recognized this island as Waghal, and the Luis of that song advanced toward us in friendship in the person of Don Luis de Torres, from whom we now copy the following reports, remembering him with sincere love and gratitude.

Luito, a seafarer from the islands situated to the south of Guaján, whose fame still lives among his compatriots, in the year 1788 again found the way to Guaján with two boats, the knowledge of which seems to have been preserved in an old song.[6] Encouraged by the success of the first voyage and the reception he had found, he returned in the year 1789 with four boats, requesting permission from the governor to return annually. The four seafarers, when they set about to return home, quarreled about the route they should steer. They separated. The sea did not return any of them to their homeland.

Thereupon the contacts they had begun were broken off.

In the summer of the year 1804 the ship *Maria* from Boston, Captain Samuel Williams Boll, Supercargo Thomas Bormann, went on a voyage of discovery, proceeding from Guaján, to search for trepang in the Caroline Islands. Don Luis de Torres went aboard the *Maria* as a passenger with the hope of again seeing the islanders, of whom he had become fond, of helping them, of learning why they had stopped visiting Guaján, and of urging them to return. . . .

Don Luis de Torres, on Ulea, whose language he understands and whose people he regards highly, took advantage of the opportunity to inform himself thoroughly and profoundly through the best informed members of this people about it and related tribes. On Ulea he used the reports of the most experienced seafarers among the natives with regard to the courses they sail to draw a map of all the islands known to him, a map that agrees strikingly with Cantova's map, which he had never seen. Since then he has lived on Guaján in continual contact with his friends on Ulea and has every year seen the most skilled seafarers, who guide the trading squadron from Lamurek to Guaján. We regret that we had so few fleeting moments to draw upon the treasure chest of his experiences and information that he so kindly opened to us; and from the French expedition under Captain Freycinet, which is promised a longer stay on Guaján, and with whose learned members we discussed this matter at the Cape, we expect gleanings that could be far more substantial than our harvest.

Don Luis de Torres learned on Ulea that Luito's failure to return in the year 1789 had been misinterpreted and laid on the doorstep of the Spaniards. The islanders, having been informed of the truth, promised to reestablish trade, and kept their word.

A passenger on board the *Maria*, an Englishman whom Don Luis calls Juan, settled in Ulea. Kadu after his return knew him there under the name of Lisol; he had taken a wife and procreated a child with her. According to his report, later on, at a time when Kadu was again absent on a voyage, this Lisol was again transported back by ship. According to the inquiries that Don Luis made about him, he died on Ulea.

On this voyage Don Luis de Torres had attempted to introduce cattle and swine and various useful plants on Ulea. Subsequently the natives diligently exterminated the cattle and swine, because they were not only of no use to them, they were also detrimental. The cattle browsed on the young coconut trees, the swine endangered the taro plots. Of the plants only the pineapple had flourished. When it bore fruit and the people were pleased with it, they transplanted the plant, which everyone wanted to possess, so often that it finally died.

Since Don Luis's voyage no new accident has interrupted the resumed contacts. The Carolinians come to Guaján in larger numbers each year. Their squadron, consisting of boats from Ulea and surrounding groups, from Lamurek and Setoan, gathers in Lamurek. The voyage out is undertaken from there in the month of April. To Fayo [West Fayu], the desolate island on which they rest a few days, the voyage lasts two days; from Fayo to Guaján three days.[7] The trip back likewise takes place by way of Fayo and Lamurek. Its time is in May, at the latest June, before the west monsoon, which must be feared, can occur.

Kadu mentioned the attempt of the chief of Fatoilep [Faraulap] to sail from this group direct to Waghal (Guaján).[8] He was lost at sea for a long time, and finally, without having found this island, he arrived on Mogemug, from where he returned home again.

The squadron once missed Guaján and drifted to leeward of this island. The mariners perceived their error in time, and, struggling with the adverse wind, they reached their goal only after considerable delay.

This long voyage was once completed by a very small boat that carried only three people. It sailed better than the two larger vessels with which it came. The seafarer Olopol from Setoan brought it to Don Luis as a gift. Olopol died in Agaña, and we saw the boat ourselves.

Toua, the king of Ulea, himself came to Guaján in 1817.[9]

It was also in this year or in the following that a boat from the eastern island Tuch [Truk] was driven ashore on Guaján. It had fifteen people on board, the pilot's name being Kulingan. The strangers were well received, but a procession, which took place in these days and occasioned artillery salvos, spread fear and terror among them. They concealed themselves in the jungle and that same night, without any provisions, they went to sea again. Fortunately, on their flight they encountered the arriving flotilla from Lamurek, which equipped them with provisions and gave them the necessary directions for their return home.

The squadron numbered eighteen sails in the year 1814.

In Guaján the Carolinians trade boats, shells, and rarities for iron, glass, cloth, etc.[10] Trepang may become an important branch of their trade. They themselves are taken in by the natives in the most hospitable fashion during their stay on Guaján.

Don Luis de Torres has undertaken with pleasure to report on Kadu's fate and his whereabouts to his friends on Ulea and to send them our presents in his name.

Furthermore, Don Luis de Torres gave us information of a high, large island of unknown name that had been seen by the brigantine *San Antonio de Manila*, Capt. Manuel Dublón, on the voyage from Manila to Guaján on December 10, 1814, at 7°20′N latitude, 151° 55′E longitude. A very high mountain towers above it.

We had heard Kadu sing a song about Feis that had reference to a ship with which the islanders had traded in sight of their island, without its having stopped there. It sang of the names José, María, and Salvador. We learned on Guaján that in the year 1808 or 1809 the *Modesto* from Manila, Capt. José María Fernández, a ship seeking the Pelew Islands to gather trepang, missed them and came in sight of Feis. When afterwards the *Modesto* reached the Pelew Islands, one of the natives from Feis, with whom they had traded, was already there to continue the trade, having hurried ahead of the ship. The governor of the Marianas, Don José de Medinilla y Pineda was on board the *Modesto*. In Manila we tried in vain to gather further news of this voyage.

We shall narrate here an incident that we have from our friend Kadu, and which might be of interest. On Eap six people wearing white clothes once arrived in a boat joined together without iron, with wooden pegs. This boat was otherwise constructed in the European fashion. The strangers were received hospitably. One of them, called Boele, was adopted by Laman, the chieftain of the region of Katepar. The latter remained on the island when the other five went to sea again after a stay of several months. Kadu, who shortly thereafter came to Eap, knew this Boele. He went around naked on the island and was tattooed on the upper part of his loins.

# CHAPTER IV
## Life in Radak.

THE inhabitants of Radak are not of large stature, nor are they especially powerful physically. They are, although slender, well-proportioned and healthy and seem to reach a ripe old age with good-natured hardiness.[1] The children are suckled for a long time and still take the breast when they are able to walk and talk. The Radakians are of a darker color than the O-Waihians, from whom they can be distinguished readily by greater cleanliness of their skin, which is not malformed either by the use of kava or any other prevalent skin diseases. Both sexes wear their long, beautiful black hair neatly tied up in the back. On children it hangs down freely in curls. Men let their beards grow, and they become long but not especially thick.[2] In general they have their teeth spoiled, the front ones often broken off, by the nature of their basic foodstuff, from chewing the fruit of the pandanus with its wooden fibers. This is less the case with the chiefs, for whom the juice of the fruit is scratched out and extracted with the edge of a shell. Men and women wear a rolled-up pandanus leaf in their pierced earlobes. For men the roll is three to four inches in diameter, for women less than half that. It is sometimes covered with a delicate tortoise-shell lamina. Some older people also had the upper edge of the outer ear pierced so that flowers could be inserted.

The artistically delicate tattooing is different according to sex, otherwise uniform for everyone.[3] In men it forms a triangle that encompasses shoulders and chest and comes to a point at the navel and consists of smaller, variously connected lines. Similar well-ordered horizontal lines frame the back and the abdomen. On women only the shoulders and arms are tattooed. Besides this regular design, which is executed only on adults and is lacking in a few, they all have groups of symbols or lines tattooed on them as children on loins, arms, or more rarely, on the face. We noticed a few times the image of the Roman cross among these symbols.[4] The tattooed spot is very dark, sharply drawn, and raised above the skin.

The men's garb consists of a belt with hanging strips of bark, which a small square mat often accompanies as an apron. Boys go completely naked until they reach the age of manhood. The women wear two longer mats fastened above the hips with a cord, the girls from the time they are quite young a smaller apron. Besides the wreaths of flowers and shells with which both sexes decorate themselves, the men occasionally wear a necklace composed of rows of dolphin teeth, with pendant plates made from bones of the same animal or of tortoise shell. For this ornament thin, round disks of seashell or coconut shell are also used. We have also encountered the tailfeathers of the tropic bird, the feathers of the frigate bird, and armbands ground down from the shell of a large univalve mollusk among their ornaments.

The *irus* or chieftains are often distinguished by taller stature, never by unsightly corpulence of the body.[5] The tattooing on them generally is distributed over parts of the body that are spared on the common man: sides, loins, neck, or arms.

The houses of the Radakians consist merely of a roof and a kind of attic freely borne by four low posts. One can do no more than sit under it. You clamber through a square opening into the upper room where the family's small possessions are stored. You sleep on this floor or below in the open hall, and a few tentlike open huts serve as detached sleeping chambers. The roofs are of coconut or pandanus branches, the floor is strewn with fine bits of coral and seashells gathered on the beach. A bare, coarse mat serves as bed and a log as a pillow.

At first we did not consider these houses, which we often found abandoned, to be the permanent habitations of the people. The boatmen move from one island to the other on their artfully constructed craft[6] with all their goods and families, so that once we had become friendly with them the greatest part of the population always congregated in our vicinity.

The wild pandanus seems to be common property. A bundle of leaves from this tree (a symbol of possession) tied to the branch on which a fruit is ripening assures the one who discovered it the right to it. We have often seen this fruit, almost the only food of the Radakians, being consumed when it was still far from being ripe. Coconut trees are private property. One occasionally sees those that are in the vicinity of dwellings, and which are laden with ripening nuts, protected with a coconut frond attached to the trunk by fastening the opposing leaves together so that the rustling noise would betray any attempt to climb them. In the populous Kaben and Aur groups, districts and orchards are often encircled with a cord in place of a fence.

Apart from their concern for food, nothing occupies our friends but their boats and songs. Their dearest, their only property are their boats and their drum, which even dominate the children's games. Especially in the evening, gathered in a circle around a brightly flaming fire, they perform their sitting dance-songs. An intoxicating joy possesses all of them then, and all of their voices blend in the choir. These songs resemble those of the O-Waihians, but they are coarser, more distorted, the gradually increasing waves of the song finally degenerating into shouts.

We got to know the charming people of Radak first and mainly on the Otdia group of Radak. The people, who approached us in a friendly and hospitable fashion, for a long time seemed to withdraw from us, feeling us to be superior. The chiefs showed the stronger courage, the greater confidence. Familiarity never made our friends pushy, never burdensome. The comparison of our excessive wealth with their need never lowered them to the point of begging, seldom tempted them to steal, never let them break faith when they were trusted. We walked daily across their islands alone, slept under their roofs with treasures beside us (knives, iron), went on long trips on their boats, and trusted their disposition the way that at home we trust the watchful protection of the law. We exchanged names with them, first urged on to do this by them. People met us hospitably wherever we appeared, and handed us coconuts. We did not trade on Otdia, we gave gifts and received gifts in return. Some seemed to have the same desire to give with fine manners that we had and still brought us presents when they could no longer expect presents in return. Others behaved more selfishly. When extraordinary events produce unheard of conditions, and the moral code has no answer, the peculiar character of a person must reveal itself independently. The women's comportment was shy and reserved; they withdrew when we first appeared and only returned under the protection of the men. In return for our small presents—rings and beads, which they seemed to esteem less than fragrant shavings from English pencils—they handed us in an elegant manner the ornaments they were then wearing, their wreaths of shells and flowers. No woman from Radak ever came on board our ship.

Wherever we went we encountered the picture of peace in a developing people. We saw their new garden plots, progressive culture, many growing children in a small number of people, the tender concern of the fathers for their progeny, charming easy manners, equality in the concourse between chiefs and vassals, no humbling of one's self before more powerful men, and along with greater charm and less self-confidence we saw none of the vices show that deface the peoples of eastern Polynesia.

We first learned on Aur that these people, barely able to feed themselves, also wage wars, that the urge to rule and conquer has also brought this curse upon them. They summoned us to intervene in their bloody feuds like the forces of fate with our fearful iron (they did not learn from us the more terrible effect of other weapons).

The powerful Lamari proceeded from Meduro to subjugate all the northern island groups of Radak with weapons. He now rules over Aur, Kaben, and the north of the chain and has his residence on Aur. The people of Meduro and Arno conduct war against him and his empire. Their expeditions on thirty boats, each one manned with six to ten people, have extended to Otdia. The new battle on Tabual has cost four people their lives, three on Meduro's side, and one on the side of Aur. In an earlier campaign approximately twenty were lost on each side.

In the beginning of 1817 Lamari traveled across the islands of his realm to call his squadron of war, also about thirty boats strong, together on Aur, from where he wished to move on Meduro. We expected to meet this chief on Eilu, but he was already on Udirik, near which group he visited us on the open sea in his boat. When we returned to Otdia at the end of the same year, the military expedition was gathered in Aur. Lamari had missed the island of Mesid, and—driven to shore on other groups—had been forced to do without the reinforcements he had hoped to secure there.

We shall report in detail everything we were able to find out about the religion, social order, customs, and morals of our friends.

The inhabitants of Radak worship an invisible god in the sky and without temples and priests bring him simple offerings of fruits. In their language *jageach* means "god," and the name of the god is Anis.[7] When wars are to be undertaken and on similar occasions solemn sacrifices are made; the actions take place in the open. One out of the assembly, not the chief, dedicates the fruits to the god by holding them up and crying out. The formula is *Gidien Anis mne jeo*. The assembled people repeat the last word. When the head of a household goes out to catch fish or undertakes something important to him, he sacrifices with his family. On different islands there are holy trees, coconut palms in the crowns of which Anis reclines. Around the foot of such a tree four logs are laid in a square. It does not seem to be forbidden to step into the space that they enclose, and the fruits of the tree are eaten by the people.

On Radak the operation of tattooing is connected with religious belief and may not be undertaken without certain divine signs.[8] Those who wish to be tattooed spend the night in a house to which the chief who is to perform the operation conjures down the god. A perceptible sound, a whistling, is said to announce his agreement. If this sign is lacking the operation also is left undone. For which reason it is never performed on some people. In the case of a transgression the sea would come over the island and all land would disappear. A well-known danger threatens all low islands from the sea, and religious belief often holds this rod above the people. But conjuring helps against this. In Radak Kadu saw the sea rise to the feet of the coconut trees, but it was abjured in time and returned to its borders. He named two men and a woman for us who understand this conjuring in Radak.

The desolate Bigar group of islands has its own god. The god of Bigar is blind, he has two young sons by the name of Rigabuil, and the people who visit Bigar call each other Rigabuil as long as they are there, so that the blind god will consider them his sons and do good things for them. Anis may not be invoked on Bigar, as the god would afflict whoever did it with severe illness and death. Under a tree in Bigar offerings of fruits, coconuts, etc., are made. Special incantations spoken without error help water to flow into the pits, and if the efforts are not successful, something was done wrong and the words were not spoken correctly. Everywhere the situation is the same as it is with us.[9] In Bigar sharks may not attack a person: God does not permit it. From all the island groups of Radak Bigar is visited by way of Udirik, except that the inhabitants of Eilu may not do so directly. They must spend a month on Udirik before they go there, and after their return they must spend another month on the same group before they consume the provisions they brought with them. These provisions consist of the flesh of birds and turtles, which is first roasted and then dried in the sun. The use of salt is unknown in Radak.

The marriages, the burial of the dead, the feasts that are arranged upon various occasions seem to be without connection with religion. We did not succeed in making ourselves understood to Kadu with regard to the concept of the continuation of life after death.

Although no particular expressions of respect are paid to the chiefs, they exercise arbitrary power over all property. We ourselves saw chiefs conceal our gifts from the eyes of those more powerful than themselves. They seem to be subordinate to one another in varying degrees, but we were unable to perceive these relationships correctly. Rarik was the mightiest on Otdia, while his father, Sauraur, perhaps the real chief of the group, lived on Aur. Rarik and his son, a boy of about ten years of age, were the only ones who wore several strips of pandanus leaves, in which knots were tied, around their necks, and it seemed a privilege. In the houses of chiefs we have seen similar strips hanging, which, like dried fish-heads, unripe coconuts, and stones, had the appearance of consecrated objects. The succession is not directly from father to son, but from the older brother to the younger, until after the death of all the brothers the firstborn son of the first again is in line. Women are excluded. When a chief arrives at an island, a signal is given from his boat, and his needs are anticipated immediately with the best at hand. This signal is given by the man in the prow, who swings his right arm and shouts. This was also observed when officers of the expedition traveled on boats of the natives. The chiefs are distinguished by freer movements in their gait, which the common man may not imitate.

For war the nobles call up their men, the chief of each group pushes out to the squadron with his boats, the attempt is made to attack a hostile group with a united force, a landing is made. Fighting occurs only on land. The women take part in the war, not only when it is a matter of warding off the enemy on their own soil, but also in the attack, and they make up a part of the military force in the squadron, even though in the minority. The men stand in front in combat. Their weapons for combat at a distance are: a sling, which they handle without skill, and a staff sharpened at both ends, which, hurled in an arc, rotates through the air like the spokes of a rolling wheel and strikes with either end. For close combat: a javelin, a five-foot-long stick that is sharpened and equipped with a barbed hook or shark's teeth; we saw a short, crooked wooden sword furnished with shark's teeth only on Mesid. The women form a second line without weapons. Some of them at the leader's bidding beat the drum, first at a slow, measured beat (ringesipinem) when the antagonists exchange throw upon throw, then with doubled rapid beat (pinneneme) when man fights against man in hand-to-hand combat. The women throw stones with their bare hands; they help their dear ones in the fight and throw themselves propitiatingly between them and the victorious enemy to succor them. Captured women are spared, men are not taken prisoner. The man takes the name of the enemy he subdues in battle. Captured islands are despoiled of their fruits, but the trees are spared.

Marriages rest on a free agreement and can be dissolved the same way they are made. A man can have several wives. The wife is the man's companion and seems to subordinate herself independently and willingly to him in a fitting relationship to the head of the family. When on the move the men walk protectively in front and the women follow them. When there is talking the men speak first, and the women, when it is requested, take part in the conversation and are listened to. In peace only what we call female occupations are imposed on them. The drum, which provides pleasure for everyone, is in their hands. Unmarried women enjoy their freedom under the protection of the moral code. The girl extracts gifts from the man, but the veil of modesty is drawn over all the relations that unite the sexes. We note that the caress by contact of noses, usual even among men in the Carolines and on the islands of eastern Polynesia, in Radak is customary only among man and wife, and only in the darkness in which intimacy is concealed.

The bond of exclusive friendship between two men, which recurs on all the islands of the First Province, in Radak imposes on the friend the obligation to share his wife with his friend but does not obligate him to participate in life-and-death feuds.

Hesitantly and shuddering we mention a law the basis of which Kadu declares to be in the pressing want and sterility of the parsimonious earth. Every mother may bring up only three children. The fourth one she bears, and every other one following, she herself must bury alive. The families of the chiefs are not subjected to this horror. Illegitimate children in general are brought up the same as the legitimate ones. When they are able to leave the mother the father takes them in with him. When no father acknowledges the child the mother keeps it. If the mother dies another woman takes over the child.

The corpses of the deceased are wrapped entirely in cords in a sitting position. The chiefs are buried on the islands. A square space marked off with large stones designates the spot under the palm trees on the inner beach. The bodies of the common people are cast into the sea. The same procedure is undergone toward enemies killed in battle, according to their rank. A staff implanted in the ground with ring-shaped notches designates the graves of the children who were not allowed to live. We ourselves have seen these types of burials.

A long time ago a European ship appeared at Kaben and tarried an entire day in the vicinity of this group without landing. The chief Sauraur, our host on Tabual, climbed aboard this ship. (We note that at the time he called himself Laelidjü, having since then received his present name through a friendly exchange with a chief of the Ralik island chain, who now is called Laelidjü after him.) The natives bartered for iron and pieces of glass from this ship. Kadu himself possessed two of these pieces on Aur, and he remembered this on an occasion when he was picking up similar pieces among us for his friends.[10] No song has preserved the memory of this ship. No names have been rescued from oblivion.

We are the first Europeans who landed in Radak and became

acquainted with its charming people. Out of principle and inclination and from real sincere love we endeavored to neglect nothing that we could do for this people. On our first visit we had put our friends on Otdia into the possession of swine, goats, and domesticated fowl; yams were planted, and melons and watermelons had sprung up and were thriving. When we returned after a few months the garden spot on the island of Otdia was desolate and empty. Not a single strange plant remained to testify to our good intention. The swine had died of thirst, the fowl were no longer present, the noble Lamari had brought the goats over to Aur and also transplanted there the few yams on Otdia that had resisted the hostile rats. On an island of his territory the old chief Laergass had discovered other yams planted there by us. He had found these roots to his taste, and after he had eaten them had carefully replanted the rest of the plant. This procedure, which is followed in the cultivation of taro, had deceived him into trusting to it here.

The real purpose of our second visit was to be helpful to our friends. We brought them goats, swine, dogs, cats, domesticated fowl, sweet potatoes from the Sandwich Islands (Ipomoea tuberosa Lour. Coch.),[11] yams (Dioscorea alata),[12] melons, watermelons, gourds of various types—those from which the fruit is used for valuable vessels and others that are eaten—sugar cane, grapevines, pineapple, the apple tree of the Sandwich Islands (not a Eugenia), the tea [ti] root (Dracaena terminalis), the lemon tree, and the seeds of various trees useful on the Sandwich Islands, such as the kukui (Aleurites triloba), the nuts of which are used as candles and furnish oil and dyestuff, and two of the species of shrubs the bark of which serves for the manufacture of cloth, etc.

With good intent we distributed the seeds, which Kadu undertook to watch over.

May Kadu proceed with wisdom and power in his fine calling, may he succeed in doing what without him would be hopeless. May this good man accomplish the good that he desires to accomplish. May he, the benefactor of an estimable people, found its prosperity, conduct it peacefully and popularly to a better era, and move it to abnegate a law abhorrent to nature, but based on necessity.

We must confess that our friend stands alone, exposed to the envy of his equals, the greed and power of his chiefs, and the treasures that our love has heaped upon him will draw a storm upon his head. Our worry can go a step further. The real wealth of iron, which we expended with pleasure on Radak, can stir up a ruinous war between the south and north of this chain, and between it and Ralik, and blood could be the fruit of our generosity.

The poor and dangerous reefs of Radak have nothing that could attract Europeans, and we wish our childlike friends the good luck of remaining in their remoteness. The charm of their customs, the gracious modesty that marks them, are blossoms of nature that are not based on any concept of virtue. They would easily prove receptive to our vices and, like the victims of our lusts, draw our contempt upon them.

# CHAPTER V
## Life in the Carolines.

CANTOVA mentions a mixture of races in the Carolines of which our reports know nothing. To be sure, Papuas from the southern lands through some sort of accident, and a few Europeans—Martin López and his companions, or others on different routes—may have come to these islands, as has happened with some frequency since that time. However, the race of the natives is the same one that is distributed on all of the islands of the Great Ocean. Their hair seems to be more kinky and curly than that of the Radakians. They all allow it to grow long and attach considerable value to this natural adornment. Only on Eap is the children's hair cut.

According to Kadu's observation the inhabitants of the area of Summagi on Eap are of exceptionally small stature. Malformed babies and birth defects are remarkably frequent on this island according to the same authority. He cited as examples: a man without arms whose head is extraordinarily large; one without hands; another without thumbs; a person with only one leg; harelips and deaf-mutes.[1] Even less striking cases are much rarer on other islands. A disease that the Europeans have spread to most of the islands of the South Seas according to Kadu does not seem unknown on Ulea.

In general the people in the Carolines are better fed and stronger than they are in Radak. Tattooing is arbitrary everywhere and bears no relation to the religious belief. The chiefs are tattooed more than the common people. A piece of banana leaf, worn like the *maro* of O-Waihi and O-Taheiti, is the usual attire; only on Pelli [Peleliu?] do the men go entirely naked, as used to also be the case in the Marianas.[2] Only on Pelli is the ear ornament of the Radakians not worn. The nasal cartilage is pierced for the insertion of aromatic flowers. The bracelet made from bone of the *Trichechus dugong*, which the chiefs of the Pelew Islands wear, is known from H. Wilson.[3] The chiefs of Eap wear a similar, broader bracelet, carved out of a seashell.

Everywhere the houses are large and enclosed. One can walk through the doors without stooping. Paved paths and square courts in front of the chiefs' houses are found on Eap as well as on the Pelew Islands, where we know of them through H. Wilson.

We must first observe this courageous seafaring people in its boats.

According to Kadu the boats on Ulea are of the same construction as those of Nugor and Tuch, whose peoples are cut off from the others by their languages, and those of the similarly speaking islands as far as Ulea, Feis, and Mogemug. The differently speaking inhabitants of Savonnemusoch [Lukunor], between Nugor and Tuch, undertake no large sea voyages and would like to have different boats.[4] The comparison Cantova makes between the boats in the Carolines and those of the Marianas allows us to draw conclusions about the latter. The boats of the Marianas were similar to those of Ulea, although of better quality, and were better sailers.[5]

The construction of the boats of Eap and Ngoli [Ngulu] deviates little from that of Ulea.[6] However, the natives of Eap like to use boats from Ulea, which they acquire by trading. Pelli has its own manner of construction, and the low-lying island to the southeast of Pelli yet another. Pelli and these islands are far behind in navigation, and their boats do not visit the more eastern islands.

The boldest seafarers are the natives of Ulea and the surrounding islands, whom Cantova, too, considers more civilized than the others.[7] The driving-rod of shipping is trade. The chief objects of trade are: iron, boats, cloth, and curcuma powder [turmeric]. In another place we spoke of the trade with Guaján, where the people from Ulea chiefly sell boats for iron. The people from Feis, Eap, and Mogemug obtain boats in Ulea for curcuma powder. Those of the eastern islands have an excess of breadfruit trees and build all their boats themselves. The people of Nugor and Tuch obtain iron in Ulea for cloth. The people of Ulea also travel to Tuch and Nugor. Those from Savonnemusoch are visited on these voyages without themselves visiting other islands. In Pelli iron, which the Europeans bring there, is traded for curcuma. On the more southwestern island groups cloth is exchanged for iron, which they lack. A squadron of ten sails, five from Mogemug and five from Eap, completed this voyage. Kadu knew these very seafarers personally on Eap.

In their navigation they are guided by their knowledge of the stars in the sky, which they divide into different constellations, each one of which has its special name.[8]

On each voyage they seem to observe the rising and setting of a different star. A misinterpreted expression of Cantova's erroneously ascribed the knowledge of the magnetic needle to them.[9] Cantova means only the division of the horizon into twelve points, such as we have furnished along with other designations for the courses and winds in our *vocabulario* according to Don Luis de Torres and Kadu. According to Don Luis the helmsman of a boat places a little piece of wood, a wand, down flat in front of him, and thinks he is guided by it as we are by the compass. It is incomprehensible to us that this wand, placed at the moment of observation, could serve to symbolize the course that must be held against the wind in an area of very constant winds.

In the Caroline Islands they count days and moons and divide the year into its seasons according to the reappearance and disappearance of the constellations. However, no one counts the years. The past is past, song names names that appeared worthy of preservation, and they drift carefree down the stream.[10]

Kadu knew his own age as little as any islander of more eastern Polynesia. The life of these islanders, free from concern, decisive, and belonging to the moment, is free of many of the torments that undermine ours. When we told Kadu that suicide was not without example among us, he thought he had heard wrong, and this remained for him one of the most ridiculous things that he had heard from us. But they, for the same reason, do not tolerate planned foreign oppression, and History has recorded in her book the suicide of the people of the Marianas under the Spanish (the messengers of the Gospel?).

On all the Caroline Islands only invisible heavenly gods are believed in. Nowhere are figures made of the gods, nowhere are human works or physical things worshipped. Kadu was poorly versed in the theosophy of his people. What we relate from him now leaves much to be desired and perhaps needs criticism. In accordance with what he said we believed it necessary to translate the word *tautup* (*jageach* in Radak, *tahutup*, Cantova) by the word *god*. According to Cantova the *tahutup* are departed souls, which are regarded as protective spirits.

The god (*tautup*) of Ulea, Mogemup, Eap, and Ngoli is called *Engalap*, that of Feis *Rongala*, that of Elath [Elato][11] and Lamurek *Fuss*, that of the desolate island Fayo *Lage*.

Is Engalap the Eliulep of Cantova, the Aluelap of Don Luis de Torres, the great god?

People have never seen Engalap. Fathers passed on knowledge of him to their children. He visits alternately the islands where he is acknowledged. The time of his presence seems to be that of fertility. He is connected with Rongala, the god of Feis, by friendship; they visit each other hospitably. He sems to have no connection with Fuss, the god of Lamurek.

On Ulea and the more eastern islands (Lamurek, etc.) there are neither temples nor priests, and no solemn offerings are made there. On Mogemug, Eap, and Ngoli special temples are built, offerings are made, and there is a religious service.

Kadu has informed us how he found things on Eap, where he spent a long period of time, and he maintains that conditions are identical on the two closest groups. Both sexes have different temples and different times for making offerings. No man is present when women make their offerings. When the men make their offering it is the chief who makes the offering. He consecrates a fruit of every kind and a fish to the god by holding it up and calling to him. The formula is *Wareganam gure Tautup.* The people repeat the last word. The fruits thus offered are not consumed but put aside in the temple. For these offerings the people stay collected and isolated in the temple for a month, obtaining their food from outside. Of all the fruits or fish that he consumes during this time each one dedicates the first bite in accordance with the custom described and then throws this bite away uneaten. Songs or dances do not take place in the temple. This solemnity is celebrated alternately one month in one region, the following month in another. Kadu, as a foreigner, did not attend the celebration in the temple. He never entered it. Except at offering times it is forbidden to everyone except the chief and the priest. *(Matamat.)*

Rongala has no temples on Feis. But there are times when he descends upon the island and is present invisible in the jungle. Then the people must not speak loudly or walk; then they may approach the jungle only when dyed with curcuma and festively arrayed.

We shall furnish the theology of Ulea faithfully and extensively according to Don Luis de Torres. Cantova, whom we ask you to compare here, tells the genealogy of the gods in almost the same way, and somewhat more completely. The attractive myth of Olifat is completely new.

Three persons are worshipped in the sky, Aluelap, Lugeleng, and Olifat. The origin of all things, however, is as follows. Before all time there was a goddess called Ligopup. She is considered the creatress of the world.[12] She bore Aluelap, the lord of all knowledge, the lord of all splendor, the father of Lugeleng.[13] But no one knows who Lugeleng's mother was, and how his birth came about. Lugeleng had two wives, one in the sky and one on earth. The heavenly one was called Hamulul, the earthly one Tarisso, who was without equal in beauty and other natural gifts.

After four days of pregnancy Tarisso bore Olifat from her skull.[14] Olifat ran away immediately after his birth, and they followed him so as to cleanse the blood off him. However, he said that he would do it himself and would not tolerate anyone's touching him. He cleansed himself on the trunks of the palm trees past which he ran, for which reason they possess their reddish color. They called out to him and followed him in order to cut off his navel cord. However, he bit it off himself; he said he would take care of himself and didn't allow any mortal to touch him. He remembered how it was the custom to have the newborn child drink the milk of the young coconut and came to his mother, who handed him the coconut to drink. He drank and turned his eyes toward the sky, in which he perceived his father Lugeleng, who called out to him. Then he followed his father's call, and his mother with him. Thus they both left the world. When Olifat had arrived in the sky, he there met some children who were playing with a shark, around whose tail they had tied a cord. In order to remain unrecognized, he pretended to be a leper. Then the children stayed away from him and did not touch him. He demanded the fish from them so that he could play with it too, and they denied it to him. However, one of them took pity on him and handed him the string to which the fish was tied. He played a while with it and then gave it back to the children, urging them not to be afraid, but to keep on playing. The fish wouldn't hurt them. But he bit all of them except the one who had been kind to Olifat. Olifat had cursed the shark, which up until then had had no teeth and had been harmless. So he went on through the sky, distributing his curse to all creatures on similar occasions, because he was irritated in his glory. As no one knew him, and he had still not come to his father, who alone could recognize him, attempts were made on his life. He came to a place where a large house was built; he asked the workers for a knife to help cut coconut leaves for the roof. They refused him, but one handed it to him, and he cut himself a load of leaves. But he cursed all the workers, except the one who had been helpful to him, so that they froze into statues. Lugeleng, however, the owner of the building, inquired about his workers, and he was told how they had frozen motionless like statues. From this Lugeleng and Aluelap realized that Olifat was walking around in the sky. They asked the man who was still at work busily carrying coconut leaves to the building if he had seen anything round about, and he answered he had seen nothing except a *canduru* (a kind of sandpiper), into which bird Olifat had transformed himself. They sent the man out to call the canduru; but when he did this the bird was frightened by his voice and flew away. The man reported this, and they asked him what he had said to the bird. He answered that he had told him to come to him. They sent him out again, and they instructed him to tell the bird to go away because he was troublesome to chiefs. He did so and the bird came up right away. He further forbade him to go inside and sit down in the presence of chiefs, and the bird did immediately what had been forbidden him. As soon as the latter had sat down, Lugeleng commanded that the workers who had remained petrified in the forest should be called together, and they came immediately, to the amazement of the bystanders. For Aluelap and Lugeleng alone knew that the other was Olifat.

The workmen now continued with the building and dug deep holes in the ground to set the posts in. For those who were out to kill Olifat because of the great mischief that he had carried out this seemed a good opportunity. However, Olifat recognized their intent and carried with him concealed colored earth, coals, and the rib of a palm leaf. Thus he dug in the pit and at the bottom made a hole at the side to hide himself in. But they believed that the time had come, pushed the post in, and poured dirt around the foot of it, attempting to crush him in this manner. But he escaped in the side hole, spitting out the colored earth, which they thought was his blood. He spat out the coals, and they thought it was gall. They believed he was now dead. With the coconut rib Olifat made himself a way through the middle of the post and escaped. He lay down like a beam across the top of the post out of which he had come, and was not noticed. When the day's work was over, the workmen sat down to their meal. Olifat sent an ant to bring him a small piece of coconut. It brought him a crumb commensurate with its strength. With his powers he increased it to form an entire nut. He then cried out loudly, "Watch out down there, I am going to split my coconut." They became aware of him at his shout and were quite amazed that he had remained alive. They considered him to be Alus, the evil spirit.[15] They stuck to their resolve to kill him, telling him he should finish his meal and afterwards they would have an errand for him. They sent him to the house of Thunder to bring him his food. Olifat took a reed with him and went there without concern. He came to Thunder's house and told him rudely and arrogantly, "I have exhausted myself to bring food for your misshapen mouth." He delivered the food and left. Thunder wished to attack him, but he hid in his reed. Thunder could not find him and gave up trying to pursue him. Olifat came forth again, and excited all the more amazement from having returned unhurt from this trial. The workmen sent him out again to bring the fish Fela his food.[16] Olifat entered the house of Fela the fish and, as he himself was not present, he threw the food down in front of those who were there, saying, "Take this for yourselves," and left. When the fish came home he asked about the one who had brought the food. The family told him that someone had thrown the food to them, but they did not know who he was or where he had gone. The fish now proceeded to cast a fishhook on a long line to all the winds, and when he finally cast the hook to the north he pulled Olifat out. Then he killed him. After four or five days had passed without Olifat's appearing again, those who had sought his death in the sky comforted themselves and thought he was now dead. But Lugeleng sought his son and finally found him deceased and full of worms. He raised him up in his arms and woke him again. He asked him who had killed him. Olifat answered he hadn't been dead but had just been sleeping. Lugeleng summoned the fish Fela and struck him across the head with his staff, breaking off his upper jaw. Hence the shape that he now has. Aluelep, Lugeleng, and Olifat now went into glory, where they are busy dispensing justice.

Others bring the number of the heavenly residents to seven, to wit, Ligopup, Hautal, Aluelap, Litefeo, Hulaguf, Lugeleng, and Olifat.

To the question as to whether other islands had a different belief, some answered: This is the belief of the entire world, and the world would perish if Aluelap decreed it.

For comparison we cite the teachings of the former inhabitants of the Mariana Islands.[17] Puntan was a very clever man who lived many years in empty space before the creation of heaven and earth. When he was at the point of death the latter commissioned his sister to fashion heaven and earth out of his breast and shoulders, the sun and moon out of his eyes, and the rainbow of his eyebrows.[18]

Although there is no public service to the gods or the godhead on Ulea, according to Don Luis de Torres the people are not without piety. The individual sometimes lays out fruits as offerings to the invisible beings, and it is not taken amiss if someone picks up this offering and consumes it.

Cantova mentions a peculiar way of consulting the auguries. The procedure involved is as follows: A person rips off two strips of a coconut leaf from each side of the rib, at the same time repeating the syllables *pue, pue, pue* rapidly; then quickly and without counting them he ties knots in each strip, repeating the question that is to be asked of Fate in audible words. The first strip is taken between the little finger and the ring finger with four knots within the hand, the second between the ring and middle finger with three knots within the hand, and the others with a decreasing number of knots between the middle and the index fingers and between index finger and thumb. According to the way the number of the knots hanging out over the back of the hand coincides with or deviates from the numbers of the fingers one, two, three, and four, the augury comes out favorable or unfavorable.

On Ulea, as among all peoples, many superstitious practices are observed, and many charms are currently in use. We have mentioned the cutting apart of the dolphin. A small fish is frequently caught that children are not allowed to play with. If it were to happen that someone would grasp one of these fish by the tail and lift it up so that the head hung downward, on the next fishing expedition all the fish would seek the depths in the same fashion with their heads down, and none could be caught. Several people may not consume fruit from the same banana stalk. When someone has eaten one of the bananas, only he may consume the others.

On the desolate island of Fayo, as well as on Bigar, charms are spoken to produce fresh water in the water pits.

There is a species of black bird that is under sacred protection, and which must not be killed.

The people of Eap are notorious because of their magical arts. They know how to conjure the wind, to conjure the storm so that it becomes silent, and in calm to evoke the wind from a favorable direction. They know how, by casting a plant into the sea with an appropriate incantation, to agitate the waves and cause endless storms. The capsizing of many vessels from Mogemug and Feis, as well as the gradual depopulation of the latter island, are ascribed to this. In some fresh water of the Sütemil area there are two fishes, only a span long, but ancient.[19] They constantly remain in a line with their heads turned toward each other. If someone ever touches one of them with a rod or something so that it moves forward, and the two of them are at an angle to each other, the island will be shaken in its foundations, and there will be no end to the earthquake until both of them have resumed their accustomed places. Above these fishes and the water in which they are located a house is built and is watched over by the chiefs, by whose deaths sometimes an earthquake is occasioned.

A certain Eonopei (he is now dead, and his son is a chief of the Eleal region)[20] once showed our friend Kadu a remarkable proof of his skill. Eonopei fashioned a round, flat cake out of taro dough. It was night and a full moon brightened the sky. While he conjured he began to eat his cake. To the extent that he attacked its round shape and bit a piece out of it, the original full circle of the moon was attacked and hollowed out more and more into a sickle shape. When he had magically eaten away on the moon in this fashion for a time, he changed his procedure and his incantations. He began to knead the remaining soft dough of his cake into the form of a complete circle again, at which time the sickle of the moon again filled in uniformly, and finally the moon appeared full again. In the meantime Kadu sat next to the conjurer, observed everything, the moon and the cake, with the greatest attention, and was amazed at the way the roundness of both was first impaired and then again renewed. We shall let the testimony of our childlike friend, which we do not doubt, rest on its own merits, leaving it up to enlightened interpreters to apply it to an eclipse of the moon, which, however, before the invention of writing on Eap, can not be assumed to have been calculated in advance.

Celebrations and feasts, which take place on different occasions, such as the piercing of children's ears and the cutting of their hair on Eap, tattooing, etc., seem to have nothing religious about them.

Song and dance, generally inseparable, everywhere make up the chief diversion, the chief entertainment. There are different kinds of festive performances that are engaged in by only one of the sexes or by both together, and each of them has a different character and special name. However, these songs are not accompanied by any musical instrument, and even the drum is unknown in the Caroline Islands.

The chiefs seem to be subordinate to one another according to a kind of feudal system. Opinion raises them high above the common people, and extraordinary tributes of respect are paid to them, known to us from Cantova's letters and (for Pelli) from the *Account of the Pelew Islands.* One falls down onto the ground before them, and may only creep up to them. In view of the island of Mogemug, the residence of the supreme chief of the group of this name, the boats lower their sails. This veneration of the noble, perhaps divine descent does not seem to enter into purely human relations, which exist between chief and commoner without detriment to the conditions of rank, which are fully observed. The supreme chiefs have great authority and administer punitive justice according to the principle of strict retribution. An eye for an eye, a tooth for a tooth.

According to Cantova criminals are punished only by exile. We relate a story according to our friend Kadu in which it becomes apparent that with great clemency the crime is less atoned for than suppressed. We could imagine we were hearing the popular fairy tale *Fin voleur* from the lips of our nurses.[21]

On an island of Mogemug the trees were regularly robbed of their best fruit without the people being able, although they observed each other carefully, to discover the culprit for some time. They finally discovered that an apparently good boy got up each night and perpetrated the theft. They chastised him and kept an eye on him. But he eluded their watchfulness and did not desist from his habit. They locked him up at night, they bound his hands behind his back, but the cunning thief knew how to frustrate all their caution, and the thefts kept on happening. They brought him to a remote, uninhabited island of the group, which scarcely could provide food for one person. They left him there alone. However, they soon noticed that this had done no good, and that their trees continued to be robbed as before. Some of them went over to the desert island and found the young man feasting in great plenty on the fruits of their property. A tree trunk served him as a boat and he departed for his harvest every night. They destroyed his vessel and left him, now rendered harmless, to his solitude. Now they had peace. After some time they desired to know how he fared and some of them traveled over to the island again. They saw and heard no sign of him. After they had cried out to him and sought him in vain in the forest, they returned to the beach, only to find that their boat was missing. The cunning thief had gone to sea with it. He sailed over to Sorol.[22] On this group he did not desist from his tricks but also thought up greater enterprises. He was able to induce the chief of Sorol to plan an attack against Mogemug. In a nocturnal incursion he was to kill the chiefs and assume the supreme power. The conspirators came in sight of Mogemug in daylight. They lowered their sails to await nightfall on the open sea. Nonetheless, the boat had been observed, and they were surrounded as they landed. The ringleader was killed. The men of Sorol returned unharmed to their island.

On Ulea and Eap as on Radak the hereditary succession passes first to the brothers, then to the sons of the firstborn.

According to Kadu the chiefs are supposed to give their firstborn the name of their father, the second son the name of the father of their wife, the third again the name of their father, and so on. The common man, on the other hand, must give his firstborn son the name of the father of his wife and the other children other names, and so it is said to have been observed on Radak as well. According to Don Luis de Torres the indication of kinship is in the names, and from them it can be told whose son and grandson someone is.

The friendly exchange of names, a general custom in eastern Polynesia, is unknown in the Carolines, and Kadu at first denied that it was customary on Radak, even though he himself subsequently cited examples of it.

Marriages are contracted without ceremony. The man makes the father of the girl a gift of fruit, fish, and similar things. The extent of this bridal portion varies according to the station of the father of the bride; for marriages also take place between those of unequal birth. If only the father or the mother belongs to the chiefly class, the children are also reckoned among this class. In the first event the man pays the external homage of respect to his wife and children born to her that pertain to her rank. A plurality of wives is allowed. Marriages are dissolved without formality, even as they are contracted without formality. The man sends his wife back to her father. The men remain with their wives even when they are expectant, but not when they have a child at the breast. The latter occurs only on Radak; the former, contrary to Wilson's testimony, is expressly asserted about Pelli. There a chief, who usually has several wives, sends a handpicked man to replace him with that one of his wives who is in this condition (ab egregie mentulato quodam ["by someone who is exceptionally endowed with a large penis"]). We shall speak separately of the customs of Pelli. Wives on the other islands are subject only to their own husbands. They are bound together by oath, and the unspoiled nature of the people seems to protect their virtue. Custom allows unmarried people to enjoy their freedom. They spend the nights in their own large houses. Infanticide is unheard of; the chief would have the unnatural mother killed.

What we have reported about funeral customs on Radak is also true of Ulea and the islands situated more to the east. According to Kadu, on Feis, Mogemug, and Eap the corpses of everyone, without any differentiation according to birth, are buried on the islands. However, on Mogemug, after the great tragedy that concluded the history of the Caroline missions, we see the customs of Ulea observed toward the bodies of the threatening strangers and must believe that Kadu errs with respect to Mogemug. On Eap the burials take place in the mountains. The inhabitants of the mountains fetch the bodies of those who die in the valley and for this service receive presents of fruit, roots, etc. It does not seem as if any of the relatives follow the procession to the gravesite.

On all of these islands an indissoluble bond of friendship is formed exclusively between two men, very strongly obligating those so joined to each other. The chief and the common man can also form such a union without damage to the conditions of rank, which continue to be observed. Although this friendship recurs on all of these islands, in different places it is connected with different rights and duties. On Eap the friend must stand by his friend in every action, and if he is wronged or slain he has the duty to avenge him. In addition to similar obligations there is a new one on Ulea.

When the friend claims the hospitality of his friend, the latter relinquishes his wife to him for the duration of his visit, something that does not occur on Feis and farther to the west. We have seen that on Radak the duty is less binding in the first respect, and otherwise is the same as on Ulea.

As on the islands of eastern Polynesia, rubbing noses is the usual expression of love.

Among the Carolines only Pelli, Eap, Tuch, and the more remote islands with which Tuch is feuding, know war. The other islands, like Ulea, enjoy undisturbed peace. "There," our good-hearted companion repeated often and gladly, "there nothing is known of war and battle, there man does not kill man, and if someone sees war his hair becomes white." War did not always prevail on Eap. Formerly the island recognized the authority of a supreme head, and there was peace. But since Gurr, the last one to rule alone, departed, the chiefs of the various regions often fight their feuds to a bloody end. When a transgression, an insult has occurred, the triton-shell horn is blown. Both factions advance toward each other in arms. There is negotiating. When satisfaction is refused and no compromise is reached, there is fighting. The war lasts until one of the class of chiefs has fallen on each side and those of the opposing side have tasted his bloody flesh. Each one merely lifts a piece to his mouth. This is an unavoidable formality. When this condition has been met peace again sets in, and marriages between both regions seal it. The character of these islands nonetheless is gentle and hospitable, as it is in the other island groups. The stranger on Eap can walk through the warring factions without danger, and here and there receives a friendly reception right away. The men of Eap throw the javelin in an arc with the help of a slotted piece of bamboo in which the blunt end of the projectile is held and receives the impulsion when it is thrown. In this way they are effective over an extraordinary distance. This weapon seems to coincide essentially with that of the Aleuts and the northern Eskimos. They also have the two-pointed javelin of the Radakians. This same javelin, when the combatants have drawn closer together, is thrown straight with the bare hand. Finally they fence man-to-man with it. The chief directs the encounter with the triton-shell horn. The war party moves out against the hostile region on boats and rafts. The attempt is made to prevent a landing. The decisive battles take place on land.

The men of Tuch use the javelin in close combat, but from a distance they use the sling. Their throw is far and certain, and they manipulate this weapon with admirable dexterity. In peacetime they always go about with this weapon tied around their heads, and they use it to kill birds, to knock fruit down from trees, and the like. On Ulea Kadu had learned to use the sling from natives of Tuch, and he often passed the time among us practicing with it, although he was very awkward with it.

Don Luis de Torres praised the same virtues in his friends on Ulea that it had pleased us to praise in our friends of Radak. They are good, friendly, handsome, and modest. Never did a woman climb on board the *Maria*. They are charming, affectionate, generous, and grateful. They have the memory of the heart. The thing, for instance the useful tool, that they possess as a gift from a loving hand, receives and bears as a late reminder for them the name of the friend who presented it to them. And thus Kadu on Radak wished to give our names to the species of animals and plants that we had introduced as an eternal reminder of us.

Cantova draws a terrifying picture of the natives of the Pelew Islands.[23] According to the reports he collected they are hostile cannibals. These same people then appear in the most favorable light, the opalescence of love, endowed with all the virtues, in the reports of a grateful Henry Wilson, who owed his return to his homeland to their generous hospitality, and the deed demonstrates that they displayed most of these virtues. We live with Wilson in the midst of these people, see with our own eyes, and judge for ourselves. Since Wilson the English, Spanish, Americans have continually visited the Pelew Islands, various Europeans have settled down there, and trepang is regularly gathered on their reefs for the Canton market. Kadu from Ulea was in the Pelew Islands, and in his verdict we behold a comparison of both peoples. This comparison, like our friend's verdict, is unfavorable to the natives of Pelli. Kadu especially berates them for being devoid of all modesty, so that they bestially satisfy their natural impulses before everyone's eyes. He evoked in us the picture of utter licentiousness, such as prevails in the Sandwich Islands.

Some pages that a Spaniard who had spent nine months on the Pelew Islands showed us in Cavite are composed abusively rather than critically. He makes less of an impression upon us than does our honest friend, whose accusations he repeats in great detail, among other things. "Men have congress with women before everyone. They are all ready to sell the favors of their wives for a trifle." Etc. But he also accuses them of eating human flesh and hardly admits to their having human shape.

We lay aside this sad work after having merely mentioned it. These are no longer the innocent, guileless friends of Wilson. What they have learned from us has not made them any better.

# CHAPTER VI
## The Penrhyn Islands.

THE tall, dense forests that the coconut palm forms on the Penrhyn Islands deceived us from a distance with the appearance of high shores. Smoke announced the presence of man. As soon as we approached land numerous boats surrounded us, and a peaceful folk desired to have contact with us.

The islanders are strong and well built, heavier than the inhabitants of Easter Island, and of the same color. They are not tattooed, but many have furrows or welts cut into the skin of the trunk or arms, which on one of them still appeared fresh and bloody. They are often missing their front teeth. Older people become obese and have fat bellies. We noticed various old men who had let their thumbnails grow, an eloquent token of their aristocratic idleness. On one of them this inwardly bent nail had attained a length of two to three inches.

We counted about thirty-six boats. In each of them there were seven to thirteen men, who seemed to belong to one family. An old man (the head of the house?) stood in the middle and conducted the conversation. He had tied the end of a coconut leaf around his neck, apparently as a sign of peace. There were women only in three boats. In these an old woman (the lady of the house?) occupied the rear seat and seemed to have an important voice in the men's affairs. The authority of no individual appeared to go beyond his own boat.

The women wear a belt to which are freely attached pendant strips of bark, similar to the men's garb on Radak; the men instead wear only a bundle of coconut leaves attached with cords. Only a few had a miserable shoulder covering. This consists of a coarse mat plaited out of a coconut leaf. A part of the central rib that bears the leaves forms the lower edge of this basketlike cloak. Occasionally bleached pandanus leaves are woven in for decoration. A few wear a headpiece of black feathers.

They came close to the ship, talking confidently the while, but no one quite dared to accept our invitations to come aboard. They had only little to exchange for our goods, which they showed themselves eager to acquire, and which they accepted with a kind of veneration. They had a few coconuts, mostly unripe, for quenching thirst, a few tools they happened to have brought along, and their weapons. These are long spears of coconut wood, at the bottom of which a grip made of some other wood is fastened with coconut fiber, the point of which is either expanded and two-edged or is tapered long and simply. At first they refused to barter these weapons and decided to do so only in return for long nails or woolen scarlet sashes. We acquired from them some fishhooks fashioned of two pieces of genuine mother-of-pearl joined together in a most attractive manner, which were completely identical with those of the Sandwich Islands.

The boats are fashioned of several pieces of wood joined together by means of cords of coconut fiber. Both ends are rounded off above the water and equipped with a jutting spur beneath the surface. They have an outrigger, and weapons are stored there.

We did not wait for a boat from one of the more remote islands that approached us under sail.

The low-lying group of the Penrhyn Islands feeds a strong population abundantly, as the aspect of the people testifies. The only products of theirs that we are familiar with are the incomparable coconut groves, which cover them, and the pandanus. We were unable to determine what other fruits and roots occur there, or if they had swine and dogs, or only the latter.

As we departed from the Penrhyns storm clouds hung over them with thunder and lightning, affording us a sublime spectacle one seldom enjoys at sea.

# CHAPTER VII
## Waihu or Easter Island.
## Salas y Gómez.

WE just about set foot on the lava beach of Easter Island and do not flatter ourselves that we can add anything of substance to the knowledge of it that has already accrued. We refer to the reports of our predecessors and seek only to make the reader aware of the impression that this cursory contact left upon us.

Easter Island rises majestically from the waves in a broadly arched triangular ridge, the corners resting against pyramidal mountains. The calmly magnificent lines of O-Waihi are repeated on a small scale. It seemed to be completely arrayed in the freshest green, the earth everywhere, even on the steepest slopes of the mountains, divided into straight-bordered fields, differentiated by charming gradations of color, many of which were in yellow bloom. We gaped in astonishment at this volcanic, stone-covered earth, notorious because of its lack of wood and water!

We believed that on the southeastern coast we could distinguish with our telescope some of the colossal sculptures that excite so much amazement. In Cook's bay on the west coast, where we cast anchor, those busts that marked the landing place are no longer present.

Two canoes (in all we saw only three on the island), each one manned by two men, had come toward us invitingly but without daring to come close to the ship. Swimmers had surrounded the boat we had set out for sounding and opened the bartering there. The deceit of one of these traders had been severely punished. To attempt a landing we dropped a second boat into the sea. A numerous crowd awaited us peacefully, joyously, noisily, impatiently, childlike, and disorderly on the shore. It is not our place to decide along with Lapérouse whether or not these childlike people are to be commiserated with as being more unrestrained than others of their brothers. It is certain that this condition makes dealing with them difficult. We approached the beach. Everyone was running, exulting, and yelling; signs of peace, threatening casts of stones and shots, expressions of friendship were exchanged. Finally the swimmers dared to approach us in groups, trade began with them and was carried out honestly. With the repeated cry of "Hoe! Hoe!" they all demanded knives or iron for the fruits and roots and the handsome fishing nets they offered in exchange. We stepped ashore for a moment.

These people, described as being so miserable, seemed to us to be of handsome facial features, of pleasant and expressive physiognomy, of well-shaped, slender, healthy build, the elderly among them without defects. The eye of the artist rejoiced to see a more beautiful nature than the bathing spots of Europe, his only school, have to offer. The bluish, broad-lined tattooing, which artistically accompanies the course of the muscle, makes for a favorable effect against the brownish background of the skin. There seems to be no lack of bark cloth. White or yellow cloaks made from it are general. Fresh wreaths of leaves are worn in the hair, which varied in length. Headpieces of black feathers are rarer, and we remarked handsome necklaces that were decorated in the front by a polished seashell (Patella). We did not note any ugly, distorting ornaments. The pierced and expanded earlobes of some old men were tied together, pushed through the aperture again, and were not very noticeable. The incisors were often broken out. Some young people stand out through a much lighter skin color. We saw only a few women, these with faces dyed dark red, without charms or attractions, and, so it seemed, without any esteem among the men. One of them held a baby to her breast. We therefore do not consider ourselves justified in drawing any conclusion as to the numerical ratio of the two sexes.

If we compare the reports of Cook, Lapérouse, Lisianskoy [Lisiansky], and our own, the supposition forces itself upon us that the population of Easter Island had increased and the condition of the islanders has improved.[1] But whether the charitable intentions of the humanitarian Louis XIV were fulfilled, he having sent this people our domestic animals, useful plants, and fruit trees through Lapérouse, we could not determine, and we must doubt it: we saw only the products enumerated by Cook: bananas, sugar cane, roots, and very small chickens.

When we weighed anchor that evening fructifying clouds rested upon the heights of the island.

We later learned the probable cause of the doubtful reception that was given us on Easter Island and had cause to blush for ourselves, we who call these people savages.

The island of Salas y Gómez is a bare cliff that rises naked from the base of the waves. It rises saddle-shaped toward each end, where the type of mountain becomes apparent, in that the center is strewn with loose rocks. It is not one of the coral reefs, which only begin to occur farther to the west. One can suppose connection and similar nature with the high volcanic land of nearby Easter Island. No beginnings of a future vegetation are perceptible on it. It serves as a roosting place for innumerable aquatic birds, which seem to prefer such bare cliffs to green, although uninhabited islands, as with plants insects also occur, and ants, which especially endanger their brood.

Seabirds, according to our unauthoritative experience, are encountered most frequently above the winds of the islands where they nest. They can be seen in the morning flying out from land against the wind and in the evening flying with the wind toward land. Kadu also seemed to observe the flight of birds in the evening.

It is said that the remains of a wrecked ship were perceived near Salas y Gómez. We hunted around for it. It makes one shudder to imagine the possibility that a human being could be cast ashore alive on it, for the eggs of the waterfowl could have sufficed to lengthen his forsaken existence all too much upon this bare, sunburned piece of stone between sea and sky.

# CHAPTER VIII
## The Sandwich Islands.
## The Johnstone Islands.

O-WAIHI rises majestically from the waves in magnificently smooth lines and forms an enormous mass with three different mountain peaks, on two of which snow is present several months of the year.

Both times we visited the Sandwich Islands late in the year and saw no snow upon the heights of O-Waihi.[1]

Mauna Roa [Mauna Loa], the large mountain, La Mesa, the table of the Spaniards, rises in a broad dome to the south in the interior of the island and rises above the other adjoining peaks.[2] Mauna Kea, the small mountain, the next one after Mauna Roa, dominates the north with its jagged peaks.[3] The third, Mauna Wororai, a volcanic peak, is on the west coast. Its crater is depicted in Vancouver's atlas.[4] On its bare slopes lava flows gleam, the last of which it spewed forth toward the sea through a lateral eruption in the year 1801.[5] The village of Powarua is built on the beach on this slaglike lava. Mauna Puoray, which forms the northwestern point of the island, adjoins the base of Mauna Kea as a minor hill.

The heights of O-Waihi generally show clean and clear during the night and in the morning. Water vapor settles down on it toward noon, so that the clouds so produced hang over the island in the evening in a thick, concealing layer and become dissipated again toward midnight.

Wherever we approached O-Waihi, sailing around the northwest tip and along the west coast to the foot of Wororai at Tiutatua, the slopes appear bare and brown. Some fields are tilled, but most of the land is covered by pale grass. High up by the clouds the forest region begins, and the eye hardly extends to the bare crowns of the gigantic structure. The shore offers an uninterrupted series of settlements, which, as one proceeds southward, are surrounded by more abundant verdure and interspersed with more numerous coconut palms.

In the volcanic mountain chain of the Sandwich Islands Wororai

on O-Waihi seems to be the only active volcano. Hot springs can be found in the Kochala section at Mr. Jung's residence on the coast south of Puoray. The chain runs from the northwestern tip of O-Waihi across the islands of Mauwi, Morotoi, and O-Wahu to west-northwest. The eastern mountain on Mauwi lacks only a little of the height of Wororai, giving a repitition of its magnificent shape.[6] The western one is lower, and its peak seems to be deeply split from north to south at two points.

The outlines of the mountains descend much lower on Morotoi down to the extremely flat western tip of this island. The mountains soar upward again on O-Wahu (Waohoo of the Englishmen), where they take on a completely different character and attain hardly a fourth of the height of those on O-Waihi. Two different mountain ranges arise on the island of O-Wahu. The low eastern range is greater in extent than the western range, which contains the higher peaks.[7] The mountains, deeply furrowed by copiously watered, beautifully green valleys, lift their jagged peaks in uneasy, restless lines. The forests descend lower on their slopes than they do in O-Waihi down to the sun-dried plains, which mostly surround the island and once were coral reefs covered by the sea; and from these plains coral reefs extend far out into the sea. A breach in the reef at the mouth of a stream of confluent mountain streamlets at the southern foot of the eastern mountainous mass forms the safe harbor of Hana-ruru, from which place our excursions extended through both parts of the island.

The next low hill behind Hana-ruru is an old volcanic crater whose stopped-up mouth and outer slopes are thickly covered with grass.[8] Another similar but larger and higher crater forms a sea-laved promontory that cuts off the view to the east.[9] Alleged diamonds, which a European is said to have found in this area, caused the taboo under which this mountain is placed. We were shown some, which were common quartz crystals.

The mountains rise behind these bare foothills in uneven, beautifully green steps to its highest ridge, which runs along the northern coast. Valleys and gorges traverse them between the peaks. The Nuanu [Nu'uanu] Valley behind Hana-ruru is by far the widest and most charming of them all. Beyond it toward the north or northeast the mountains plunge down so steeply that the descent can be made only by clambering barefoot down dizzying paths and rocky trails.

Low hills, covered with sun-dried savannahs, unite the two mountain ranges of the island. South of these hills the inlet of the sea that the English call Pearl River winds its several branches up to the bottom of the hills through a broad plain that is a coral reef forsaken by the sea, the top of which may have been ten feet higher than the present surface of the water. The passes between the peaks are high and steep and can be traversed only by dangerous paths. The luxuriousness of the vegetation, which seems to remain unchanged at the height of 300 toises [approx. 1,919 feet] to which we climbed, distracts the geognost's eye from the object of his investigation, and the type of mountain seldom is apparent.

In these parts of the island we observed only diorite and clay porphyr. Black spots, which we saw from the sea on the eastern slope and foot of the larger old crater, seemed to us to be a kind of lava.

Clouds gather around the mountain peaks, and rain falls in the interior of the island while a blazing sun singes the beach.

The temperature changes perceptibly as soon as one steps from the outer plains into the mountain valleys.

We already possessed three approximate measurements of Mauna Roa, varying considerably, taken by King, Marchand, and Horner.[10] Mr. von Kotzebue's more precise measurement agrees down to six toises with the median of the three former ones, and his trigonometric work on the other peaks of the Sandwich Islands makes an interesting list.[11]

The short time that was allotted to us both times permitted us only to look sadly at the mountains of O-Waihi, which seemed to us to deserve to be the goal of a special trip to the Sandwich Islands. On the very spot, we had to refrain from doing anything about them.

To climb Mauna Roa from Tiutatua demands a trip of at least two weeks (cf. Vancouver), and if from Tiutatua and Powarua at the very foot of Wororai we might hope to climb the peak of the latter in a short time, the trip to the ship in Hana-ruru in a native double canoe remained unreliable, as there is no way of commandeering such a vessel, frequent taboos hinder traveling by sea, and the trip from O-Waihi to Mauwi and from Morotoi to O-Wahu can be hampered and long delayed by the winds. The plants that Archibald Menzies, the learned companion of Vancouver, gathered in various trips to the heights of O-Waihi and Mauwi, are still buried along with so many other treasures, in Bank's herbarium, and although the venerable *doyen* of natural scientists opens his Gazophylacium to all scholars with equally unlimited hospitality, no one has yet undertaken the task of making us acquainted with the alpine flora of O-Waihi.[12]

The flora of O-Wahu has nothing in common with that of the closest continent, the coast of California. The leafless form of the acacias, the genera *Metrosideros, Pandanus, Santalum, Aleurites, Dracaena, Amomum, Curcuma, Tacca,* impress upon it the seal of its origin and its natural relatives.[13] There is a prominence of the families Rubiaceae, Contortea, and Urticeae, of the last of which many varied wild-growing species are used for the manufacture of bark cloth.[14] Some treelike milky Lobeliaceae are outstanding.[15] The outer edge of the island produces only a few species of grasses and weeds. In the interior the flora is rich without, however, being comparable in luxuriant abundance with Braziliian nature. Only low trees can be found in the valleys, among them the *Aleurites triloba*, which with its whitish foliage forms distinctive clumps at the feet and on the slopes of the mountains. Here and there in the high mountain gorges there are wonderful groves of banana trees, their trunks pressed so closely together that they harbor an area of darkest night beneath their widespread leaves. This plant, which, when it is cultivated on the shore, hardly attains a height of five feet, in such places attains three times this height. The acacia, out of whose trunks the natives' large canoes are fashioned, attains the height necessary for this purpose only in the high mountains, and only there, too, is the sandalwood tree found, whose wood, so greatly prized in China, helps the ruler of these islands to accrue treasures while the oppressed people who must collect the wood become poverty-stricken because it is removed from their agriculture and their crafts.

The taro root *(Arum esculentum)*, pounded to a sticky paste after it has been cooked, constitutes the chief food of the people. The most fertile of the islands is O-Wahu, from which O-Waihi draws a part of its requirements of taro. The cultivation of the valleys behind Hana-ruru is admirable. Even on the hills artificial pools that are also fishponds maintain the taro plants, and all sorts of useful plants are now cultivated along with the indigenous ones, but the people, who adhere to their old way of life, make use of few of them. Among these tobacco may be accounted the main one, all the people of the earth having demonstrated themselves to be equally willing to adopt its use. The watermelon, the melon, and fruit in general have found the most ready reception next to tobacco. Beside the ruinous kava, fermented drinks are made from the ti root *(Dracaena terminalis)*, but the sugar cane is still not utilized for this purpose.

The Sandwich Islands in general, and O-Wahu, his present place of residence, in particular, owe much to Mr. Marini's activity as a planter. He has tirelessly introduced and increased our animal and plant species. Near Hana-ruru he possesses numerous herds of cattle. (The goats seem to be more generally distributed.) He possesses horses and will increase the number of donkeys and mules, which are more useful in these mountains. Many foreign trees and plants are cultivated in his plantations. Some that he introduced can already be found growing wild all over, for example, *Portulacca oleracea*.[16] (Two other species of the same genus are all that belong to the group of indigenous flora.) He recently saw rice grow up from Chinese seeds, after several futile attempts. He has planted vineyards of considerable extent, but he is still not adept in the art of making wine. On our journey we have often found that everywhere the art of using the products that are present is a much more urgent need than the introduction of new products and seize this opportunity to give this hint to philanthropic travelers. A few books of instruction are all that is needed.

The only indigenous wild mammals on the Sandwich Islands are a small bat and the rat. The latter has now been joined by our house mouse, even as the flea, species of *Blatta*, and other parasites have found their way here.[17] Cattle have now run wild on the island of O-Waihi, where the king occasionally has some of them hunted down for his table.[18] Among the land birds we observed the *Nectarinia coccinea*, whose highly prized feathers form a part of the tribute the chiefs exact. The sea is rich in fish, many of which are endowed with an extraordinarily magnificent coloration. They are among the favorite foods of the natives, who raise several species in the taro pools and in fishponds that are formed on the reefs along the shore when walls are constructed.

Among the crabs, beautiful *Squilla* and *Palinurus* species stand out;[19] among the mussels, the small mother-of-pearl mussel, which is found only in Pearl River, and from which small pearls of slight value are obtained.

The sea worms and zoophytes probably comprise the most abundant and interesting part of the fauna. Here in general species different from those in Radak seem to occur. The progressive growth of the reefs themselves seems not to have escaped the notice of the natives. We were told that the people who at the king's command were constructing a wall for which they had to procure the stones from the sea at one time remarked that they would regrow by themselves and increase in size.

About the Sandwich Islands we possess only the reports of fleeting visitors who in their fidelity merely show us pictures where we await more thorough information and are more and more desirous of obtaining it. Cook discovered these islands and an unfortunate quarrel caused him to lay down his life among the strong and warlike O-Waihians.[20] They had honored him like a god, and they still honor his memory piously. Trade followed in Cook's wake to the northwestern coast of America, and the Sandwich Islands, which offered all sorts of refreshments to the ships that traveled there, at once assumed the important position that their discoverer had attached to them. With Vancouver we are made to feel at home on them. A great man, whom we encountered as a youth in Cook's account, had seized the reins of power on O-Waihi and strove for complete sovereignty over the entire group. Tameiameia assured himself of the protection of Great Britain by independently, voluntarily, and solemnly doing homage to King George through the person of Vancouver.[21] Later travelers, including Lisianskoy, informed by the Europeans settled on the Sandwich Islands, expand our knowledge of them and report on the course of events. Our avaricious adventurers busily stir up war in order to keep up the price for the weapons with which they pay for their cargoes. Tameiameia completes the conquest of all the islands, and the king of Atuai (the separate group in the west) hurries to subject himself voluntarily to the foe he cannot resist. To be sure, he is led to rebel under the banner of the Russian-American company, but he soon atones for his dereliction and does homage to his feudal lord anew (1817).

Tameiameia, favored by the position of his kingdom, and by the sandalwood that it produces, has amassed astounding riches. With cash he buys cannon and ships, himself builds smaller ships, which, when he lacks the copper to sheath them, he preserves by having them pulled ashore into sheds at Tiutatua, Karakakoa, and other spots on the island of O-Waihi. He sends out his ships, manned half by natives and half by Europeans, and tries, up until now unsuccessfully, to gain entrance for his flag into Canton. He chooses with great perspicacity from the Europeans who offer him their services, but he is very generous with fiefs and salaries to those whom he picks. He is magnanimous, and for all the matters he has learned from foreigners, he remains true to the spirit of his people and the customs of his ancestors.

But after the death of this old hero his kingdom, founded on and held together by force, the division of which has already been decided and prepared, will fall apart.

Kareimoku, otherwise called Naja (Bill Pitt of the Englishmen), a scion of the royal blood of Mauwi, after the conquest of this island when he was still a boy, was spared by Tameiameia and kindly treated and brought up. He has bestowed love, property, and power upon him and has raised him to an eminence scarcely less than his own. He has put into his hands the right to decide over life and death. He always found him faithful. Kareimoku, governor of O-Wahu and master of the fortress of Hana-ruru on this latter island, the most important because of its harbor, is prepared to assume power over it and is purchasing cannon and ships on his own account. In concert with him, and united with him in close friendship, is Teimotu, who, from the royal line of O-Waihi and a brother of Queen Kahumanu, will receive the island of Mauwi as his share. The king of Atuai will reassert his independence over his inherited kingdom. And the natural heir to the throne, the weak, characterless Lio-Lio (*Prince of Wales* of the English), grandson of the last king of O-Waihi, son of Tameiameia and the high queen Kahumanu, before whom his father may appear only when unclothed, will be limited to the hereditary island of O-Waihi. No foreigner, many as there are who can be counted among the mightiest chiefs and royal vassals, can exercise any claim to rule over the natives.

For all these impending political upheavals, the Sandwich Islands will remain what they are: the free harbor and stockpiling place for all those mariners who sail these seas. If any foreign power should foolishly take it into its head to take possession of them, to frustrate this undertaking there would be no need of the jealous alertness of the Americans, who have taken over almost exclusively the trade of these seas, nor would there be any need of the certain protection of England. The conquest might indeed be successful. The fort in the background of the harbor of Hana-ruru, which Mr. Jung designed without any technical knowledge, a mere square of dry masonry without bastions or towers and without a moat, does not meet the double purpose of the ruler of protecting himself from attack from without and enemies from within. The fort, where it stands, would have to be constructed in a proper manner, and there should be a battery on the outermost edge of the reef to defend the entrance of the harbor. For all their supply of cannon and small arms the natives are still inexperienced in the use of artillery and our military tactics. A serious attack might appear to be decisive, but the victors would only have conquered the ground for their own graves. This people will not subject itself to foreigners, and they are too strong, too numerous, and too fond of warfare to be quickly extirpated, like the natives of the Marianas.

This is the historical situation of the Sandwich Islands. That which appears in the Missionary Register for 1818, page 52, to the effect that a son of Tamari, king of Atuai, who now is being educated in the school of the Board of Foreign Missions (Connecticut, North America) along with other O-Waihians, is the natural heir to all the Sandwich Islands, betrays inconceivable ignorance.[22]

No missionaries have as yet come to the Sandwich Islands, and, indeed, they could promise themselves that their efforts would bear but little fruit among these sensual people. On the islands of Eastern

Polynesia Christianity could flourish only upon the downfall of everything now in existence there. We do not doubt the events in O-Taheiti, but neither do we comprehend them, and Mr. Marini, who earlier visited these islands, tells us, which seems very logical to us, that the natives mostly visited the missionaries only from the desire to amuse themselves later by imitating their habits.

We owe the most valuable contribution to our knowledge of Polynesia to the accounts of William Mariner and the admirable industry of D. John Martin in the satisfying *Account of the Natives of the Tonga Islands* (London, 1818). This important work was not extant at the time of our journey, and the need of a similar work on the O-Waihians is all the more urgent. The desire both to study thoroughly the legends and the history, the common and the liturgical language, the religion and customs, the social order, and the nature of this people on the one hand, and the longing to explore the history of plants and their wanderings on the heights of O-Waihi impelled the naturalist of the expedition on the occasion of our first visit to the Sandwich Islands to offer to sojourn there until the return of the *Rurik*. This idea, which the prevailing political conditions would have frustrated anyway, was found to be irreconcilable with the purpose of the expedition.[23] It is now high time under the high-minded King Tameiameia and with the assistance of the Europeans who have settled in his kingdom, whose experience and knowledge would give the learned scholar a big advantage, to undertake this task and to put in writing what the O-Waihians still know about themselves; for where monuments and writing are lacking languages change under foreign influence, legends die out, customs are leveled out, and someday the European will find only Europeanized people who have forgotten their origins and their ancestors.

Among all the Europeans residing there, Mr. Marini seems to possess the most comprehensive knowledge of the people of O-Waihi. He has studied them in many respects and has had the opportunity on various journeys to compare and enrich his experience on other islands of the South Seas, from O-Taheiti to the Pelew Islands. Mr. Marini had done some writing: we lament along with him the loss of his manuscripts. He had promised us on our first stay in Hanaruru to answer in writing the questions we had addressed to him and to hand us the answers upon our return. But we were deceived in the hope that he had entitled us to cherish. He had not managed to find the time for this task, and during our second sojourn he was busy with the ships in the harbor to such an extent that we could scarcely enjoy his conversation for a few fleeting moments.

Mr. Marini lamented the recent death of an old man who was especially well versed in the old legends of his people, and with whose demise a part of the orally transmitted history may have been lost forever. The old legends are told in very different ways. There was a flood during which only the top of Mauna Roa had projected above the waves. People saved themselves upon this peak. Before this flood there had been another cataclysm in which the entire earth remained in darkness for forty days.

In ancient times strangers, whose names are not mentioned, arrived on the Sandwich Islands in a boat. Mr. Marini heard a legend on O-Taheiti according to which seafarers from this island who had become lost at sea were the ones who were cast ashore on the Sandwich Islands.

The conditions of a social order that is not based on any written law or mandates but, mightier than force, on belief and tradition, can be looked upon and interpreted differently. Mr. Marini counts four castes in the people of O-Waihi. *De sangre real* ["of royal blood"], the royalty; *de hidalguía*, the nobility; *de gente media*, the middle class (which makes up by far the largest part of the population); and *de baxa* [*baja*] *plebe*, the lower class, a disdained race, which is not numerous. Formerly every white person was immediately regarded as a member of the nobility, but now his condition depends upon his personality.

The word *hieri, jeri, erih, ariki* or *hariki* [*ali'i*] ("head, chief") might best be translated by "lord." The king is *Hieri ei Moku*, the lord of the island or islands. Every powerful prince or chief is a *Hieri nue* [*ali'i nui*], "great lord"; and this is the way, without distinction, Tameiameia, Kareimoku, Haul Hanna (Mr. Jung), and others are called.

The land belongs to the lord of the island; the nobles possess land only as fiefs. The fiefs are hereditary but inalienable. If there is no heir, they revert to the crown. Powerful lords may well revolt and defend what they possess. Might makes the right that supports the lord of the island. The great lords feud among themselves with weapons. These small wars, which used to be numerous, seemed to have stopped since 1798. The lord leads his vassals in war, and no commoner can possess a fief or lead vassals. He can be only a manager of property. Those who till the earth are renters or peasants of the fief-owners or directly of the king. Tribute is paid the king from everywhere. High-ranking chiefs are placed as governors over the various islands and regions. The people are virtually subject to the whims of the lords, but there are no slaves or serfs *(Glebae adscripti)*.[24] Peasant and servant can move about as they please. A man is free—he can be killed, but he cannot be sold or imprisoned. Nobles or lords without land serve those more powerful than they are. The lord of the island maintains many of them, and his paddlers belong exclusively to this caste. Of course, the castes are segregated in such a way that there is no possibility of passing from one to the other. A nobility that can be given and taken away is no nobility. A woman does not share her husband's class. The class children belong to is determined by certain very definite laws, for the most part by the class of the mother but also by that of the father. A noble-woman who marries a commoner loses her class only in the event that she bears him children, in which case she and her children pass over into the man's caste. It is not primogeniture, but rather, where there is polygamy, it is the more noble birth on the side of the mother that determines the right of heredity. The inequality of the members of the nobility and the different degree of taboo or conse-cration due each high-ranking chief by birth and without regard to his power are matters that have not been sufficiently explained. Tameimeia's predecessor on O-Waihi was taboo to such an extent that he could not be seen by day. He showed himself only at night, for anyone who accidentally beheld him by daylight would have had to die immediately—a sacred commandment that nothing could prevail against. The human sacrifices, which upon the death of kings, princes, and noble chiefs are traditionally made and interred with their corpses, are from the lowest caste. In certain families of this caste members inherit the fate of dying along with the various members of this or that noble family, so that from the time of birth it is decreed at whose death they shall be sacrificed. The victims know their fate, and their lot does not seem to have anything terrify-ing for them. The progressive spirit of the times has already made this custom antiquated, so that it scarcely survived the death of the most sacred of chiefs. When upon the death of Kahumanu's mother three victims voluntarily reported to fulfill their destiny, Karei-moku did not allow it to happen, and no human blood flowed. Prob-ably human sacrifices still take place, but it would be unjust to reproach the O-Waihians for this. They sacrifice law-breakers to their gods, while in Europe we sacrifice them to justice. Every land has its customs. What were the *autos de fe* among Christians, and when did they stop? Moreover, the custom of eating human flesh had ceased long before Cook's death. The last historical vestiges of this can be seen on the island of O-Wahu.

Every prominent chief has his own gods *(akua)*, whose idols are set up in all his morais. Others have different ones. The cult of these idols seems to be more a matter of prestigious swank than religion.

The common people must do without these images and make various creatures—birds, chickens, etc.—the objects of their cults. On the Sandwich Islands superstition takes many forms. As the guest of Kareimoku we attended the celebration of a *tabu-pori* [*kapu poli*], which lasts until sunrise of the third day. The kind of sanctity that during this time is invested in a man who has shared in this concourse with the gods is familiar. If he were to touch a woman even accidentally she would have to be killed right away. If he were to enter a house for women the flames would have to consume it straightforth. We expected some solemnity during these prayers and sacrifices, and were put off by the profane mood that prevailed, the ignoble fun that was poked at the images, and the foolishness into which they had great delight in drawing us during the sacred proceedings. Children show more piety when they play with their dolls.

The old inhibiting laws of the taboo still hold undiminished sway.[25] We ourselves saw the corpse of a woman floating around our ship who had been killed because in a drunken state she had entered her husband's eating-house. However, the women, when they know they are unobserved, do not hesitate to transgress the many prohibitions with which they are burdened. Up until now traffic with Europeans has had little apparent effect upon the social order or the customs of this people. Certainly we have contributed to the development of vice, to the arts of corruption that are so outrageous in these childlike people. *Ingens nostratium Lupanar! Turpissimis meretricum artibus, foetidissimis scortorum spurcitiis omnis instructa est femina vel matrona. Omnis abest pudor, aperte avideque obtruditur stuprum, precio flagitato. Aperte quisque maritus uxorum offert, obtrudit solventi.* [One big brothel of the natives! Every woman, even every matron, is well versed in all the vilest artifices of whores, all the filthiest, dirty tricks of prostitutes. They all lack shame; openly and avidly sex is offered for a fixed price. Openly every husband offers his wife, presses her upon one for a price.]

An event that transpired toward the year 1807 is related in various ways by rumor. We follow Mr. Marini's account.

A nephew of the king was found in Kahumanu's arms. He himself escaped, but his clothing remained behind and betrayed him. Three days after the event he was seized by the leaders of the realm and strangled. A soldier of the guard reported the punishment and the crime to the king at the same time. Everything was in order this way. Tameiameia lamented the death of the poor youth and wept tears for him.

In comparison with our friends from Radak we found the O-

Waihians self-serving, graceless, and unclean. In their relations with strangers from whom they wish to derive an advantage they have forgotten their natural hospitality. Their great mimic talent and the practice they have had makes it easy for them to make themselves understood to us. They are an incomparably more powerful people than the Radakians. From this is derived their great self-confidence and their more inconsiderate merriment. The chiefs especially are of an exceedingly handsome and powerful build. The women are beautiful but without charm.

Earlier travelers have noted that natural malformations are more frequent in the Sandwich Islands than on the other islands of Eastern Polynesia. On O-Wahu we saw several humpbacks, an idiot, and several members of one family with six fingers on each hand.

The O-Waihians are sparsely and irregularly tattooed. It is remarkable that this indigenous adornment has borrowed foreign patterns. Goats, muskets, even letters, their names and places of birth, are frequently tattooed along the arm. The men shave off their beards and cut their hair into the shape of a helmet, the crest of which is often bleached to a blond or whitish color. The women wear theirs cut short, except that around the forehead they display a fringe of longer hairs projecting stiffly like bristles and burned white with undissolved lime. Often a fine long lock in the middle of the forehead is singled out, dyed violet, and combed back. To please the Europeans some let their hair grow and tie it into a braid in the back similar to that which was regulation in the Prussian Army in 1800. In general the O-Waihians have wisely remained true to their native costume as well as their way of life. Their chiefs appeared in fine English clothes neatly done up only to honor us, and they imitated our customs with dignity. Otherwise, when at home they remained dressed in their native fashion, and only the foreign guest is served with porcelain and silver. Fashion also holds sway in O-Waihi with changing fads, especially over the ladies. The jewelry that the queens and the noblewomen wear soon increases enormously in value. All now wear a mirror and a pipe bowl tied in a European cloth around the neck. The Europeans go around clad in the European fashion and do not disrobe before those whose rank usually demands this mark of reverence.

Many O-Waihians understand some English, but none of them is a complete master of the language, not even those who have served on American ships, as very many have done. No one seems to have learned the letters of the alphabet.[26] It is only our ships that draw their complete attention. At Tiutatua we watched in admiration as children drew ships in the sand with a stick. Two- and three-masters

were drawn in correct proportions and equipped with the most minute details of rigging. Still, the O-Waihians continue to make their
boats in their old fashion, single and double. The king's larger double canoes, which serve the purpose of maintaining connections
among the various islands, are rigged in the European manner. We
must not make Zimmermann's mistake (Australia) in confusing the
boats of eastern Polynesia (Friendly Islands, Sandwich Islands, etc.),
which are propelled by paddles and use sails only when the wind is
behind them, with the artfully crafted vessels of the First Province
(the Ladrones, etc.), which can travel with any wind. We are amply
familiar with the former through Cook and the more recent travelers, the latter from Dampier, Anson, and others.[27] The warlike O-
Waihians take pleasure not only in their boats, but also in their
weapons, their javelins. They take pleasure in contests at arms,
which are not without danger, and already practice throwing their
javelins when they are children. The favorite game of boys and
youths, which consists of throwing light reeds, which the wind
catches, at a moving target, seems to point toward this weapon.
They have few other games. The only board game that has been discovered among them is now being displaced by our European game
of checkers.

Poetry, music, and dance, which in the South Sea Islands still go
hand in hand to embellish people's lives, deserve to be highly
regarded. The spectacle of the *hurra*, the festive dances of the O-
Waihians, filled us with admiration.

The words, like Pindaric odes, generally glorify the fame of some
prince. Our knowledge of the language is not sufficient for us to be
able to judge their poetry. The song itself is monotonous. With the
drum-beats that accompany it, it measures off the twists and turns
of the dance, at the same time bearing a high harmony on its waves.
In the sinuous dance the human body unfolds in a most magnificent
manner according to this rhythm, exhibiting itself in the flow of
easy, unforced motion in all its natural and beautiful positions. We
could believe that we see a transformed Antiquity before us; feet
merely bear the dancer. He strides along calmly. His body moves, all
his muscles stir, his countenance is animated. We look him in the
eye, the way we do a mime when his art holds us in its grip. The
drummers sit in the background, the dancers stand before them in
one or several rows. They all contribute their voices to the chorus.
The song starts in slowly and softly and is gradually and uniformly
accelerated and intensified as the dancers step forth and their
motions become more animated. They all carry out the same
motions. It is as if the same dancer stood before us several times

recurrent. These festive spectacles of O-Waihi remind us of the chorus of the Greeks, of tragedy before dialogue was added, and if we turn our regard toward ourselves we recognize what a ridiculous aberrant road we have taken in restricting the dance to the movement of the feet. These festive spectacles intoxicate the O-Waihians with joy. Their usual songs are danced to in the same way, standing or sitting. They are of a very different character but always accompanied by pleasant motions of the body and the arms. What a school opens up here for the artist, what enjoyment is offered to the lover of art!

This beautiful art, the only one the islanders have, is the bloom of their lives, which belong to the senses and to pleasure. They live in the present, without reckoning time, and an old woman with regard to her age only knows that she has lived beyond the first period of enjoyment, beyond the age of twelve.

The O-Waihians are included in the charge that our seafarers make against the South Sea Islanders in general, namely, that they are devoted to thievery. That we had no occasion to join in this lament can probably be ascribed to the protective care that Tameiameia took of us, unselfishly and high-mindedly honoring in us the successors to Vancouver. Europeans who have settled here give honorable testimony to the honesty of the natives. Without worry they leave doors and drawers unlocked. These people allow themselves thievery only against the rich foreigners on the well-laden ships. Why shouldn't our abundance of iron, this precious metal, not excite the desire of the South Sea Islanders? "How can you see the mote in your brother's eye and not see the beam in yours?" We are not thinking here of the Spanish conquests of the past, but rather we are concerned about the deeds that greedy adventurers perpetrate in these seas, where our laws do not reach them. We have touched on some of them in these pages, others are covered by darkness. By our office we are attorney for the weaker part. Discard our testimony, but scan without prejudice the accounts of all the mariners who have sailed these seas since they were opened to trade. From Vancouver's *Journey* to Nicolas' *New Zealand*. Judge for yourself. While we judge and punish, people of our color engage in kidnapping, robbery, deceit, force, treason, and murder. The arts and sciences have given us this power over our weaker brothers.

The commerce of this oceanic basin is said to engage two hundred North American ships, but this seems too high an estimate to us. The chief elements of this commerce are the smuggling on the Spanish coast of both Americas, which on the Spanish side is carried out by the monks; the fur trade of the northwest coast, the export of the

pelts assembled in the Russian-American trading posts; the sandalwood in the Sandwich and Fiji Islands and other islands. The field is
open to the boldest enterprise. New discoveries are attempted and
followed (be reminded of the ship that according to Mackenzie's
account was seen about the year 1780 in the Polar Sea)[28]; Aleuts or
Kadiakans are taken to the Californian coast to hunt sea otters, etc.
Canton is the common market, Hana-ruru a free harbor and storage
depot. The captain is generally in charge of the business affairs, so
that none of the wrangles need be feared that occur between captain
and supercargo when these offices are separated. In the dangerous
trade of the northwest coast neither side is to be trusted, and one
must be on his guard against the weapons that are sold. Neighboring
tribes are often at war with each other. One negotiates with the
leader of the one tribe and delivers him up to his enemy, whom one
then tries to get in one's power by ruse or force to hold for a suitable
ransom. One entices chiefs on board and frees them again for a suitable ransom, etc. Also, people who are bought on the southern coast
are said to find an advantageous market on the northern coast. We
mentioned kidnapping on the South Sea Islands in our essay on
Guaján. It was no American who on an island along the coast of California had all the male inhabitants rounded up and shot.[29] Captain
Door (with the *Jenni* from Boston) landed on Guaján in the year
1808, after he had taken aboard a cargo of sandalwood in the Fiji
Islands. In the year 1812 he made the same journey with another
ship. Upon his return he told Don Luis de Torres that he had been
hostilely received this time and had lost a boatswain's mate and four
sailors. The natives had told him that in the ensuing time they had
come to know white men and had decided to show them no mercy
henceforth. (On the Fiji Islands see Mariner's *Tonga*.)

In a European cemetery near Hana-ruru this simple inscription for
Mr. Davis can be read:

The remains
of
Mr. Isaac Davis
who died at this
Island April 1810
aged—52 years[30]

When we sailed away from Hana-ruru we left the aged Mr. Jung in
a very feeble condition. Both friends, whose names together shone
brightly in the history of these islands, will rest side by side. Mr.
Jung's children, although heirs to his property, will be lost among

the people without any fame, because they were not born of a noble mother.

The islands that Captain Johnstone discovered in the frigate *Cornwallis* in the year 1807 to the WSW of the Sandwich Islands, and which we sought out again in the late fall of 1817, are, like the island Salas y Gómez, completely bare rocks, which do not seem to have anything to do with the formation of the other islands. The reefs that adjoin them form shallows at a great distance from them, which threatens danger to shipping.

# NOTES

Introduction

1. See J. C. Beaglehole, *The Exploration of the Pacific*.
2. Krusenstern, known in Russia as Ivan Fedorovich Kruzenshtern, tells of this journey, in which the young Kotzebue took part as a cadet, in his work *Reise um die Welt in den Jahren 1803, 1804, 1805, 1806, und auf Befehl seiner Kaiserlichen Majestät Alexanders des ersten auf den Schiffen Nadeshda und Newa*, 3 vols. and Atlas (St. Petersburg, 1809–1814). Kotzebue's expedition was the second one under the Russian flag, and it partially overlapped a third one under Captain Vasilii M. Golovnin.
3. George Vancouver (1758?–1798), having sailed with Cook to the Hawaiian Islands, afterwards led an expedition of discovery to the Pacific (1791–1792). His work was entitled *A Voyage of Discovery to the North Pacific Ocean and round the World*, 3 vols. with Atlas (London, 1798).
4. See Louis Choris, *Voyage pittoresque autour du monde*.
5. See *Peter Schlemihl*, trans. Leopold von Löwenstein-Wertheim (New York, 1980).
6. See Otto von Kotzebue, *Entdeckungs-Reise in die Süd-See und nach der Berings-Strasse . . . in den Jahren 1815–1818*.
7. See Adelbert von Chamisso, *Werke*, vols. 1 and 2.
8. See Otto von Kotzebue, *A New Voyage round the World in the Years 1823, 24, 25 and 26*.
9. See Luis Galdames, *A History of Chile*, trans. and ed. Isaac Joslin Cox, pp. 141–204.
10. See Hector Chevigny, *Russian America: The Great Alaskan Adventure, 1741–1867*.
11. See Warren A. Beck and David A. Williams, *California: A History of the Golden State*, pp. 30–65.
12. See H. David Tuggle, "Hawaii," in *The Prehistory of Polynesia*, ed. Jesse D. Jennings, pp. 167–199, and Peter Bellwood, *The Polynesians: A Prehistory of an Island People*, pp. 96–109.
13. See Ralph S. Kuykendall, *The Hawaiian Kingdom*, vol. 1, *1778–1854: Foundation and Transformation*, pp. 1–70.
14. See Richard A. Pierce, *Russia's Hawaiian Adventure, 1815–1817*.
15. See Nicklaus R. Schweizer, *A Poet among Explorers: Chamisso in the South Seas*, p. 13 and passim, and Gisela Menza, *Adelbert von Chamissos "Reise um die Welt mit der Romanzoffischen Entdeckungs-Expedition in den Jahren 1815–1818,"* pp. 85–121.

16. Otto von Kotzebue, *A New Voyage round the World*, 2:217–219.

17. Ibid., pp. 256–257.

18. See Schweizer, *Poet among Explorers*, pp. 23–27, 33–35.

19. See Samuel Elbert's Introduction to the 1969 reprint edition of Chamisso's *Über die Hawaiische Sprache*, p. xvii.

20. Adelbert von Chamisso, *Bericht über die zur Bekanntmachung geeigneten Verhandlungen der Königlichen Preussischen Akademie der Wissenschaften zu Berlin aus dem Jahre 1838*, pp. 45–46; reprinted in Chamisso's *Sämtliche Werke in zwei Bänden*, 2:524–532.

21. See Gunther Schmid, *Chamisso als Naturforscher. Eine Bibliographie.*

22. Chamisso, *Sämtliche Werke*, 1:468–476.

23. Ibid., pp. 520–522.

24. Ibid., pp. 226–228.

25. Ibid., pp. 410–414.

26. See Schweizer, *Poet among Explorers*, pp. 44–45.


# PART I

## BY WAY OF FOREWORD

1. This essay, entitled "Uber die Korallen-Inseln," appears anonymously in the appendix to Chamisso's "Notes and Opinions" under the rubric "Anhang von anderen Verfassern" [Appendix by other authors] in Kotzebue's *Entdeckungs-Reise in die Süd-See*, 3:187–189 (3:331–336 in the English translation). The false attribution to Chamisso is retained by Charles Darwin, *The Structure and Distribution of Coral Reefs. Being the First Part of the Voyage of the Beagle* (London, 1842), p. 63. Chamisso's own views appeared in an essay entitled "Notice sur les îles de corail du grand Océan," which appeared in *Nouvelles Annales des Voyages, de la Géographie et la Histoire* 10 (1821): 159–163; reprinted in Chamisso, *Werke*, 2:392–396. The main points of contention were assertions by Ivan Ivanovich Eschscholtz, the *Rurik*'s doctor, that coral grows more rapidly on the surf side than on the lagoon side of a reef, and that it does not grow in great depths—in both of which points he was right.

2. Kotzebue's *Entdeckungs-Reise in die Süd-See* was published by Wilhelm Hoffmann, in Weimar. Chamisso's friend was Louis de la Foye (ca. 1780-1847), French mathematician and physicist. The matter is discussed in their correspondence. See René Riegel, ed., *Correspondance d'Adalbert de Chamisso. Fragments inédits*, pp. 211–226.

3. This is an allusion to the murder of Kotzebue's father, August von Kotzebue. He was stabbed to death on March 23, 1819, in Mannheim by Karl Ludwig Sand, a fanatic student of theology who regarded Kotzebue as the archenemy of liberalism because of his ridicule of the patriotic and liberal views of the German student associations *(Burschenschaften)* in the conservative journal *Literarisches Wochenblatt* ("Literary Weekly") that he edited.

4. The review (vol. 26, pp. 341–364) is ascribed by Chamisso in *Werke*, 5:194), in a letter to Karl Bernhard Trinius (1778–1844), German naturalist and poet, to Sir John Barrow (1764–1848), English traveler and geographer.

5. Cacciaguida appears in cantos 15–17 of the "Paradiso" in the *Comme-*

*dia divina.* Dante refers to him as *la luce* "the light, brightness" (XVII, 121–123):

> La luce in che rideva il mio tesoro
> ch'io trovai lí, si fó prima corusca,
> quale a raggio di sole specchio d'oro

("The light in which my treasure, which I found there, first smiled and shone gleamingly, like a golden mirror in the rays of the sun.")

6. Chamisso was suffering from a lung ailment that eventually caused his death.

### By Way of Introduction

1. The correct date is actually 1792.

2. Frederick William II (1744–1797) succeeded his uncle, Frederick the Great, as king of Prussia, 1786–1797. His consort was Friederike Louise of Hessen-Darmstadt. His son Frederick William III (1770–1840) succeeded him as king and reigned from 1797–1840.

3. Through a coup d'état in 1799 Napoleon had himself named first consul in a consulate of three, a step toward obtaining absolute power as emperor.

4. Chamisso's *Faust* is a short "poem in dramatic form" in which Faust sells his soul to an "evil spirit" and commits suicide. See Chamisso, *Sämtliche Werke*, 1:500–509.

5. Karl August Varnhagen von Ense (1785–1858), together with Chamisso, Julius Eduard Hitzig, and others, formed a literary circle in Berlin called the *Nordsternbund* ("North Star Alliance") to promote the ideas presented in the Berlin lectures of August Wilhelm Schlegel (see n. 6 below). After serving as an officer in the Austrian army in the Napoleonic Wars Varnhagen von Ense distinguished himself as a literary critic and political liberal.

6. Published in Leipzig, it was called "der grüne Musenalmanach," or "der Grünling," because of its green cover. It was patterned after *Musenalmanach für das Jahr 1802* (Tübingen, 1802), edited by two leaders of the Romantic movement in Germany, August Wilhelm Schlegel (1767–1845) and Ludwig Tieck (1773–1853).

7. Johann Gottlieb Fichte (1762–1814), the well-known German philosopher, frequented Romantic circles in Berlin and contributed anonymously to the *Musenalmanach* of 1804.

8. The almanacs for 1805 and 1806 were published in Berlin by Heinrich Frölich. The year 1805 was the year of the War of the Fourth Coalition, which ended with a disastrous defeat for Prussia in the battle of Jena. Chamisso served in the Prussian military and was stationed in the city of Hameln when it surrendered to the French.

9. Napoleon closed the University of Halle in 1806.

10. The man seems to have been Friedrich Schleiermacher (1768–1834), a Protestant theologian and member of the Romantic circles of Berlin. His *Über die Religion. Reden an die Gebildeten unter ihren Verächtern* (Berlin, 1799) (in English, *On Religion: Speeches to Its Cultured Despisers*, trans. John Oman [London, 1893]), was influential in disseminating Romantic theories.

11. The friend was Julius Eduard Hitzig (1780–1849), Chamisso's life-long confidant.

12. A town adjacent to the town of Pontivy, 30 miles NNW of Vannes, Napoléonville was constructed by Napoleon as the military headquarters of Brittany. The "old friend" was Louis Marquis de Fontanes (1757–1821), a French writer and statesman created a marquis by Louis XVIII.

13. This famous French writer, Anne Louise Germaine (née Necker), Baronne de Staël-Holstein (1766–1817), was married to a Swedish minister to France. Having fled from France during the Revolution (1793), she returned in 1795 but was banned from Paris because of her opposition to Napoleon.

14. Mme de Staël was residing in Chaumont Castle in Blois on the Loire River in central France when Napoleon banished her from France (September 24, 1810) because of her book *De l'Allemagne*. Amable Guillaume Prosper Brugière, Baron de Barante (1782–1866), was a French historian and diplomat in Mme de Staël's coterie. Napoléon is the former Napoléon-Vendée (now La Roche-sur-Yon), a commune in Vendée Department, western France. It was founded by Napoleon in 1804 to serve as the capital of Vendée. Coppet is a Swiss town on Lake Geneva, for years a center for intellectuals who gathered around Mme de Staël. To escape police surveillance Mme de Staël on May 23, 1812, fled from Coppet to Vienna.

15. Auguste de Staël (1790–1827) was Mme de Staël's son by her lover, Louis, Comte de Narbonne-Lara (1755–1813), French nobleman and statesman. Chamisso addressed himself seriously to the study of botany at the University of Berlin.

16. Chamisso's most famous work first appeared as *Peter Schlemihl's wundersame Geschichte*, mitgetheilt von Adelbert von Chamisso und herausgegeben von Friedrich Baron de la Motte Fouqué (Nürnberg, 1814), and in English as *Peter Schlemihl*, trans. Sir John Browning (London, 1823).

17. This was the year in which Napoleon regained power after having been exiled to Elba. After the famous "Hundred Days" he was defeated at Waterloo on June 18, 1815.

18. Prince Maximilian von Wied-Neuwied (1782–1867) was a German naturalist and traveler. His journey to Brazil (1815–1817) is described in his book, *Reise nach Brasilien in den Jahren 1815–1817*, 2 vols. (Frankfurt, 1820–1821). It was published in English as *Trends in Brazil in the years 1815, 1816, 1817*, 2 vols. (London, 1820 and 1825).

19. Krusenstern organized many other Russian trips around the world. Nikolai Petrovich, Count Rumiantsev (1754–1826), Russian statesman, historian and writer, belonged to the high nobility, and was chancellor of Russia from 1809–1812, when his Francophile policies led to his dismissal.

20. Karl Friedrich von Ledebour (1785–1851) was a German-born professor of botany in Tartu, Estonia.

CHAPTER I

1. Wilhelm Gottfried Tilesius von Tilenan (1769–1857), physician and naturalist, participated in the Krusenstern expedition that circumnavigated the globe in 1803–1806.

2. Auguste de Staël hoped to make his settlement, named for his mother's maiden name, a refuge for escaped slaves.

3. Barthold Georg Niebuhr (1776–1831) was a Prussian historian and statesman, son of the explorer Carsten Niebuhr (1733–1815).

4. Ludwig Robert (Marcus Levin) (1778–1832), brother-in-law of Varnhagen von Ense, was also a member of the *Nordsternbund.*

5. Johann Kaspar Spurzheim (1776–1832), German physician and phrenologist.

6. According to Horace (*Odes*, III, 5), Marcus Atilius Regulus (d. ca. 250 B.C.), a Roman consul, was tortured to death by the Carthaginians by being thrown about in a box studded inside with nails. Georg Christoph Lichtenberg (1742–1799), German satirist, described this action by saying that they would "enclose him in a kind of German stagecoach and roll him down the mountain in it."

7. A German mile was 7,532 meters long, compared with the English mile of 1,609 meters.

8. Lenzen is a small town on the Löcknitz River a few miles northwest of the city of Wittenberge.

9. Friedrich Christoph Perthes (1772–1843) founded his publishing house in Hamburg in 1796.

10. Mungo Park (1771–1806) was a Scottish explorer of Africa, the author of *Travels to the Interior Districts of Africa in the Years 1795, 1796, and 1797* (London, 1799). (A German version appeared in Hamburg the same year.) He drowned in the Niger River while trying to escape an attack by natives near Bussa in the province of Sokoto, Nigeria.

11. The reference is probably to "Stimme der Zeit" [Voice of the times] (1834), a poem commissioned in honor of a retiring Prussian minister of state, Friedrich Hermann, Count Wylich und Lottum (1767–1841). See Chamisso, *Sämtliche Werke*, 1:488–490. Chamisso mentions the Lapp preacher again in Chapter XII.

12. Joachim Christian Nettelbeck (1738–1834), Prussian mariner and distiller in Kolberg (now Kołbrzeg in northwestern Poland), was a superpatriot during the Napoleonic Wars.

13. A galleass is a small coastal freighting vessel used in the Baltic in Chamisso's day.

14. Jens Wilken Hornemann (1770–1841) was a professor of botany at the University of Copenhagen; Christoph Heinrich Pfaff (1773–1852) was a professor of chemistry at the University of Kiel.

15. Adam Gottlob Oehlenschläger (1779–1850) was Denmark's most famous writer of the period. He wrote numerous poems and dramas and was a leading figure in the Romantic movement in Europe. Baron Friedrich de la Motte Fouqué (1777–1843) often frequented Berlin Romantic circles and was a friend of Chamisso's. *Undine* (1811), probably his most famous work, is a fairy tale about a water nymph who falls in love with a mortal.

16. Frederick VI (1768–1839) was regent of Denmark from 1784 to 1809 after his father, Christian VII, became incurably insane. After his father's death he was king from 1808 to 1839 (also king of Norway, 1808–1814). Even though Denmark had lost a good deal in the war, there was a feeling of relief in the land because the worst was over and their national existence was assured.

17. Morton Wormskiold (1783–1845) was a Danish botanist who had

traveled to Norway in 1807 and to Greenland in 1812–1815. He left the *Rurik* expedition on Kamchatka, where he was picked up two years later by Golovnin. See V. M. Golovnin, *Around the World on the* Kamchatka, *1817–1819*, trans. and ed. Ella Lury Wiswell, p. 94.

18. At the Treaty of Tilsit (1807) France and Russia secretly agreed to force Denmark and Norway (then united under the Danish crown) to close all their ports to English ships. The Dano-Norwegian government refused, but the British (who may have heard of the Franco-Russian demand) themselves demanded that Denmark and Norway enter into an alliance with them and rent them their fleet for the duration of hostilities for £100,000. When Denmark refused, the British sent a fleet to Denmark and landed a large army on the island of Sjælland. This army bombed Copenhagen, killing over 1,600 civilians and forcing the surrender of the city. The British then commandeered almost the entire Dano-Norwegian fleet, which was in Copenhagen harbor. The only ship of the line not lost at this time, the *Prins Christian Frederik*, was later (March 22, 1808) surrounded and defeated by five British men-of-war at the battle of Sjællands Odde. It was run aground and later caught fire and exploded. See Palle Lauring, *A History of the Kingdom of Denmark*, 3d ed., trans. David Hohnen (Copenhagen, 1968), pp. 193–200.

19. In 1809 Sweden was forced by France and Russia to depose its anti-French king, Gustavus IV Adolphus and elect his uncle, Charles XIII (1748–1818). It also accepted Marshal Jean Baptiste Jules Bernadotte (1763?–1844), a Frenchman, as heir to the Swedish throne. Bernadotte turned Sweden away from Napoleon and in 1814 insisted on having Norway joined to Sweden as the price for helping Britain. King Frederick VI renounced Denmark's right to Norway in the Treaty of Kiel that year, and Norway entered into a union with Sweden under the Swedish king that lasted until 1905, when Norway secured its complete independence. See Lauring *History of Kingdom of Denmark*, pp. 200–205, and Karen Larsen, *A History of Norway* (Princeton, 1948), pp. 365–395.

## CHAPTER II

1. According to Kotzebue's account, *Entdeckungs-Reise in die Süd-See*, 1:98 (English trans. 1:94), the envoys were Count Dohna (Russia), Count Boribell (Austria), and Admiral Lowenor (not further identified), van Brien (secretary of the Russian embassy), General Tawast (Swedish envoy).

2. Shishmarev (1781–1835) later commanded the ship *Blagonamerennyi* in a voyage around the world led by M. N. Vasilyev on the sloop *Otkrytie* (1819–1822).

3. Sakharin (d. 1857) rose to the rank of vice admiral.

4. Baron Friedrich August Marschall von Bieberstein (1768–1827), German traveler and botanist, described his trips to the Caucasus in *Beschreibung der Länder zwischen den Flüssen Terek und Kur am Caspischen Meere* (Frankfurt a/M, 1800).

5. Helsingør (Elsinore) is a city on North Sjælland Island, Denmark.

6. Horatio Nelson, Viscount Nelson (1758–1805), the hero of Trafalgar, was famous for his seasickness.

7. Napoleon was brought from Rochefort to Plymouth on the *Bellerophon*, where he had surrendered to the British on July 15, 1815. On

August 7 he was transferred to the *Northumberland*, on which he was transported to St. Helena, where he was landed on October 16 and lived until his death on May 5, 1821.

8. See Gilbert Martineau, *Napoleon Surrenders*, trans. Frances Partridge (New York, 1971), pp. 180–182.

9. Eliza O'Neill (Lady Eliza Bechera, 1791–1872) was an Irish actress who specialized in tragic roles. *Menschenhass und Reue* (1789) (*The Stranger; or, Misanthropy and Repentance*, trans. G. Papendick [London, 1798]), was one of August von Kotzebue's most famous plays.

10. Edmund Kean (1787–1833) was the greatest English tragedian of his day, a star of the Drury Lane Theater in London.

11. Eulalia is a character in *Menschenhass und Reue.*

12. See *Hamlet*, Act III, Scene 2, where Hamlet says: "Suit the action to the word, the word to the action; with this special observance, that you o'erstep not the modesty ["moderation"] of nature: for anything so overdone is from the purpose of playing, whose end, both from the first and now, was and is, to hold, as 'twere, the mirror up to nature. . . ."

13. Kotzebue's plays were very popular both in England and the United States. See Bayard Quincy Morgan, *A Bibliography of German Literature in English Translation* (Madison, 1922), pp. 301–311.

14. *Alarcos* is a play (1802) by Friedrich Schlegel (1772–1829), one of the principal writers of the Romantic movement in Germany. The play *Ion* (1803) was written by his brother, August Wilhelm Schlegel.

15. An allusion to a poem of Chamisso's (written in 1832), entitled "Roland ein Rosskamm" [Roland, a horse-dealer], in turn based on a passage in *Orlando furioso* (1516) (canto 30, 5) by the Italian poet Lodovico Ariosto (1474–1533).

16. Kotzebue's oldest brother, Wilhelm (1785–1813), was a colonel in Russian service when he was killed.

17. *The Vicar of Wakefield* (1766) is the famous novel by Oliver Goldsmith (1728–1774). A reference to gooseberry wine occurs in Chapter 1, where the vicar writes: "As we lived near the road, we often had the traveller or stranger visit us to taste our gooseberry wine, for which we had great reputation."

18. The Eddystone lighthouse was rebuilt in 1759 by John Smeaton (1724–1792), English engineer. It rose to a height of over 78 feet.

## Chapter III

1. *Hakon Jarl hin Rige* [Earl Hákon the rich] is a drama (1807) by Adam Oehlenschläger. Earl Hákon (ca. 937–995) ruled Norway from 970–995. *Correggio*, a tragedy (1811), is also by Oehlenschläger. Antonio Allegri, il Correggio (1494–1534), was an Italian artist.

2. CHAMISSO'S NOTE: "Sea miles" refers to English nautical miles of which there are sixty in a degree of the Equator; minutes of the Equator.

3. Literally, "taking no part in the baths of Ocean" (*Iliad* 18, 489).

4. Salpas are any of a genus of transparent barrel-shaped or fusiform free-swimming oceanic tunicates common in warm latitudes, specifically here *Salpa pinnata*.

CHAMISSO'S NOTE: See Chamisso, *De animalibus quibusdam e classe vermium. Linnæana* Fasc. I. *de Salpa* (Berol., 1815). [On some animals of the

Linnaean class of Vermes. Fascicle I. On *Salpa* (Berlin, 1815, recte 1819).
Comments on this work are in Oken's *Isis* (a scientific journal) 1 (1820), 3
(April), cols. 273–276. Fasc. II: "reliquos vermes continens" (containing the
rest of the Vermes), together with C. G. Eisenhardt in the *Nova Acta Phy-
sico-Medica* of the *Transactions of the Imperial Leopold and Caroline Academy of Naturalists* (Vienna) 10, div. 2 (1821): 343–374.]

5. This story appears as a supplement ("Die Doppeltgänger") to vol. 1 of
Paul's famous novel *Titan* (1800). See *Jean Pauls sämtliche Werke*, ed.
Eduard Berend, series 1, vol. 8 (Weimar, 1933), pp. 245–250.

6. Gavrill Andrevich Sarychev (1763–1831), Russian explorer, comman-
der of the second ship on the expedition to Siberia and the Arctic under
Joseph Billings, wrote *Puteshestvie flota kapitana Sarycheva po severovos-
tochnoi chasti Sibiri* (St. Petersburg, 1802), translated into English as
*Account of a Voyage of Discovery to the North-East of Siberia, the Frozen
Ocean and the North-East Sea*, 2 vols. (London, 1806–1807).

7. Friedrich Heinrich Alexander von Humboldt (1769–1859), German
naturalist, traveler, and statesman, undertook an expedition to Central and
South America (1799–1804) with Aimé Bonpland (Goujaud) (1773–1858),
French naturalist. Together they published *Voyage aux régions equinoxials
du Nouveau Continent, fait en 1799–1804*, 30 vols. (Paris, 1805–1834).
Chamisso here refers to vol. 1.

8. The Salvages (Selvagens) are a group of small uninhabited islands in
the Madeiras.

9. Baron Christian Leopold von Buch (1774–1853), a German geologist
who studied volcanic processes in the Canaries, wrote *Physikalische Beschreibung der Kanarischen Inseln* [Physical description of the Canary
Islands] (Berlin, 1825).

10. *Cactus opuntia*: the prickly pear. Today *Opuntia* designates a genus
comprising numerous species of cacti bearing pulpy, edible fruits.

11. The Guanches, probably related to the Berbers, inhabited the Canary
Islands until they were wiped out or absorbed by the Norman and Castilian
conquerors of the fifteenth century.

12. The Spanish formal second person pronoun *usted* is a contraction of
*vuestra merced*, "your grace."

CHAPTER IV

1. Canaria, Grand Canary Island, 40 miles ESE of Tenerife.

2. San Iago (São Tiago) is the largest of the islands, with an area of about
359 square miles.

3. *Physalia arethusa*: a species of siphonophore of the genus including the
Portuguese man-of-war.

4. A janissary is a kind of Turkish soldier. According to *Webster's Third
New International Dictionary*, janissary music features "shrill fifes and
loud oboes and drums, cymbals, triangles, and Turkish crescents."

5. "Marlborough s'en va-t-en guerre" [Marlborough goes to war], a folk
song honoring John Churchill, first Duke of Marlborough (1650–1722),
English military commander in the War of the Spanish Succession. Holtei's
"Cloak Song" refers to "Mantellied" from the play *Lenore* (Berlin, 1829),
by Karl von Holtei (1798–1880), German poet, novelist, and playwright,
member of the *Mittwochgesellschaft* ("Wednesday Society"), a Berlin literary club.

6. Cape Frio is an island in the Atlantic Ocean in Rio de Janeiro state, Brazil.

7. Infusoria: a group of protozoans, differing in extent in different classifications.

8. *Planaria:* a genus of flatworms.

9. The Channel of Santa Catarina lies between the island of Catarina and the Brazilian mainland. The island, the site of present-day Florianópolis, is about thirty miles in extent and is located between 27° and 28°S latitude.

10. *Cocos Romanzoffiana M. (Arecastrum romanzoffianum):* The *M.* stands for Karl Friedrich Philipp von Martius (1794–1868), German botanist, director of the Botanical Garden in Munich. He took part in an Austrian expedition to Brazil (1817–1820) and wrote many books about the flora of Brazil. In *Historia naturalis palmarum* (1823–1853) he accepted Chamisso's designation.

11. *Melastoma:* a genus of Asiatic shrubs with coriaceous leaves and large purple flowers.

12. Bromeliaceae: family of plants to which the pineapple belongs. *Tillandsia usneoides:* Spanish moss.

13. Aroideae: a subfamily of plants of the *Arum* family (Araceae), including the cuckoopint and jack-in-the-pulpit.

14. Augustin François César Prouvençal de Saint-Hilaire (1799–1853), French botanist, traveled through Brazil and wrote *Flora Brasiliae meridonalis*, 3 vols. (Paris, 1825–1832), and *Plantes usuelles des Brasiliens* (Paris, 1824–1828). Christian Gottfried Daniel Nees von Esenbeck (1776–1858), German botanist, was the author of *Agrostrologia brasiliensis* (Stuttgart, 1829). Johann Baptist Emmanuel Pohl (1782–1834), a German botanist who traveled in Brazil (1817–1820), was author of *Plantarum Brasiliae icones et descriptiones hacfenus ineditae Zires* (Vienna, 1827–1831), and *Reise im Innern von Brasilien*, 2 vols. (Vienna, 1832–1837). Diedrich Franz Leonhard von Schlechtendal (1794–1866) was a German botanist in Berlin and editor (from 1826) of the journal *Linnaea,* in which Chamisso published some of the results of his trip. De Candolle may refer to Augustin Pyrame de Candolle (1778–1841), Swiss botanist, or to his son Alphonse Louis Pierre Pyrame (1806–1893), who edited vol. 4,1 of Saint-Hilaire's *Flora Brasiliensis.* Adrien de Jussieu (1797–1853) was a French botanist in Paris.

15. The city of Nostra Senhora do Destero [Destêrro] is now Florianópolis. See n. 9 above.

16. San Miguel (São Miguel) is a city and district in the state of Rio Grande do Norte, Brazil.

17. *Armação* literally means "arming; equipment, outfit."

18. Goethe wrote the ballad "Bride of Corinth," "Die Braut von Korinth," in 1797.

CHAPTER V

1. At the time of this voyage, ownership of the Falklands was disputed among Spain, Argentina, and England, which occupied them in 1833.

2. Staten Island (Isla de los Estados) is an Argentine island about 45 miles long off the eastern tip of Tierra del Fuego. The chief town, located at the eastern end, is San Juan de Salvamento.

3. William Smith, English navigator, discovered the South Shetland Islands in 1819. The South Shetland Islands are located about 550 miles

southeast of Cape Horn (between 61° and 63°S latitude and between 54° and 63°W longitude) and form part of the Falkland Islands Dependencies.

4. Cape Victoria is a promontory in Tierra del Fuego.

5. *Ramphastos:* a genus of birds comprising various toucans. *Simia capucina (Cebus capucinus):* the capuchin monkey.

6. The Reaumur thermometric scale was invented by René Antoine Gerchault de Réaumur (1683–1757), French naturalist and physicist. On this scale the freezing point of water is 0° and the boiling point is 80°.

7. *Fucus pyriferus (Macrocystis pyrifera)* and *Fucus antarcticus (Durvillea antarctica):* species of kelp.

8. Dante's *Purgatorio* I,22 ff. The verse in Italian is from Dante Alighieri, *La Commedia secondo l'antica vulgata,* ed. Giorgio Petrocchi (Turin, 1975), and the English from Dante Alighieri, *The Divine Comedy,* illustrated by Umberto Romano (Garden City, 1947), p. 150:

> I' mi volsi a man destra, e puosi mente
> a l'altro polo, e vidi quattro stelle
> non viste mai fuor ch'a la prima gente.
> Goder pareva 'l ciel di lor fiammelle:
> oh settentrïonal vedovo sito,
> poi che privato se' di mirar quelle!

> To the right hand I turn'd, and fix'd my mind
> On the other pole attentive, where I saw
> Four stars ne'er seen before save by the ken
> Of our first parents. Heaven of their rays
> Seem'd joyous. O thou northern site! bereft
> Indeed, and widow'd, since of these deprived.

9. The Botocudos are a tribe of Indians in Brazil named from the labrets they wore.

10. Records note only the date of his baptism. He was born between January 27 and 30, 1781. See Ludwig Geiger, *Berlin 1688–1840,* 2:16–17.

11. See Chamisso, *Werke,* 2:1 ff.

12. Spain lost most of its colonies during the reactionary reign of Ferdinand VII (1784–1833), king of Spain from 1808 to 1833.

13. Coblenz was a center for exiled French nobility during the War of the First Coalition, 1792–1797.

14. "Patriots" refers to those on the side of the revolutionaries under Bernard O'Higgins (1778–1842) and José Miguel Carrera (1785–1821). The revolutionaries, who gained control of Chile in 1810, were defeated in 1814, but they were soon to gain the ascendancy again through the campaign of 1817–1818 under the leadership of José de San Martín (1778–1850), a South American soldier and statesman born in Argentina.

15. In a letter to Julius Eduard Hitzig from June or July, 1816 (*Werke,* 6: p. 40), Chamisso added the following lines: "d'un desdichado/ la voz oí." ("In the shade of a green meadow/ I heard the voice of an unhappy person.")

16. Valdivia was the Chilean province where Concepción and Talcahuano were located.

17. The Araucanians were an Indian people occupying parts of Chile and Argentina. The *Civil History of Chile, Saggio sulla storia civile del Chili* (Bologna, 1787), was written by Giovanni Ignazio Molina (1740–1829), an Italian naturalist.

18. *Bomba*, literally, "bomb," also means "impromptu verse."

19. Alexander I (1777–1825) was tsar of Russia from 1801 to 1825. The Biobio (Bío-Bío) is the most important river in Chile. It rises in Argentina and empties into the Pacific a little south of Concepción. Alonso de Ercilla y Zúñiga (1533–1594), Spanish poet and soldier in Chile, was the author of *La Araucana* (1569–1590), an epic poem dealing with the war waged by the Araucanian Indians against the Spanish.

20. The Greek word means "sharp," and the Greek word for vinegar is derived from it.

21. Cartagena is a city in Colombia, the surrender of which to the Spanish troops in 1815 was a major setback to the revolution.

22. In Book 10 of the *Odyssey* the sorceress Circe turns Odysseus' men into swine.

23. Chamisso to Julius Eduard Hitzig, February 25, 1816. See *Werke*, 6:34–36. "Thou art to me father and lady mother, yea, and brother." These words were spoken by Andromache to Hector, *Iliad* VI, 429–430. See Andrew Lang, Walter Leaf, and Ernest Myers, trans. *The Complete Works of Homer* (New York: Modern Library, n.d.), p. 113.

CHAPTER VI

1. Avatcha Bay, situated on the east coast of Kamchatka Peninsula, contains the smaller bay on which Petropavlovsk is located.

2. Romanzov Island, a coral atoll now called Tikei, is part of the Tuamotu Archipelago. Kotzebue believed he had discovered what he called the Krusenstern Islands, including Romanzov. See his account in Kotzebue, *Entdeckungs-Reise in die Süd-See*, 1:119–120 (English trans., 1:149–153). The Penrhyn Islands, also called Manihiki or Northern Cook Islands, are a group of seven islands north of the Cook Islands in the central Pacific. The chief island is Tongareva or Penrhyn. They are administered by New Zealand as part of the Cook Islands. Radak (Ratak) consists of eighteen atolls forming an eastern chain of the Marshall Islands and extending 700 miles.

3. Salas y Gómez (Sala-y-Gómez) is an uninhabitable rocky island in the Pacific, 210 miles ENE of Easter Island, belonging to Chile.

4. Krusenstern's "Analysis of the Islands Discovered by the *Rurik* in the Great Ocean" is contained in Kotzebue, *Entdeckungs-Reise in die Süd-See*, 2:149–160 (English trans. 2:291–313).

5. Ibid., 2:221 (English trans. 3:425).

6. Ibid., 2:125 (English trans. 2:226–228).

7. Ibid., 2:160. La Caldera de Apra on Guaján was the name for Apra Harbor, on the west coast of Guam, constituting the best anchorage on the island.

8. Actually, the instructions are included in vol. 1 of the Russian version of Kotzebue's account, pp. cxxv–cxlviii.

9. Juan Fernández is a group of three islands, Más Afuera, Más a tierra, and Santa Clara (Goat Island), about 400 miles west of Chile and belonging to Chile. Chamisso seems to mean Más a tierra by the designation.

10. Jakob Le Maire (1585–1616) and Willem Corneliszoon Schouten (ca. 1567–1625) were Dutch navigators who first rounded Cape Horn on their way to the East Indies (1615–1617). Schouten wrote *Iournael ofte beschrijvinghe van de wonderlicke reyse gedaen door Vvillem Cornelisz. Schouten*

*van Hoorn, inde jaren 1615, 1616. en 1617. Hoe hy bezuyden de strate van Magallanes een nieuwe passagie tot inde groote Zuyd-zee ontdeckt, en voort den geheelten aerdt-kloot om gheseylt heeft* . . . (Arnhem and Amsterdam, 1618).

11. "The doubtful island" is Pukapuka, a coral reef in the northern part of the Tuamotu Archipelago.

12. Spiridov Island is Takapota, an atoll in the northern part of the Tuamotu Archipelago.

13. Pallisers is the former name of the Tuamotu Archipelago. The Rurik chain is Arutua, a coral reef in the northern part of the Tuamotu Archipelago.

14. The Dean chain is Rangiroa, an atoll of the northern part of the Tuamotu Archipelago.

15. Mulgrave Islands is the former name of parts of the Marshall Islands.

16. *Procellaria:* a genus of petrels.

17. Cf. pp. 299–300, where Chamisso narrates that the islanders at first hesitated to come close to the *Rurik* party.

18. The Russian word *kotik* is a derivative of *kot* "cat" (Max Vasmer, *Russisches etymologisches Wörterbuch*, 1:645). The animal referred to is a fur seal.

19. CHAMISSO'S NOTE: A typographical error in the date, which must be presumed here or above, does not detract from the plausibility of the story.

20. According to Volker Hoffmann's notes in Chamisso's *Sämtliche Werke*, 1:628, Mearn refers to "islands north of the Marianas."

21. *Fringilla:* a genus of birds including the chaffinch.

22. St. Peter and Paul (Petropavlovsk-Kamchatski), a seaport town on the eastern end of Kamchatka Peninsula, now Khabarovsk Territory, USSR.

23. The voyage of Russian navigator Vasilii Mikhailovich Golovnin (1776–1831) was interrupted by captivity in Japan (1811–1813), which he wrote about in *Puteshestvie Rossiiskago Imperatorskago shlyupa "Diany" iz Kronshtadta v Kamchatku, Sovershennoe pod nachal'stvom Flota Leitenenta (nynie Kapitana 1-go ranga) Golovnina v 1807–1808 i 1809 godakh* [Voyage of the Russian Imperial sloop *Diana* from Kronshtadt to Kamchatka performed under the command of Lieutenant (now Captain, 1st rank) Golovnin in 1807, 1808 and 1809], 2 vols. (St. Petersburg, 1819; reprinted Moscow, 1961); and *Zapiski flota kapitana Golovnina o priklucheniiakh ego v plenu u yapontsev v 1811, 1812 i 1813 godakh, Spriobshcheniem zamiechanii ego o yaponskom gosudarstve i narode* (St. Petersburg, 1816), published in English as *Memoirs of a Captivity in Japan, during the Years 1811, 1812, and 1813; with Observations on the Country and the People,* 2d ed. (London, 1824; reprinted London and New York, 1973). Golovnin captained the *Kamchatka* on the third Russian expedition to circumnavigate the globe (1817–1819). See Golovnin, *Around the World on the Kamchatka*, trans. and ed. Ella Lury Wiswell.

24. Jeanne Françoise Julie Adélaide Récamier, néc Bernard (1777–1849), was a French society beauty and wit.

25. Vitus Bering, a Danish navigator in Russian service, led expeditions (1725–1730 and 1734–1743) that explored the area on either side of the strait named after him.

26. Louis Augustin Guillaume Bosc (1759–1828), French zoologist and botanist, wrote *Histoire naturelle des vers* [Natural history of worms], 3 vols. (Paris, 1802). Peter Simon Pallas (1741–1811), German naturalist and

traveler, wrote *Reise durch verschiedene Provinzen des russischen Reiches* [Journey through various provinces of the Russian Empire], 3 vols. (St. Petersburg, 1771–1776). Johann Georg Gmelin (1709–1755), German chemist and botanist, wrote *Flora Sibirica sive Historia plantarum Sibiriae* [Siberian flora or history of the plants of Siberia], 4 vols. (St. Petersburg, 1747–1769).

27. Heinrich Julius Klaproth (1783–1835), German Orientalist and traveler in Asia, was a friend of Chamisso in Berlin.

28. Ivan Ivanovich Redovsky (1774–1807) was a Russian botanist.

29. In Russian this is *baidara*, probably a derivative of *baidak* "riverboat," and an Oriental loan-word in Russian (Vasmer, *Russisches etymologisches Wörterbuch*, 1:40). Chamisso uses the word to designate both the Eskimo umiak and the much smaller Aleutian kayak.

## Chapter VII

1. Torres Sound, a strait about 80 miles wide between New Guinea and the northern tip of Australia, is dangerous to navigation because of its many reefs, shoals, and islands.

2. Chamisso Island is a small island south of Baldwin Peninsula in Alaska.

3. Captain (later Rear Admiral) Frederick William Beechey (1796–1856), English naval officer and geographer, wrote *Narrative of a Voyage to the Pacific and Behring's Strait*, 2 vols. (London, 1831).

4. The Chukchis (Chukchees) are a people of the Kamchatka Peninsula.

5. See Kotzebue, *Entdeckungs-Reise in die Süd-See*, 1:134–168 (English trans., 1:187–244), and Choris, *Voyage pittoresque autour de monde*.

6. See Chamisso, *Werke*, 2:380–382, and Chamisso, *Sämtliche Werke*, 2:495–496.

7. The Nukahiveans are the natives of Nukahiva or Nuku Hiva, the largest of the Marquesas Islands.

8. A *yurta* is a sod-covered underground house used by the Aleuts. The Russian word is of Turkic origin and in Central Asia designates a skin or felt tent stretched over a collapsible framework.

9. King's Island is a steep rocky island at the southern end of Bering Strait off the western coast of Seward Peninsula, Alaska. Cape Wales (Cape Prince of Wales) is the westernmost point of Alaska, the tip of Seward Peninsula on the Bering Strait.

10. Karl Friedrich Gauss (1777–1855), German mathematician and astronomer, was director of the observatory in Göttingen.

11. Sarychev Island (Sarichef Island) lies at the entrance to Shishmaref Inlet halfway between Cape Prince of Wales and Kotzebue Sound. Shishmarev Bay (Shishmaref Inlet) is located on the northwest coast of Seward Peninsula.

12. Linum is a village in the Havelland district in the west of Brandenburg province, Prussia. Chamisso and two of his friends, Friedrich Hoffmann (1797–1865), German mineralogist, and Hans Christian Poggendorf (1796–1877), German chemist and physicist, published their investigation of the peat bog there: "Über das Torfmoor zu Linum" [On the peat bog of Linum], in the *Archiv für Bergbau und Hüttenwesen* 5 (1822): 253–277.

13. Matthew Flinders (1774–1814), an English mariner and hydrographer

who surveyed the coast of Australia, was the author of *Voyage to Terra Australis* (London, 1814). Sir John Ross (1777–1856), a Scottish Arctic explorer who undertook expeditions (1818; 1829–1833) to discover the Northwest Passage, wrote *A Voyage of Discovery . . . for the Purpose of Exploring Baffin's Bay and Inquiring into the Probability of a North-West Passage* (London, 1819); *Narrative of a Second Voyage in Search of a North-West Passage, and of a Residence in the Arctic Regions during the Years, 1829, 1830, 1831, 1832, 1833 . . .* (London, n.d. [1833]). William Scoresby (1789–1857), an English explorer, traveled to the Arctic and Australia.

14. See Kotzebue, *Entdeckungs-Reise in die Süd-See*, 1:152 (English trans., 1:233–234).

15. Cape Espenberg is the northern promontory of Goodhope Bay, Alaska.

16. See Chamisso, *Werke*, 2:333–335.

17. CHAMISSO'S NOTE: Please compare what I said in *Linnaea* 4 (1829): 58 ff., and the authorities cited on page 61. [This is a note entitled "Vorerinnerung" (Preliminary discourse), which prefaced an article by Heinrich Mertens on Norfolk Sound.]

18. The work Chamisso refers to, by Georges Léopold Chrétien Frédéric Dagobert, Baron de Cuvier (1769–1832), French scientist, is *Recherches sur les ossemens fossiles*, 4 vols. (Paris 1812; 4th ed., 10 vols., 1834–1836).

19. Eschscholtz Bay is an inlet on the east end of Kotzebue Sound, Alaska.

20. See Chamisso, *Werke*, 2:362.

21. Cape Deception is the promontory at the southern end of Goodhope Bay, Alaska.

22. East Cape (Cape Dezhneva), in the Soviet Union, is at the northeastern extremity of Asia, projecting into Bering Strait. St. Lawrence Bay is southwest of Cape Dezhneva.

23. See Kotzebue, *Entdeckungs-Reise in die Süd-See*, 1:157.

24. Kariakish (Koryak) is the dialect of the Americanoid Koryak people in the northern part of the Kamchatka Peninsula.

25. See Kotzebue, *Entdeckungs-Reise in die Süd-See*, vol. 1, facing p. 140.

26. The reference is to the following lines from *Gargantua* (1535) by François Rabelais, French humorist and satirist:

> "Mieux est de ris que de larmes escripre,
> Pour ce que rire est le propre de l'homme."

("It is better to write of laughter than tears, for laughter is peculiar to man.") See Book 1, "Aux Lecteurs," in François Rabelais, *Œuvres completes*, ed. Jacques Boulanger and Lucien Scheler (Bruges, 1955), p. 2.

27. *Colymbus:* the type genus of Colymbidae, a family of aquatic birds comprising the grebes.

28. Sitka, on Baranof Island in Alaska, at this time was the chief commercial center on the Pacific coast.

29. *Kornak* is a variation of *carnac*, "elephant-driver," borrowed through French *cornac* from Portuguese *cornaca*, probably a modification of a word from an Indian dialect, possibly Singhalese.

30. Kodiak is the site of the first Russian colony in America, founded in 1784.

31. "Spanish flies," *Lytta vesicatoria*, a species of South European blister

beetle; the source of cantharides, it was formerly much used as a rubefacient and a vesicatory as well as an aphrodisiac.

32. M. William Mariner (fl. 1800–1860), English traveler in the South Pacific; the work Chamisso refers to is *An Account of the Natives of the Tonga Islands in the South Pacific Ocean, with an Original Grammar of Their Language*, compiled from the communications of M. W. Mariner by John Martin (London, 1817).

33. Kotzebue, *Entdeckungs-Reise in die Süd-See*, 1:167.

### CHAPTER VIII

1. Akun and Unimak are members of the Fox group of the Aleutians, separated from each other by the Unimak Pass.

2. The highest point on Unimak Island is Shishaldin Volcano, 6,600 feet high.

3. See Kotzebue, *Entdeckungs-Reise in die Süd-See*, 2:5 (English trans., 1:275–276).

4. CHAMISSO'S NOTE: All of this and much besides I have already said in a work, "Ansichten von der Pflanzenkunde und dem Pfanzenreiche" [Views on botany and the plant kingdom], which has appeared in a compilation in Berlin (published by Dümmler), 1827 [pp. 3–98]. [The "compilation" is *Übersicht der nutzbarsten und der schädlichsten Gewächse, welche wild oder angebaut in Norddeutschland vorkommen.* (Survey of the most useful and harmful plants which occur wild or cultivated in North Germany].

5. Ostyak refers to a Finnic people of the Ural Mountains and western Siberia. Georg Adolf Erman (1806–1877) was a German physicist and world traveler who wrote *Reise um die Erde durch Nord-Asien und die beiden Oceane, in den Jahren 1828, 1829 und 1830*, 5 vols. (Berlin, 1833–1848]. The reference here is to vol. 1, p. 721.

6. Chamisso is referring to Sir William Edward Parry (1790–1855), English Arctic explorer and searcher for the Northwest Passage, author of *Four Voyages to the North Pole*, 5 vols. (London, 1833), and Sir John Ross, the Scottish Arctic explorer.

7. Alta California or Upper California, contrasting with Baja California.

8. A *presidio* is a "garrisoned fortress"; the San Francisco presidio was founded in 1776. See Oscar Lewis, *San Francisco: Mission to Metropolis* (Berkeley, 1966), pp. 8–9.

9. Don Luis [de] Argüello, a California-born Spaniard, was chosen interim governor by the Mexican government (1822–1825).

10. The Feast of Saint Francis is celebrated on October 9.

11. See Choris, *Voyage pittoresque autour du monde*, sect. 1, plate 13.

12. Ibid., sect. 1, p. 5.

13. Monterey was one of the four provinces of California under Spanish (1774–1822) and Mexican rule (1822–1846). Don Pablo Vicente de Solá (1815–1822) was the last governor of California under Spanish rule.

14. Ivan Aleksandrovich Kuskov (1765–1823) was an official of the Russian-American company. Port Bodega (Fort Ross) was the Russian trading center north of San Francisco.

15. Kotzebue, *Entdeckungs-Reise in die Süd-See*, 2:9, note. Aleksandr Andrevich Baranov (1746–1819), Russian fur trader, was head of the Russian-American company and first governor of Russian America. See P. A.

Tikhmenev, *A History of the Russian-American Company*, trans. Richard A. Pierce and Alton S. Donnelly; and Hector Chevigny, *Russian America: The Great Alaskan Venture, 1741–1867*, and *Lord of Alaska: Baranov and the Russian Adventure*.

16. See Kotzebue, *Entdeckungs-Reise in die Süd-See*, 3:192. Moritz von Engelhardt (1749–1842) was a German mineralogist and geologist (professor at Dorpat after 1820) who published an essay on the nature of the rocks of California in ibid., 3:189–196 (English trans. 3:337–345).

17. Georg Heinrich Freiherr von Langsdorff (1774–1852), German botanist, accompanied Krusenstern on his trip around the world. His account of the voyage is *Bemerkungen auf einer Reise um die Welt in den Jahren 1803–1807* [Notes on a trip around the world in the years 1803–1807], 2 vols. (Frankfurt, 1812).

18. Sophie Dorothea Friederike Krüger (1789–1848) enlisted in the Prussian army under the name of August Lübeck to fight in the War of Liberation of 1813. When she was wounded, her sex was discovered, but by royal decree she was allowed to remain in the army and was promoted to corporal after her recovery.

19. *Potentilla ansarina:* silverweed.

20. The text was printed and translated in August C. Mahr, *The Visit of the "Rurik" to San Francisco in 1816*, pp. 116–121.

21. The Pacific Fur Company, founded by John Jacob Astor (1763–1848), German-American fur trader and financier, established Fort Astoria at the mouth of the Columbia River. During the War of 1812 the company's representatives in Astoria, fearing they would lose everything to the British, sold out to the rival Canadian North West Company in October 1813, prior to the arrival of the British naval sloop *Racoon* under Captain Black in November. The fort was renamed Fort George and flew the British flag. In the Treaty of Ghent (1815) it was returned to the United States. See Dorothy O. Johansen and Charles M. Gates, *Empire of the Columbia: A History of the Pacific Northwest*, pp. 133–141 and 188–190.

## CHAPTER IX

1. Jean Paul Friedrich Richter (1763–1825) was perhaps the most popular German novelist of his time. Volker Hoffmann in Chamisso, *Sämtliche Werke*, 2:562, n. 122, supposes that the allusion is to the servant Flex in *Dr. Katzenbergers Badereise* (Summula 7), who has such short legs that he is described as giving the appearance of walking on his knees when he wears a coat with long tails.

2. Pearls, mostly of low grade, were found in the Pearl River on Oahu.

3. Jung is a Germanized form of the name of John Young (d. 1835), a British sailor on the American ship *Eleanora* who in 1790 was detained on shore at Kealakekua, Hawaii, by King Kamehameha. He became Hawaiianized, married a Hawaiian woman, and became a trusted advisor to Kamehameha. His Hawaiian name, 'Olohana, supposedly was derived from the English "All hands!" which he, as a boatswain, often called out to his crew. See Mary K. Pukui, Samuel H. Elbert, and Esther T. Mookini, *Place Names of Hawaii*, pp. 169–170, and Ralph S. Kuykendall, *The Hawaiian Kingdom*, 1:25–26. Tokahai is unidentifiable, but Kochala (Kohala) is a district in the northwest of the island of Hawaii.

4. Karakakoa (Kealakekua), literally, "the pathway of the god," is a village in the Kailua district of Hawaii on the bay of the same name, where Captain Cook was killed.

5. Tiutatua (Kaiakekua) is the beach area near Kealakekua. Wororai (Hualālai), a volcano (2,519 meters high) in Kailua quadrant, Hawaii, last erupted in 1801.

6. Morai is the word Chamisso uses to designate the Hawaiian temples. Actually, it is derived from Tahitian *marae*, and presumably Chamisso and Kotzebue had learned the word from accounts of previous travelers in the South Seas. It appears, for instance, in George Forster, *A Voyage round the World*, p. 162, as *marai*. The Hawaiian designation for the temple is *heiau*.

7. Tapa *(kapa)* is the designation applied primarily to the cloth itself and also to any article made from it (see Mary K. Pukui and Samuel H. Elbert, *Hawaiian Dictionary*, s.v. *kapa*). This cloth was known all over Polynesia and was fashioned from the bark of the paper mulberry *(Broussonettia papyrifera)*, the māmaki tree *(Pipturus spp.)*, and several other trees. See David Malo, *Hawaiian Antiquities*, pp. 48–50 and Peter H. Buck, *Arts and Crafts of Hawaii*, pp. 161–213.

8. Sir Joseph Banks (1743–1820), English naturalist, accompanied Cook around the world (1768–1771) in the *Endeavour*, for which he bore the cost. Chamisso met him in London on the *Rurik*'s return journey. Chamisso met French officer and statesman Marie Joseph Paul Yves Roch Gilbert du Motier, Marquis de Lafayette (1757–1834), in Paris in 1825.

9. This famous portrait of Kamehameha I, often reproduced, appeared first in Choris' *Voyage pittoresque autour du monde*, sect. "Îles Sandwich," Plate 2. Kamehameha was also portrayed by Mikhail Tikhanov, the artist on board the *Kamchatka*. The portrait is reproduced in Golovnin, *Around the World on the* Kamchatka, trans. and ed. Ella Lury Wiswell, p. 420.

10. Georg Anton Schäffer (1779–1836) was a German surgeon and adventurer in the employ of the Russian–American company in Hawaii. He ended his days in Brazil. Mikhail Petrovich Lazarev (1788–1851), Russian naval officer, commanded the *Suvorov* on a round-the-world voyage to Sitka (1813–1816).

11. For an excellent detailed account plus supporting documents of the Schäffer affair, see Richard A. Pierce, *Russia's Hawaiian Adventure, 1815–1817*.

12. Tamari (Kaumuali'i, d. 1824) was king of Kauai from 1794 until he ceded his kingdom to Kamehameha in 1810. In 1821 he was brought to Oahu, where he later married Ka'ahumanu (see n. 14 below).

13. Cyperacea: a large family of monocotyledonous plants including the sedges.

14. Kahumanu (Ka'ahumanu, d. 1832) was Kamehameha I's favorite queen. After his death she became *kuhina nui* ("premier"). When Kamehameha II (Liholiho) traveled to England she became regent and retained this post after his death during the minority of Kamehameha III (Kauikeaouli). See Kathleen Dickenson Mellen, *The Magnificent Matriarch: Kaahumanu, Queen of Hawaii*.

15. After his father's death (1819) Lio-Lio (Liholiho, 1797–1824) became king as Kamehameha II. He abolished the taboo system at the urging of Ka'ahumanu. He traveled to England with his favorite wife and half-sister, Kamamalu, where they both died of measles. See Kuykendall, *The Hawaiian Kingdom*, 1:61–78.

16. Mr. Marini is Don Francisco de Paula Marín (1774–1837), a Spanish sailor who settled in Hawaii. For an account of his life, see Ross H. Gast and Agnes C. Conrad, *Don Francisco de Paula Marin: A Biography, with the Letters and Journal of Francisco de Paula Marin.*

17. Manuja (Manuia) was "commander of the fort of Honolulu under Boki. He went to England with Kamehameha II in 1823 and returned on the *Blonde* in 1825. He was engaged in trading ventures in the Pacific, and is sometimes referred to as 'acting governor' " (Gast and Conrad, *Don Francisco de Paula Marin*, p. 326). Boki, the younger brother of Kalanimoku, was governor of Oahu. See Gavan Daws, *Shoal of Time: A History of the Hawaiian Islands*, pp. 82–87.

18. Mr. Herbottel (John Herbottle, d. 1830), an Englishman who settled in Hawaii in 1793, was port captain under Kamehameha I. See Gast and Conrad, *Don Francisco de Paula Marin*, p. 321.

19. This ship is mentioned on p. 68.

20. Kareimoku (Kalanimoku or Kālaimoku, d. 1827), Hawaiian chief, was called Billy Pitt by foreigners. Loyal friend and advisor to Kamehameha I, when the king died he led Liholiho's army to victory in 1819 in the insurrection that followed Liholiho's abolition of the kapu system and served as prime minister until his death. See Kuykendall, *Hawaiian Kingdom*, 1:53, 69.

21. The volcano Chamisso is referring to is Punchbowl, called Pūowaina, literally, "hill of placing [human sacrifices] (for which this hill was famous)." See Pukui, Elbert, and Mookini, *Place Names of Hawaii*, p. 195.

22. Teimotu (Ke'eaumoku, d. 1824) was a close friend of Kamehameha I. He was governor of Maui, 1820–1824.

23. This taboo is frequently mentioned; cf. Malo, *Hawaiian Antiquities*, pp. 27–30.

24. *Tabu-pori (kapu poli):* a period of extreme taboo.

25. *Aleurites triloba:* now called *Aleurites moluccana*, the candlenut or kukui tree is widespread in the Pacific. The handsome nuts were (and still are) also used for necklaces in Hawaii, as well as in a relish called '*inamona* (see Pukui and Elbert, *Hawaiian Dictionary*, s.v. *kukui*).

26. See Choris, *Voyage pittoresque autour du monde*, sect. "Îles Sandwich," plates 5–8. See also J. Halley Cox and William Davenport, *Hawaiian Sculpture.*

27. The classical work on the hula is Nathaniel B. Emerson, *Unwritten Literature of Hawaii: The Sacred Songs of the Hula, Collected and Translated with Notes and an Account of the Hula.*

28. Kotzebue, *Neue Reise um die Welt*, 1:91–92 (English trans., 1:201–205), about Tahiti, and 2:142–144 (English trans., 2:251–262) about Hawaii.

29. See Choris, *Voyage pittoresque autour du monde*, sect. 8, plate 12, "Danse des hommes des Îles Sandwich," and plate 16, "Danse des femmes des Îles Sandwich."

CHAPTER X

1. C. J. Johnston, English mariner, discovered Johnston and Sand islands in 1807. They are an atoll formation 715 miles southwest of Hawaii, now an unincorporated territory of the United States.

2. San Pedro: unidentifiable.

3. Excerpts from this essay are included in Part II (pp. 263–274). By his First Province Chamisso means essentially Micronesia, "the islands east of the Philippines between the Equator and the Tropic of Cancer as far as the Greenwich meridian" (*Werke*, 2:40). His Second Province contains roughly most of Melanesia and Polynesia.

4. Arno is an atoll of the southern Ratak chain in the Marshall Islands. For Kotzebue's map, see *Entdeckungs-Reise in die Süd-See*, vol. 2, opposite pp. 44 and 72.

5. Mesid (Mejit) is an isolated island northeast of the Wotje Atoll of Ratak.

6. *Yalik*, in Russian, refers to a "skiff, dinghy, yawl."

7. Otdia (Wotje) is a group of atolls in the central part of the Ratak chain. One of the islands is also called Wotje.

8. See Choris, *Voyage pittoresque autour du monde*, sect. "Radak," plates 11, 12, and 18.

9. Aur is an atoll of Ratak south of Maloelap Atoll, containing the islands of Aur and Tabal, among others.

10. *Mäl (māāl)*. See Takaji Abo et al., *Marshallese-English Dictionary*.

11. Oromed (Ormed) is an island of the Wotje group.

12. Goethe, *Wilhelm Meisters Wanderjahre* (1829), Book I, chapter 10.

13. Kotzebue, *Neue Reise um die Welt*, 1:184 (English trans., 1:331).

14. Erigup (Erikub) is an atoll south of Wotje.

15. See Kotzebue, *Neue Reise um die Welt*, 1:171 (English trans., 1:309).

16. Lithophytes: plants or plantlike organisms having a stony structure, such as coral. *Millepora coerulea*: a species of hydrozoan coral, dark blue in color. *Tubipora Chamissonis Ehrenb.*: a species of organ-pipe coral. Christian Gottfried Ehrenberg (1795–1876), German physician and naturalist, was the author of many books, including *Über die Entwicklung und Lebensdauer der Infusionsthiere* (n.p., 1832).

17. *Scaevola*: a genus of tropical shrubs having succulent drupaceous fruit and belonging to the family of the Goodeniaceae.

18. *Mogan (mokwan)*, according to Abo et al., *Marshallese-English Dictionary*, "A food, pandanus juice, cooked and preserved" (p. 209). It is often mixed with grated coconut.

19. This poem, entitled "Generalbeichte" ["General Confession"], was written by Goethe in 1802 for the so-called *Mittwochgesellschaft* ("Wednesday Society"). It consists of six seven-line strophes, from the penultimate of which Chamisso cites the last two lines. (*Vollen* should be replaced by *Guten*, the "fully" of the translation by "well.")

20. The Strait of Lagediak is located to the southwest of Egmedio in the Wotje group.

21. Shishmarev (Schischmarev) Strait is located to the west of Lagediak Strait in the Wotje group.

22. *Egil's Saga* is an Icelandic saga written in the thirteenth century, probably by Snorri Sturluson (1178–1241), medieval Iceland's greatest writer. It narrates the story of the life of Egill Skalagrímsson (ca. 900– ca. 980), a skaldic poet, some of whose verses are incorporated in the saga.

23. Kaben (Maloelap) consists of a group of atolls southeast of the Wotje group in the Ratak chain.

24. See Kotzebue, *Entdeckungs-Reise in die Süd-See*, 2:83 (English trans., 2:117–118).

25. *Arum*: a genus of plants including the cuckoopint. Chamisso includ-

ed taro, which he called *Arum esculentum*, in this genus, but it is now called *Colocasia esculenta.*

26. Airik is a reef-island at the southeastern tip of the Maloelap group.

27. Torua (Taroa), Tian, and Olot (Ollot) are reef-islands of the Maloelap group.

28. Ulea (Woleai) is an atoll in the Caroline Islands.

29. Meduro (Majuro), Arno, and Mille (Milli) are groups of islets in the southern part of the Ratak chain. In his "Notes and Opinions," Chamisso discussed this war; see below, pp. 278, 280.

30. Eilu (Ailuk) is the name of a group of islets north of the Wotje group, containing the islets Ailuk and Kapeniur (Kapen Island).

31. Temo (Jemo) is an isolated island of the western part of the Ratak chain, situated between Wotje and Ailuk, and Ligiep (Likiep) is an atoll in the central part of the Ratak chain.

32. Kapeniur (Kapen) is an islet in the Ailuk group; see n. 30.

33. Ralik is the western chain of islands in the Marshall Islands.

34. See below, p. 264.

35. Sauraur is the same as Tiuraur, mentioned on p. 152. See also p. 281, where Chamisso states that before he assumed the name Sauraur he had called himself Laelidjü.

36. See Kotzebue, *Neue Reise um die Welt,* 1:171 (English trans., 1:309).

37. According to Abo et al., *Marshallese-English Dictionary,* p. 188, Ļa is a prefix to masculine names.

38. See below, pp. 264–265.

39. Eap (Yap) is an island group in the Carolines, about 225 miles northeast of the Palau Islands, comprising four islands, of which Yap is the largest.

40. Bigar (Bikar) is an atoll of the Marshall Islands.


CHAPTER XI

1. The Pelew Islands (Palau or Belau Islands) are a group of about 100 islands and islets often considered part of the Carolines (Western Carolines), about 1,000 miles southeast of Manila.

2. Jean-Antoine Cantova (1697–1731), was an Italian Jesuit missionary in the Philippines, the Marianas, and the Carolines, where he was killed. A long letter of his from the Marianas was published in the series founded by Charles Le Gobien, *Lettres édifiantes et curieuses, écrites des Missions Etrangères, par quelques Missionaires de la Compagnie de Jésus* [Edifying and curious letters of the foreign missions, written by some missionaries of the Society of Jesus], Collection 18, ed. J.-B. du Halde (Paris, 1728), pp. 188–248. Here, however, Chamisso appears to refer to a different letter, "Lettre du 10 janvier 1731," published in Pedro Murillo Velarde, *Historia de la provincia de Philipinas de la Compañía de Jesvs* (Manila, 1749), Book 4, chap. 23, no. 867. Cantova also wrote letters from the Carolines in early May 1731; see Francis X. Hezel, *The First Taint of Civilization: A History of the Carolines and Marshall Islands in Pre-Colonial Days, 1521–1885,* p. 57.

3. Mogemug (Mogmog) is one of the islets in a large atoll of the Palau Islands northeast of Yap known as Ulithi Atoll. Cantova was killed on Mogmog.

4. *Tetrodon (Tetraodon) mola L.:* a species of tropical maritime fish.

5. Kotzebue, *Entdeckungs-Reise in die Süd-See*, 2:99.

6. See ibid., 2:100. Kotzebue gives the date as April 18.

7. Unalga is a small island in the Aleutians to the east of Unalaska.

8. *Empetrum nigrum:* crowberry, according to *Webster's Third New International Dictionary*, "an undershrub of arctic alpine regions with an insipid black berry."

9. *Maja vulgaris:* a species of a nearly cosmopolitan genus of crabs.

10. *Uvullaria (Uvularia) amplexifolia:* a species of North American herb having yellowish bell-shaped flowers.

11. *Rubus spectabilis:* a species of shrubs belonging to the genus that contains the blackberry, dewberry, and raspberry.

12. *Heracleum:* a genus of plants containing the cow parsnip.

13. *Verhandlungen der Akademie der Naturforscher* 12, 1 (1824): 247–262. Chamisso's article was entitled "Cetaceorum Maris Kamtschatici Imagines ab Aleutis e ligno fictas, adumbravit recensuitque Adelbertus de Chamisso" [Models of whales of the Kamchatka Sea, drawn and discussed by Adelbert von Chamisso]. It contains five drawings.

14. See n. 12, p. 331, above. Chamisso also surveyed two other peat bogs under government contract and reported on them in the *Archiv für Bergbau und Hüttenwesen* 8, 1(1824):129–139, and 11, 1 (1826): 3–26.

15. *Leo marinus Stelleri (Eumetopias jubata):* Stelleri sea lion.

16. "And who told you to take care of my family?"

17. *Uria:* a genus of guillemots (narrow-billed auks) comprising the murres.

18. By "mouth buttons" Chamisso means ornaments inserted in perforations near the corners of the mouth.

19. Kotzebue, *Entdeckungs-Reise in die Süd-See*, 1:105.

20. See *Quarterly Review* 24 (January 1824): 363. Chamisso gives both the English original and a German translation, but he does not translate the last sentence in the quotation.

21. See Kotzebue, *Entdeckungs-Reise in die Süd-See*, 2:106.

22. *Tarbassi:* in Russian, *tarbasi*.

## CHAPTER XII

1. Mauna Puoray: unidentifiable.

2. Powarua: unidentifiable.

3. *Cordia sebestena:* a species of a large genus of chiefly tropical shrubs and trees that have fleshy and often edible fruits.

4. This is Kalanimoku, governor of Oahu. See n. 20, p. 336, above.

5. The *Kadiak (Kad'iak* or *Mirt-Kad'iak)*, formerly the *Myrtle*, was a British ship purchased at St. Paul, Kadiak Island, by Baranov in 1807.

6. George Beckley, American seaman, resident in Hawaii, was the builder and the first commander of the Honolulu fort, 1816.

7. See Kotzebue, *Entdeckungs-Reise in die Süd-See*, 2:113–114 (English trans., 2:195–198).

8. Timofei Tarakanov, Russian-American company employee, served under Schäffer on Kauai until June 1817. This quote is from Kotzebue, *Entdeckungs-Reise in die Süd-See*, 2:113 ff.

9. See Kuykendall, *Hawaiian Kingdom*, 1:41–42.

10. Both doubloons and maravedíes are Spanish coins no longer in use;

the doubloon, made of gold, was of great value; the maravedí, a small copper coin, had little value.

11. Mme de Staël traveled to Italy in 1816 in the hope of restoring her health.

12. *Chaetodon:* the type-genus of Chaetodontidae, a large family of percoid tropical marine fishes.

13. *Dracaena terminalis (Cordyline terminalis):* the ti plant.

14. Pierre Jean de Béranger (1780–1857), French lyric poet of liberal views, called poets men of the future in a letter to Chamisso. See *Correspondance de Béranger,* ed. Paul Boiteau, 2:180–181.

15. By order of Catherine de Médici (1519–1589), mother of Charles IX (1550–1574), king of France, Huguenots were massacred in Paris on St. Bartholomew's Day, August 24, 1572. *Auto da fe,* literally, "act of faith" in Portuguese, refers here to the execution of heretics in Spain and Portugal at the time of the Inquisition.

16. Robert François Damiens (1715–1757), a French fanatic, attempted to assassinate King Louis XV at Versailles, January 5, 1757. On March 28, 1757, he was cruelly tortured to death.

17. *Tamon* is apparently a word for "chief" or "noble" in the language of the Carolines. See Kotzebue, *Entdeckungs-Reise in die Süd-See,* 2:132.

18. Malte Conrad Bruun (1773–1826) was a Danish geographer and political writer who settled in Paris. The review of Choris' work probably appeared in the journal *Nouvelles Annales des Voyages, de la Géographie et de l'Histoire* (Paris, 1819–1826), of which he was one of the editors.

19. "A Day of Judgment on Huahine" ("Ein Gerichtstag auf Huahine") is a poem of 142 lines based on an account in William Ellis' *Polynesian Researches* (2:457) of the introduction of missionary law on the island of Huahine, about 80 miles WNW of Tahiti. Ellis (1792–1872) was an English missionary in the South Seas, 1816–1824.

20. Sir Walter Scott, *Life of Napoleon Buonaparte,* 2 vols. (Exeter, 1834).

## CHAPTER XIII

1. *Sartor Resartus or the Life and Opinions of Herr Teufelsdröckh,* by Thomas Carlyle (1795–1881), Scottish essayist and historian (first appearing in *Fraser's Magazine,* 1833–1834), is "a speculative discussion of creeds and systems of philosophy under guise of a philosophy of clothes" (*Webster's Biographical Dictionary,* p. 251).

2. *Paniers,* literally, "baskets," were the frames upon which the hoopskirts of the rococo era rested. The *frisure à la grecque* ("Greek-style hairdo") was a style in which the hair was swept up into knots in imitation of that of ancient Greek women. It was popular as part of the resurgence of classicism after the French Revolution. *Ailes de pigeon,* literally, "pigeon wings," was a hair style for women that featured two large puffs of hair on either side of the head. It was popular in France in the mid-eighteenth century.

3. August Jules Armand Marie, Comte (later Prince) de Polignac (1780–1847), as minister of foreign affairs under Charles X of France promulgated the Ordinances of July 1830 that caused the revolution that drove Charles from his throne. Henriette Sontag (ennobled in 1826 as Henriette Sontag von Lauenstein, 1806–1854) was a German operatic coluratura soprano.

4. *Inga* is not a Hawaiian word. Chamisso lists it in *Werke*, 2:98, as a Radakian word meaning "yes." Abo et al., *Marshallese-English Dictionary*, p. 77, lists *iññā* as the word for "yes" in Eastern Marshallese dialect only.

5. The line appears in a poem by Goethe entitled "Vier Jahreszeiten. Winter" ("Four Seasons: Winter"), Distich 93.

6. *Professeurs de physique amusante:* "masters of legerdemain."

7. The Saint Simonians were adherents of the idealistic socialism developed by French philosopher Claude Henri de Rouvroy, Comte de Saint-Simon (1760–1825).

8. *Rhizophora gymnorhiza:* a species of mangrove tree.

9. See pp. 269–270, 282–283.

10. See Kotzebue, *Neue Reise um die Welt*, 1:161–190 (English trans., 1:289–341).

11. See ibid., 1:172 (English trans., 1:310–311).

12. See ibid., 1:171 and 184 (English trans., 1:308–309, 331–332).

13. Odia is an islet in Ailinglapalap Atoll.

14. See Kotzebue, *Neue Reise um die Welt*, 1:191 (English trans., 1:378).

### CHAPTER XIV

1. Sarpane (Sarpana) or Rota is an island in the southern end of the Marianas, about 35 square miles, midway between Guam and Tinian.

2. Kotzebue, *Entdeckungs-Reise in die Süd-See*, 3:226 (English trans., 3:420–421).

3. Agaña (or Agana) is a town on the west coast of Guam about 8 miles northeast of Apra Harbor.

4. "Island of the lateen sails."

5. The Tagals (Tagalogs) are a people of central Luzon in the Philippines.

6. See Chamisso, *Werke*, 2:139–143.

7. José de Medinilla y Pineda was governor of the Philippines from 1812–1822.

8. Lamurek (Lamotrek) is an atoll in the Western Carolines. For a good discussion of the trade between Lamotrek and Guam in these times, see Hezel, *The First Taint of Civilization*, pp. 106–108.

9. Trepang, also called bêche-de-mer or sea cucumber, refers to any of several large holothurians, mostly of the genera *Actinopyga* and *Holothuria*.

10. *Verhandlungen der Akademie der Naturforscher* 10, 2 (1821): 353. Chamisso's article was called "De animalibus quibusdam e classe vermium Linnaeana, in circumnavigatione terrae . . . annis 1815–1818 peracta, observatis, Adelbertus de Chamisso et Carolus Guilelmus Eysenhardt, . . . " [On some animals of the Linnaean class of Vermes, observed on a circumnavigation of the earth in the years 1815–1818, by Adelbert de Chamisso and Karl Wilhelm Eysenhardt]. Fasciculus secundus.

### CHAPTER XV

1. Aaron Arrowsmith (1750–1823), English cartographer, founded a firm that published atlases and maps.

2. Kotzebue, *Entdeckungs-Reise in die Süd-See*, 2:136.

3. Bashees (Bashi) Islands was the earlier name of the Batan Islands, a

group in the northern Philippines separated from the southern end of Taiwan by Bashi Channel. The Babuyanes (Babuyan) Islands are a group of twenty-four islands of volcanic origin north of Luzon.

4. The "telegrapher" sent signals by various semaphoric devices. The word *télégraphe* was first applied by French engineers Claude (1763–1805) and Ignace Urbain Jean Chappe (1760–1828) in 1792 to a signaling device they invented.

5. *Nectarinia:* a genus of Old World sunbirds.

6. In May 1832 the Tories in the House of Lords defeated the Reform Bill promoted by the Whigs under the Prime Minister, Earl Grey (1764–1845). However, the Tories under the Duke of Wellington were unable to form a government, and five days later the Whigs were back in power, and the Reform Bill was passed.

7. Taal is a volcano 984 feet high with a crater $1\frac{1}{4}$–$1\frac{1}{2}$ miles in diameter on Volcano Island in the center of Lake Taal in central Batangas province, Luzon.

8. *Doctor naturalista* and *facultativo:* "naturalist" and "physician."

9. Mesmerism was a system for treating maladies by "animal magnetism" and hypnosis, named after its founder, Franz Anton Mesmer (1734–1815), Austrian physician.

10. See Choris, *Voyage pittoresque autour du monde*, section entitled "Îles Marianes," pp. 11–16, and plate 5.

11. Chamisso's brother, Charles Louis Chamisso (1774–1822), had become prefect of Lot, a department of south central France, whose chief city was Cahors.

12. See pp. 251–253, 350–352.

13. Father Juan de Noceda and Father Pedro de San Lucar, S.J., *Vocabulario de la lingva tagala* (Manila, 1754).

14. *Eugenia:* a genus of tropical trees and shrubs of the myrtle family bearing baccate fruit. Here the rose apple *(Eugenia jambos)* is meant.

15. This quotation is from Horace, *Epistles*, I, 17, 36.

16. What is probably meant is *Mémoires concernant l'histoire, les sciences, les arts, les mœurs, les usages des Chinois* [Memories concerning the history, sciences, arts, customs, and usages of the Chinese], 16 vols. (Paris, 1776–1814), by Jean Joseph Marie Amiot, S.J. (1776–1814), French missionary.

## CHAPTER XVI

1. Pulo (Pulau) Sopāta is an island in the South China Sea.

2. Pulo Timon, Pisang, and Aora are islands in the South China Sea lying just east of the Malay Peninsula.

3. The Gaspar Strait, now the Kelasa Strait, is a channel about 45 miles wide between Belitung (Billiton) Island and Bangka Island, east of southern Sumatra, Indonesia.

4. See *Entdeckungs-Reise in die Süd-See*, 2:142 (English trans., 2:269–271).

5. Rhizophores: mangroves, trees of the genus *Rhizophora*, especially *R. mangle*, tropical maritime trees or shrubs that throw out many aerial roots.

6. See Eschscholtz, "Beschreibung einer neuen Affengattung Presbytis mitrata" [Description of a new genus of monkeys, *Presbytis mitrata*], in

Kotzebue, *Entdeckungs-Reise in die SuLDd-See*, 3:196–198 (English trans., 3:353–356).

7. Chamisso saw the comedian Masurier in Paris in 1825. He mentions him in a letter to his wife October 21, 1825 (Chamisso, *Werke*, 5th ed., 6:103).

8. Crocotoa (Krakatoa), an island volcano in the Sunda Strait, was the site of the most tremendous volcanic eruption of modern times (August 26–28, 1883).

9. Cape Agulhas is the southernmost point of Africa, 100 miles ESE of the Cape of Good Hope.

10. Adamastor, a giant transformed into a cliff, is the personification of the Cape of Storms in canto 5, strophes 37–61 of *Os Lusíadas* ("The Lusiads"), by Luís de Camões (Camoëns) (1524–1580), Portuguese poet.

11. See Kotzebue, *Entdeckungs-Reise in die Süd-See*, 2:145.

12. Karl Heinrich Bergius (1792–1818) had been in Cape Town since 1816.

13. Louis Claude de Saulces de Freycinet (1779–1842), French naval officer, directed an expedition around the world in 1817–1820 and gave an account of it in *Voyage autour du monde . . . pendant les années 1817–1820*, 13 vols. (Paris, 1824–1844).

14. Charles Gaudichaud-Baupré (1789–1854) was a French botanist.

15. This is a quote from *Dya-Na-Sore, oder; Die Wanderer*, 3 vols. (Leipzig, 1787–1791), a novel published anonymously by Wilhelm Friedrich von Meyern (1762–1829), German writer. *Dya-Na-Sore*, ostensibly translated from Sanskrit, narrates the life of a young, idealistic patriot.

16. L. Krebs, in 1816, was the apothecary in Grahamstown, Cape Province.

17. The Dutch-Malayan grammar Chamisso refers to was probably the one by George Henric Werndly (1694–1744), Swiss theologian and Orientalist, *Maleische spraakkunst uit de eige schriften der Maleiers opgemaakt* [Malayan grammar composed from the Malayans' own writings] (Amsterdam, 1736).

18. *Sphaerococcus:* a genus of red algae. *Conserva:* in former classifications, a genus of filamentous green algae, now usually placed in the genus *Tribonema*. Chamisso alludes to views expressed on the basis of his own seaweed findings by the Swedish botanist Carl Adolph Agardh (1759–1859) and his pupil Joachim Åkerman in their work *Dissertatio de metamorphosi algarum* [Dissertation on the metamorphosis of algae] (Lund, 1820).

19. *Protea argentea (Leucadendron argenteum):* the silver tree, a South African tree cultivated for its long, silvery silken leaves.


CHAPTER XVII

1. Byron, in his "Ode to Napoleon Buonaparte" (1814) upbraids Napoleon for having abdicated rather than fight to the death. The reference to Prometheus is in strophe 16:

> Or, like the thief of fire from heaven [Prometheus],
>> Wilt thou withstand the shock?
> And share with him, the unforgiven,
>> His vulture and his rock!

> Foredoom'd by God,—by man accurst,
> And that last act, though not thy worst,
>    The very Fiend's arch mock;
> He in his fall preserved his pride,
> And, if a mortal, had as proudly died!

[*The Complete Poetical Works of Byron*, ed. Paul Elmer More (Boston, 1933), p. 181].

2. Jamestown, a seaport town, was the capital of St. Helena.

3. Mme de Staël died July 14, 1817.

4. Cowes is an urban district on the Isle of Wight, 9 miles WSW of Portsmouth.

5. Chamisso to Julius Eduard Hitzig, June 6, 1818.

6. Sir Robert Brown, Scottish botanist (1773–1858), was the naturalist on Matthew Flinders' expedition to Australia (1801–1805) and later curator of the botanical department in the British Museum.

7. This work by Burney (1750–1821) was published in five volumes in London (1803–1817).

8. August Wilhelm Otto (1786–1845) was a professor of medicine at the University of Breslau.

9. Antonio Canova (1757–1822), Italian sculptor, probably made this statue of Napoleon in the year 1803. Napoleon is nude, with a chlamys fastened over his shoulder, a lance in one hand, and the palm of victory in the other. The sculpture is pictured in Armand Dayot, *Napoléon: Illustrations d'après des peintures, sculptures, gravures, objets, etc., du temps* (Paris, n.d.), p. 292. Arthur Wellesley, first Duke of Wellington (1769–1852), British general and statesman born in Ireland, was Napoleon's victor at Waterloo (1815).

10. The "old sergeant of the guard" is the stereotype of the veteran French soldier loyal to Napoleon, affectionately called the "Little Corporal" in the poetry of Pierre Jean de Béranger, some of whose poems Chamisso rendered into German.

11. Grand Duke Nikolai Pavlovich (1796–1855) was the third son of Tsar Paul I; he became tsar in 1825.

12. The Duke of Wellington, prime minister from 1828–1830, was forced to resign because of his opposition to electoral reform.

13. *Las narices del volcán*, in Spanish, literally, "the nostrils of the volcano."

14. In this year Prussia entered into an alliance with Russia against Napoleon, who was soundly defeated in the Battle of Leipzig.

15. Thomas Cochrane (1775–1860) was the tenth Earl of Dundonald and a British naval commander.

16. *Alcidor* (1825) was written by Gasparo Luigi Pacifico Spontini, Conte di Sant'-Andrea (1774–1851), an Italian composer active in Berlin from 1820 to 1841.

17. Johann Reinhold Forster (1729–1798), German traveler and scholar, professor at the University of Halle after 1780, accompanied Cook on his first voyage around the world (1772), along with his son George, and wrote *Observations Made during a Voyage round the World on Physical Geography, Natural History and Ethic Philosophy* (London, 1778).

18. Eschscholtz, *System der Acalephen* (Berlin, 1829). Acelephae are a group of coelenterates including the jellyfishes.

19. Eschscholtz died in 1831.

20. Swinemünde, now Świnoujście, Poland, is a harbor town in Pomerania near Stettin.

21. The poems appear in vols. 3 and 4 of Chamisso's *Werke* (1836).

## PART II

### CHAPTER I

1. CHAMISSO'S NOTE: On California see: *Noticia de la California y de su conquista temporal y espiritual hasta el tiempo presente*, by Padre Miguel Venegas (Madrid, 1757), translated as *A Natural and Civil History of California* (London, 1759); *Diario histórico de los viages de mar y tierra hechos al Norte de la California*, by Don Vicente Vila (Mexico, 1769); *Nachrichten von der amerikanischen Halbinsel Californien, von einem Priester der Gesellschaft Jesu, welcher lange darin diese letztere Jahr gelebt hat* (Mannheim, 1772); and the journeys of Lapérouse, Vancouver, and Langsdorff. [Miguel Venegas (1680–ca.1764) was a Spanish Jesuit in Mexico. The work mentioned by Chamisso was edited and published from Venegas' manuscript by Andrés Marcos Burriel in 3 vols. (Madrid, 1757). An English translation of the work by Vila is *The Portola Expedition of 1769–1770; Diary of Vicente Vila*, ed. Robert Seldon Ross (Berkeley, 1911). The third volume was published in English as *Nachrichten: An Account of the Aboriginal Inhabitants of the California Peninsula, As Given by Jacob Baegert, a German Jesuit Missionary Who Lived There Seventeen Years during the Second Half of the Last Century*, trans. Charles Ron (Washington, 1865–1875). Baegert(1717–1772) was a missionary in California from 1751 to 1767.]

2. CHAMISSO'S NOTE: At St. Barbara (34°N latitude) a still active volcano rises from the coast, whose foot is swept by the sea, and in other parts of the peninsula volcanic action is evident.

3. James Burney, English naval officer; see his *Chronological History of the Discoveries in the South Sea*, 1:354. Sir Francis Drake (ca. 1540–1596) sailed along the California coast in 1577 and claimed it for the British crown.

4. Punta de los Lobos is a point of land south of San Francisco.

5. Punta de los Reyes (Point Reyes) is a point of land northwest of San Francisco.

6. CHAMISSO'S NOTE: *Ceanothus, Mimulus, Oenothera, Solidago, Aster, Rhamnus, Salix, Aesculus*, etc. Wild grape species, which we ourselves did not encounter, are said to be frequent farther in the interior, and to bear delicious fruit. *Abronia, Eschscholtzia Cham.*, and others are yet to be described. [*Ceanothus*: a large genus of American vines, shrubs, and small trees of the family Rhamnaceae, containing the New Jersey tea. *Mimulus*: a genus of American herbs of the family Scrophulariaceae, containing the monkey flower. *Oenothera*: a genus of mostly North American annual or biennial herbs of the family Onagraceae, containing the evening primrose. *Solidago*: a very large genus of chiefly North American herbs of the family Compositae, containing the goldenrod. *Aster*: a large genus of chiefly fall-blooming herbaceous plants of the family Compositae, containing the Michaelmas daisy. *Rhamnus*: a genus (the type of the family Rhamnaceae)

of trees and shrubs containing the buckthorn. *Salix:* a genus of shrubs and trees (the type of the family Saliaceae) containing the willow. *Aesculus:* a genus of trees and shrubs of the family Hippocastanaceae, containing the buckeye and horse chestnut. *Eschscholtzia:* a genus of poppies named by Chamisso after his colleague, Eschscholtz. *E. californica:* the California poppy.]

7. Archibald Menzies (1754–1842), an English botanist, made many trips to the Pacific, including the coast of North America. Langsdorff: see n. 17, p. 334.

8. Carl Asmund Rudolphi (1771–1832) was an anatomist and botanist at the University of Berlin. Cuvier recognized this species as the grizzly bear *(Ursus horribilis)* in an article, "L'Ours gris de l'Amérique Septentrionale," in Choris, *Voyage pittoresque autour du monde,* sect. 1, and reprinted with translation ("The Grizzly Bear of North America") in Mahr, *Visit of the "Rurik" to San Francisco in 1816,* pp. 178–181.

9. *Oriolus phoeniceus:* a species of passerine bird.

10. CHAMISSO'S NOTE: Each mission is presided over by two Franciscan monks who have obligated themselves to spend ten years in this world. They are given dispensation from the rule of their order, and each receives 400 piasters from the crown. Several missions are under one presidio. The commandant of the presidio, captain of the company, has under him an artillery officer, a commissaire *(officier payeur),* a lieutenant, an *alférez* (ensign), and eighty men. The Spaniard is always on horseback. Here horses and cattle are kept in herds, and are almost wild. They are caught with the lasso. The weapons are lance, shield, and musket. The presidios do not engage in agriculture, the officers scarcely even make gardens; they consider themselves exiles waiting for their speedy recall. The *pueblos,* of which there are few, are villages of Spaniards. A few colonists sent out in the early days and retired soldiers make up the population. Their wives are mostly Indian women. The governor of New California in Monterey, like that of Old California in Laretto, is under the viceroy of Mexico. In San Francisco at the time the lieutenant, after the death of the captain, was the interim commandant, and the *alférez* was absent.

11. CHAMISSO'S NOTE: The Californian sea otter pelts are really inferior to the northern ones, but the difference is not so great.

12. CHAMISSO'S NOTE: Judge for yourself: a hundredweight of flour, which costs 6 piasters in the missions here, costs 40 piasters in San Blas and 50 piasters in Acapulco.

13. San Blas is the narrowest section of the Isthmus of Panama.

14. In 1789, several ships belonging to John Meares (ca. 1756–1807), an English mariner and founder of a Pacific trading company, were seized by the Spanish in Nootka Sound on Vancouver Island. Meares protested in England in 1790, and, when reparation was not immediate, the British assembled a large fleet under Lord Howe, whereupon the Spanish acceded to all Britain's demands.

15. CHAMISSO'S NOTE: A sermon given in the Spanish language in the mission of San Francisco on the name day of the saint, in which the patron saint was put next to Christ, provided us with more annoyance than edification.

16. CHAMISSO'S NOTE: One example among others: The fathers sent their Indians on their boat to our anchorage just so that they might look at our ship, a new sight for them. The Indian in the mission dances his

national dances on Sunday under the eyes of the fathers, plays his accustomed games of chance (always for a stake); the only thing he is forbidden to gamble away is his clothing, a piece of coarse woolen cloth from the factory of the mission; he can enjoy his customary steam bath. The dances are wild, different for each tribe; the melody sung or whispered along with it was generally without words. The game is played by two opponents with sticks that they show rapidly, odd or even. A judge sits nearby and keeps tab with other sticks. The usual bath of the Indians, like that of other northern peoples, is as follows: At the entrance to a cave at the seashore a fire is made. When they have sweated long enough they let it go out and jump across it to plunge into the sea. Steam baths, similar to the Russian, were formerly customary among most of the peoples of Europe. Erasmus Roterodamus *Coll. Diversoria:* Atqui ante annos viginti quinque nihil receptius erat apud brabantos quam thermae publicae, eae nunc frigent ubique, scabies enim nova docuit nos abstinere. ("Twenty-five years ago nothing was more popular among the Brabantians than public baths. They now stand cold everywhere, for the new pox has taught us to abstain from them.") [See Desiderius Erasmus (ca. 1466–1536), *Opera Omnia*, part 1, vol. 3, *Colloqvia*, ed. L.-E. Holkin, F. Bierlaire, and R. Hoven (Amsterdam, 1965), p. 336.]

17. CHAMISSO'S NOTE: No territory is assigned to the various missions. The Indian goes to one or another according to whim.

18. CHAMISSO'S NOTE: Two invalids, man and wife, who seemed to be approaching the proximate end of their days, being incapable of completing the journey, had remained behind from the party of those on leave. Nor had they returned to the mission: naked as they were they had camped down on the damp earth of the shore next to our tents, without any protection from the stormy, rainy nights. Their glances remained fixed on those blue mountains; they saw their fatherland and they comforted their hearts, as they had not been able to reach it. The padre, his attention having been called to them after a few days, sent them back to the mission, admonishing them gently.

19. Syphilis is said to have made its first appearance in 1493 in Europe among the sailors returning with Columbus from the New World. It was introduced into the South Seas by European sailors, and it may well have been brought to California by Europeans as well.

20. On the Cholovones and other Indian groups, see n. 23 below.

21. CHAMISSO'S NOTE: De Lamanon has furnished us with valuable contributions concerning the languages of the Achastlers (?) and the Ecelmachs near Monterey in Lapérouse's *Voyage*. For other works, s. *Mithridates*, 3, 3, p. 182. [Robert de Paul, Chevalier de Lamanon (1752–1787), French traveler, accompanied Jean François Galaup, Comte de La Pérouse (1741–1788), French explorer, on the voyage around the world (1785–1788) in which he perished. See his *Voyage autour du monde pendant les années 1785–1788*, ed. by Millet-Mureau, 4 vols. and Atlas (1797). The other work Chamisso refers to is *Mithridates oder allgemeine Sprachenkunde mit dem Vater Unser als Sprachprobe in beynahe fünfhundert Sprachen und Mundarten* (Mithridates or general linguistics with the Lord's Prayer as example in almost five hundred languages and dialects), ed. Johann Christoph Adelung and Johann Severin Vater, 4 vols. (Berlin, 1806–1817).]

22. CHAMISSO'S NOTE: A fort, erected at a well-chosen site, now blocks San Francisco harbor.

23. There is a good deal of confusion in the classification of Indian tribes

of California. Many of the names appear in various forms, and often they refer to a village allied with others to form a tribe, so that there is considerable overlap in the terminology. Chamisso's divisions are reliable on the whole, but there are apparently some mistakes. According to Robert F. Heizer, *Handbook of North American Indians*, vol. 8, *California*, the coastal Indians spoke Penutian languages, of which there were five diverse families: Yokuts, Miwok, Costanoan, Maiduan, and Wintuan (p. 446). Of the tribes Chamisso mentions, the following are subdivisions of the Coast Miwok or Olamentke division of the Moquelumnan or Miwok family: Guimen, Utchium, Olumpali, Numpali, Tamal (ibid., p. 424). The Saclan were a group of the Costanoan family inhabiting the shore of San Francisco Bay (ibid., pp. 495-496; Frederick W. Hodge, *Handbook of American Indians North of Mexico*, 2:402). The Cholovones were a tribe constituting a portion of the Mariposan or Yokuts family (Hodge, 1:290; Heizer, p. 446), of which the Bolbones were a subdivision (Hodge, 1:158). The Pitemis were a group of Northern Valley Yokuts (San Joaquín Valley) (Heizer, p. 470), and the Suisun spoke a division of the Patwin language of the Wintuan family (Heizer, p. 82).

I have been unable to find any reference to the other names mentioned by Chamisso.

CHAPTER II

1. Malacca is an area on the southwest coast of the Malay Peninsula.

2. The Haraforas were the original inhabitants of Celebes and the Moluccas. Chamisso here refers to discussions of John Leyden, "Dissertation on the Languages and Literature of the Indo-Chinese Nation," in *Asiatick Researches*, 10:217-218, and William Marsden, *Grammar of the Malayan Language* (London, 1812), p. 22.

3. The Aetas are a Negrito people of Zambales, Pampanga and Bataan provinces. Fra Juan de la Concepción, a Spanish Augustinian, had been in the Philippines since 1752. Joaquín Martínez de Zúñiga (1760-1818), also a Spanish Augustinian, had been in the Philippines since 1786.

4. Forster (see n. 17, p. 344) called the Negroid peoples of the South Seas "the second race," as opposed to the lighter-skinned peoples of Polynesia and elsewhere in the Pacific.

5. William Marsden (1754-1836) was an Irish Orientalist and numismatist and also an official of the East India Company in Sumatra who wrote a grammar of the Malay language. See n. 2 above.

6. CHAMISSO'S NOTE: see Hervas, *Arithmet. d. nat.* and the table of comparisons in Cook's *Third Voyage*, Appendix I [recte III, 3:549-553]. [Hervas: probably the work of Lorenzo Hervas y Panduro, *Catálogo de las lenguas de las naciones conocidas, y numeración, división y clases de estas según la diversidad de sus idiomas y dialectos* (Catalogue of the languages of known nations, and the numeration, division, and classes of them according to the diversity of their languages and dialects), 6 vols. (Madrid, 1800-1805).]

7. John Leyden (1771-1811) was a Scottish naturalist, poet, and Orientalist in India and Indo-China. See n. 2 above.

8. See Marco Polo, *The Adventures of Marco Polo, as Dictated in Prison to a Scribe in the Year 1298*, ed. Richard J. Walsh (New York, 1948).

9. Antonio Pigafetta (1491-ca.1534) participated in the first circumnavi-

gation of the globe (1519–1522). His account, *Primo viaggio intorno al globo terracqueo*, edited by Carlo Amoretto, was first published in full in Milan, 1800. It appeared in English as *Magellan's Voyage around the World*, trans. James Alexander Robertson (Cleveland, 1906). Tidori (Tidore) is a small island of the Moluccas, known in Europe as the Spice Islands.

10. William Marsden, *History of Sumatra* (London, 1783); Sir Thomas Stamford Raffles (1781–1826), *The History of Java* (London, 1817) (Raffles was the founder of Singapore and lieutenant governor of Java from 1811 to 1816); *Asiatick Researches; or, Transactions of the Society Instituted in Bengal for Inquiring into the History and Antiquities, the Arts, Sciences and Literature of Asia*, 20 vols. (Calcutta, 1788–1839); and *The Asiatic Journal and Monthly Register for British India and Its Dependencies*, 31 vols. (London, 1816–1845).

11. Chamisso here gives a long list of such works in a footnote; see *Werke*, 2:63–64.

12. The Pampangos (or Pampangans) were a Christianized people of central Luzon; the Zambals or Sambals, a people of Zambales province, western Luzon; the Pangasinans, a Christianized people of western Luzon; the Ylocos (Ilocanos), a major people of northern Luzon; and the Cayayanes, a people in northern Luzon.

13. Father Francisco de San Joseph (San Josef, San José, 1560–1614), an Augustinian in the Philippines, wrote *Arte y reglas de la lengva tagala* (Partido de Bataca, 1610; reprinted Manila, 1832), and sermons in Bisayan in manuscript. Pedro de Herrera (d. 1648), a Spanish Augustinian who also worked in the Philippines, wrote *Confesionario en lengua tagala* (Manila, 1639); *Ramillete de flores en tagala*; and made translations into Tagalog. Some of the works attributed to Dionysius Areopagita (fl. first century A.D.), but forged in his name (probably in Syria) by a Christian Neoplatonist (Pseudo-Dionysius), became of importance for the theology of Eastern Orthodoxy and Western Catholicism.

14. See Leyden, "Dissertation on the Languages and Literature of the Indo-Chinese Nation," p. 207. Bugis (Buginese) is the Austronesian language of the Buginese people in the southern Celebes, Indonesia.

15. CHAMISSO'S NOTE: These two plurals of the first person are found, apart from the language family in question, also in the Quichuan or Peruvian language.

16. See Chamisso, *Werke*, 2:94.

17. Chamori (Chamorro): the language of the Chamorro people on the Mariana Islands. The Chamorro people violently opposed Spanish rule in the Marianas, and the Spaniards used military force against them. The last resistance was crushed in 1695. See Hezel, *The First Taint of Civilization*, p. 48.

18. Chamisso furnishes vocabulary lists for a number of Pacific languages; see Chamisso, *Werke*, 2:96–111.

19. CHAMISSO'S NOTE: *An Account of the Pelew-Islands from the Journals of Captain Henry Wilson [and Some of His Officers Shipwrecked There in August, 1783 in the Antelope]*, by George Keate, 5th ed. (London, 1803), supplement, p. 63. [The first edition of this work was published as *An Account of the Pelew Islands in the Western Part of the Pacific Ocean, and the Shipwreck of the Antelope, East-India Packet, There* (Catskill, 1797). Its author, Captain Henry Wilson (1729–1797), English mariner, ran aground in the *Antelope* in Palau in 1783.]

20. CHAMISSO'S NOTE: See Arrowsmith, *Chart of the Pacific Ocean*

(1798) and Meares, *Voy.*, p. 293. [John Meares, *Voyages Made in the Years 1788 and 1789, from China to the North West Coast of America. To Which Are Prefixed . . . Observations on the Probable Existence of a North West Passage; and Some Account of the Trade between the North West Coast of America and China; and the Latter Country and Great Britain* (London, 1790).]

21. CHAMISSO'S NOTE: *An Account of the Natives of the Tonga Islands from the Communications of M. W. Mariner,* by T. Martin, M.D. (London, 1818).

22. Chamisso was later to change his views as to the "childish" quality of Hawaiian; see Introduction, p. xxii.

23. CHAMISSO'S NOTE: Obviously we cannot equate the limits of our knowledge of the language of the Sandwich Islands with those of the language itself, but in other language samples of Polynesia, especially in Nicolas' *Voyage to New Zealand* (London, 1817), we also find only two pronouns. Pronoun of the first person: O-Waihi *Wau*, New Zealand *Aou*, Tonga *Au*, perhaps the Tagalog *Aco*, Malayu *Ku*. (Tonga also has among others *Gita*, Tagalog *Quita*, Malayu *Kita*.) Pronoun of the second person: O-Waihi *hoe* ['oe], New Zealand *Eakoe* or *Acquoi*, Tonga *Acoi* and *coi*, Tagalog *Ycao*, Malayu *Ankau*. What confuses us most in the study of these languages is the diversity of orthography among the different word-collectors and linguists. One must often know the word in order to recognize it.

24. CHAMISSO'S NOTE: *Moku-moku*, "war"; *moku*, "island" and "European ship."
*Make-make*, "love, like" ["desire, want, wish, like"];
*Make* or *mate*, "kill, beat."
*Mire-mire*, "look, see."
*Moe-moe* [*moemoe*, "ambush, lie in ambush, lurk"] and *moe*, "sleep."
*Nome-nome*, "speak, say" [*nomenome*, "to eat a little at a time"].
*Hane-hane*, "make, do" [the simplex *hana* means "work, do," etc.; *hana-hana*, "hot, warm, vehement" and "sour, stinking"].
*Mi-mi* [*mimi*], mingere, "to urinate."
*Wite-wite* [*wikiwiki*], "fast, quick."
*Rike-rike* [*likelike*], "like, resembling."
[The bracketed words and definitions are from Pukui and Elbert, *Hawaiian Dictionary*.]

25. CHAMISSO'S NOTE: The letters *r* and *l* and *n*, *k*, and *t* are of like value. Examples of such words are *kau-kau*, Chinese *tschau-tschau* for *païni*, "to eat" ['*ai* = "to eat," *pā'ina* = "meal, dinner"]; *pane-pane*, Chinese for *aïni* "coitus," which foreign word still seems to be euphemistic, as more proper matrons avoid the other one out of general modesty [Pukui and Elbert, *Hawaiian Dictionary*, lists *panipani* as a native Hawaiian word, the reduplicated form of *pani* "to close"; *ai* is the only form listed for "coition"]; *pihi*, English fish for *haiïna*, "fish" [the usual Hawaiian word for "fish" is *i'a*; I can find nothing resembling Chamisso's word in ibid.]; *neipa*, English, "knife"; *pikenene*, Spanish *pequeño*, for *kaea*, "small." We are surprised that we not only find the same word in New Zealand (Niclas), but also among allegedly Greenland words that are listed by Bernard O-Reilly, *Greenland, the Adjacent Seas and the Northwest Passage* (London, 1818). [Pukui and Elbert list *pikanini*, "small," from the English *pickaninny*, which in turn is probably derived from Portuguese *pequenino*, diminutive of *pequeno* "small." I can find nothing resembling *kaea* in the *Hawaiian Dictionary*.]

26. CHAMISSO'S NOTE: We cite the testimony of Mr. Marini, of whom we will speak further below.

27. CHAMISSO'S NOTE: Thus we can adduce only inadequate examples of this entire linguistic process, which, although adequately attested for us, exceeds the measure of our imagination so much that we do not presume to demand credence.

| Usual Language | New Language |
|---|---|
| *kanaka* | *anna* "man" |
| *waheini [wahine]* | *kararu* "woman" |
| *kokine* | *amio* "go" |
| *irio ['ilio]* | *japapa* "dog" |

Mr. Marini says *irio*, but otherwise one hears *lio*. [*Kokine* is not listed in Pukui and Elbert, *Hawaiian Dictionary*.]

28. CHAMISSO'S NOTE: We mention supplementarily a similar custom of arbitrary linguistic changes that are demonstrated among a people and in a language that are not suspected of having anything in common with the peoples and languages of Polynesia. M. Dobrizhoffer's *History of the Abipons* has been translated into all languages and can be looked up by anyone. This custom of the Abipons is mentioned in the seventeenth chapter of the second part. The language itself is dealt with extensively in the sixteenth to eighteenth chapters. [Martin Dobritzhofer, S.J. (1777–1791), Austrian Jesuit missionary in Paraguay, *Historia de Abiponibus, Equestri Bellicosaque Paraquariae natione*, 3 vols. (Vienna, 1784); English trans., *An Account of the Abipons, an Equestrian people of Paraguay*, trans. Sam Coleridge (London, 1822).]

29. CHAMISSO'S NOTE: It is undecided, whether pigs and dogs were found in Chile, and Humboldt has proved that the *musa* (the banana) was at home in Mexico before the African one was brought from the Canary Islands (in the year 1516) to the West Indies. The breadfruit tree and the paper mulberry decidedly belong exclusively to East Asia, where the related species still only occur. The Indian sugar cane was transplanted to Sicily in the Middle Ages and brought to America by us. Various species of *Arum*, *Dioscorea*, *Convolvulus*, and *Ipomoea* (taro, yams, and sweet potatoes) occur in both hemispheres and demand a more detailed investigation than space allows here.

30. *Hibiscus populneus (Thespesia populnea)*: a species of hibiscus.

31. Forster, *A Voyage round the World*, p. 266, has *gooree*. Eric B. Shumway, *Intensive Course in Tongan* (Honolulu, 1971), cites the word as *kulī* (p. 650).

32. See Forster, *A Voyage round the World*, p. 320.

33. CHAMISSO'S NOTE: We mention incidentally, without trying to draw any conclusions from it, that the word *tabu* in the same sense as on the islands of the South Seas, also appears in the books of Moses—which has not been unnoticed by the scholars.

34. CHAMISSO'S NOTE: Mariner's *Tonga*, p. 330. [See n. 21, above.]

35. CHAMISSO'S NOTE: *Giru* and *ghuri* cannot definitely be derived from Malay *kuyuk*, Bisayan *iro*, Tagalog *aso* or *ayam*. *Irio* or *lio* of the Sandwich Islands are closer to the Bisayan.

36. CHAMISSO'S NOTE: In the second chapter of the *Historia de las Philipinas* [by Zúñiga; see n. 3 above].

37. Giovanni Ignazio Molina, *Saggio sulla storia civile del Chili*. See n. 17, p. 328.

38. *Tighi* apparently is the Tahitian *ti'i*, "statue, image." See D. T. Tryon, *Conversational Tahitian* (Berkeley and Los Angeles, 1970), p. 159.

39. CHAMISSO'S NOTE: The Patagonians, the Puelci or Puelchi, the Easterners, as the Araucanians call them, belong to the Chilean people and speak the same language.

40. CHAMISSO'S NOTE: For the Araucanian language we have used the following books: Bernhard Havestadt [1714–post 1775, Jesuit missionary in Chile from 1746–1768], *Chilidugu* (Münster, 1777); Molina, *Saggio sulla storia civile del Chili; Mithridates* 3:403. For the Quichua language, *Mithridates* 3:519.

41. José de Acosta (ca. 1539–1600), a Spanish Jesuit in Peru, wrote *Historia moral y natural de las Indias* [Moral and natural history of the Indies] (Seville, 1591).

42. CHAMISSO'S NOTE: The swine is called *babi* in Malay, in Tagalog and Bisayan *babui*, and in the languages of the South Seas *bua, buacca, buaha,* and *pua* [Hawaiian, *pua'a, pū'a*]. For the names of the dog compare a preceding note.

43. See James Burney, *Chronological History of the Discoveries in the South Seas,* 3:187; Hendrik Brouwer, *Journael ende historis verhael van de reyse gedaen by oosten de straet le Maire naer de custen van Chili* (Amsterdam, 1646), p. 72. Brouwer (1581–1683), Dutch navigator and merchant, was a colonial official in the Dutch East Indies. *Cici* is perhaps the Spanish *chicha.*

44. *Piper methysticum:* kava, an Austronesian shrubby pepper from the crushed root of which the intoxicating beverage is made. *Piper latifolium:* a broad-leafed pepper.

45. CHAMISSO'S NOTE: In Europe one can only call the Canabrians (Basques) and the Celts autochthonous, and only because their immigration and derivation cannot be demonstrated. The Chudi tribe can be traced to other Asiatic peoples.

46. CHAMISSO'S NOTE: Humboldt, *Vue des Cordilleres,* p. 152, etc. [Alexander von Humboldt, *Vue des Cordillères, et monumens des peuples indigènes de l'Amérique* (Paris, 1810).]

## CHAPTER III

1. Feis (Fais) is an island of the Western Carolines situated northwest of Woleai.

2. Nugor (Nukuoro) is an atoll in the Eastern Carolines.

3. CHAMISSO'S NOTE: When, having returned to the ship from the island of St. George, we discussed the sea lions, by the whimsical and skillful imitation of whose gait and cries Kadu amused himself and us, he was asked with apparent seriousness if he had observed their nests and eggs under the cliffs by the beach. Uninformed though he was in the natural history of mammals, this question still astounded him; he immediately discovered it to be a jest and laughed heartily at it.

4. CHAMISSO'S NOTE: Kadu had easily learned how to communicate with the Hawaiians and he himself pointed out the similarity between various words in their language and the languages of the islands of the First Province.

5. CHAMISSO'S NOTE: πολύχμητός τε σίδηρος ("iron wrought with fire"), Homer, *Iliad,* 10, v. 379.

6. CHAMISSO'S NOTE: Compare Espinosa, cited in Krusenstern, *Beyträge zur Hydrographie*, p. 92. [José de Espinosa y Tello (1763–1815), Spanish mariner and hydrographer, *Memorias sobre las observaciones astronómicas hechas por los navegantes españoles en distintos lugares del globo* (Madrid, 1809). Adam Johann von Krusenstern, *Beyträge zur Hydrographie der grösseren Ozeane als Erläuterungen zu einer Charte des ganzen Erdkreises, nach Mercators Projection* (Leipzig, 1819).]

7. Fayo (West Fayu) is an island in the Western Carolines.

8. Fatoilep (Faraulap) is an island in the Western Carolines.

9. CHAMISSO'S NOTE: Don Luis de Torres calls him *Roua*, even as he calls that island *Rug*, which we write as *Tuch* according to Kadu.

10. CHAMISSO'S NOTE: These shells, among which the most beautiful species occur, are sent by the governor of Guaján to Manila, from where our museums and collections obtain them.

## CHAPTER IV

1. CHAMISSO'S NOTE: We must mention a natural malformation that we observe on numerous women of the chiefly caste of various groups and on a chief of the Eilu group: it concerns the forearms. The ulna appears to be twisted upward at the wrist, and the crooked forearm, more or less impeded in its growth, in some cases is scarcely a span long. The hand is small and twisted outward. A child on Otdia had a double row of teeth in his mouth. An example of deaf-muteness may also be cited.

2. CHAMISSO'S NOTE: They also told us of a man from Meduro, who had been left behind in a battle on Tabual, whose beard hung down to his knees.

3. CHAMISSO'S NOTE: In the spring of 1816 we had perceived this tattooing on Udirik (Kutusov's islands).

4. CHAMISSO'S NOTE: Natives of the Mulgrave Islands, who climbed on board the *Charlotte*, wore a cross hanging on their necks in the manner of the Spanish. We did not observe this adornment on Radak and endeavored in vain to discover any connection with Christians and Europeans in the sign that we mentioned.

5. CHAMISSO'S NOTE: The chief of the Ligiep group is said to form an exception in this regard and to be an exceptionally obese man.

6. CHAMISSO'S NOTE: The author of these essays leaves it up to people more expert than he to describe accurately these vessels, which in essence agree with the often-mentioned proas of the Mariana Islands.

7. *Jageach* and *Anis*: I can find nothing similar to *jageach* in Abo et al., *Marshallese-English Dictionary*, which, however, lists *Anij* with the meaning of "god" (p. 15).

8. CHAMISSO'S NOTE: Our friends always refused under various pretexts to bestow this adornment upon us. They often pleaded the serious consequences, the swelling of the limbs, the severe illness. Once a chief on Aur directed one of us to spend the night with him, so that he could tattoo him the next morning. The next morning he repeatedly evaded his guest's urging.

9. CHAMISSO'S NOTE: As an example, the belief in medicine, the last to which the nonbeliever still clings.

10. CHAMISSO'S NOTE: You can scrape wood with glass shards and use them about the way we do a plane. They have a real value.

11. *Ipomoea tuberosa Lour. Coch. (Ipomoea batatua):* sweet potato.
12. *Dioscorea alata:* a species of yam.

CHAPTER V

1. CHAMISSO'S NOTE: On Eap Kadu also saw a monstrosity of a *kaluv* [a kind of lizard, *Hydrosaurus marmoratus*], which had two tails and two tongues.

2. Pelli (Peleliu?) is one of the Palau Islands (Western Carolines).

3. *Trichechus dugong:* a species of manatee. Captain Henry Wilson was the English mariner who spent three months in the Palau Islands in 1783 after his ship, the *Antelope*, was wrecked there. The account of his sojourn in Palau was well known. See Hezel, *The First Taint of Civilization*, pp. 66–74.

4. Savonnemusoch (Lukunor) is an island in the Eastern Carolines.

5. CHAMISSO'S NOTE: The two boats, which Cantova had seen, together with four others, had been caught up by the wind and scattered apart on a trip from Fatoliep to Ulea. Most of the people on them were natives of both of the groups mentioned, and we assume that the boats themselves had come from these islands. The first, larger boat, which carried twenty-four people, had three cabins, and is described carefully because of its remarkable nature, is called "a strange boat, little different from the Mariana boats, but higher"; the other smaller one is called "a strange boat, although similar to those of the Marianas." It is further stated, where the distance between the islands is to be estimated: "I have called attention to the construction of their boats, which do not have the lightness of those of the Marianas," and we believe we have demonstrated at another point that, where no other criterion was given, the distances were assumed to be too large. Ulea itself is noted to be at a lesser distance from Guaján, apparently because of the false determination of Fatoilep by Juan Rodríguez in 1696, upon which Cantova relied.

6. Ngoli (Ngulu) is an atoll between Yap and the Palau Islands.

7. CHAMISSO'S NOTE: "The inhabitants of the Island of Ulea and the neighboring islands seemed to me to be more civilized and more reasonable than the others."

8. CHAMISSO'S NOTE: According to Cantova astronomy is taught: "The pilot of the boat has a sphere on which the principal stars are traced."

9. CHAMISSO'S NOTE: "They use a compass which has twelve points."

10. CHAMISSO'S NOTE: "Carpe diem."

11. Elath (Elato) is an atoll in the Western Carolines.

12. CHAMISSO'S NOTE: According to Cantova, Ligopud is the sister and not the mother of Eliulep. The first of the gods, however, are Sabucur and his wife Halmulel, parents of Eliulep and Ligopud. [Chamisso uses Cantova's spelling in his notes.]

13. CHAMISSO'S NOTE: Lugueileng according to Cantova, who calls his mother Leteuhieul, born in Ulea.

14. CHAMISSO'S NOTE: Oulefat—Cantova. He does not name Lugueileng's wives but has Oulefat's earthly mother born in the island of the province of Hogoleu. This island is unknown to Kadu; it is called Felalu on D. L. de Torres' map. [Hogoleu is Truk Island.]

15. CHAMISSO'S NOTE: This is a name they give to the devil.

16. CHAMISSO'S NOTE: This is a fish whose upper jawbone is much shorter than the lower one.

17. Pedro Murillo Velarde (1696–1753), Spanish Jesuit, historian and professor of theology in Manila; see his *Historia de la provincia de Philipinas de la Compañía de Jesvs*, 2:291.

18. CHAMISSO'S NOTE: So in our northern mythology:

| | |
|---|---|
| *Or Ymis holdi* | Out of Ymer's flesh |
| *Var iörth vm scavputh* | Was the earth created |
| *enn or beinom biörg,* | And from his bones the cliffs, |
| *Himinn or havsi* | The sky from the skull |
| *ins hrímkalda iotvnns,* | Of the ice-cold giant, |
| *Enn or sveita sviór.* | And from his blood the sea. |

(Vafthrusdismal XXI, *Edda sæmundar*, p. 13.)
[The *Vafthrúdnismál* ("The sayings of Vafthrúdnir," a giant who disputed with Ódinn), is one of the mythological lays in the collection of mythological and heroic lays known as the *Edda* or *Elder Edda* or *Edda of Sæmund*, written down in Iceland in the thirteenth century, but containing many poems which were composed much earlier. Chamisso cites (with a few mistakes) from *Edda Sæmundar hinns Fróda* (Copenhagen, 1787). The best edition today is *Edda. Die Lieder des Codex Regius nebst verwandten Denkmälern*, ed. Gustav Neckel, vol. 1, *Text*, 4th ed., revised by Hans Kuhn (Heidelberg, 1962); English trans., *The Elder Edda: A Selection*, trans. Paul B. Taylor and W. H. Auden (New York, 1970).]

19. Sütemil is a district on the island of Yap.

20. Eleal is a district on the island of Yap.

21. *Fin Voleur*: See Volker Hoffmann's notes in Chamisso's *Sämtliche Werke*: cf. Grimm's *Kinder und Hausmärchen*, Nr. 192, "Der Meisterdieb."

22. Sorol is an atoll west of Woleai in the Western Carolines.

23. CHAMISSO'S NOTE: "A numerous people, but inhumane and barbarous. The men and the women there go entirely nude and feast upon human flesh. The Indians of the Carolines regard this nation with horror, as the enemy of the human race, with which it is dangerous to have the least commerce. This report seems faithful to me and in accord with what Father Bernard Messia has related, as can be seen in his account." This report cannot be found anywhere and does not seem to have ever been printed.

## CHAPTER VII

1. Yuri Teodorovich Lisiansky was the commander of the *Neva* when it circumnavigated the globe under Krusenstern (see p. xii). He wrote an account of the voyage in *Putemestape kokrug sveta na korable "Neva" v 1803–1806 godakh* (St. Petersburg, 1812). English trans.: *A Voyage round the World in the Years 1803, 4, 5, & 6 . . . in the Ship Neva* (London, 1814).

## CHAPTER VIII

1. CHAMISSO'S NOTE: In November 1816 and September 1817.

2. Mauna Roa [Mauna Loa], literally, "long mountain," is an active volcano and the second highest mountain in Hawaii, "probably the largest sin-

gle mountain mass on earth, rising 13,677 feet above sea level and about 29,000 feet above its base on the ocean floor" (see Pukui, Elbert, and Mookini, *Place Names of Hawaii*, p. 149).

CHAMISSO'S NOTE: O-Waihi and the Sandwich Islands, La Mesa or La Mira and Los Monges of the old Spanish maps (San Francisco of Anson's map might also be O-Waihi) must have been often sighted by the galleons on their trip from Acapulco to Manila. It should be noted that Mr. Marini was unable to find any memory of former contact with Europeans in the folk tales of O-Waihi.

[George Anson (1697–1762), a British admiral, sailed around the world 1740–1744; see George Anson, *A Voyage round the World in the years 1740–44*, compiled from his papers by Richard Walter (London, 1748). The map Chamisso mentions had been obtained by Anson from the Spanish in 1743, and some islands in the approximate position of Hawaii were noted on it.]

3. Chamisso erroneously believed that Mauna Loa was higher than Mauna Kea.

4. See George Vancouver, *A Voyage of Discovery to the North Pacific Ocean and Round the World.*

5. CHAMISSO'S NOTE: In the year 1774 according to Choris, *Voyage pittoresque. Îles Sandwich*, p. 2.

6. This is of course Haleakalā, 10,025 feet high.

7. The eastern range is the Koʻolau Mountains and the western range the Waiʻanae Mountains.

8. This is Punchbowl Crater. See n. 21, p. 336.

9. This is the world-famous Diamond Head, a tuff crater 760 feet high at its highest point.

10. King (according to Volker Hoffmann's notes in Chamisso's *Sämtliche Werke*, 2:593) is perhaps Philip Parker King (1793–1856), English sea captain; Marchand is Étienne Marchand (1755–1793), French navigator who circumnavigated the globe (1790–1792) in the ship *Le Solide* (see Charles-Pierre Claret, Comte de Fleurieu, *Voyage autour du monde par Étienne Marchand*, 6 vols. (Paris, 1798–1800); Johann Kaspar Horner (1774–1834), Swiss navigator, was cartographer on the Krusenstern expedition around the world in 1803–1806.

11. CHAMISSO'S NOTE:

| | | |
|---|---|---|
| On O-waihi Mauna Roa | 2482.4 | toises |
| Mauna Kea | 2180.1 | " |
| Mauna Wororai | 1687.1 | " |
| Mauna Puoray (oral communication) | 817.3 | " |
| The eastern higher peak of Mauwi | 1669.1 | " |
| On O-Wahu, the highest peak in the NW | 631.2 | " |
| The highest peak in the SE | 529.0 | " |

[A toise is 6.396 feet.]

12. Chamisso visited Sir Joseph Banks' library in London; see p. 304. Gazophylacium, in Greek literally means "treasure chamber," as it is used in the New Testament books Mark 12, 41; Luke 21, 1; John 8, 20. The King James Version renders it as treasury.

13. *Metrosideros:* a genus of trees, shrubs and vines (family Myrtaceae) chiefly of the Pacific islands, including the lehua tree. *Santalum:* a genus of trees to which the sandalwood belongs *(Santalum album)*. *Dracaena:* a genus of shrubs containing the *ti* plant. *Amomum:* a genus of plants with over ninety species belonging to the family Zingeraberaceae. *Curcuma:* a

genus of plants belonging also to the family Zingeraberaceae and containing *C. longa*, turmeric. *Tacca:* a genus (type of the family Taccaceae) of tropical herbs containing pia, the source of Otaheite arrowroot.

14. Rubiaceae: a very large family of plants, including gardenias and the coffee tree. Contortea: a synonym for Gentianales, an order of plants containing the gentians. Urticeae (Urticaceae): a family of plants including the nettles.

CHAMISSO'S NOTE: The paper mulberry tree *(Broussonetia papyrifera)* is cultivated in the Sandwich Islands, as it is on most of the islands of the South Seas, for the manufacture of cloth. However, it is erroneous to believe that cloth can be made from its bark only.

15. Lobeliaceae: a family of widely distributed herbs, shrubs, or trees including the lobelias.

16. *Portulaca oleracea:* the common purslane.

17. Chamisso is here referring to cockroaches.

18. Vancouver introduced cattle into Hawaii, giving a bull and six cows to Kamehameha I (see Vancouver, *Voyage of Discovery*, 2:120–121, 127). The Hawaiians, fearing the beasts, allowed them to run wild on the island of Hawaii, where they proliferated. Later, Mexican vaqueros were introduced to capture and control them. See Francis Allyn Olmsted, *Incidents of a Whaling Voyage*, pp. 233–235.

19. *Squilla:* a genus of stomatopod crustaceans. *Palinurus:* a genus of crustaceans including the spiny lobsters.

20. See Kuykendall, *Hawaiian Kingdom*, 1:16–17, for an account of Cook's death.

21. See ibid., pp. 41–42.

22. This "son of Tamari" (Kaumuali'i), likewise called Kaumuali'i, was known to the missionaries as George Tamoree (d. 1826). He went to the U.S. in 1803 and returned with the first companies of missionaries in 1820. In 1824 he led an abortive revolution in Kauai. See ibid., pp. 102, 118.

23. Cf. Chamisso's account above, pp. 123–126.

24. *Glebae adscripti*, in Latin, literally "those consigned to the soil."

25. CHAMISSO'S NOTE: They are known from the travel narratives (Cook, Vancouver, Turnbull, Lisianskoy, et al.). A family must of necessity have three houses, as the men's eating house is forbidden (taboo) to the women. The dwelling house is the common one; the women's house is not barred to men, but a decent man does not go into one. Each sex must prepare its own food and must use separate fires. On board ship the prohibition (taboo) is less severe. Both sexes may not consume the flesh of the same animal. Pork (or dog meat, which is no less prized) and turtle meat, as well as several kinds of fruit, coconuts, bananas, et al., are forbidden (taboo) to women. The male servants of the women in many respects are subjected to the same limitations as they are. Etc. [John Turnbull (d. 1823), English traveler, was author of *A Voyage round the World in the Years 1800–1804* (London, 1805).]

26. CHAMISSO'S NOTE: Tameiameia understands English, without being able to speak it. Lio-Lio learned to write two lines in English, in which he requests a bottle of rum from the ship's captain. As a child Louis XIV learned to write, "L'hommage est dû aux Rois, ils font ce qu'il leur plait." (Manuscript of the Dubrowski Collection in the St. Petersburg Imperial Library.)

27. Eberhard August Wilhelm von Zimmermann (1743–1815), German

geographer and naturalist, was author of *Die Erde und ihre Bewohner nach den neuesten Entdeckungen*, 4 vols. (Leipzig, 1810–1812). William Dampier (1652–1715) was an English mariner and buccaneer who twice circumnavigated the globe. He wrote *A New Voyage round the World* (London, 1697); *A Voyage to New Holland* (London, 1703); and *A Continuation of a Voyage to New Holland* (London, 1709).

28. Sir Alexander Mackenzie (1764–1820), Scottish explorer and discoverer of the Mackenzie River, wrote *Voyages on the River St. Lawrence and through the Continent of North America to the Frozen and Pacific Ocean in the Years 1789 and 1793* (London, 1801).

29. CHAMISSO'S NOTE: I expected that Mr. von Kotzebue, from whose mouth I heard this horror story, would write it down. Shuddering, he allowed a veil of silence to enshroud it. The perpetrator was an official of the Russian–American Trading Company, who was commissioned with hunting the otter along the California coast; the scene, one of the larger islands in the region of Santa Barbara. Cf. Kotzebue's *Entdeckungs-Reise in die Süd-See*, 2:35.

30. Isaac Davis, a British seaman on the American ship *Fair American*, was the sole survivor of an attack on the crew by Hawaiians under Kame'eiamoku in 1790, when the ship was becalmed off the coast of North Kona. Davis was taken under the protection of Kamehameha and later became one of his most cherished chiefs. See Kuykendall, *Hawaiian Kingdom*, 1:24–25; 43–44.

# BIBLIOGRAPHY

Abo, Takaji, Byron W. Bender, Alfred Capelle, and Tony Debrum. *Marshalese-English Dictionary.* Honolulu: University Press of Hawaii, 1976.
Beaglehole, J. C. *The Exploration of the Pacific.* 3d ed. Stanford: Stanford University Press, 1966.
Beck, Warren A., and David A. Williams. *California: A History of the Golden State.* Garden City, New York: Doubleday & Co., 1972.
Bellwood, Peter. *The Polynesians: Prehistory of an Island People.* London: Thames and Hudson, 1978.
Béranger, Pierre Jean de. *Correspondance de Béranger.* Edited by Paul Boiteau. Vol. 2. Paris: Garnier, 1860.
———. *Œuvres de Pierre Jean de Béranger.* New ed. 2 vols. Paris: Garnier, 1876.
Buck, Peter H. [Te Rangi Hiroa]. *Arts and Crafts of Hawaii.* Bernice P. Bishop Museum Special Publication 45. Honolulu: Bishop Museum Press, 1957.
Chamisso, Adelbert von. *Reise um die Welt mit der Romanzoffischen Entdeckungs-Expedition in den Jahren 1815–18 auf der Brigg Rurik, Kapitain Otto von Kotzebue.* Leipzig, 1836.
———. *Reise um die Welt.* Edited by Walther Migge. Stuttgart: Deutsche Verlags-Anstalt, 1970.
———. *Sämtliche Werke.* Edited by Jost Perfahl, with notes and bibliography by Volker Hoffmann. 2 vols. Munich: Winkler Verlag, 1975.
———. *Über die Hawaiische Sprache.* Abhandlungen der Preussischen Akademie der Wissenschaften zu Berlin, 1837. Leipzig: Weidmannsche Buchhandlung, 1837. Reprint with Introduction by Samuel H. Elbert. Amsterdam: Halcyon and Philo Press, 1969.
———. *Werke.* 6 vols. Vols. 5 and 6 edited by Julius Eduard Hitzig. Leipzig: Weidmannsche Buchhandlung, 1836–1839.
———. *Werke.* 5th ed. Edited by Friedrich Palm. Berlin: Weidmannsche Buchhandlung, 1864.
Chevigny, Hector. *Lord of Alaska: Baranov and the Russian Adventure.* New York: Viking, 1942.
———. *Russian America. The Great Alaskan Venture, 1741–1867.* New York: Viking, 1965.
Choris, Louis. *Voyage pittoresque autour du monde.* Paris: Firmin Didot, 1820–1822.
———. *Vues et paysages des régions équinoxiales recueillis dans un voyage autour du monde.* Paris: Renouard, 1928.
Cox, J. Halley, and William Davenport. *Hawaiian Sculpture.* Honolulu: University Press of Hawaii, 1974.

Dahnke, Hans-Dietrich, Thomas Höhle, and Hans-Georg Werner. *Geschichte der deutschen Literatur.* Vol. 7. *1789 bis 1830.* Berlin: Volk und Wissen Volkseigener Verlag, 1978.

Dayot, Armand. *Napoléon. Illustrations d'après des peintures, sculptures, gravures, objects, etc., du temps.* Paris: E. Flammarion, n.d. [193?].

Elbert, Samuel H., and Mary Kawena Pukui. *Hawaiian Grammar.* Honolulu: University Press of Hawaii, 1979.

Ellis, William. *Polynesian Researches during a Residence of Nearly Eight Years in the Society and Sandwich Islands.* New York: J. & J. Harper, 1833.

Emerson, Nathaniel B. *Unwritten Literature of Hawaii: The Sacred Songs of the Hula, Collected and Translated with Notes and an Account of the Hula.* Bureau of American Ethnology, Bulletin 38. Washington: Smithsonian Institution, 1909. Reprint. Rutland, Vt. and Tokyo: Charles E. Tuttle Co., 1964.

Forster, George. *A Voyage round the World.* 2 vols. London: B. White, J. Robson, P. Elmsly, and G. Robinson, 1777. Reprint. *Georg Forsters Werke.* Edited by Robert L. Kahn. Vol. I. Berlin: Akademie-Verlag, 1968.

Galdames, Luis *A History of Chile.* Translated and edited by Isaac Joslin Cox. Chapel Hill: University of North Carolina Press, 1941.

Gast, Ross H., and Agnes C. Conrad. *Don Francisco de Paula Marin: A Biography,* with *The Letters and Journal of Francisco de Paula Marin.* Honolulu: University Press of Hawaii for Hawaiian Historical Society, 1973.

Geiger, Ludwig. *Berlin 1688–1840. Geschichte des geistigen Lebens der preussischen Hauptstadt.* 2 vols. Berlin: Paetel, 1893–1895.

Golovnin, Vasilii Mikhailovich. *Puteshestvie vokrug svieta, po poveleniyu Gosudariya Imperatora sovershennoe, na voennom shlyupye "Kamchatkie," v 1817, 1818 i 1819 godakh.* 2 vols. St. Petersburg: Morskoi Tipografii, 1822. English translation: *Around the World on the Kamchatka, 1817–1819.* Translated and edited by Ella Lury Wiswell. Honolulu: Hawaiian Historical Society and University Press of Hawaii, 1979.

Heizer, Robert F., ed. *Handbook of North American Indians.* Vol. 8. *California.* Washington: Smithsonian Institution, 1978.

Hezel, Francis X. *The First Taint of Civilization: A History of the Caroline and Marshall Islands in Pre-Colonial Days, 1521–1885.* Pacific Islands Monograph Series, No. 1. Honolulu: University of Hawaii Press, 1983.

Hodge, Frederick Webb. *Handbook of American Indians North of Mexico.* Bureau of American Ethnology, Bulletin 30. 2 vols. Washington: Smithsonian Institution, 1907–1910. Reprint. New York: Greenwood Press, 1969.

Johansen, Dorothy O., and Charles M. Gates. *Empire of the Columbia: A History of the Pacific Northwest.* New York: Harper & Row, 1957.

Kotzebue, Otto von. *Entdeckungs-Reise in die Süd-See und nach der Berings-Strasse zur Erforschung einer nordöstlichen Durchfahrt. Unternommen in den Jahren 1815, 1816, 1817 und 1818, auf Kosten Sr. Erlaucht des Herrn Reichs-Kanzlers Grafen Rumanzoff auf dem Schiffe Rurick.* 3 vols. Weimar: Gebrüder Hoffmann, 1821. English translation: *A Voyage of Discovery into the South Seas and the*

*Beering's Straits, for the Purpose of Exploring a North-East Passage.* 3 vols. London: Longman, 1821. Reprint. Amsterdam: N. Israel and New York: Da Capo, 1967. Russian translation: *Puteshestvie v Yuzhnyi Okean i v Beringov Proliv dlya ot'iskaniya Syevero-vostochnago morskago prokhoda, predprinyatoe v 1815, 1816, 1817 i 1818 godakh izhdiveniem gr. N.P. Rumyantsova na korablye Ryurikye, pod nachalstvom Flota Leitenanta Kotsebu.* 3 vols. St. Petersburg: N. Grecha, 1821–1823.

———. *Neue Reise um die Welt, in den Jahren 1823, 24, 25 und 26.* 2 vols. Weimar: Wilhelm Hoffmann, and St. Petersburg: J. Brief, 1830. English translation: *A New Voyage round the World in the Years 1823, 24, 25 and 26.* 2 vols. London: H. Colburn & R. Bentley, 1830; Reprint. Amsterdam: N. Israel and New York: Da Capo Press, 1967.

Kuykendall, Ralph S. *The Hawaiian Kingdom.* Vol. 1. *1778–1854: Foundation and Transformation.* Honolulu: University of Hawaii Press, 1968.

Lewis, Oscar. *San Francisco: Mission to Metropolis.* Berkeley: Howell-North Books, 1966.

Mahr, August C. *The Visit of the "Rurik" to San Francisco in 1816.* Stanford University Publications. University Series. History, Economics, and Political Science. Vol. 2, No. 2. Stanford: Stanford University Press, 1932. Reprint. New York: AMS Press, 1971.

Malo, David. *Hawaiian Antiquities (Moolelo Hawaii).* Translated by Nathaniel B. Emerson. Bernice P. Bishop Museum Publication 2. 2d ed. Honolulu: Bishop Museum Press, 1975.

Martineau, Gilbert. *Napoleon Surrenders.* Translated by Frances Partridge. New York: St. Martin's Press, 1971.

Mellen, Kathleen Dickenson. *The Magnificent Matriarch: Kaahumanu, Queen of Hawaii.* New York: Hastings House, 1952.

Menza, Gisela. *Adelbert von Chamissos "Reise um die Welt mit der Romanzoffischen Entdeckungs-Expedition in den Jahren 1815–1818": Versuch einer Bestimmung des Werkes als Dokument des Überganges von der Spätromantik zur vorrealistischen Biedermeierzeit.* Frankfurt am Main, Bern and Las Vegas: Peter Lang, 1978.

Olmsted, Francis Allyn. *Incidents of a Whaling Voyage.* New York: 1841. Reprint. Rutland and Tokyo: Charles E. Tuttle Co., 1969.

Onions, C. T., ed., with the assistance of G. W. S. Friedrichsen and R. W. Burchfield. *The Oxford Dictionary of English Etymology.* Oxford: Oxford University Press, 1966.

Pierce, Richard A. *Russia's Hawaiian Adventure, 1815–1817.* Berkeley and Los Angeles: University of California Press, 1965.

Pukui, Mary Kawena, and Samuel H. Elbert. *Hawaiian Dictionary. Hawaiian-English, English-Hawaiian.* Honolulu: University Press of Hawaii, 1975.

Pukui, Mary Kawena, Samuel H. Elbert, and Esther T. Mookini. *Place Names of Hawaii.* Revised edition. Honolulu: University Press of Hawaii, 1974.

Riegel, René. *Adalbert de Chamisso. Sa vie et son œuvre.* 2 vols. Paris: Les Éditions Internationales, 1934.

———, ed. *Correspondance d'Adalbert de Chamisso. Fragments inédits.* Paris: Les Éditions Internationales, 1934.

Schmid, Günther. *Chamisso als Naturforscher. Eine Bibliographie.* Leipzig: K. F. Koehler Verlag, 1942.

Schweizer, Niklaus R. *A Poet among Explorers: Chamisso in the South Seas.* Bern and Frankfurt a/M: Herbert Lang, 1973.

Shumway, Eric B. *Intensive Course in Tongan.* Honolulu: University Press of Hawaii, 1978.

Tikhmenev, Petr Aleksandrovich. *A History of the Russian-American Company.* Translated and edited by Richard A. Pierce and Alton S. Donnelly. Seattle: University of Washington Press, 1978.

Tryon, D. T. *Conversational Tahitian.* Berkeley and Los Angeles: University of California Press, 1970.

Tuggle, H. David. "Hawaii." In *The Prehistory of Polynesia.* Edited by Jesse D. Jennings. Cambridge, Mass. and London: Harvard University Press, 1979.

Vancouver, George. *A Voyage of Discovery to the North Pacific Ocean, and round the World . . . Performed in the Years 1790, 1791, 1792, 1793, 1794 and 1795, in the* Discovery, *Sloop of War and Armed Tender* Chatham *under the Command of Captain George Vancouver.* 3 vols. London: G. G. & J. Robinson, 1798.

Vasmer, Max. *Russisches etymologisches Wörterbuch.* 3 vols. Heidelberg: C. Winter, 1953–1958.

*Webster's New Biographical Dictionary.* Springfield, Mass.: G. & C. Merriam Co., 1983.

*Webster's New Geographical Dictionary.* Springfield, Mass.: G. & C. Merriam Co., 1972.

*Webster's Third New International Dictionary of the English Language.* Springfield, Mass.: G. & C. Merriam Co., 1981.

# INDEX

# ABOUT THE AUTHOR

HENRY KRATZ is a professor of Germanic languages at the University of Tennessee. He received his Ph.D. in Germanic languages and literature from Ohio State University and has taught Germanic languages in five state universities. In addition, he spent five years writing etymologies for *Webster's Third New International Dictionary*. He has been a Hawaii buff since his first visit to the Islands in 1976. His interest in the Hawaiian language led him to Adelbert von Chamisso, who in addition to the present work wrote the first grammar of the Hawaiian language.